MomStrong *365*

TYNDALE
MOMENTUM®

A Tyndale nonfiction imprint

Heidi St. John

MOM STRONG

A DAILY

DEVOTIONAL

TO ENCOURAGE

AND EMPOWER

EVERYDAY MOMS

365

Visit Tyndale online at tyndale.com.

Visit Tyndale Momentum online at tyndalemomentum.com.

Visit the author's website at heidistjohn.com.

Tyndale, Tyndale's quill logo, *Tyndale Momentum*, and the Tyndale Momentum logo are registered trademarks of Tyndale House Ministries. Tyndale Momentum is a nonfiction imprint of Tyndale House Publishers, Carol Stream, Illinois.

MomStrong 365: A Daily Devotional to Encourage and Empower Everyday Moms

For information about special discounts for bulk purchases, please contact Tyndale House Publishers at csresponse@tyndale.com, or call 1-855-277-9400.

ISBN 978-1-4964-1268-3 (sc)

Printed in the United States of America

29	28	27	26	25	24	23
7	6	5	4	3	2	1

Motherhood.

*It's one part exhilaration, one part exhaustion, and one part experimentation.
As a mother to seven precious children, and now, as "Mamsi" to my
grandchildren, I have come to appreciate the impact that my mom and my
grandmother had on my life.*

*Mom, you may not realize it right now . . . but
you are doing something amazing
that will reverberate for generations.
You are raising parents for your grandchildren.
I pray that as you model unconditional love for your children,
you get a glimpse of how much God loves you.
Precious mom, you are loved.
Never forget who you are.
You are a life giver, a truth teller, a meal maker, and an owie kisser.
You are a grace giver and a memory maker.
In His wisdom, God hand-picked you to be a mother for such a time as this.
You are extraordinary.
This book is for you.*

Introduction

When my publisher approached me about the possibility of writing a 365-day devotional, my heart soared. *I love devotionals*, I thought to myself. In fact, some of my favorite books are devotionals I was given when I was a young mother.

Naively, I thought that I would be in my Bible every single day—and even more naively, I thought I would have something to write for you. As you may have guessed, that wasn't always the case. Some days, I struggled to have anything good to say, let alone write, but the Lord was faithful to encourage my heart through the many, many months that I spent working on the book you're holding in your hands.

Motherhood is like that too, isn't it? I thank God for the women in my life who understand the struggle, don't you? Some days, we feel like we've got it down—we're reading our Bible faithfully, discipling our kids, and trying new recipes just for grins… and other days, we wonder what in the world God was thinking when He gave us kids! The good news, of course, is that God is consistently with us throughout the ebb and flow of motherhood. When He sees you, mom, He sees beyond the work-in-progress. He sees what you are becoming.

I hope that as you read these daily devotions, your heart will be reminded that God has made you for this time in history and that He is always at work. I hope you laugh too—at the mistakes I've made along the way and at God's kindness in redeeming all of it.

As you read, be sure to pay attention to the Bible verses that correlate to these short little devotions every day. Truth is, I don't have any wisdom to give you on my own. God's Word is life giving and powerful. I pray that what the Holy Spirit gave me is of encouragement to you as you raise your children up in the wisdom of the Lord.

Precious mom, there's never been a more important time to study God's Word. There's never been a more important time to ask for His wisdom, and there's never been a more important time to commit to being the mother that God has raised you up to be for such a time as this. You may be a new mother, or you may have been at this for a while. You may have transitioned to the wonderful role of grandmother, or you may still be actively discipling young children. No matter where you are on the journey, it's very clear—this generation of young people needs mothers who are grounded in the rich soil of God's Word and who are committed to teaching it to their children and grandchildren.

It is my prayer that we would all become the mothers and grandmothers and the teachers, mentors, and friends that these children need for such a time as this.

Where's Your Confidence?

My heart is confident in you, O God; no wonder I can sing your praises with all my heart!

PSALM 108:1

MY ALARM WENT OFF AT 6:30 on a dark, cold January morning. With all the new-year enthusiasm I could muster, I slowly made my way to the shower. Mornings are not my thing, but like many people, I had made a few promises on January 1, and I was determined to keep them. Promise number one: get up earlier.

This might be a mistake, I thought to myself. After all, the kids had me up late talking the night before. How could I get up earlier if I couldn't go to bed earlier?

As the shower steamed, my "to do" list grew. Maybe getting up at 6:30 was not going to work. Maybe I needed to get up at 5:30. I laughed out loud. It was only 6:53 a.m., and already I was wondering how I could do all that was in front of me. The self-talk started again. *Come on, Heidi! You can do it!* Yes, this was going to be the year "I" would keep all of my resolutions.

By 7:30 a.m. the kids were arguing. Fifteen loads of laundry sat coldly staring at me. I was frustrated, defeated, and discouraged when I finally did the thing I should have done *first*: I sat down and opened my Bible.

In Psalm 108:2-3, I read, "Wake up, lyre and harp! I will wake the dawn with my song. I will thank you, LORD, among all the people. I will sing your praises among the nations."

As I read, the gentle voice of the Holy Spirit comforted and convicted me. I noted that David sang praises because his confidence was in God! I knew that I was placing my confidence in my own ability—not in God. David's confidence moved him to thank the Lord "among all the people" as he greeted the day with a song. I had not greeted "my people" with a song. Instead, they were greeted by a grouchy mom who had not focused her attention on the One who could give her direction. Have you been that mom too?

As you think about your day today, consider the life of David. When our confidence is in Christ, we can relax, knowing that He will give us the direction we need. A mom who finds her confidence in God can start her day with a song and teach her children to do the same.

Lord, teach us to come to You first, knowing that You guide and direct us.

The Gospel: The Greatest Privilege

You are all one in Christ Jesus. And now that you belong to Christ, you are the true children of Abraham. You are his heirs, and God's promise to Abraham belongs to you.

GALATIANS 3:28-29

PRIVILEGE. IT IS A SOURCE OF much conversation in our world today, but when was the last time you considered the privilege you have under the gospel? Christ's death on the cross and resurrection from the dead secured an incredible privilege for those who claim His name: we are no longer slaves to sin, but rather, we are seen as sons and daughters of God. We are *heirs* of God, and as such, God's promise to Abraham belongs to us.

Think of it! Through faith alone—dependent on *nothing* that we could do—the moment we declare our faith in God, He grants us the *privilege* of being adopted into His family. The apostle Paul teaches that this is like "putting on new clothes" (Galatians 3:27). I don't know about you, but a new outfit that fits perfectly makes me stand a little taller. As mothers, we know why this matters, don't we?

It's even better to be dressed as children of God. Because of the death and resurrection of Jesus, we are able to "put on" the righteousness of God. It's a miracle, really—a privilege that we should celebrate every day. The good news is simply this: *anyone* can belong to Christ. This is the heart of the gospel—and it's available to us all, regardless of ethnicity or economic background. Even the most hardened criminal or most rebellious child can become a son or daughter of Abraham and inherit the promises of God.

How about you? Are you trusting in the promises of God? Are you living your life in view of the amazing inheritance that's waiting for you in heaven?

As I consider my earthly lineage in light of my heavenly destiny as a co-heir with Christ, the things of this world do indeed grow "strangely dim," as the old hymn says. I can only say *thank you* to the One who adopted me into His family. Me. A child of God. What a privilege.

As mothers, the best gift we can ever give our children is to explain to them the nature of true privilege and the great love of the One who has given us the greatest privilege of all: the chance to be called the sons and daughters of God.

There can be no greater joy than to see our children grasp this truth, accept the free gift of salvation through faith, and believe in the promises of God themselves.

That's privilege.

All Will Be Well

Now, O Jacob, listen to the LORD who created you.
O Israel, the one who formed you says, "Do not be afraid."

ISAIAH 43:1

THE PROPHET ISAIAH SEEMS TO HAVE a window into our weary, sometimes discouraged human hearts as he shares God's heart and reminds us of God's extravagant love for His children. The echo that comes back to my heart after reading Isaiah 43:1 is simple: "All is well."

Mothers know the power of this gentle reassurance. When your child comes to you in the middle of the night, afraid of the dark or worried about tomorrow's math test, you cradle your child in your arms or look into your teen's worried expression to offer the confident reassurance that *all will be well.*

When we know how loved we are, that God has a plan, and that it will be accomplished, we can rest. When we understand the power of this promise, we find comfort. Allow me to offer a very loose translation of Isaiah 43:1 for your mama soul: *Now, precious mom, listen to the Lord who created you. Remember, that just as you were present while your children were formed in your womb, God was present as you were being formed. Do not be afraid.*

Remember the first time you heard your child's heartbeat and how strong the bond was with this child you had never even seen? Remember that first kick? Even the searing pain of childbirth paled in comparison to hearing that first cry, didn't it? The agonizing wait for that precious adoption to be finalized was worth every tear you cried and every prayer you sent heavenward.

I will never forget meeting my first child. After two agonizing days of back labor, my husband gently lifted her to my breast. I still cry as I write about it, more than thirty years later. "Shhhhh, Savannah. Don't be afraid. Mama's here. I love you. I know your name. *You. Are. Mine.* All will be well."

What we say to our children is exactly what Isaiah is telling us about the boundless love of God. To His flailing child He gently says, *"Shhhhh. Don't be afraid. I know your name. You. Are. Mine. All will be well."*

Love is the great motivator, isn't it? Apart from God Himself, no one knows the depths love will go to for a child as a mother does. Just as your heart toward your child is good, God's heart toward you is also good. The love that you have for your children is only a glimpse into God's heart for you.

The One who formed you says, "Don't be afraid."

All will be well.

Enough Already!

Be wise enough to know when to quit.

PROVERBS 23:4

"WHERE DOES A MOTHER GO TO RESIGN?" I yelled. After a long day of homeschooling, chores, errands, and refereeing sibling squabbles, it was finally dinnertime at the St. Johns'. I had planned a peaceful dinner—even going so far as to put candles on the table and jazz music on the stereo. I don't know what I was hoping for, but I can say with certainty that I was hoping for more than I got in return.

Hot tears ran down my face as I slammed the dishwasher shut.

Instinctively, my husband sensed I had reached my breaking point. "Babe, why don't you sit this round out?" he said, looking up from his work.

I exploded. "Sit it out?! Really?! I've been working all day on this meal! No one ever listens to me! No one ever helps! I quit!"

My patient husband watched silently as I blew the candles out, grabbed my keys, and headed to the car. I wasn't going anywhere, but I sure wished I could. Tahiti sounded good. Or Target. I didn't care, if it meant I could sit in relative peace and be asked what *I* wanted for a change. For two hours, I sat in the driveway, working out my salvation and my motherhood. When I went back in the house, it was sparkling clean—and the kids had all written apology notes. You'd think I felt better, but deep down, I was embarrassed. This was *not* the mother I wanted them to remember.

Sometimes, we just want to quit—and sometimes, quitting is the right thing to do. We may need to quit trying to be the Pinterest Mom. Maybe it's time to step down from leading that small group in order to embrace a season of little ones. Or maybe, just maybe, we need to quit being so hard on ourselves.

Let's be honest: most of us battle burnout at some point in our mothering. Sometimes, the day-to-day burdens are simply heavier than we expected. Sometimes, unexpected trials take us by surprise. No season of motherhood is immune to burnout.

We need wisdom in every stage—and praise God, He offers the wisdom we need through His Word. In Proverbs 23:4, Solomon wisely advises us to "know when to quit." Although he's not saying to quit mothering, we can take it as a reminder to know our limits and to seek counsel *before* an emotional explosion instead of after. Knowing when to quit isn't a sign of weakness; it's a sign of strength. Knowing your boundaries—first for you, and then for your family—is a blessing.

Precious to God

Others were given in exchange for you. I traded their lives for yours because you are precious to me. You are honored, and I love you.

ISAIAH 43:4

HAVE YOU EVER HAD A MOMENT where you wondered if there was something else—something "more important" that you could be doing instead of shepherding and raising children? If so, you're not alone.

Quietly, we have relinquished our right and responsibility to be the primary influence in the lives of our children—no matter how innocently—and yielded it to youth pastors and schoolteachers. And what message are we sending? Motherhood is a precious responsibility, and the window we have to influence our children closes quickly. If you have forgotten, even for a moment, how precious your role is, let's look to God's Word for a change in perspective.

In Isaiah 43, the prophet makes a reference to "others" who were given in exchange for "their lives." But who were the "others"? Most Bible scholars believe it's a reference to the Egyptians. God seems to be trying to get through to the Israelites, who tended to forget that God had ransomed them from a life of slavery and servitude. Because of His love, God would go to great lengths for the people He chose as His. He was saying, in essence, "Look! I gave up the Egyptians, and I'm ready to give up others too, if it becomes necessary. That's how much I love you."

God has gone to extravagant lengths, even His own Son's death on the cross, to ransom and redeem us. God's love isn't mere words. When God says, "I love you," you can count on it being backed up by actions.

My question is—do our children know how precious they are to us? Are we ready to give up whatever God asks us to give up for our family to flourish and grow strong in Christ? Sometimes, we find we are in a season of real sacrifice. Over time, those small decisions to prioritize our children will yield huge dividends.

Love requires sacrifice. In a self-centered culture, love requires us to look beyond a temporary goal of more money or a bigger house and instead focus our gaze far into the future as we make daily choices for the good of our children and family.

If our ultimate aim is to grow to be more like Christ, let's do it in every area of our lives, starting with our marriages and our children. Yes, you may trade some things in this season of your life to make time for training tender hearts, but I promise you, the trade will be worth it.

A Prayer for Every Season of Motherhood

This is the confidence we have in approaching God:
that if we ask anything according to his will, he hears us.

1 JOHN 5:14, NIV

THERE'S NOTHING LIKE HAVING CHILDREN to test where our confidence lies, is there? Before my first daughter was born, my confidence in God felt unshakable. My joy was palpable.

Thank You for this baby, Lord! Please protect my baby as the pregnancy progresses. I am so excited to meet her!

When I was an expectant mother, the world didn't feel too big for my God. As with many other moms, my conversations with God centered around what I *anticipated* motherhood would bring. I asked God to calm my heart and assuage my fears about an upcoming birth. I asked for a smooth delivery and a healthy baby.

But after the baby's arrival, many of my conversations with God took place in the middle of the night as I tearfully confessed to an unexpected struggle—I often felt inadequate for the tremendous responsibility He had given to me. I worried if I would have the physical and emotional, let alone spiritual, endurance that I would need for the road ahead.

Lord? Are you listening? I'm so tired, Lord. I need Your help.

As the years go by, motherhood's changing seasons alter the nature of the way we pray. Our prayers may change, but God wants one thing to remain the same: He desires that our confidence be placed always in Him. He wants us to know that He is listening. Because as much as our hearts have invested in our children, God has even more invested. After all, He has planted eternity in their hearts (see Ecclesiastes 3:11).

As our children grow into their teen years and our gaze shifts to the edge of the parenting horizon, a new confidence in Him is required. Can you feel it, precious mom of teens? At sixteen, the harvest is close.

Oh Father, how I long to see my children walking in the truth. Protect their hearts. Draw them close.

I pray that my young trees will flourish and grow in righteousness—that they would be like the "cedars of Lebanon" that the prophet wrote about in Psalm 92:12.

Lord Jesus, help me to place my confidence in You. Remind me that You hear me, and help me to live out my life in a way that says, "I trust You."

God understands the seasons of motherhood, precious one. No matter what season you are in, His heart is for you. Confidence in God is well placed. As your children grow, let your confidence in God grow with them.

Who Has Held You Back?

You were running the race so well. Who has held you back from following the truth? It certainly isn't God, for he is the one who called you to freedom.

GALATIANS 5:7-8

HAVE YOU EVER LOST MOMENTUM? I have. One minute, I'm cruising along, just killing it at this motherhood gig: dinner's in the slow cooker, homeschooling is all caught up, laundry's done. Okay—that was pushing it. Laundry is never done, and we all know it, right? But just about the time I'm ready to collect my motherhood medal, something happens, and I'm a mess, lying in the fetal position behind my closet door with a bag of Double Stuf Oreos.

Please tell me you understand.

When I fall off the mommy wagon, it's easy for me to look around in an effort to cast the blame somewhere, when most of the time, even discipline issues I'm struggling through with my kids can be traced back to . . . you guessed it . . . my own disobedience.

When I realize this, it's time to take a step back and hit the reset button. Maybe you're there now too. If you are, take a deep breath. God understands—even when that "momentum" you've lost has resulted in a departure from God's truth.

I love Paul's honest emotion in Galatians 5. You can almost hear the tone of a parent in his voice. *You were running the race so well! What happened?* And then, as if he knows the inner struggle we all face, he jumps in and says, *Hey. This is not God's fault. He has more for you!*

The world tries to drown out the truth of Scripture, but hear me, loved child of the living God—you must cling tightly to it. God's ways bring freedom with them. Freedom from worry. Freedom to rest. Freedom from the fear of failure. Freedom to cling tightly to the truth. Cling to it, precious mom—for in the Truth, you'll find the Life, also.

Jesus understands the weariness of the race, and through the apostle Paul, He gently says, *"I love you."* Can you hear His voice, sweet mom? Can you hear Him above the noise of a busy household and the demands of motherhood? Lean in. He's here. He will help and encourage you to get back on the path He has set before you. His Word will be a lamp to your feet and a light to your path (see Psalm 119:105).

Stay in His Word, and you'll stay on the path. Keep running the race! God is for you!

I Am Trusting the Lord

I am trusting the Lord to keep you from believing false teachings.
God will judge that person, whoever he is, who has been confusing you.

GALATIANS 5:10

THIS IS A VERY CONFUSING TIME to shepherd children. Every day, I interact with parents who are struggling to navigate the turbulent waters of a culture in spiritual crisis.

The Bible teaches us that Satan is a master deceiver. From the time of Eve, the devil has been delighting in misleading human beings. Turns out that, like Eve, we are easily deceived. In every generation, there are false teachers whom Satan uses to sow seeds of confusion and draw us away from the truth. Shepherding children in the midst of this can make us fearful of our sons and daughters being led astray.

I find it's easy to focus on the evil that is around me instead of the victory that has already been won for those who are in Christ. Can you relate? I know it's easy to become fearful. I'm often tempted to react to false teaching in fear and frustration instead of remembering that, ultimately, God will have His way. If you're discouraged by what you see happening in a faraway city or even in your own backyard, I want to encourage you.

Keep trusting the Lord. Allow your weary heart the grace necessary to lay your burden at His feet. When we do this, what we are really doing is showing our children that in a world of confusion, our hope is secure. *God* is well aware of the struggles you are facing. And while we do have a primary role in teaching and training our children in righteousness, when all is said and done, God alone is the One who keeps them from believing the false narratives around them. God will carry your children through, just as He is carrying you.

Trust the Lord to guide you as you teach and train your children, sweet mom. Ultimately, it is the Holy Spirit who will guide the hearts of our sons and daughters as they grow to recognize His still, small voice for themselves.

And when it's hard, remember this: God *will* make things right one day. He will judge those who have made deceit their mission. Truth belongs to God. He is the One who defines it. The ground on which you stand as a child of God is solid ground. Stay close to Him, precious mom! When your heart falters, turn your eyes back to Him.

You can trust Him.

Throughout Our Lifetime

I will be your God throughout your lifetime—until your hair is white with age.
I made you, and I will care for you. I will carry you along and save you.

ISAIAH 46:4

MY GRANDMOTHER WAS A FORCE FOR the Kingdom, and I loved her deeply. If I close my eyes, I can see her challenging my older brother to an arm-wrestling match or bringing home yet another stray animal from the field near our home in Boring, Oregon. Grandma's eyes wrinkled when she smiled, almost to the point of disappearing. She made us feel loved and wanted.

As the years went by, her laugh lines grew deeper, and her pace slowed. Eventually, she traded in constructing tree forts (yes, she climbed the tree) for creating cardboard houses. When her hands became too full of arthritis to use scissors, she transitioned to command central: teaching her great-grandkids to build them. I marveled at the way she enjoyed every stage of her life and how she had such a joyful outlook.

Grandma had learned about the brevity and preciousness of life as a child when she lost most of her siblings to scarlet fever. Because the undertaker could not come to their quarantined house in rural Nebraska, she had to help her grief-stricken mother prepare the bodies for burial. The memories of that terrible time remained with her—but so did her faith. God strengthened her and prepared her for other valleys she would encounter. After a car accident that nearly took her life, she learned that God is the healer.

When I lost a baby to miscarriage, Grandma's words of comfort soothed my soul. "There's no time in our life that our God will fail you, Heidi," she said to me as the tears poured down my face. "He's with you now, and He's with your baby. Don't let this painful thing cause you to doubt the love God has for you. God's heart toward you is always, ever, only good." Grandma spoke with authority when it came to suffering. Her perseverance in trials gave her the ability to help me through my own struggle. She knew the One who can heal a broken-hearted mom, and she pointed me back to Him.

The day the Lord called Grandma home, she was ready to go. I know she heard, "Well done, good and faithful servant."

If you're struggling to understand God's heart for you, look up and believe the promises in God's Word. God will be with you throughout your lifetime. He made you. He will carry you. He will save you. His heart toward you is *always, ever, only . . . good.*

Night-Light

O LORD, you are my lamp. The LORD lights up my darkness.

2 SAMUEL 22:29

I HAVE STRUGGLED WITH FEAR MY whole life. As an adult, I realized my brain still seemed hardwired for trauma and panic. This was especially true at night. I struggled to fall asleep. I also startled easily.

Turns out, we bring 100 percent of ourselves into motherhood, don't we? Our fears, along with our bruised egos, insecurities, past hurts. *We bring it all.* It's why we need Jesus. The moment we realize we've brought "all of us" into motherhood, God can start to work.

Many years ago, I noticed that my daughter Sierra struggled with an irrational fear of the dark. Every night after we put her to bed, she would get up and toddle to wherever we were, wrap herself in her blanket, and go to sleep. This happened over and over. We had night-lights in nearly every room to help her sleep.

It frustrated me that I could not help her overcome this fear. I didn't want her to grow up and struggle with the crippling anxiety I was plagued with. How could my children be set free from fear if I couldn't free myself? I began to take my insecurity to the Lord in prayer.

Over a few months, the Lord graciously opened my eyes. First and foremost, I was not letting my children see me process my own struggle. Of course, they saw obvious things (like the fact that I was on medication), but because I was embarrassed by my apparent weakness, I rarely invited them into the conversations I had with the Lord about my fear and anxiety.

One morning, I was praying about my daughter's fear of the dark. The Lord's kind voice of conviction spoke to my spirit. "*Heidi,*" I heard Him say, "*Teach your kids that I AM their lamp.*"

My heart began to buzz with Holy Spirit–inspired ideas for how I could impart this truth to our children. Over the next few weeks, we memorized Bible verses about God's light—and we talked about how light always overcomes darkness. One night, Sierra said to me, "Mama! *God is our night-light!*" Yes, beautiful girl. Yes, He is. God lights up the darkness in our hearts as we recognize our sin and our need for Him. Then, He begins to free us from our fears. God is light.

Soon after, the night-lights seemed less important to Sierra. She was more at ease at bedtime—and so was I. Sierra is a beautiful young woman now, but I will always remember the season where she—and I—learned to trust God through the night together.

Pray Boldly!

"Do not be afraid of them," the LORD said to Joshua, "for I have given you victory over them. Not a single one of them will be able to stand up to you."

JOSHUA 10:8

We can learn a lot from the prayer of Joshua—and so can our kids. Allow me to set the story up: the king of Jerusalem was worried. He had heard that Joshua, an Israelite, had captured the large city of Ai, on the heels of complete victory over Jericho. The king's response was to be afraid of Joshua, especially after he heard that the city of Gibeon had entered into a peaceful alliance with Israel. King Adoni-zedek called upon five Amorite kings to join him and attack Gibeon.

What would you do if you knew that five kings from some of the most feared people groups around were coming to destroy your town? Chances are good that, like the Gibeonites, you would be begging for help from your allies. The Bible records that the Gibeonite men were strong warriors—but even a strong warrior is susceptible to fear. Look at their very human response to their situation in Joshua 10:6: "The men of Gibeon quickly sent messengers to Joshua at his camp in Gilgal. 'Don't abandon your servants now!' they pleaded. 'Come at once! Save us! Help us! For all the Amorite kings who live in the hill country have joined forces to attack us.'"

Joshua's response was just what they were hoping for. He gathered his entire army and set out from Gilgal to Gibeon. The Lord was with Joshua. Notice His bold promise in verse 7: "Not a single one of them will be able to stand up to you."

That's powerful—but the best part was yet to come as the Lord performed what Joshua could not. The Bible records that God threw the Amorite army into a panic, and He didn't stop there. As the Israelites chased the retreating army, the Lord caused a hailstorm that killed more of their enemies than even their own swords!

Emboldened by this mighty work of God, Joshua prayed a prayer of faith in front of all the Israelites. "'Let the sun stand still over Gibeon, and the moon over the valley of Aijalon.' So the sun stood still and the moon stayed in place until the nation of Israel had defeated its enemies" (Joshua 10:12-13). God answered Joshua's bold prayer.

How boldly are you praying, precious mom? If you want your children to learn to believe in the power of prayer, it needs to start with you. Let your children see that your trust is in the Lord.

Good News

The L%%ORD%% is in his holy Temple; the L%%ORD%% still rules from heaven.

PSALM 11:4

I HAVE ALWAYS WATCHED THE NEWS. My grandparents loved them some Walter Cronkite, so I grew up watching him and listening to my grandparents' wise post-news analysis whenever I was at their house for dinner. Grandpa was a pastor for many years. His heart burned with passion for the people God put in his life. If the news brought to light something we could actively work to improve, such as a community crisis, we were taught and encouraged to do so. My grandparents were the first people in my life who got #offthebench and fought for what was right.

Whether the news was national or international, my grandparents' first response was to pray. No matter what was happening, Grandma and Grandpa knew how to give it to the Lord and leave their worries with Him.

We can all learn from their example, can't we? Have you given something to the Lord and then struggled to leave it there? You're not alone. If we're not careful, we can easily feel discouraged by the stories coming across our screens and on the covers of magazines. It's easy to feel like things are spinning out of control, isn't it?

David was troubled by the news in his time too. I love David's honest assessment of his situation in Psalm 11:1-2. First, he affirms where his protection rests, and then, the cry of his heart is put to paper: "I trust in the L%%ORD%% for protection. So why do you say to me, 'Fly like a bird to the mountains for safety! The wicked are stringing their bows and fitting their arrows on the bowstrings. They shoot from the shadows at those whose hearts are right.'"

I can identify with his frustration—can you? He's essentially asking God, "What can I even do about this?" Have you ever felt helpless in your situation? God understands. David answers his own question in verse 4: "But the L%%ORD%% is in his holy Temple; the L%%ORD%% still rules from heaven."

The Lord still rules from heaven. In other words, *be still.* If you're struggling with the sin around you, *be still.* God is on His throne. He is in control. As Christians, our hope is not here on this earth. Our hope is in heaven. Our hope has a name. His name is Jesus—and He still rules from heaven.

That's good news.

Nothing Is Too Hard for God

O Sovereign LORD! You made the heavens and earth by your
strong hand and powerful arm. Nothing is too hard for you!

JEREMIAH 32:17

HAVE YOU EVER HAD A DREAM that was bigger than your resources?

In May 2016, my husband and I felt a strong call from God to open a resource center for families in Vancouver, Washington. Our hearts were burdened for parents who desired to homeschool their children but needed support that was not currently available. The vision was a big one—we would need a building large enough to hold at least twelve classes simultaneously, a bookstore, a coffee shop where parents could encourage each other, and an auditorium.

Jay and I gathered the kids and told them that we sensed the Lord was giving us a God-sized assignment. In just a few minutes, our kitchen became holy ground as each of our children joined us in asking God to provide what was certainly impossible by human standards.

Less than twenty-four hours later, God surprised us when a Christian couple in Vancouver caught the vision and began to support it financially. The kids were ecstatic to see such an immediate answer to prayer. Encouraged, we began to plan a series of informational and prayer meetings that would begin a few days after we arrived home from my four-month speaking trip.

In June, we found a few vacant properties and began to pray about them. Once a week, parents and children from our community gathered and walked the perimeter of the property we felt would be best for our needs, asking God with one voice to provide us with this building. The price tag? Just over a million dollars—well beyond what the homeschool families could afford on their own . . . but we knew we were *not* on our own.

Our community experienced many ups and downs in the months that followed—but our faithful God answered our prayer with amazing specificity—right down to the coffee shop. We received the keys to a beautiful 17,000-square-foot building right in the heart of Vancouver on October 1, 2017—and we opened our doors to the community less than a month later. Since that time, we have served thousands of children in the name of the Lord Jesus Christ.

Our family learned many lessons during that miracle-filled season—but the greatest lesson has impacted us forever: God answers seemingly impossible requests. If you are dreaming about something that only God could make happen, be encouraged! Involve your children in your prayers and let them see that your faith is strong. God is able!

Learning to Be Led

Teach me to do Your will, for you are my God. May your
gracious Spirit lead me forward on a firm footing.

PSALM 143:10

MOTHERS ARE MANY THINGS. We are nurturers, chauffeurs, short-order cooks, and first-aid providers. We are shoulders to cry on, advice givers, driver's ed teachers, and broken heart menders. But the most important role we play in the lives of our kids is the role of teacher.

As a homeschool mom, I learned a lesson very early in my homeschooling journey: where students and teachers are concerned, it's the teacher who learns the most. After all, we can't teach what we don't understand. David acknowledges his need to be taught by the Lord in Psalm 143:10: "Teach me to do Your will, for you are my God. May your gracious Spirit lead me forward on a firm footing."

I love the humility in this passage. I would imagine that by this time in his life, David had become keenly aware of his deep need for guidance from the Lord. As I think back on the thousands of decisions—large and small—that I have made in more than thirty years of mothering, one thing is for sure: my wisdom is not reliable. God's wisdom, on the other hand, is.

Life teaches us many things, and some of them are hard lessons to learn. Most of us have probably admitted to periods of sporadic "quiet times," usually during busy seasons of life or times of change, such as welcoming a new child into the family. One of the harder lessons I have learned is how important it is for me to seek God's help every. single. day. In truth, I have discovered that I am utterly lost without the guidance of the Lord.

Human as we are, our tendency to rely on ourselves is great, especially when we're not facing a giant. If you're not facing a giant right now, it's time to hunker down and prepare for the time when you will be. Throughout Scripture, we are encouraged to seek God for wisdom. I want to encourage you, precious mom, to seek the Lord today and every day, asking Him to lead you forward on firm footing.

As we cry out to the Lord, we can be assured that He is listening, longing to teach and guide us along every step of this journey we are on. The most important role we'll ever play in the lives of our children is to teach them what it looks like to be led by the Holy Spirit.

Let's learn to be led so we can teach our children to do the same.

Rarely Early, Never Late

I am with you always, even to the end of the age.

MATTHEW 28:20, NKJV

MANY YEARS AGO, I READ *The Hiding Place*, the true story of Corrie ten Boom and her courageous family. The ten Booms boldly hid Jews during the Nazi occupation of the Netherlands, rescuing them from almost certain death. The ten Boom family saved nearly eight hundred lives.

Sadly, the ten Booms lost everything when they were betrayed by a fellow Dutch citizen. On February 28, 1944, the Gestapo raided their home. Corrie and her family (including her eighty-four-year-old father, Casper) were arrested and imprisoned by Hitler's regime. Casper died in the Scheveningen prison near The Hague, the administrative capital city of the Netherlands.

Corrie and her sister, Betsie, were sent to Ravensbrück concentration camp. Located near Berlin, Ravensbrück had a reputation for cruelty. Betsie died there on December 16, 1944, at the age of fifty-nine. Just twelve days after Betsie's death, Corrie was miraculously released. She was the only one of her family to survive.

Corrie had a tremendous testimony of forgiveness and trusting God, and I have always been moved by her incredible witness. For one thing, it puts my own struggles into perspective. It's amazing how God uses suffering to do that, isn't it? Over the years, I have read the story to my own children, sparking conversations about the sufficiency and grace that God offers His children in every circumstance.

We all tend to worry about tomorrow, don't we? We wonder if God will really show up when we need Him, even though He has promised us that He will never leave.

This explanation Corrie's father gave her about facing death is one of the important stories I have reminded my own children about whenever they face fearful situations: "'Corrie,' [Father] began gently, 'when you and I go to Amsterdam— when do I give you your ticket?' I sniffed a few times, considering this. 'Why, just before we get on the train.' 'Exactly. And our wise Father in heaven knows when we're going to need things too. Don't run out ahead of Him, Corrie. When the time comes that some of us will have to die, you will look into your heart and find the strength you need—just in time'" (Corrie ten Boom, *The Hiding Place*).

No matter what is ahead of us, God is already there. Praise the Lord. We need not fear death or any other calamity, because we know God will be with us. He will give us the strength we need—just in time. Rarely early, but never late.

In the Grip of Grace

So we do not lose heart. Though our outer self is
wasting away, our inner self is being renewed day by day.

2 CORINTHIANS 4:16, ESV

MY FRIEND CLINT BIDLEMAN GREW UP in San Luis Obispo, California, in the late seventies and early eighties. For Clint, life was filled with skating, drugs, alcohol, and stealing wood to build skateboard ramps. But at age seventeen, he and his best friend, Paul Anderson, underwent a radical lifestyle change when they individually came to know Jesus Christ as Savior.

Clint and Paul moved to Portland, Oregon, to attend Bible college. There, they began informally skateboarding with local neighborhood skaters. Eventually, Clint and Paul would start Skatechurch, an outreach dedicated to sharing Christ with the skate culture in Portland.

With a ministry just beginning, the two young men were excited about all that God had ahead for them. But Clint's life had its share of tragedy. During his freshman year at college, Clint learned that he had contracted the AIDS virus from a blood transfusion he had received in 1983 after a near-fatal motorcycle accident.

As Clint's body deteriorated, I witnessed the Lord at work in and around him. One evening, he came over for dinner. I served the usual starving student supper: grilled cheese and tomato soup. When the plate was passed to him, Clint politely declined. "Heidi, I've got these reminders that I'm heading to heaven—bad thing is, they keep me from enjoying tomato soup! Got any baby food?" The painful open sores in Clint's mouth made eating anything acidic almost unbearable.

As I searched my pantry, Clint played with our toddler in the other room. His eyes were full of joy. While the rest of us railed against the obvious unfair nature of the disease ravaging his body, Clint was at peace. God's unfailing grace was holding him tight.

Eventually, Clint's disease required hospitalization. On one of our visits, he asked if Jay would lead worship. By this time, Clint's labored breathing and persistent struggle with nausea made it hard to sing, so he whispered the songs with us. As he did, the presence of the Lord filled that room. It was miraculous. Through our tears, we watched as Clint closed his eyes and lifted his face heavenward.

Clint found his hope in Jesus, and we can find our hope in Him too. We know that this world is not all we have, praise the Lord! He broke the chains of sin and death, and He is preparing a place for us to be with Him forever. Glory to God! And Clint, my friend—we'll see you soon.

Discipline = Love

The LORD disciplines those He loves.

HEBREWS 12:6

"DON'T TELL ME WHAT TO DO! You are not the boss of meeeee!"

I listened with a twinge of frustration as my children engaged in what felt like the millionth prideful argument over who was "boss" in their shared bedroom. Having three girls in one room has its ugly moments, and this was definitely one of them. Even though I had warned the girls that there would be consequences for bickering, the arguments escalated as if I hadn't.

I had given them twenty minutes to tidy up their room. Now they were down to three minutes, and not a single item had been picked up off their bedroom floor. There was no way they had done what I asked.

As the clock ticked, my frustration turned to anger. Finally, I yelled (with all the maturity of a ten-year-old), "I am in charge of you! You are about to receive a consequence!"

Silence. It's a universal truth that kids know when they have pushed too far. We all know "the tone" that moms take when it's about to go down . . . and it was. I told the kids to meet me in the kitchen and sat down with a sigh so loud I'm sure the neighbors heard it.

Truthfully, I didn't want to enforce a consequence. I wanted to finish my cup of tea. I wanted to read a book and listen to quiet music. I wanted to take off my mother hat for the day and take a hot bath.

I wanted a break—but I knew this was not the time. When the kids came downstairs, I gave them additional chores (honestly, requiring even more oversight on my part). I corrected attitudes and explained that bad attitudes would incur even more unpleasant consequences.

There were tears, but ultimately, there was peace.

What a job we mothers have. We are referees, nurses, cooks, and counselors. In this particular instance, my job required that I stop what I wanted to do and turn my attention to discipline. It's my least favorite part of being a mom—but God says that when we discipline our children, it's a way to show them that we love and care about them.

Bottom line? In a culture that promotes passive parenting, God says to be anything but passive. Godly discipline is not a suggestion. It's a command. If God prioritizes discipline, so should we.

If you're struggling to follow through with loving discipline today, be encouraged. The fruit that comes from following through will be worth the effort. Your kids will thank you later, and God will bless your obedience.

In My Weakness He Is Strong

Each time he said, "My grace is all you need. My power works best in weakness."
2 CORINTHIANS 12:9

SOME DAYS, DESPITE OUR BEST INTENTIONS, everything seems to go wrong.

One day in particular, nothing I did seemed to work. I began my day by spending time with God. I prayed with the kids. I made a plan—right down to dinner. I had checked all the boxes, but apparently, no one noticed.

One of my teens was disrespectful. I caught a child in a lie. The daily tasks I had assigned to the kids were done, shall we say, *halfway*. Our seven-year-old lost her math book again. All this was before ten in the morning! I was so discouraged.

"I know better!" I muttered. Stomping up the stairs, I locked myself in the master bedroom. Mature, I know, but even moms who have been at this thing called motherhood for a while make a mess of it sometimes.

Thank God for my husband. He has the key to my heart—and also to our bedroom door. He let himself in and found me furiously scrubbing the master bathroom sinks.

"You okay, babe?" he asked.

"Do I *look* okay?" I whined.

Jay chuckled cautiously.

I smelled like bathroom cleaner. In fact, I barely recognized the harried mom staring back at me from above the sink.

Jay grinned at me. "You know," he said, "I heard this awesome message on the radio today. A mom was talking about her weaknesses and how God used them to show Himself faithful. She said that bad days don't make bad moms. She said that God delights in meeting us when we feel at our weakest point. She was really good! I think you would be encouraged."

I took the bait.

"Okay," I said, feeling a little embarrassed at my behavior. I thought it might be good for me to check this mom out. Maybe she would fill in for me for a while so I could take a vacay. "Where did you hear her?"

"On your podcast. It was *you*, babe. Answering a question from a tired mom."

God used my husband to recalibrate my heart. I realized that Christ wanted me to have victory—not failure. His strength was there for me, *but I needed to want it* more than I wanted my kids to feel sorry for me. I needed to reach out and ask for it. God is so faithful. You can start over, mom. His mercies are new every morning. He'll forgive you—and your kids will too.

Living Boldly in Babylon

Your threat means nothing to us. If you throw us in the fire, the God we serve can rescue us.

DANIEL 3:16, MSG

SOMETIMES IT FEELS LIKE WE'RE LIVING in Babylon, doesn't it? Of course, attacks against God and God's people aren't new—it's an age-old battle—but the question remains: Will we serve the gods of this world or the living God?

I've been thinking about the three young men who refused to bow down to the golden statue of King Nebuchadnezzar. Shadrach, Meshach, and Abednego were subjects of Babylon, but along with Daniel, they were determined to serve only the living God. The king hated them for it because he wanted their worship. And so, three charges were brought against the young men:

1. They paid no attention to the king and his commands.
2. They did not serve the gods of Babylon.
3. They refused to worship the golden statue, which the king himself had erected.

The penalty for defying the king was severe: to be thrown into a fiery furnace. Nebuchadnezzar's pride was fueling what would turn out to be an epic story of God's ability to deliver His people.

Consider the profound courage these three had in responding to the king: "If you throw us in the fire, the God we serve can rescue us from your roaring furnace and anything else you might cook up, O king. But even if he doesn't, it wouldn't make a bit of difference, O king. We still wouldn't serve your gods or worship the gold statue you set up" (Daniel 3:17-18, *The Message*).

This infuriated the king, and he had the furnace heated seven times hotter than normal!

Because Shadrach, Meshach, and Abednego trusted God, the power of God was revealed to everyone there. I can imagine that it astonished unbelievers and reassured those who did believe.

Nebuchadnezzar was amazed that the fire did not consume the men, and even more amazed because he saw not three, but four people in the flames! "'Look!' he answered, 'I see four men loose, walking in the midst of the fire; and they are not hurt, and the form of the fourth is like the Son of God'" (Daniel 3:25, NKJV).

The Lord will never leave you or forsake you! Does your heart need some reassurance today? No matter what you're facing, you can have confidence that God has the power to affect the outcome. Don't be afraid! Live boldly for the Lord, like Shadrach, Meshach, and Abednego did in Babylon.

Acquainted with Grief

He was . . . a man of sorrows and acquainted with grief.

ISAIAH 53:3, ESV

I WAS A FEW MONTHS INTO my fourth pregnancy when I headed to a routine prenatal appointment. All indicators reassured me that the pregnancy was progressing well, and I was looking forward to seeing our baby on an ultrasound. My joy turned to sorrow less than an hour later. Just a few minutes in, I knew something was wrong as the technician searched in silence for a heartbeat. As I lay watching the screen, I knew the truth too.

"I'm sorry," he said. "I'll be right back with the midwife."

As I waited, I begged God for a different outcome—but when the midwife came, the awful truth was unavoidable.

"I'm sorry, Heidi. Your baby appears to have died about a week ago."

The minutes that followed are a blur. Instructions were given, pain medication was prescribed, the hospital was called. I left the clinic with a profound sense of loss.

There's nothing quite like the "empty" pain of miscarriage. As my body did the painful work of losing our precious child, I learned a hard lesson. Sometimes, we don't get what we're praying for.

In the weeks and months that followed our loss, God met us in extraordinary ways: we saw His love in other people and felt His peace when the waves of grief crashed over us. God is present! Rather than serve a distant god, we serve a living God who is familiar with our suffering. Jesus never promised us a world without suffering—instead, He promised that He would be with us through it all.

I can say with tender certainty: our hope is still in Jesus. He died on the cross and was raised from the dead because He loved us so much. Through the Cross He set us free from sin and death so that those who love Him can live with Him forever, resurrected in new bodies. It's just a matter of time until we see our little one and our Savior in eternity.

Don't be afraid to ask God questions, precious mom, but please don't let your questions get in the way of believing in God's goodness and love. He understands your pain. God understands how it feels to lose a child.

It's been many years since we lost that precious little one. We have encountered more losses along the way, yes, but we have also experienced the indescribable peace and presence of God.

Whatever is ahead, God says, *I will be there while you grieve too.*

What Quiets Your Witness?

There is therefore now no condemnation for those who are in Christ Jesus.

ROMANS 8:1, ESV

IT'S EASY TO TALK TO OUR kids about forgiveness. We do it frequently as mothers, don't we? As we instruct our children in how to walk in right relationship with others, forgiveness is a natural part of what we teach. At the St. John house, we teach our kids that forgiveness is one of the most important aspects of relationship restoration.

What's not so easy, though, is forgiving ourselves. We struggle with inner restoration, and if our failure to forgive ourselves is left unchecked, it can quiet the witness that God wants us to have.

Our struggles are often all too common: a past sin, or a sense of failure that eats away at our self-confidence. It's not long before fear creeps in—after all, *what would happen if they knew?* Fear leads to shame, shame leads to apathy—and apathy (the feeling that no one would want to hear what you have to say anyway) leads to a sort of soul-shrink. Do you know the shrink I'm talking about? It's the feeling you can't shake when your head knows you've been forgiven but your heart can't believe it's really true.

Well, you really have been forgiven. Paul reminds us in Romans 8 that "there is therefore now *no* condemnation for those who are in Christ" (emphasis added). If you're in Christ, you are forgiven. No strings attached. You are free and clear. When we don't accept God's forgiveness, we often become tangled up in feelings of loathing that do two things: (1) keep us from walking in victory, and (2) keep us from sharing God's love with others.

Ultimately, that's what Satan wants: to keep us from sharing God's love with others! When we live in self-condemnation, we allow the enemy of our soul to quiet our witness. Mom, you've got a redemption story to tell. You've been forgiven! Are you living like it? Do your kids see you walking in victory?

If not, you may be hearing a voice of condemnation that isn't from God. Remember: condemnation will push you down, but the gentle voice of God's Spirit will lift you up.

You don't have to be perfect to experience freedom. You just have to say yes to God. Remember, mom: you can't pass on what you don't possess. Do you want your children to be free? Let them see you live like you've been set free too.

New Morning Mercies

His mercies begin afresh each morning.

LAMENTATIONS 3:23

Before I got married I had six theories about raising children; now, I have six children and no theories.

JOHN WILMOT

Parenting, by its nature, is humbling. Sometimes, it's downright humiliating. There was a time I thought I had this motherhood thing pretty much nailed down. Until my fifth child was born, my "theories" seemed to be working out, so naturally, I became prideful. I danced the victory dance all the way up to her second birthday . . . until we hit something that, until this child, I had assumed was an old wives' tale. I mean, *how hard could the terrible twos actually be?*

As it turns out, they can be pretty hard. Nothing that worked with my other four seemed to work with my fifth. If I said sit, she would stand. If I called her, she ignored me. Every method of discipline I was familiar with was scoring ZERO. If strong-willed had a face, I was sure it would look like my blue-eyed beauty. She was a force of nature—made in the image of God with the strength to match.

One day, in absolute frustration, I prayed, "Lord! She is more than I know how to handle! Help me shape her to be a force for Your Kingdom!" For three years, this was the cry of my heart. Oh, the tears we shed! Sometimes, they were tears of frustration (hers and mine), and sometimes, I cried over the sin that God was exposing in my own life.

It turns out I like my life to be as easy as possible. I wanted compliant, first-time obedient, easy-button kids, and instead, I got human beings. Motherhood has shown me how absolutely selfish I can be. It's driven me to the end of my physical, emotional, and spiritual resources—which I believe is exactly what the Creator intended.

You see, precious mom, where our strength and wisdom ends, God's are only just beginning. The steep learning curves of mothering don't throw God for a loop, and with God's help, we can have the wisdom, perseverance, and love we need. God isn't looking for perfection; He is looking for surrender.

My darling Summer Anne is now on the cusp of adulthood—a beautiful, blue-eyed firecracker who is a bright light for the Lord. Mothering her has been one of my greatest challenges and joys. God answered my prayer, because she is indeed a force for the Kingdom.

If you're at the end of your human resources today, talk with the Lord. His new morning mercies are waiting for you.

Attitude Changes Everything

A cheerful heart is good medicine.

PROVERBS 17:22

A FRIEND OF MINE WAS TALKING with me the other day about the never-ending challenges of raising children. She's not quite as far into her motherhood journey as I am. Most of her struggles center around the sheer physical demands of chasing toddlers around the house and rescuing babies from . . . well . . . themselves! My challenges, on the other hand, have moved to a new place as I mentor our adult children and continue to have a middle schooler at home. Really, we're all tired, but for different reasons! As we laughed about our near-constant state of adrenal fatigue, the ongoing battle of chores, homework, and attitude adjusting, she joked, "So what I hear you saying is, little kids wreck your house, but big kids wreck your mind!"

Oh man, how we laughed. I mean we were doubled over laughing. I hadn't laughed that hard in such a long time, but as my grandma used to say, "Every joke has an element of truth in it."

She was right, of course. We do have wrecked houses, and if I'm honest, I'll admit to being in various stages of a "wrecked" mind. That's the nature of the job we call motherhood. I suppose we could sit around and talk about how hard it is and how much we miss sleeping through the night—but in the end, our attitude will play a huge part in how our children remember their growing-up years.

Solomon wisely reminds readers that "a cheerful heart is good medicine" (Proverbs 17:22), and then he goes on to say what happens when we suffer from something I like to call *motherhood martyrdom*. In the second part of the verse, he warns, "but a broken spirit saps a person's strength."

Oh, it's so true, isn't it? I can think of dozens of times where my attitude ruined not only my day but my husband's and children's day too. As mothers, our attitude affects every single person in our home.

How's your attitude today, precious mom? If you've lost your ability to laugh at yourself or at the chaos that sometimes defines life, may I make a suggestion? Look for more ways to laugh. Step back and count your blessings. Yes, motherhood is hard, but it's also one of the greatest blessings this life offers. I have found laughter to be a reviving balm—that, just like Solomon said, is *good medicine*. In fact, God's prescription for laughter not only restores joy, but it also helps set a positive tone for the rest of the family.

A cheerful heart really is good medicine.

Praise the Lord!

You have taught children and infants to give you praise.

MATTHEW 21:16

WHEN OUR KIDS WERE LITTLE AND we wanted to help them take off their shirts for a bath or bedtime, we would say, "Praise the Lord!" Instantly, their eyes would light up and their hands would raise high. Over the years, it became something of a family identifier—whether we were in church or at the grocery store, if our little ones heard "Praise the Lord!" they would lift their hands and smile broadly, knowing they would get a smile in return.

Imagine my delight the other day when our little grandsons were spending the night and I heard "Praise the Lord!" coming from the master bedroom. Curious, I peeked around the corner to see my oldest daughter getting her boys ready for bed.

"Yes, Mommy!" I heard, as Wesley's little arms raised high.

As mothers, we have a precious opportunity to teach our children to praise the Lord from a young age. Worship is important to God. When we worship Him, we give Him honor, reverence, praise, and glory. God demands worship because He alone is worthy of it. We are responsible for teaching our children to acknowledge these things about God by praising and worshiping Him.

How do we do this? It starts with our example. It starts with our own acknowledgment of God's amazing power and love. Do you recognize the majesty of the creation around you? *Praise the Lord!* Do the stars shine brightly at your home? *Praise the Lord!* Has God answered a prayer that you prayed as a family? *Praise the Lord!* Did your child reach a milestone academically or personally? Praise Him together!

As mothers, we are the primary teachers at home. Our children will delight in what they see us delighting in. What an awesome, precious opportunity we have been given—to teach our children how much God loves it when we praise Him is a blessing that we can see passed on to our children and eventually our grandchildren.

Do you want to see your children learn to give praise and honor to God? It starts with you. Use every opportunity you are given to praise the Lord. Open your mouth, lift your hands high, and let Him know that you honor and love Him. And don't stop there—teach your children to praise Him also. Our children will naturally mimic what they see us doing. Teaching them that God is worthy of their praise—not only for the beauty they see around them but because their Creator loves them—is a wonderful place to start their own journey of faith.

Thank You, Holy Spirit!

The Holy Spirit produces this kind of fruit . . .

GALATIANS 5:22

HAVE YOU EVER BEEN FRUSTRATED BY the lack of spiritual "fruit" in your children's lives? You know what I mean—love, joy, peace, patience, kindness, goodness, faithfulness, gentleness, and self-control. (Never mind that we're also responsible for showing these fruits in our own lives!) As mothers, we spend a lot of time tending the fruit "orchards" that are the hearts of our children, don't we? Sometimes it can be downright discouraging! Other times, when we see hopeful little buds beginning to sprout on our saplings, we are encouraged to keep praying and pruning.

I can't help but laugh when I think of a situation with one of my elementary school–age children. For weeks, we had been focusing on the fruit of self-control. My child's lack of self-control was affecting every area of her life. Whether it was getting up when the alarm went off or finishing schoolwork *before* moving on to other things, we were struggling to make progress.

After several days of back-to-back coaching, discipline, and correction, I was weary. It seemed that my daughter wasn't interested in what I was trying to teach her—in fact, I felt as if she wasn't even listening! Looking back, I can see clearly that my pride was on the line. I felt I was failing as a mother, when the reality was simply this: I had forgotten a core truth about parenting. The heart issue wasn't up to me. It was up to the Lord.

How thankful I am for the Word of God! As I opened my Bible, the words about the fruit of the spirit took on fresh meaning. "The Holy Spirit produces this kind of fruit in our lives. . . . There is no law against these things" (Galatians 5:22-23).

Do you see? The first four words of this beautiful verse tell us so much about our job and God's job when it comes to parenting. We can work and work at the heart issues with our kids, but ultimately, it's not our job to produce such a fruitful outcome in the lives of our children. It's the job of the Holy Spirit.

This is so freeing! If you have put yourself in the role of the Holy Spirit, if you're taking on too much responsibility, if the pressure is too great—step back and assess your heart. Are you asking the Holy Spirit to give you wisdom and peace as you shepherd the hearts of your children? If not, you're carrying too much. *The Holy Spirit produces fruit.* Pray and see what He will do!

Parenting Well: Teen Edition

Look to the LORD and his strength; seek his face always.

1 CHRONICLES 16:11, NIV

I'VE ALWAYS SAID THAT IF PARENTING doesn't drive you to your knees—you're doing it wrong. This truth hit me one afternoon as I was thinking back over many seasons of motherhood. The first "season," of course, is pregnancy. We pray for strength and for a healthy outcome. Little ones require supernatural physical endurance with a splash of "adult conversation, please," but as the littles grow into *sort-of-big*, new seasons arrive with them. Teaching (read: *modeling*) the fruits of the Spirit (see yesterday's devo) and offering course corrections as needed will test our resolve and bring delight at the same time.

Motherhood is always changing.

There's something about the teen years, though, that many moms dread. We've been told teens are *dreadful*, so it makes sense that when the time comes, we tread carefully into it. But here's the thing—parenting teens well requires that we allow God to parent *us* well.

Teens are facing a world that many of us parents barely recognize. We are grappling with everything from faith in God to human sexuality to the preciousness of life—and our teens are doing it largely in front of an audience, thanks to social media.

Oh, how we need the wisdom of God.

Thankfully, God knew that we would be facing times like these. The hot-button issues of the day don't take God by surprise. Nothing your teen does will be outside of God's ability to redeem and restore. So if you discover that your teen has viewed pornography, don't panic: *pray.* When your teen questions your authority or pushes just the right button on the parenting dashboard, pray. If your child has made a poor decision, don't compound it by making a poor decision of your own. Instead, take it to the Lord in prayer and listen for His wisdom.

The teen years are chock full of opportunities to build rock-solid relationships with our children. Is the time you have with your teen drawing to a close? Don't waste it, precious mom! Ask the Lord to help you reach the heart of your older child. He will give you what you need to not only survive parenting teens, but to thrive in the teen years.

God understands the challenges we face in *every season* of motherhood. If you need wisdom and strength, take a page from God's handbook: "Look to the LORD and his strength; seek his face always." Notice that little word *always*? The verse doesn't say "occasionally" or "when things get really bad."

God's Word tells us to *always* seek Him—and He means it.

I'm Sorry

Be kind to each other, tenderhearted, forgiving one another,
just as God through Christ has forgiven you.

EPHESIANS 4:32

I HAVE NEEDED MANY DO-OVERS IN more than thirty years of mothering—but one stands out.

Jay and I always dreamed that our house would be the house that our kids wanted to bring their friends to. We hoped our house would be full of teens and movie nights and . . . well, all the things. (I was nineteen, and he was twenty-one when we got married. We had no idea that having children would age us overnight.)

When our oldest daughters were new high schoolers, we were still having babies. This complicated our young dreams of being "that house," but we soldiered on. One night, our oldest asked if youth group friends could come over. They planned on baking cookies and watching a movie in our family room. It seemed like a great idea, so we agreed.

The kids started arriving around seven on a Thursday night, and I greeted everyone with a smile—in my pajamas. The newborn was getting ready for her next feeding, and I was looking forward to the possibility of three glorious hours of uninterrupted sleep.

As you can imagine, fifteen-plus kids in the kitchen does not make for great sleep. I carefully laid the baby in her bassinet and tiptoed into the kitchen. "Hey, kids," I said, "can you please keep it down? The baby just fell asleep, and the toddler is in bed too. Thanks!"

Of course, the kids didn't stay quiet, and after several visits from *Nice Mommy*, they got *Mean Mommy*. I yelled, "Be quiet!!!" along with a few other exclamations. The kids quickly shuffled out of the kitchen, leaving the cookie dough churning in the mixer.

My work was done . . . until the Holy Spirit's gentle conviction prompted me. My face was red as I opened the door to the girls' room and offered a tearful apology. I tried not to make excuses. After all, there were fifteen pairs of eyes staring, and three of those were my kids'. I noticed a sixteen-year-old girl quietly crying near the back wall. I felt so ashamed!

"I'm sorry," I gently repeated. "I'm so glad you're here. Really! Please forgive me."

And then it happened. "No, you don't understand," the girl said. "I would give anything to hear my mom apologize just one time. Thank you for saying you're sorry." I could hardly believe it. It taught me an important lesson: when we humble ourselves to say we're sorry, God does the rest.

There's power in your words, sweet mom. Do you need to apologize today? Don't wait.

God's Ways Are Best

"My thoughts are nothing like your thoughts," says the LORD.
"And my ways are far beyond anything you could imagine."

ISAIAH 55:8

IF THERE'S ONE THING MOTHERHOOD HAS taught me, it's this: I am a woman in need of the grace and correction of the Lord. I like to be in control. In March of 2003, I gave birth to a beautiful baby girl. She came into the world right on time—but it was God's timing. Eight months earlier, I wasn't so sure I appreciated God's timing. In fact, I hope you won't think less of me if I admit that I was not at all pleased when I saw the "+" sign appear on a pregnancy test.

My hunch is I'm not alone in my visceral reaction to this unexpected news. I was hip-deep in potty training, relatively new to homeschooling, and still recovering from my last pregnancy and birth, which had been difficult.

In tears, I called my mom.

"Hello?" My mom's voice on the phone was comforting—she would understand. With seven kids of her own, she had been down this road before. I was surprised, though, by the emotion that overwhelmed me. A lump the size of Oregon seemed to fill my throat. After a few attempts, I whispered, "I'm pregnant."

"Oh honey!" my mom began. "You're not ready for this, are you?"

I so appreciated her willingness to acknowledge that sometimes, even good things don't feel very good. Mom knew that my heart needed a change of perspective. "Do you know what you need to do right now?" she offered. When I didn't answer, she offered an answer of her own. "*Breathe. I'm listening.*"

I told her all the reasons why I doubted myself as a mother. As the words tumbled out, my emotional equilibrium seemed to return. It wasn't the fact that I was pregnant, it was the fact that I had not decided to be pregnant. My control freak roots were showing! In truth, I wanted to make the decision—and instead, it had been made for me. (And yes, I know how it happened.)

Can you relate? As we continued to talk, my mom offered a gentle course correction, reminding me that God works all things together for our good. She was right, of course. In my desire to be in control of my plans, I had forgotten that God's plans are much better than mine!

If you're struggling to allow God to be God, breathe His mercy in deeply with me. God's heart toward you is always good. If you're rearranging your plans for His right now, rejoice! *Good things are coming.*

One Day

He will wipe away every tear from their eyes, and death shall be no more, neither shall there be mourning, nor crying, nor pain anymore, for the former things have passed away.

REVELATION 21:4, ESV

It is my speaking season. As Jay drives through the mountains en route to Nashville, my heart is heavy. A dear friend reached out to me last night. Her son had taken his life. No warning. No explanation. The grief is incomprehensible. *It's an epidemic*, I think. *Lord, make it stop!*

In the last three years, I've been touched by suicide more than I ever imagined I could be. A homeschool mama who left two amazing kids and a grief-stricken husband, the daughter of a well-loved leader in the homeschool community, the son of a pastor. Suicide is no respecter of station in life, religion, economic status, or even past hurt.

If you've been touched by the pain of suicide, or if you know someone who has, lean in close. Hear my heart, because we have to talk about the demon behind this epidemic. As mothers, we can help to remove the stigma of suicide by linking arms and allowing the topic into our moms' groups and organizations without shrinking from it. We do this by acknowledging grief in light of God's mercy and healing. As Christians, we know death is not the end.

About two months ago, my friend George announced that his teenage son had taken his life. I was amazed at his ability to redirect his community's pain, grief, and shock toward the hope we have in Jesus.

At the funeral, he acknowledged his son's pain and the particularly acute pain of suicide—but up against the grace and mercy of God. I believe some of George's son's friends heard the gospel for the first time at that service.

The main thing is that this world is not our home, and it's not our hope. Our hope is in Jesus. And while the hurt is unescapable, we have the ultimate escape in Jesus. Jesus knows this is unbearable. He has been there. God knows what it's like to lose a son.

I've never seen the devil so hard at work to take out a generation of young people. Ultimately this battle is spiritual. It's Ephesians 6 on the big screen. It's hard, but we will have victory. In the meantime, we cling to the only real hope we have: one day, God will settle the score. We will see our sons and daughters, friends and loved ones again because Christ has defeated death.

We don't need to understand right now. God promises that one day we will.

The Original Pinterest Mom

Who can find a virtuous and capable wife? She is more precious than rubies.

PROVERBS 31:10

PROVERBS 31, THAT FAMOUS PASSAGE IN the Bible that seems to be guilt inducing and inspiring at the same time, depicts a mother who appears to have it all, starting with servants and some spare cash for vineyard purchasing. As if that weren't enough, her children stand and bless her! Her husband adores her, and she's got great business savvy. She also has her emotional house in order—a rare combination indeed.

Like browsing picture-perfect images on Pinterest, it's easy to read this passage and see all the ways we don't measure up, isn't it? There have been days when load after load of cold, wrinkled laundry seems to mock my resolve, when I can't muster up the energy to make dinner or check that the kids' chores are done. Sometimes I wonder what my kids will say when they look back at the way I mothered them— especially when I compare myself to others.

Precious mom, don't fall into the trap. We don't grow by comparing ourselves to others—we grow when we look to Jesus for approval instead of to people. We learn to discern the voice of conviction from the guilt-inducing voice of condemnation. Condemnation pushes us down—but God's gentle voice of conviction lifts us up. If you struggle to see yourself as someone who could identify with the Proverbs 31 woman, it's likely because of false guilt. Satan uses it to trap us in a never-ending cycle of insecurity.

When we read Proverbs 31 through the eyes of insecurity, we miss the heart of the passage. What is more precious than rubies? A virtuous and capable wife. Do you doubt your ability to do what God has called and equipped you to do? Do you struggle to see yourself as the virtuous woman God created you to be?

The way out of the cycle of insecurity is through the door of grace.

God, who knew you from before the foundations of the earth, *chose you* to mother your unique and precious children. He chose you, knowing your propensity to wait on a dinner plan. He chose you, knowing that you would lose your temper and shout in your anger. He knows your struggles and insecurities. He wants to help you find victory.

Knowing that we are chosen by God helps us to reframe the way we see ourselves. We are full of promise and possibilities, not only for our children but for every aspect of influence God gives us. So long, insecurity! Today, I choose to believe I am who God says I am.

Pass the Baton

Paul came to Derbe and then to Lystra, where a disciple named Timothy lived.

ACTS 16:1, NIV

HAVE YOU NOTICED A GAP IN generational mentoring? There's the greatest generation, the boomers, Gen X, the millennials, and Gen Z. We're divided, all right—and yet God's Word paints a more inclusive picture for how we should be interacting across generational divides. According to the Bible, we need each other.

One of my favorite examples is found as we study the life of the apostle Paul. He was always forward thinking when it came to passing the baton. It was through Paul that Timothy's mother, Eunice, and his grandmother, Lois, had become Christians. Paul wrote about this important influence in Timothy's life: "Paul reminded him, 'I call to remembrance the genuine faith that is in you, which dwelt first in your grandmother Lois and your mother Eunice, and I am persuaded is in you also'" (2 Timothy 1:5, NKJV).

Timothy and Paul became very close friends. Paul was older than Timothy, and he described their friendship as being like that of a father and son (see Philippians 2:22). Paul described Timothy as "my son whom I love" (1 Corinthians 4:17, NIV).

Often, we think of "mentoring" as something that can happen only after we've been down the road a long way—but that's not the case at all in God's economy. If you've only been a mother for a year, you have more experience than the mom who just found out she is pregnant with her first child. If you're a grandmother—boy howdy—get out there and share what you've learned!

Mentoring can be as simple as having another mom over for coffee, or hosting a MomStrong Bible study in your home once a week. The key is to involve the younger moms in your effort to grow in Christ and in your skill as a mother.

By the time Paul became friends with Timothy, his own life was drawing to a close. Perhaps this is why he involved Timothy in his work right from the start. God blessed this unique friendship, and the Bible records the impact. Speaking of their shared mission, Paul wrote, "Day after day the congregations became stronger in faith and larger in size" (Acts 16:5, *The Message*).

How amazing would it be if we saw Bible study groups of mature, Christ-following mothers become "stronger in faith and larger in size" as a result of our partnership in ministry? Who can you mentor today? Our time here is brief, so let's get off the bench and onto the battlefield, moms! Let's be sure to pass the baton!

Stay on the Path!

They do not compromise with evil, and they walk only in his paths.

PSALM 119:3

"STAY ON THE PATH!" I HOLLERED at my son as we walked along the trails that meandered up and down the South Rim of the Grand Canyon. I could tell by his movements that he was contemplating whether those "keep off" signs were serious or not. The risk of falling seemed, at least momentarily, worth the "reward" of a good picture and a few likes on Instagram. "Remember—no compromise!"

The South Rim of the Grand Canyon truly is one of the most spectacular things I have ever seen. Only a few feet of dirt, trees, and rocks make up many of the paths along the rim's edge. In places, the rim is lined with blocks of jagged, unstable rocks. Is it dangerous? Obviously. But the siren song of the majestic canyon, with its layers of red and green rocks that seem to go on forever, draws hikers off the path and closer to the edge every day.

It's not like we were unaware of the dangers. For months, we had been planning to visit the canyon. As we drove from Washington State to Arizona, we talked about the importance of staying on the path. Good mom that I am, I even printed some articles to read about people who fell to their deaths at the Grand Canyon— all because they refused to stay on the path. One foolish, prideful compromise could have deadly results.

Compromise in our Christian walk can have serious consequences too. To compromise is to violate our own set of guiding principles and agree to something we know is foolish because we think that the consequences won't be lasting or severe. Many Christians today are engaging in compromise with regard to God's design for marriage, for example. It's easy to compromise to stay comfortable, but we need to be very careful about this! Just like walking too close to the edge of the South Rim can put us at risk of falling, compromise with the world puts our walk with God at risk. It's a lot like walking on the edge of sin. When we flirt with sin, we demonstrate that we don't understand the danger it puts us in.

The world will tempt you to compromise. It will tell you that you only need enough of Jesus to stay out of hell but not enough to walk in victory. Stay on the path! Do not compromise with evil. The risk isn't worth any brief moment of reward.

A Time to Sow, A Time to Reap

Only the tribe of Judah remained loyal to the house of David.

1 KINGS 12:20, NIV

PARENTING CHILDREN IS ONE OF THE most important things you will ever do. All throughout the Bible, we see examples of good parenting and the fruit it produced—and we see examples of parents who neglected their responsibilities. We can see these same things happening around us today. In many cases, we need only to look one generation back to get to the root of serious issues in our churches and our government today. Nowhere can we see the importance of parenting better than in the life of Solomon.

For all of Solomon's amazing qualities, he was not a very good father. He seemed to misunderstand the basic wisdom of "sowing and reaping," and as a result, generations after him suffered.

One of the most poignant examples of this is found in his son, Rehoboam. Rehoboam, Solomon's heir to the throne, was a disgrace to his father. He rejected the advice of experienced elders and instead foolishly chose to accept the unwise counsel of friends. The results of his immature leadership proved to be devastating for the nation when the northern kingdom (Israel) chose to rebel, plunging the nation into idol worship (see 1 Kings 12:1-24).

We can't lay this solely at the feet of Rehoboam, of course. Thanks to the poor leadership of his father, he had inherited a mess. For all the wisdom that Solomon displayed, his son was unwise. He did not deal wisely with his opponents. He failed to listen to wise counsel and chose instead the company of fools.

Rehoboam did not listen to the people either.

When the counsel of Israel approached Rehoboam asking for relief, he "turned a deaf ear to the people" (1 Kings 12:15, MSG). They realized that he "hadn't listened to a word they'd said" (verse 16) and rebelled.

I have to wonder if the reason Rehoboam did not listen was that his father did not listen to him.

As a result of the rebellion against Rehoboam, most of Israel rallied around his rival, Jeroboam. "Only the tribe of Judah remained loyal to the house of David" (1 Kings 12:20, NIV).

Yet again, war broke out (see 1 Kings 12:21), and the kingdom was divided. Solomon's son, and the nation, reaped the consequences of poor leadership. We too reap what we sow. What are you sowing right now in the lives of your children?

Don't Give Up!

When I was in deep trouble, I searched for the Lord.

PSALM 77:2

HAVE YOU EVER FELT LIKE QUITTING? Giving up? Throwing in the towel? Crying uncle?

I have. Maybe it's a strong-willed child or that struggle to get into an exercise routine. Maybe you're reading this right now and your marriage is struggling. Maybe you're a homeschool mom wondering if the job you're doing will ever bear fruit.

Whatever it is you're struggling with today, I want to encourage you to stay in the fight. You see, the fight you're fighting matters more than you know.

In 2021, I announced a run for Congress. Having never run for a political office before, I did the best I could to prepare: I spoke with former and current state and federal representatives. I sought counsel from men and women in positions of influence. My husband and I prayed for weeks, and then I made my announcement to run.

Nothing could have prepared me for the onslaught to come—and I mean *nothing*. The lies in the paper, the horrifying television commercials, friends who turned their backs on me, and more. The Lord and I spent a lot of time together in the months that followed. Over and over, I found myself in the Psalms, pouring my heart out to the Lord. Precious hours of prayer passed during that time in my life. In some ways, it reminded me of other seasons of stress and struggle. You know, the ones that we go through during the different seasons of motherhood.

In the moments when I felt I could not go on, God would show me just the right psalm for my particular situation. Come to think of it, God has been picking me up, dusting me off, and reminding me that the battle I'm facing is spiritual for nearly all of my life.

I have a hunch He's doing that for you too. You see, God wants you to be victorious in the battles that you are facing. Be in His Word, mom! Ask the Lord to speak to you through the pages of the Bible. If He calls you, He will equip you, but more than that, He'll encourage you every step of the way. He's good like that.

Strength through Trust

David strengthened himself with trust in his GOD.

1 SAMUEL 30:6, MSG

IS MOTHERHOOD OVERWHELMING? Maybe it's not motherhood, per se, but the combination of motherhood and a culture careening into darkness that is so overwhelming. Everywhere I look right now, the culture seems to be fixated on reaching my children and my grandchildren.

In 1 Samuel 29–30, we read about some terrible times for the people of God. David has reached a low point in his life. After a series of ill-advised decisions, he is in a real crisis of his own making. (Sound familiar?)

It's easy for us to feel like we are living in a particularly wicked time, but when we study the Bible, we see that the brutality brought into this world by sin has been here for a long time. The answer then is the same answer now, and David modeled it well, even in the face of his own sin and failure. In the middle of all David's problems, the Bible records how he kept going: "David strengthened himself with trust in his GOD" (1 Samuel 30:6, MSG).

I don't know about you, but if I am not in the Bible, I can quickly feel overwhelmed, outnumbered, outmanned, and outmaneuvered. Like David, I need to strengthen myself in the Lord—but even more important than that, my children need to see me doing it. After all, our kids are learning how to navigate this crazy world by watching us do it. You don't have to have the answers, dear one! You just have to go to the One who does.

How are you doing in the midst of the day's headlines and challenges? Are you trusting in God? Are you finding your strength in Him and His Word, or are you scrolling mindlessly through social media in an attempt to distract yourself from the hard work of learning to trust the One who made you?

Today, let's purpose to follow David's oh-so-human example and spend time in the Bible. That's where you will find new morning mercy and strength to face whatever is coming next. That's where your heart will be renewed. No matter what struggle you're walking through right now, God has strength for you as you trust in Him.

Can't Sleep

In peace I will lie down and sleep, for you alone, O LORD, will keep me safe.
PSALM 4:8

ARE YOU TIRED, PRECIOUS MOM? Maybe the kids have been keeping you up—maybe it's a recurring nightmare or simply the pressure of this weighty world we're living in. Stress, financial issues, health concerns, or loss can steal precious time from us in the middle of the night. If you're struggling to find perspective from a place of sleep deprivation, be encouraged. God works the night shift too.

Sometimes we forget that God cares about every little nuance of our mothering journey, including the restless nights when sleep eludes us and the morning comes too soon. God knows very well our human condition. He hears the cries of weary mothers, up all night from worrying or caring for a sick child. His Word is relevant. I have always marveled at the way Scripture addresses our felt needs. We can go to His Word for encouragement.

In 2018, our family was going through a painful time. We were grieving the loss of a friendship while at the same time struggling to keep what felt like fifteen balls in the air. One by one, the balls began to drop as night after night, I was awakened by thoughts of insecurity stemming from the pain in my heart. I wanted the Lord to rescue me. Like David, I was weary. I needed God's help to quiet my mind and spirit so that I could rest and be restored.

In some ways, my lack of sleep was pride. It was me saying to God, "I don't think You can handle this, so here, I'll stay up all night and think about it." What I *should* have said was much simpler: *Lord, I am in need of rest. Help me to rest in You.* When we learn to do that, things change.

God understands your sorrow. He knows your innermost fears and struggles—and He says, *Rest in Me.* He knows that the enemy of our soul isn't a fairy-tale enemy. Jesus promises us that we can lie down and sleep in peace, for *He* is the one who keeps us safe. When He makes a promise, we can take it to the bank.

So if you're struggling to find peace, and if that lack of peace is robbing you of sleep, know that God is able to restore you.

Worn Out

I am worn out waiting for your rescue, but I have put my hope in your word.

PSALM 119:81

IT WAS FOUR O'CLOCK ON A Tuesday afternoon when I decided that I was no longer interested in what any of my children had to say. The dishes were piled up in the sink and on the countertop. Every laundry hamper in the house was overflowing. At least two of my children had been what my mama would have called "mouthy" to me. Schoolwork sat unfinished at the kitchen table, and speaking of the kitchen table, I had no plan for dinner.

I hate it when I have no plan for dinner. Come to think of it, that's probably what provoked my screaming fit. It wasn't my best mom moment, if you know what I mean.

"Get down here!" I yelled. "Every. single. one. of. you!" One by one, six of our seven children gingerly made their way downstairs. They looked worried, and with good reason. I outlined my grievances, addressing everyone—from toddlers to teenagers. I wasn't kind. In fact, I said things I wish I hadn't. I was at the end of my rope.

After my rant/lecture was over, I gave the kids their marching orders and retreated to my bedroom, feeling like an utter failure as a mom. Why was I so angry? Why was my soul so weary? Hot tears ran down my face. Reaching for a blanket, I caught a glimpse of my dust-covered Bible, sitting on the nightstand.

In a moment, I knew a nap was not what I needed. I needed Living Water.

In the day-to-day busyness, I had allowed pride to sneak into my life. Pride says, "I don't need to spend time with the Lord today. I've got this thing figured out." And before I knew it, a day turned into a week, and a week into a month of me trying to do it all myself. Suddenly, I realized how in need of God's help I really was. Without Living Water, my spiritual eyes had grown dim, and my perspective was skewed.

I'm so glad God understands. As I came to Him in prayer, His grace washed over me. "Lord, I'm sorry for thinking I could do this without You," I prayed. "Please help me to see my children with fresh eyes. Help me to put my hope in You alone."

Ask yourself, *Have I been drinking Living Water?* Is your hope in God's Word? Are you resting in Him and asking for wisdom and help daily? I promise, precious mom—He's waiting with open arms. Let your weary heart find rest in God alone.

A Peaceful Home

A wonderful future awaits those who love peace.

PSALM 37:37

HAS YOUR HOME BECOME A PLACE filled with strife and bickering? It's amazing how quickly it happens. One minute, you've got a perfectly compliant, cheerful child, and the next she turns three. Tantrums begin. Back talk disobedience. It can be frustrating and bewildering. Can you relate? I can!

Something that is sorely lacking in our world today is the *pursuit* of peace in our homes. As a speaker, I am privileged to hear from thousands of mothers every year at events and through my podcast. You might not be surprised to learn that upwards of 80 percent of the moms who talk to me say their homes are not peaceful.

Recently a young mom confessed that her husband no longer looked forward to coming home after work because his kids were mouthy and disrespectful. To make matters worse, they were constantly bickering with one another. "What can I do?" the mom lamented. "They won't listen to me." She went on to talk with me about all the positive things she was doing to encourage her children to choose peace and kindness. With everything from sticker charts to special lunch choices, this mom was going all-out for her kids.

"I'm trying to be their friend!" she said. Bingo. We'd found the problem.

Mom, your kids do not need your friendship when they are under your direct care. They need your loving guidance. After all, we are not raising children to stay childish; we are training them for adulthood. This requires consistency regarding your expectations and follow-through when the guidelines you give are not respected or followed.

Is it hard? YES! Mothering is hard—but the peaceful fruit of righteousness is worth pursuing. If your home is a place of strife and yelling, it's time to take a hard look at how it got that way and begin to take steps of obedience in your own life as you focus on loving your children enough to correct their behavior.

This mom went home that afternoon and began to implement sweeping changes with her children. She put an immediate stop to the yelling and began to consistently follow through when the children slipped back into old habits. The benefits of her hard work could soon be seen not only in her children but also in her marriage.

A peaceful home is worth the work it takes to get there. Don't let strife and disrespect continue in your home. Ask God to help you be the mom He made you to be. God's Word is true, mama—a wonderful future awaits those who love peace.

What to Tell a Tattletale

Why worry about a speck in your friend's eye when you have a log in your own?

LUKE 6:41

"Moooommm! She hit meeeee!" my daughter sobbed, running up the stairs to the laundry room where I stood surrounded by at least six loads of cold, wrinkled laundry waiting to be folded and put away. (At least it was clean, right?)

"What happened?" I asked. For the next several minutes, my daughter lamented all the wrongs that had been done to her that day by her siblings—culminating, of course, in the fight that sent her running to me. I was mad. I was tired of the tattling, and frankly, I had a hard time thinking my other child had instigated the brawl.

She tattled some more—this time being sure to include that her sister had disobeyed me the night before and, instead of unloading the dishwasher, had gone outside to play. And that was it. The proverbial "last straw" that seemed to ruin my ability to see the situation clearly. One child told the story one way, while the other child had a completely opposite version. What was I supposed to do?

Well, to make a long story short, let's just say I spanked the wrong child. I know. I know. Let's keep this between us, okay?

In a classic "he said, she said," I took the bait and was manipulated by a very cute kid with eyes that *just would not tell a lie to me*. Except that I missed a key clue in the very beginning: the tattletale was not concerned one bit with her part in the altercation. She was out for revenge.

And I'd say she got it.

Mothers, we need the wisdom of Solomon to know how to make wise judgments when our children tattle on each other—and we also need to ban tattling unless the offense is truly serious. See what I mean about needing wisdom?

God's Word instructs us to remove the plank in our own eye before removing the speck in our friend's eye. It's human nature, and frankly, it's easier to see the faults in others and miss our own part in the problem. As mothers, we know that this does not get easier as we get older either! We need the Lord's help to model this well for our children, teaching them to be introspective rather than focused on the sin of other people. The next time your kids tattle, ask them, "What was *your* part in this? Because if *your* heart is wrong, tattling will make your offense greater in the end."

Rapture Ready

You also must be ready all the time, for the Son of Man will come when least expected.
MATTHEW 24:44

MY GRANDMOTHER LOVED THE WORD OF GOD. Some of my fondest memories include going to Sunday school with her. I loved the sound her Bible made as she opened it and thumbed through the worn pages until she found the passage she was looking for. The smell of ink and leather on her hands at the end of the day told me she had been studying her Bible.

When I was about seven, Grandma started talking to me about the imminent return of the Lord Jesus. If you're not familiar with the term *Rapture*, it's the word Christ-followers use for when the Lord returns for His people. I imagine that I was about the same age when I noticed that she lived in such a way as to be ready for His return. "Heidi, are you ready?" she would ask. She taught me that the unsaved would not be ready for the Rapture. Instead, the Bible teaches that the day of the Lord (which begins with the Rapture) will come upon the unsaved "like a thief in the night" (1 Thessalonians 5:2, NIV).

Those who have not accepted Jesus as their Savior will be left behind in the Rapture because they will not have the Spirit of Christ dwelling within them. Christians will be ready, however: "You, brothers and sisters, are not in darkness so that this day should surprise you like a thief" (1 Thessalonians 5:4, NIV).

We need to teach our children what it means to be ready for the Lord's return. Are you "Rapture ready?" Are your kids? Here's how we become ready for the Lord's return:

1. Receive Jesus as your Lord and Savior. The Rapture is only for believers (see John 10:14).
2. Know the Word of God. Place a high priority on knowing God, because you're going to see Him face-to-face someday (see 2 Timothy 2:15)!
3. Love others as Jesus loves you (see John 15:12).
4. Tell others about Jesus so they can receive Jesus as their Lord and Savior too (see 2 Corinthians 5:20).
5. Examine your life regularly. You will want to hear "Well done, good and faithful servant" when you finally see God face-to-face (see Matthew 25:23).

Are you ready for the Rapture? Jesus knows His own—and He's coming back for them!

Let the Redeemed of the Lord Say So

Has the LORD redeemed you? Then speak out!
Tell others he has redeemed you from your enemies.

PSALM 107:2

MANY CHRISTIANS HAVE BEEN LED TO believe that because we trust in Christ, our lives will be easy. This couldn't be further from the truth. Many early Christians were killed for their faith. In Matthew 16:24-25, Jesus warned his disciples: "Whoever wants to be my disciple must deny themselves and take up their cross and follow me. For whoever wants to save their life will lose it, but whoever loses their life for me will find it" (NIV).

In 2017, our family walked through terrible suffering when my nephew was involved in a devastating and life-threatening car accident. At the beginning of our ordeal, we opened our lives to the public, inviting them to watch and pray with us as my nephew fought for his life. The reason we did this was threefold: we believe in the power of prayer (and decided to unashamedly ask for answers), we wanted to be an encouragement to people who were in the trenches and fighting their own personal battles, and we wanted to proclaim that we serve the Living God.

For months, we shared heartbreaking losses and miraculous victories with complete strangers from around the world. The response was incredible. Ultimately, the Lord answered our prayers for a miracle—and over many months, we were able to witness my nephew's physical healing. However, as God is the ultimate multitasker, and as He healed Bobby, He was also healing many who were watching this miracle unfold.

When we share what God is doing in our lives, others are strengthened and encouraged. In Psalm 107:2, the psalmist writes, "Has the LORD redeemed you? Then speak out!" I can almost hear the urgency in his voice; it's as if David senses that the time to speak out about what God has done for us will soon be over. It's as if the psalmist is saying, *Don't miss it! Share what God has done!*

Women! We have been redeemed! Because of the incredible sacrifice of the Lord Jesus on the cross, we have been saved from the eternal punishment of our sin. Because we serve a powerful God, we can see His hand in miracles that He's performed in our lives. If you are one of the redeemed, say so. Speak out!

In Pursuit of Wisdom

Teach us to realize the brevity of life, so that we may grow in wisdom.

PSALM 90:12

PSALM 90 IS THE OLDEST PSALM, written by Moses around the year 1440 BC. It is recorded as "A prayer of Moses, the man of God." What does it look like to be a man (or in this case, a woman) of God? Moses gives us a little insight in the psalm, which is good, because as moms, we're not just invested in our own walks with God but also heavily invested in our children's walks too.

If you have a Bible nearby (or a Bible app on your phone), take a look at Psalm 90. The first thing I notice as I glance at it is that Moses is very aware of the fragility of human beings. Verse 5 says, "You sweep people away like dreams that disappear. They are like grass that springs up in the morning." Moses gets it. We're here on the earth for only a little while. The time we have to train our kids while they are young is even shorter.

Moses points out in verse 8 that we are sinful. Moms, let's teach our kids that they are born sinful, in need of a Savior!

Next, Moses seems to linger on the fact that our lives are short, especially in comparison to God's eternal nature. He says, "Seventy years are given to us! Some even live to eighty. But even the best years are filled with pain and trouble; soon they disappear, and we fly away" (Psalm 90:10).

As we teach our children that life passes quickly, let's also remind them that as Christians, we have a destination! This world is not our home—someday, we're going to "fly away"! Praise the Lord!

This is our hope—and the hope we have for our children too.

Finally, Moses asks the Lord to help him have the right perspective. Oh, how we need this as mothers. We can learn a lot from Moses' simple prayer: "Teach us to realize the brevity of life, so that we may grow in wisdom" (Psalm 90:12).

Moses got it right. He knew what to ask for, and he knew who to ask. With God's help, we can grow in wisdom too.

Babies = Blessing

Children are a gift from the LORD.

PSALM 127:3

IN THE SPRING OF 2010, my wonderful husband and I learned that we were going to have another baby. Our oldest daughter was a high school senior. Yep. That's nineteen years between our oldest and youngest. Believe me when I say that I never planned on having a baby in my forties. When I married at nineteen, I hoped to be done having babies by the time I was thirty.

That was then.

Most people thought that this pregnancy must have been some sort of accident. I assure you, it was not. This seventh child was wanted and prayed for. I was forty-one years old (so no spring chicken), and this was my eighth pregnancy. Honestly? We thought we would be "done" after four kids, but something transformative happened in our hearts as our family grew. We began to see children as God sees them—not as burdens, but as blessings.

As we leaned into the blessing of family life, God taught us that He can be trusted. He provides. He guides. According to God, children are synonymous with blessing, and who doesn't want to live a life of blessing?

We believe that children equal blessing too, so, in the fall of 2009, knowing that the window was beginning to close on the time that I could bear children, we humbly asked God if He would be so kind as to give us one more child. God answered our prayer, blessing us with a little girl whom we named Saylor Jane.

As soon as we saw the positive sign on the pregnancy test, our hearts overflowed with joy. The reaction our announcement brought from family and friends was swift. Many people were genuinely happy for us. We soaked up encouraging words whenever we heard them.

But there were condescending comments too. In a public post on Facebook, one of my acquaintances said, "You're so . . . brave!" Now listen. Telling someone she's "brave" when she announces a pregnancy is a little like saying, "Bless your heart." We all know she didn't mean "brave," right?

I'll be honest: for a few days, comments like that threatened to steal my joy. But not for long. I believed too much in the blessing to live very long in a lie. Mom, if the culture has clouded your view of children, look to the Bible. God's heart is revealed in it—and His heart can change yours. God sees children as a precious blessing, and as His children, so should we.

Slow Down

Jesus said, "Come to me, all of you who are weary
and carry heavy burdens, and I will give you rest."

MATTHEW 11:28

You won't mind if I just pray here for a moment, will you? Maybe the conversation that I am having with the Lord will encourage you too. And if it does, I'm grateful.

Lord, I'm tired.

If I tell you why I'm weary, will You still hear my heart? Will I still hear Yours?

I know I am doing too much. Last week when You clearly said, "Say no," I said yes.

I'm sorry, Lord.

I don't know why I fight my flesh so much. I push myself to keep going when I really need to take a nap. I don't know how to slow down. I don't know how to be still, and yet—somehow—I know that when I come to You, I am.

My heart is burdened by the struggles that my adult children are facing. Help me come to You before I phone a friend or search the Internet for answers.

The little ones, oh Lord—You know how much I love being their mama—the little ones need more of me. Help me slow down and be present with them. I need to put my phone down, and I can't do it without a gentle reminder from You.

Search my heart, Lord. Show me where I'm off Your path. Father, teach me how to be the mother that You see when You see me.

Father, I need rest. Physical rest for sure, but I need spiritual rest too. I know what it's like to rest in Your arms, but somehow—in my effort to "do"—I forget to simply "be." Help me come to You and know that I am loved and accepted. Let me fall into Your arms of grace and be at rest.

Thank you, Lord, that You are aware of every circumstance of my life. You see the laundry piles and the half-painted railing on my back porch. You know the deadlines and commitments and hurry-up that I feel. I need Your help to know what to do and what to let go of.

Thank You that Your forgiveness is available and that Your strength is made perfect in my weakness. Let me lean hard into You. Help me to slow down and enjoy every good thing You have given. I don't want to be busy for the sake of being busy. I want to be busy doing what You want me to do. As I pray this prayer, I have confidence that You will help me sort things out. Thank you, Lord. Amen.

A Lasting Foundation

When the storms of life come, the wicked are whirled
away, but the godly have a lasting foundation.

PROVERBS 10:25

WE HAVE ALL HEARD STORIES OF men and women who once claimed the name of
Jesus but were "whirled away" by the storms of this life.

As mothers, it's easy to worry that our children will be whirled away when they
encounter their own storms. It seems that the enemy of our soul intently focuses
on deceiving the next generation.

If your heart is frightened, precious mom, look to Jesus. The Bible teaches us
that as God's children, we have a lasting foundation. Our foundation is Christ.
He is the solid rock on which we stand. His Word is infallible and unfailing, His
truth never changes, His love is everlasting, and His mercies are new each morning.

God promises us that though others around us may be whirled away by the
storms of this life, if we remain in Him, our foundation is secure. This is something
we must impress on our children. We need to teach them that there will be storms,
and that the enemy is real, but *without* frightening them. As children of God, we
are assured the victory in Jesus.

Our children must not see us living in fear of the storms around us. Instead,
they need to see that our confidence and shelter are found in Christ. How do we
do this? By reading the Word with our children, by taking our fears and frustrations
to the Lord, and by praising His name.

When was the last time you praised the Lord in the middle of a storm? Would
your children say that you trust God no matter what circumstances you are facing?
Praise is the antidote to panic. Praise lets the enemy know that you trust in the
Lord of heaven's armies.

Let the storms rage around you, beloved. The godly have a lasting foundation.
We are safe, secure, and sealed forever in Christ.

Like Smoke in the Eyes

Lazy people irritate their employers, like vinegar to the teeth or smoke in the eyes.
PROVERBS 10:26

HAVE YOU EVER HAD SMOKE GET in your eyes or cringed as a shot of vinegar rolled past your teeth? Talk about irritating! The Bible says this is what laziness is like. Solomon noted that lazy people irritate their employers like "smoke in the eyes."

There wasn't a lot of this kind of "smoke" in my house growing up. Idleness did not go over well with the matriarchs in my family. Between my mom and my grandmother, there was a double layer of protection against it. We were well aware that we were a necessary *and loved* part of making sure the house was running and in order. We also discovered early on that the consequences for failing to do our part were not worth the thirty minutes of ease that we had chosen.

It's easy to think that childhood is for childishness rather than a training ground for adulthood, and in many ways, culture accepts this idea. "Helicopter moms" hover over their children, and so-called "lawnmower" moms go ahead of their children, even into the teen years, "mowing down" any obstacles in the way of their children getting what they want. Nowhere was this better seen than in 2019, when the FBI arrested well-known actresses, prominent business people, and several college coaches in an investigation dubbed "Operation Varsity Blues."

Reports alleged that parents caught in the scheme had used bribery to ensure that their kids got spots in some of the United States' most prestigious schools. The problem was, their kids didn't earn those spots, and in the process, other students were cheated out of an opportunity they had worked for.

There's something to be said for valuing hard work. For earning what we have—and for teaching our children to do the same. Obstacles are what force us to grow. Chores, even for young children, accomplish much more than folded laundry or a clean kitchen—they help our kids gain confidence. This comes when they know they have something to offer and they work on the skill to do it well. When we insist that our children take the time to study for a test or finish the job they've been assigned completely (not halfway), we are teaching them skills that will help them thrive as adults.

Let's teach our kids the value of a job well done. As we do this, we are also saying that we value their role in our families and instilling the confidence they'll need to move into adulthood knowing that they're ready to tackle whatever comes next.

Today

Give us today the food we need.

MATTHEW 6:11

Do you like to plan things out? I sure do. It satisfies my type A personality and gives me the illusion that I'm in control—even though I'm not! When all seven of our kids were still at home, I loved to create menus and chore charts (which worked for approximately ten minutes), schedule dentist visits, and plan birthday parties. Even today, I like to keep my pantry full and my freezer stocked. With a household to run, planning is what. I. do.

What feels downright scary to a planner like me is to have just enough for today. I don't want to have enough for today—I want enough for next month too! I like to know that my family has been well taken care of and provided for.

Planning ahead isn't a bad thing in and of itself, but if we're not careful, it can take the place of reliance on our loving Father. Sometimes, planning so far in advance reveals a deeper spiritual problem within our mama heart: a trust issue.

The Bible is full of verses that highlight how God provides for us. In Matthew 6, Jesus models how to pray—in dependence on God and the belief that we do not need to worry about anything beyond today. God can handle it. The Father knows your needs, precious mom. He is not unaware of the mortgage payment that's coming up or the fact that your husband just lost his job. God can be trusted, right now, today.

Like a good father, God knows the difference between what we want and what we need. In a culture obsessed with getting our wants met quickly, it's easy to think we "need" something, when really, it's just something we wish we could have. It's easy to forget to ask the Lord about these things, isn't it? Remember, mom, God wants good things for us as His children. He knows what is best for us, and He wants to help us in our decision making. Isn't that amazing! How quickly we forget how loved we are!

As mothers, we need to be sure and teach our children how God's care extends to all His creation. From the beating of our hearts to the distance the sun is from the Earth, God has His eyes on it all. He has never failed us, and He never will. As you make your meal plan for next week, keep in mind that God is in it all. Thank Him for all He has provided and for all He will provide in the months and years to come. God can be trusted!

Rescue Me!

Don't let us yield to temptation, but rescue us from the evil one.
MATTHEW 6:13

ARE YOU EVER FRUSTRATED BY YOUR own sin nature? I am! Over and over, I struggle with temptations that come my way: jealousy that pops up out of the blue, gossip that I engage in, the lack of contentment that leads to this purchase or that grumbling.

God's Word tells us that we have an adversary who is unyielding in his pursuit of God's people. In Ephesians 6:12, we're reminded that we're up against spiritual forces of evil in heavenly places—more than we can handle, apart from the saving power of Jesus and indwelling help of the Holy Spirit.

As part of this ongoing spiritual battle, we are tempted daily—but there is a way out of that temptation. It is found in yielding to the Spirit of God. In Matthew 6, Jesus is teaching us how to pray. I love that He uses the word "rescue." It's humbling to be in need of rescue, isn't it?

Listen. I've been in need of rescue a few times in my life. Trust me, it's embarrassing to shut down both sides of the interstate and watch helplessly while the traffic backs up and firefighters work to put out the flames that are leaping up from your RV. (Yeah. That happened.)

Truth is, we don't need to be rescued unless we've depleted our own resources. (Check.) We don't call for rescue unless we know for sure that the person next to us can't fix the problem. (Check.) Rescues aren't cheap. (Check.)

Because of our own sin, our resources have been depleted, and the people in our lives are helpless to fix our sin problem. God's rescue of us wasn't cheap either—it cost Him His only Son. Jesus gave His life to rescue us from sin. Our response to a rescue should be two things: gratefulness and humility. If we don't respond to this amazing rescue with gratefulness and humility, we don't fully grasp our need to be rescued. Because we have been rescued, we can be free from the grip and the consequences of our own sin. Praise the Lord!

Sometimes, we hide our struggles from our kids, but I want to encourage you to let your children know that you need rescuing too. Our kids need to know that they're not the only ones who need rescue. God will rescue them too.

True Beauty

You are altogether beautiful, my darling; there is no flaw in you.

SONG OF SONGS 4:7

DO YOU HAVE A DAUGHTER WHO is old enough to understand the concept of beauty? Does your son know where true beauty is found? The culture has it backward right now—and today, I want to encourage you to talk to your kids about their perception of beauty. You might be surprised.

God does not see beauty the way we define it. The world focuses on outer beauty. If we are honest, we would admit that we tend to focus on it too. It's been reported that sales of cosmetic products in the world will reach $863 billion by 2024.[1] That's a lot of mascara, mama!

Don't misunderstand—there's nothing wrong with the pursuit of outer beauty. I have been married for over thirty years now, and I hope I will always be beautiful in the eyes of my husband. I take care of myself with both my husband and myself in mind! Turning that boy's head is a top priority for me, and he knows it.

God made women different from men in many ways. Women display a beauty that is unique to the feminine form. Solomon showed us that our femininity is something to be celebrated and enjoyed. It's a gift from the Lord.

However, the Bible teaches us that not only is the beauty we have in this life temporary, but it can also trip us up when we focus on it. Our focus should be on our inner beauty! As mothers, we can model this for our daughters. Are we known for our kindness? Does our outer beauty reflect a heart of submission to the Lord Jesus—or does it serve to mask an ugliness beneath?

Solomon was so attracted to beautiful women that it caused him to sin. In Proverbs 11:22, he noted that outer beauty can't hold a candle to true inner beauty, comparing a beautiful woman with no discretion to a gold ring . . . in a pig's nose! Bottom line? A beautiful woman who lacks discretion *isn't beautiful at all*. Why? Because inner beauty is much more desirable and, ultimately, longer lasting than anything we can put makeup on.

Beauty, as defined by God, comes from within because it comes from God. We can enhance or eclipse beauty by our ability to be discerning. Let's check our hearts before we check the mirror, and teach our daughters to do the same. Ultimately, that's where true beauty originates.

---

[1] "Global Cosmetic Products Market Will Reach USD 863 Billion by 2024: Zion Market Research," GlobeNewswire, June 22, 2018, https://www.globenewswire.com/news-release/2018/06/22/1528369/0/en/Global-Cosmetic-Products -Market-Will-Reach-USD-863-Billion-by-2024-Zion-Market-Research.html.

God Disciplines Those He Loves, But I Can't!

Hope does not disappoint.

ROMANS 5:5, NKJV

HAVE YOU EVER STRUGGLED TO FOLLOW through with disciplining your child? If so, you're not alone. Parenting can be challenging at every stage, but God has given us a clear mandate to love and correct our children as they grow.

Listen, mom. I get it. We had no idea when we took on this role how completely exhausting and frustrating it could be to follow through with discipline and correction. But here's the thing: God wants us to lovingly discipline our children.

In 1 Samuel 2, we are introduced to Hophni and Phinehas, the sons of Eli. Eli was not your ordinary dad. He was a priest in the house of the Lord. His sons also served in the tabernacle, but the Bible records that they did not know the Lord (see verse 12). In fact, these boys were known throughout the city for their reckless and sinful behavior.

Worse than that, we learn that when word got back to Eli, he rebuked his sons but failed to make them stop their behavior—and so it continued. *God held Eli responsible for this.* Eli's unwillingness to discipline his own children demonstrated that some part of his heart was more concerned with his sons' pleasure than with correcting them as God required.

God sent a prophet to Eli with an urgent message regarding his family: "I will cut short your strength and the strength of your priestly house, so that no one in it will reach old age. . . . And what happens to your two sons, Hophni and Phinehas, will be a sign to you—they will both die on the same day" (1 Samuel 2:31, 34, NIV).

Eventually, the Philistines came against Israel to attack them. Eli's sons went to battle and took the Ark of the Covenant with them, thinking it would ensure their protection. God was not with them, and they were killed. When Eli learned that his sons were dead and the Ark had been lost, he fell off his seat, and his neck was broken. At the same time, Phinehas's wife died in childbirth—but not before naming her son Ichabod, saying, "The Glory has departed from Israel" (1 Samuel 4:21, NIV).

Why would I tell you this story? Because God takes parenting seriously—and so should we. If you notice your children struggling in their character, correct them. We cannot determine the paths our kids will take when they're older, but we can obey God's clear instruction to train them while they're young. You may feel like you can't follow through on discipline, but with God's help, you can!

Parental Discretion Advised

Discretion will watch over you, understanding will guard you.

PROVERBS 2:11, NASB

parental discretion *noun*

a parent choosing whether or not they want their child to do or see something;
e.g., Because of sexual themes in the movie, parental discretion is advised.

ONE NIGHT OUR HIGH SCHOOL GIRLS had invited some friends over to watch a movie. Jay had recently finished a project that we had dreamed about for many years: a big screen in our family room. While we watched in anticipation, the screen silently came down from the ceiling with the push of a button. The teens oohed and aahed, which was the response Jay had been waiting for. We want our home to be a place where the teens love to gather and where everyone feels welcomed and wanted.

After the movie was over, my husband and I decided to turn in for the night. Since it was *only* around ten thirty, the teens were up for another movie. I decided it sounded okay*ish* and headed up to bed. Did you catch my hesitation? That *ish* on the end of *okay* was the Holy Spirit.

About fifteen minutes into the movie, I decided to go down to watch for a bit. Something in my spirit was not at peace. Within a few minutes, I knew why. The movie contained an abundance of coarse language, adult themes, disrespect toward parents, and normalization of teen sex. No one seemed fazed.

I fidgeted. I *did not* want my kids watching this, but I didn't want to embarrass our guests and ask them to turn it off. After all—who wants to be *that mom*!? I don't—but I do. I believe God has given parents the responsibility for shepherding their children. I realized the only reason I wasn't being a great shepherd was because I was worried about what the kids would think of me.

That's not a good reason, moms. It's a human reason, but it's not a godly one. Proverbs 2:11 says that "discretion will watch over you." Discretion is the ability to make a wise decision. When we don't use discretion, God's Word warns us that we are left *unguarded*. I don't want my children left unguarded, so I let the kids know they would need to choose a different movie. I explained my concerns, and the teens, who clearly were struggling with their own consciences, thanked me for helping them make a better choice.

Mom, the Lord is holding you responsible for what your kids watch, how they dress, how they speak, and even what they listen to. Don't be afraid to step in. Listening to the Holy Spirit is always the right choice.

When There Are No Answers

You will not grieve like people who have no hope.

1 THESSALONIANS 4:13

On Mother's Day in 1986, a group of teenagers from an Episcopal school near Portland, Oregon, assembled just before midnight to embark on an expedition. Destination? Mt. Hood. They hoped to summit the majestic mountain, climbing 11,249 feet above sea level, as part of the school's adventure program for the sophomore class.[2]

This tradition was a test of endurance that would make "round the campfire" stories. In the months preceding the climb, students were taught basics of mountaineering: how to step-kick an ascent, self-arrest during a fall, administer basic field first-aid. The expedition was supposed to be a celebration. But it didn't turn out that way.

The group left under clear skies, but as they approached the half-way point, a fierce storm descended, bringing 103 mph winds—the same as a category 2 hurricane. The inexperienced climbers dug a snow cave in an attempt to wait out the storm. Nine died on the mountain, seven of them teenagers. As the news broke, I turned on the radio and listened for names of survivors. Only two made it out alive. My friend Richard was not one of them.

Richard was the last to be recovered off the mountain. When he was found, he had no pulse. His body temperature was barely above freezing. The brutal three-day search and rescue operation did not yield the happy reunions parents and friends were hoping for. The grief was unimaginable. The questions unbearable. Sixteen years old—and he was gone.

Sometimes, there are no answers.

Even though it has been decades since the tragedy on Mt. Hood, the lessons I learned during that time will stay with me forever. I was thankful my parents talked openly and honestly with me about death—and that they allowed me to grieve. The Bible teaches us that we will all be touched by death. In the months that passed, I watched as those who had no hope of ever seeing their son or daughter again grappled with the grief and pain of their terrible loss—and I watched those who knew Jesus try to understand. Sometimes, there is no understanding. As Christians, we grieve, but we do so with hope.

We have the hope of heaven. We know that because Jesus rose from the dead, death no longer carries the sting of permanence that sin requires. Precious mom, talk to your children about the hope they can have in Jesus.

We cannot know what tomorrow brings—but we can know who holds tomorrow. He is our hope.

---

[2] Pauls Toutonghi, "Mount Hood's Deadliest Disaster," *Outside*, November 2, 2018, https://www.outsideonline.com /outdoor-adventure/exploration-survival/mount-hood-disaster-1986/.

Friendship Is Worth Praying For

A sweet friendship refreshes the soul.

PROVERBS 27:9, MSG

I WAS FIVE YEARS OLD WHEN I met Annette. Our parents had enrolled us in kindergarten at Portland Christian Grade School in 1975. Annette was friendly and outgoing. She liked my orange plaid skirt and saddle shoes, and she noted right away that we both had glasses. She wasn't afraid to climb to the highest point on the play structure or challenge the boys to a rousing game of "boys chase the girls." It didn't take long for a friendship to form that would endure through decades.

For years, we played a game we made up with an imaginary adversary—a bush, if you must know. The bush had a name: Black Cape. Black Cape showed up without fail every. single. night. on the sidewalk just behind Annette's house. We pretended to be shocked every time we saw him. Who knew so much fun could be had with a large plant? We hid from BC in terror and jumped out at him when we felt particularly brave—though now I can't remember why. Before long, the other kids in the neighborhood were also playing the game.

I want my kids to have friends like Annette. I am always keeping an eye out and sending a prayer heavenward for good friends for my children. Friends shape our hearts for good, or for bad. Friendships are a huge part of our childhood memories. Today's verse says that "a sweet friendship refreshes the soul." How true that is.

Today, Annette is two states away from me. She and her husband have done a wonderful job raising their beautiful daughters, and I expect she'll join me in Club Mamsi before too long. Once in a while, we see each other in real life, and we're able to pick up wherever we left off.

Even today, this sweet friendship is a source of refreshment to my soul. Are you praying for friends for your children? If not, start today. Pray that your children experience godly friendships that will bring them refreshment and encouragement their entire lives.

Battle Ready

He trains my hands for battle.

PSALM 18:34

WHAT ARE THE HEADLINES IN YOUR neck of the woods right now? My hunch is that if you were to turn on the news or search the Internet for trending hashtags, most of what you would discover would be troubling. The Bible teaches us that the spinning sphere we call *home* is a war zone.

Since the fall of Adam and Eve, Satan has been waging war against God's image-bearers. He's still at it, of course, battling for the hearts and minds of human beings, but his tactics change with the times. Sin creeps into our hearts in new ways. Selfishness says, *"They don't appreciate me"* as I fold another pile of laundry, grumbling under my breath about the burden of taking care of my family. Distraction tries to keep me from focusing on things that carry eternal significance as I get caught up in a temporary argument on social media. At some point, I notice that it's actually hard to pry my eyes away from my phone.

How easy it would be, how *restful and weightless*, to trade my birthright as God's chosen ambassador for a moment of ease and acceptance by the world. After all, I am often battle weary. I am often tired of the fight. This world can be a wearying place to live.

Are you tired too? *Thank God, He understands.* God knows your human heart, right down to the tiniest temptation. He knows, better than anyone else, that we are only dust. He knows you're tired.

It's easy to lose sight of the real war and the real enemy—and God understands that too. That's why He gave us His Word. When I open my Bible, my heart is refreshed and my mind is renewed. When I take the time I thought I could not spare and spend it with Jesus, I am reminded that not only am I loved, but I was born for this.

I ask God for victory—starting with the unseen battles. I ask for His help to see my husband and my children through the lens of grace. I ask for wisdom. For love. For joy. As I pray, my eyes are opened, and I know He is listening, because my heart becomes soft again.

You see, beloved, God never designed you to engage in the battle on your own. He wants to train your hands and your heart for the battle you're facing today, and He wants to help you to be ready for the battles that lie ahead. Do you want to be victorious? Let God train you in His Word.

God's training leads to victory!

Kindness Matters

Show me unfailing kindness like the LORD's kindness as long as I live.

1 SAMUEL 20:14, NIV

NOT LONG AGO, I HAD TO CALL a utility company. I'll be honest: I can't stand making calls to utility companies—especially Internet and phone companies. I usually end up crying before I get an actual person who can help. Can you relate?

The call went as I'd expected. After weaving through the automated obstacle course and being on hold for over forty minutes, I was transferred to a call center in the Midwest. By this time, I was getting irritated. I was straight-up asking God to help me hold my tongue and choose kindness. I remembered my grandma saying, "You never know who's on the other end of the line. Be kind!"

With God's help and Grandma's wisdom, we got things sorted out. After two hours (yes, two hours) the call was finally coming to an end.

"May I have your email for a confirmation notice?"

"Sure," I said.

"Ummm, are you 'The Busy Mom'?"

Hesitation. "Yes."

"I've heard of you!" (At that moment I was very glad I had not been *that* customer.)

"I'm wondering if you can help me! What do you do?"

"Well—I love to help moms (and dads) learn how to be the parents God wants them to be. I believe that Jesus changes lives and that He can help us navigate a very confusing culture. He's the healer!"

"Wow!" she said. "I was just asking the Lord to send someone to help me. I minister to at-risk mamas—women who have fled abusive relationships and need a fresh start. I've been telling them about Jesus, and they're ready to go deeper! Do you have any resources? They want to grow!"

We spent the next fifteen minutes talking about our online Bible study community, momstronginternational.com, and some of the books I've written for mamas.

I sent her some books, and hopefully we'll be in touch for many years to come. She is making a difference in the lives of the women around her! Encouraging her was worth the two hours of my time spent on the call.

"I can't believe how God answered my prayer today!" she said as we hung up. "I was just on my break, asking the Lord to send help, and here you are. Thank you!"

And I thought it was just a call to fix my Internet. Be kind, friends! You never know who's on the other end of the line.

The Antidote to Despair

Then Elisha prayed, "O LORD, open his eyes and let him see!"

2 KINGS 6:17

ARE YOU WEARY, PRECIOUS MOM? I'm guessing even if you're in a season of rest, you have experienced a season of despair. There's a reason, and it goes beyond the daily grind of diapers, dishes, and discipline. In fact, one of Satan's primary goals is to drive God's people to despair. The Bible teaches us that we are engaged in a spiritual battle that rages around us night and day.

We must have our eyes open to see the weapons that cause us to grow weary. Even the Lord was tempted to the point of exhaustion. Satan wanted Jesus to question whether He was the Son of God. Can you imagine?

What was his key weapon? The word *if.*

"If you are the Son of God . . ." (see Matthew 4:1-11). Satan's schemes are crafted to cause us to question God, to cause us to become worn and weary. And just as he did with the Lord Jesus, Satan cleverly uses that little word *if* all the time to drive us to despair.

See if you have heard the oh-so-familiar voice of the enemy as you wrestle with thoughts that are not from the Lord: "*If* you were a good mother, your child would not have sinned. *If* you are the right person to raise your kids, you would not have so many struggles. *If* you tell anyone how hard it has been, you'll be looked down on. *If* your child was going to walk with God, there would be fruit by now. Just give up!"

Oh, how we need our spiritual eyes to be open as we raise our children! Don't let the enemy's accusations cause you to lose sight of the goal! You are raising parents for your grandchildren right now. Link arms with other mothers and grandmothers. Ask for help. Be real. Satan cannot encroach upon your thoughts if you guard your heart and mind in Christ Jesus.

Through the power of prayer, you can ask God to turn your "if" moments into "because" moments. God's tender voice will remind you that you are His child. "*Because* I am at work in you, your labor for Me is not in vain. *Because* I chose you, you are the right mother for your kids. *Because* I died for you, there is no longer any condemnation over you. *Because* you will fail from time to time, my mercy will always be available to you. *Because* my strength is found in weakness, you will have all the strength you need.

God's *because* is the antidote to Satan's *if.*

Everything's Going to Be Alright

We know that in all things God works for the good of those who love him..

ROMANS 8:28, NIV

A FEW YEARS AGO, WE WERE in a season of life that looked a lot like a scene from a home renovation show gone wrong: plumbing failures, siding worries, roof issues. It was not very much fun, and the stress level seemed to rise with each receipt from Home Depot.

One night, after a particularly busy day of home repairs, Jay decided we needed to take a break from it all. I came upstairs to find that Jay and the kids had drawn a beautiful bath for me, complete with Epsom salts and tealight candles. The kids were set to watch a movie with their dad while I relaxed in the tub. It was wonderful, and I grinned from ear to ear. My husband was grinning too. "Relax!" he said, as I got into the tub. "Take it easy." He was definitely scoring some big points in the marriage department!

I was thanking the Lord for that lavender epsom salt bath as I rested my head and closed my eyes. Suddenly, I noticed this weird smell in the air. *That's vaguely familiar*, I thought to myself. *It reminds me of the time my friend BURNED HER EYEBROWS OFF while opening her grill.*

Moment of silence. You guessed it. It was vaguely familiar—because my HAIR WAS ON FIRE! I had rested my head on a candle. There I was, in a dream state of sorts, hoping my ponytail was still attached to my head, splashing water everywhere. I got out of the tub in a pretty big hurry. (Try not to picture it.) I turned on the lights to assess the damage. There were black ASHES floating on the water. "That's hair ash," I whispered to myself. Yep. It. was. my. hair.

Jay came in. "What's that new perfume you're wearing?" He grinned. I was not grinning. "It smells like a cross between rosemary and campfire."

"That's because I sprayed rosemary ON MY HAIR before my bath!!!!" I wailed.

"Well," my sweet husband said, as I pulled clumps of hair off my head and threw them in the trash, "now when we say we run around like clowns with our hair on fire, YOU can actually mean it!" Funnyman. That's my husband.

But even in the craziness, I could see God. God knew this was going to happen because a sweet friend of mine—who happens to be a hairdresser—actually texted me the week before and offered to cut my hair for free. My appointment was already scheduled for the next morning!

Isn't God good? He doesn't miss a thing. Everything's going to be alright. God promises that He's working things out. Trust Him.

Who's Leading You?

The LORD must wait for you to come to him so he can show you his love and compassion.
ISAIAH 30:18

CAN YOU REMEMBER A TIME RECENTLY when you failed to ask the Lord which direction to go? I can. I've said yes when I should have said no. If I had spent just a little time with Jesus in prayer, I would have known the right answer. Instead, I felt too busy and relied on my own wisdom rather than seeking the Lord.

The result? Weariness that could have been avoided and unnecessary stress and tension in our home. All because I wanted to be my own boss. It's easy to think that we're "in charge" of our everyday lives, but God wants to lead and shepherd us through the hills and valleys we face.

The prophet Isaiah also noticed that God's people were prone to going their own way. Even though God had given them instructions to seek Him in all things, they failed to do so (see Isaiah 30:1-2). In fact, they disobeyed God's command to seek His counsel not once, but over and over.

We are so like God's chosen people, aren't we?

In this instance, the result of their unwillingness to let God lead them was truly disastrous. They headed off in the wrong direction, straight to Egypt without so much as a sideways glance toward God. The Israelites did not want the prophets to warn them. They wanted to make their own decisions.

I wonder if these bad decisions stemmed from the same spiritual laziness that I battle with. I tell myself that I don't have time to pray. I reason that the decision isn't that big of a deal. I talk myself into going my own way . . . even though I know better. It just seems faster and easier.

The result? More stress. More frustration. And the worst part? All of that can be avoided by simply letting the Lord direct my path.

Like the Israelites, we are a stubborn people. We resist God's plans for us because we want to be our own boss, when God wants to lead us in the right path—the path that leads to blessing and peace.

Thankfully, there is hope for our stubborn hearts. The Lord is a faithful God. He is actively looking to bless you and keep you on the path He has chosen. His condition? We must come to Him. We must wait on His instruction and listen for His voice.

God will never lead us where His grace will not sustain us. You can trust Him. Lean in, precious mom. Let Him lead.

Do You Believe?

Jesus said to her, "I am the resurrection and the life. Whoever believes in me, though he die, yet shall he live, and everyone who lives and believes in me shall never die. Do you believe this?"

JOHN 11:25-26, ESV

IT HAD BEEN LESS THAN SEVENTY-TWO hours since my wonderful father-in-law had been rushed to the hospital in the middle of the night. His sudden passing left us bewildered and exhausted. Just days earlier, we were around the dining room table, chatting with Dad about nothing in particular—and now, we were planning his memorial service. Now, I was holding a weeping little girl.

"What do you think heaven will be like, sweetie?" I asked as I gently wiped my nine-year-old daughter's tears. "What do you think Grandpa is doing right now?" Sydney looked at me with that beautiful, childlike faith that God loves and said, "I think heaven will be just like here, only better, because that's where Grandpa is. I think Grandpa is talking to God about us. He wants us to be okay."

She paused. "But, Mom, I am sure going to miss him!"

"I'll miss him too, sweet girl," I said. "Do you remember what Jesus said about death?"

She paused. "Yes, Mama," she said. "But it still hurts."

My heart was to "fix" the hurt my daughter was feeling. I wanted to soften the blow, but honestly? The hurt we feel at death is real. What we believe about death is a powerful force when we face it. It is never easy, but as Christians, we know it is not the end for those of us who have put our faith in Christ Jesus. Our children need to know this truth!

It's tempting to run from the topic, but I want to encourage you to impart the truth about the temporary nature of this life to your children. Listen to the tenderness in Jesus' voice as he comforts and exhorts the sister of Lazarus in John 11:25-26: "Jesus said to her, 'I am the resurrection and the life. Whoever believes in me, though he die, yet shall he live, and everyone who lives and believes in me shall never die. Do you believe this?'" (ESV).

Do you believe this? If we believe what Jesus taught about life after death, the lens through which we see death will change how we respond. The grief we suffer at the loss of a loved one can feel overwhelming, but God hasn't left us to suffer alone. If your heart has been shattered by grief, hold on to God's Word. His promises are for you. Whoever dies in Christ will live again. Do you believe?

Moved to Action

Phinehas stood up and intervened.

PSALM 106:30, NIV

TUCKED AWAY IN THE BOOK OF Numbers is the story of a faith-filled man named Phinehas. Phinehas was the grandson of Aaron, high priest of Israel. The Bible records that Phinehas did something that impressed God to the point that God made a covenant specifically with Phinehas and his descendants. Can you imagine? Here's what happened.

In Numbers 25, we find the Israelites camped out at a place called Shittim, in a territory occupied by the warmongering Moabites. The Moabites were well-known for their sinful behavior, especially regarding sex. Eventually, the Israelite men rebelled against God by engaging sexually with the women of Moab (see Numbers 25:1). Soon, many of God's people were enticed to sin until, eventually, they committed the grievous sin of idolatry as they worshipped false gods. God's anger burned against Israel, and a plague broke out among them.

God does not mess around with sin, mama. Moses was commanded to instruct the judge of each tribe to put to death each member who had committed idolatry. Then a man brazenly sinned by bringing a Moabite woman into the camp, in front of Moses! God was so angry, He was ready to punish the whole nation—when a godly man named Phinehas, filled with righteous anger, killed the man and woman who were openly mocking God and sinning in front of the people.

Enough! God was so impressed with this bold defense of His glory and His law that He made a covenant of peace with Phinehas, saying, "Since he was as zealous for my honor among [the Israelites] as I am, I did not put an end to them in my zeal. Therefore tell him I am making my covenant of peace with him. He and his descendants will have a covenant of a lasting priesthood, because he was zealous for the honor of his God and made atonement for the Israelites" (Numbers 25:11-13, NIV).

Did you catch that? Phinehas's righteous indignation saved the lives of many of God's people!

Our culture is awash in the kind of sin that Phinehas was driven to respond to. It's important to note that he did not react for his own glory; he did it for the glory of God. I pray that God would give us the strength, wisdom, courage, and zeal of Phinehas. I pray that we would raise men and women who are so zealous for the honor of God that they would be moved to action.

Let's be zealous in our defense of the glory and righteousness of our Lord, and by God's grace, let's teach our children to do the same.

Like Their Teacher

The student who is fully trained will become like the teacher.

LUKE 6:40

Every time I open my Bible, God shows me something new. I can read the same psalm a hundred times, and each time, the Holy Spirit offers fresh insight as something else is revealed. I credit my grandmother for passing on this love of Scripture to me—and I often wonder, *Am I passing this love on to my children?*

Every day, I pray that our children would grow to love and obey God's Word. I pray that they would see the power available to them because of Jesus—and I pray I can make the Bible come alive for them. As mothers, we have an awesome opportunity to help our children learn how much God has done for them and how powerful He is. I pray that they would be moved to action on behalf of the Lord Jesus—but mama, lean in close—*it's not enough to pray.*

The Bible teaches us that when our kids grow up, they will be like their teacher. We are their first teacher, aren't we? If we're going to pass on a love of the Bible to our kids, we need to actively engage in conversation with them about the Bible. They need to be in the Word with us—and they need to "catch" us in the Word ourselves.

When was the last time you sat down to read the Bible with your children, precious mom?

When I founded MomStrong International, it was with the hope that moms would get off the bench and onto the battlefield in the fight for the hearts and minds of our kids. Every month, we write "KidStrong" for the sole purpose of helping moms talk with their children about the truths that are in the Bible. I love hearing from moms who are beginning to see the changes that happen when we prioritize God's Word in our homes and hearts!

Ultimately, the Bible says that we will bear responsibility for teaching and training our kids. It will not happen without intention. It will not happen by prayer alone. God requires that we actively teach our children to follow and obey His Word.

When a student is fully trained, they will be like their teacher. If you want your child to be a student of the Word, let them see you studying your Bible. If you want your child to love God, let them see you love Him first by the priority you place on the things of God. We have a short window in which to influence our kids. Let's use it with eternity in mind.

Love Your Neighbor

Love your neighbor as yourself.

MARK 12:31

IT WAS A QUIET SUNDAY AFTERNOON when I got a phone call from the mother of a young girl at our homeschool co-op. We exchanged "how are yous" and commented on the weather. It took a moment for her to get to the reason for her call. After all, no one likes to be "that mom."

Apparently, my little girl had been unkind. I could feel my heart rate quicken. According to this mom, my child had passed a note to her daughter at the co-op. The note had been passed by three other kids before my daughter finally got it and gave it to the intended recipient. The note decried my friend's daughter as "weird, funny, and ugly."

Not exactly a lesson out of our family devotion time.

I'll be honest: my first instinct was to protect my child—but I have learned that even when we have given correct instruction, our kids are still responsible for their own choices and sometimes have to learn lessons the hard way.

We called our daughter to a place where we could talk to her. Within a few minutes, tears were flowing. "I didn't mean to hurt her feelings!" my daughter said. "Well, how would you feel if she handed you that note?" I asked. My daughter looked down. "I'd feel bad," she said.

"Yes," I said. "God wants us to treat everyone with kindness. That girl is as precious to God as you are—and you need to make this right. Here's what we're going to do: you're going to write a note to her and apologize when you see her next. You will also need to apologize to the other girls for setting a bad example. God's children are not to treat others unkindly."

"Yes, mama," came her tearful reply.

My daughter spent the next hour carefully crafting an apology. She picked out stickers and colored a flower to tuck inside the card. The next day, she gave it to the girl. Her conscience was cleared, and she learned a valuable lesson: people should be treated with kindness.

We are living in a culture that encourages us to be unkind and selfish. Let's be countercultural in the way we raise our children. Let's teach them that all people are precious and should be treated as such. And when we see that our children are failing to do so, let's look long and hard at ourselves even as we correct our kids. Truth is, our kids are watching and listening.

People are precious to God. And if they are precious to Him, they should be precious to us too.

No Longer Slaves

You say, "I am allowed to do anything"—but not everything is good for you.
And even though "I am allowed to do anything," I must not become a slave to anything.

1 CORINTHIANS 6:12

EVEN THOUGH WE'VE BEEN SET FREE through Jesus' death and resurrection, we struggle to stay free. Even things that are not sinful can sign us up for a life of slavery if we're not careful. The apostle Paul understood this. When he was teaching the Christians in Corinth, he wrote, "You say, 'I am allowed to do anything'—but not everything is good for you. And even though 'I am allowed to do anything,' I must not become a slave to anything" (1 Corinthians 6:12).

We must remember we are Christ's ambassadors in every area of life. I have struggled with the time I spend on social media. It is a cultural sinkhole for many mothers. Before we know it, our fifteen-minute break has turned into two hours—and the laundry is still not done. We're looking for validation—on everything from the new recipe we found to the choice we made in a movie . . . but unfortunately, social media has enslaved us.

According to a 2021 survey, more than 4.2 billion people use social media. That's 55 percent of the world's population! Statistics also tell us that the average user spends two hours and thirty-two minutes a day on social networking and messaging. Some of our teens are using it up to nine hours a day.[3]

Social media is as addictive and deadly as cigarettes—it's killing our ability to have meaningful relationships *in real life* with the people closest to us. Many moms commit relationship suicide simply by spending more time online than in real life with their kids.

When I think of the thousands of hours I have wasted on social media, I'm ashamed. I finally admitted to my husband that I needed an accountability partner. Doing this helped me get my life back from the social media sinkhole I was constantly dancing around.

But more than that, I know God wants us to be focused on serving Him and loving the people He has put in our lives. We can't do that if we have become a slave to something else.

Ask God to help you keep short accounts with things that cause you to waste this life that He has given you. Maybe it's alcohol, entertainment, social media, or even food. Take a moment and honestly evaluate yourself. If God speaks, listen. He will help you make a change.

---

3 "Latest Social Media Addiction Statistics of 2021," FameMass, accessed December 9, 2021, https://famemass.com/social-media-addiction-statistics/.

Sex Is Precious

This explains why a man leaves his father and mother
and is joined to his wife, and the two are united into one.

GENESIS 2:24

IT WAS 7:45 ON A MONDAY NIGHT. The kitchen was being cleaned by the "night crew" (or, as we like to call it, *the teens*), and I was perusing my box of teas for just the right day-ender. It had been an "I hope there's a tea for that" kind of day, if you know what I mean.

I was about to give up, when my husband snuck up behind me and started kissing my neck. "I love you, you gorgeous woman!" he declared for all to hear. I blushed. Sensing the kids were staring, Jay pressed his lips against mine. "Let's give them a reason to leave the room," he whispered. I wasn't hard to convince.

"Ewwwww, Mom and Dad! That's gross!" our youngest daughter hollered from her perch on a kitchen barstool. "Stop it!" As Jay predicted, the teens left the room, leaving our eight-year-old staring with her mouth hanging open.

Confession time: I love it when my kids are a little bit embarrassed by our public displays of affection. When they're in elementary school, they don't get it. And that's fine with me. When they're little, we want them to know one basic thing: Mom and Dad are committed to each other. Our little displays of affection show our kids they can feel secure at home.

Here's the thing: Jay is my best friend, my confidante, my lover. I want to make that man glad to come home to me at the end of a long day. To that end, I've spent my whole adult life in the precious pursuit of his affections. For over thirty years, we've been nurturing our marriage in every way that we can—including sexually.

Our world has devalued the preciousness of sex. Parents bow out of the conversation, often leaving sacred discussions about sex and marriage up to peers or sex ed curricula.

We've got to do better than this. Our kids need to see sex the way God sees it. God said that sex is precious. It's sacred. It's for marriage between a man and a woman. Sex is not something we engage in casually. In marriage, it's given and received freely. It's not something to manipulate our spouse with to gain an advantage or issue a punishment. Sex is the means by which God gives us new life. Its bond cannot be broken, and it's nothing to be taken casually.

Mom, teach your children to see sex the way God intended. It's a beautiful, precious gift by God's design.

When the Time Is Right

Let us not become weary in doing good, for at the
proper time we will reap a harvest if we do not give up.

GALATIANS 6:9, NIV

WHEN LONG NIGHTS TURN INTO LONG days, or when long days turn into long months, it's easy to lose sight of what we're doing. It's easy to be defined by the wearying moments of motherhood, but God says, "Don't give up! Good things are coming."

When God makes a promise, you can count on it, even when the way does not seem easy. The apostle Paul understood this, and when he wrote to the Galatians, he wrote from experience. I'm sure that Paul was tempted to give up and give in. The temptation must have been enormous.

As we raise our children in a sinful world, it's easy to become discouraged. It's easy to leave the hard conversations up to the youth pastor and to keep our eyes on our phones when our kids are trying to engage in conversation with us. I want to challenge you not to take the easy way. Motherhood is hard—but when we keep our eyes on the harvest, we are walking in obedience to Christ. God says that parents are the ones responsible for the upbringing of their children.

Here in Washington State, we are well known for our apples. The family who owns the apple orchard knows two things for certain about growing a tree that will bear good fruit:

1. Good fruit develops when the time is right.
2. Planting happens with the harvest in mind.

As parents, we are raising the next generation: we're hoping for good fruit. It takes time. The same is true for parenting! If you have a toddler, the harvest is years away! The time is not right.

Sometimes, it's only when we look back that we see that the seeds we have been watering have finally produced a harvest. Watching your adult children flourish as disciples of the Lord Jesus is worth every ounce of time and energy and prayer you put into it.

Keep sowing. Keep doing good, and hold on to God's promise that, at the proper time, you will reap a harvest *if you do not give up.*

Keep Looking to God

We do not know what to do, but our eyes are on you.

2 CHRONICLES 20:12, NIV

WHAT BATTLES ARE YOU FACING IN your motherhood journey? Does victory seem impossible? Has "that child" driven you to your knees again? Have you raised your hands to heaven in surrender?

If so, be encouraged. You are right where God wants you to be.

The Bible is replete with stories of ordinary men and women who were faced with extraordinary odds: Noah, Joseph, Ruth, Esther, Mary. God is good with the odds being against Him. He's got it figured out, even when we have no idea what to do.

Take King Jehoshaphat, for example. In 2 Chronicles 18–20, we can see that he had some daunting issues. He was facing the Moabites, for one thing. I think I may know a few modern-day Moabites. You too? If you step into the cultural and spiritual divide, you will quickly see that the arrows begin to fly. Truth is caught in the crosshairs right now.

If you're trying to teach your children to know God's Word, expect to be attacked. Don't forget, this is war! Just like you were born for this time in history, and for the battles you are facing, Jehoshaphat was born for the battle of his day. Like you, he was a threat to Satan's evil agenda. The Bible records that Jehoshaphat turned the people "back to the LORD" (2 Chronicles 19:4). He appointed godly judges. He called them to righteous living. In short? He was doing serious damage to the devil. He was a threat in the spiritual realms as well as the physical!

Maybe you are raising a modern Jehoshaphat! Have you ever stopped to consider it?

Look at the spiritual wisdom he led with: as the army came closer, Jehoshaphat cried out to God. He spoke *out loud* that he had no power to succeed against the army except that which God would give to him. God answered: "Do not be afraid or discouraged because of this vast army. For the battle is not yours, but God's. You will not have to fight this battle. Take up your positions; stand firm and see the deliverance the Lord will give you" (2 Chronicles 20:15, 17, NIV).

In response, Jehoshaphat worshiped the Lord! Worship is a weapon, precious mom. Do you feel outnumbered and overwhelmed? Take a page from Jehoshaphat's book and praise the Lord! Wait and see what God will do!

The Cure for Selfishness

Don't be selfish; don't try to impress others.
Be humble, thinking of others as better than yourselves.

PHILIPPIANS 2:3

WHEN OUR CHILDREN ARE LITTLE, they tend to believe that they are the center of the universe. Don't believe me? Follow a two-year-old around for an hour or so. Toddler rules dictate their reality: "If I saw it first, it's mine. If you saw it first, it's mine. If it belongs to you and I want it, it's mine." On and on it goes. It could be a little thing, like a cookie that was dropped on the floor, or it could be another toddler's sacred blankie. The rules remain the same. I have always marveled at the way my little ones could be confident in their selfish behavior and at the same time demonstrate a total lack of self-awareness.

Come to think of it, this seems to be a big issue for adults these days. Don't believe me? If you spend ten minutes on any social media platform, it becomes painfully obvious that we are a culture consumed with ourselves. The term "selfie" is relatively new, but the sin behind it has been around since the Garden of Eden, when Eve's selfishness caused her to put her own desires above God's clear command. We are still living with the results of her catastrophic decision.

Before you get too frustrated with your selfish children or your own selfish nature, consider this: according to the Bible, we come into this world hard-wired for selfishness. We're prone to it, aren't we? I mean, unless I am being led by the Holy Spirit, I will be selfish from sunup to sundown. My bent is to serve myself, not others, first. Can you relate?

As mothers, part of our job is to make sure our children eventually become aware of their selfish behavior. We want our children to be devoted to Christ so that they will desire to put others' needs above their own. This happens when we teach our children God's heart as it's communicated through the Bible, but it's also "caught" by our children as much as it is taught.

Remember, we can't pass on what we don't possess. If you're struggling with selfishness today, chances are good that your children will struggle with it too. Take a moment and confess it as sin before the Lord. You can approach Him with full confidence, knowing He stands ready to forgive and help you overcome it.

The cure for selfishness is the Savior. When it comes to living a selfless life, He is the ultimate example for us. Follow His example today!

Don't Procrastinate—Investigate!

Be very careful, then, how you live—not as unwise but as wise.

EPHESIANS 5:15, NIV

My husband and I live in a smallish community in Southwest Washington state. We moved into a wonderful home on a few acres with Jay's parents about three months after Dad found the house on Craigslist. Our Craigslist house is a miracle—but that's a story for another time. For over a decade, we've shared life together in our miracle home. For the most part, it's been smooth sailing.

For the most part.

In April 2016, we started having some . . . shall I say . . . issues with the house. First, we noticed small changes in the water pressure. It was a bit concerning that the toilets flushed slower and the water pressure in the sink was a little bit off.

"It's no big deal," we told ourselves. There were no obvious signs of trouble, after all. We're busy people, so after a cursory check, we decided that things must be fine.

Fine, except that, in addition to the curious lack of water pressure, the hot water seemed to run out faster than usual. Now, I'm a girl who loves her hot showers. I was certain that I was turning the dial to "H" sooner than I usually did. So, after a few weeks of me wondering why the hot water wasn't very hot, Jay checked the water heater. It was working just fine.

Hmm. Well, I guess I'm just colder than usual, I thought, as I put that little voice in my head to bed and decided to ignore it.

As you have guessed by now, it was a big deal. Two weeks later, our daughter was playing outside near the back of the house. She came running inside to tell us that she heard a "spraying noise" coming from underneath the house—you know, the place where the spiders live and human beings stay out of? Yes. That part.

As it turned out, a hot water pipe under our house had failed, causing water to spray on the walls in our crawl space. The damage was extensive—and expensive.

If only we had listened to that still, small voice. We could have avoided a costly repair.

Is there a "still, small voice" giving you pause today? A character issue in your child? A concern for your marriage? A "small" sin issue that's gradually getting bigger? Don't ignore something because it seems inconsequential. You can avoid costly relationship repairs by making sure you act at the first sign of trouble. Don't procrastinate—investigate!

The Pollyanna Principle

If you search for good, you will find favor.

PROVERBS 11:27

In 1960, Walt Disney Productions released a feature film based on Eleanor H. Porter's 1913 novel *Pollyanna*, starring child actress Hayley Mills. I discovered this delightful story when I was seven years old, but the lessons I learned from it made a lasting impression. Pollyanna taught me that my circumstances don't need to determine my attitude.

Pollyanna was sent to live with her wealthy, unmarried, and rather uptight aunt after she was orphaned by missionary parents. Pollyanna works to win the hearts of the grumpy townspeople around her through relentless optimism.

Instead of wallowing in disappointments, she teaches them to play the "glad game," which her father taught her. The point was to learn to find something about everything to be glad about—no matter how disappointed, sad, or frustrated she felt. It began when crutches came instead of the doll that Pollyanna wanted so much. Her father gently used this disappointment to prepare her for life's inevitable disappointments. Whenever things were sad, they would play the game by saying a "glad" word in every sentence.

Proverbs 11 teaches us that if we search for the good, we will find favor! I wonder, mama, if the "glad game" would be as useful now as it was then!

Let's give it a try—for ourselves and our kids:

Frustration: Your son or daughter is struggling to learn a new skill.
Glad game: "Even slow progress is still progress! I'm so glad to see you improving!"

Frustration: You have been up all night with a newborn. You're exhausted and angry.
Glad game: "I'm very glad God gave me this precious baby! I'm also glad this season of sleepless nights is just that—a season."

Perspective is everything, mama! In the words of Pollyanna, "When you're hunting for the glad things, you sort of forget the other kind." The "Pollyanna Principle" may have been written in 1913, but it still applies today. Let's model it!

Not Just a Hearer

Don't just listen to God's word. You must do what it says.
Otherwise, you are only fooling yourselves.

JAMES 1:22

FEW VERSES CARRY MORE CONVICTION THAN James 1:22. We might rewrite it to say, "Don't just read God's Word—do it!" Ouch!

As difficult as obedience can be for us as adults, our role as parents shows us how difficult obedience is for our children sometimes. We remind our children to hang up their clothes four times a week, and hopefully they reply with a cheerful, "Okay, Mom!" but somehow the clothes never get hung up. I probably don't need to tell you how frustrating it is to repeat the same thing over and over and always have your child acknowledge your direction . . . and then go right on about their business. It would almost be better if they stuck their fingers in their ears and said, "La la la la la." If they don't intend to obey, why do they even acknowledge my words? Sound familiar?

Context is everything. So now, perhaps you can have just a tiny bit of understanding of the Lord's response when we acknowledge His Word again and again and again but continue our business as usual. I would never say God gets "frustrated," because I don't think that's in His nature. But I'm sure He must hurt for us when He realizes we're simply not growing up.

Today, let's go back to the most basic principles of living the Christian life; let's purpose in our hearts to obey whatever we read in the Word. It sounds easier than it is, of course, so let's ask the Lord to use our desire to open conversations about obedience with our kids. Today, let's talk with them about how often we fail at obeying His Word and how today, we are going to try to do better at listening for and obeying His voice.

Remember: wisdom is caught more than taught! So today, let's pitch truth every chance we get.

Oh Lord, help me to be not just a hearer of your Word, but a doer also.

In Pursuit of Holiness

The Scriptures say, "You must be holy because I am holy."

1 PETER 1:16

IN THE PAST SEVERAL YEARS, I'VE grown more and more concerned about the state of God's people, particularly as it relates to something we call *holiness*. Like most authors, I spend quite a bit of time studying words, so I looked up the word *holiness*, of course, and according to the dictionary, *holiness* is "the state of being sinless; purity of moral character, perfect freedom from all evil."

Well, the dictionary just described God, because I can't relate to that definition at all. Thank goodness, that's not what the Bible means when it calls Christians to live a life of holiness. God isn't looking for "the state of being sinless," because He knows we cannot attain such a thing on this earth. Rather, the Greek word used for holy is *hagios*, which means simply this: we are to be a "set apart" people. It means we're not to be like the world we live in; rather, we're to be *different*, as God is different. Truly, there is no one else like Him!

Oh, how we need to be set apart!

There are moments when we find ourselves at a crossroads in our Christian walk—like an old Ford pickup truck out in the middle of nowhere. It's like we pause at a four-way stop on a dirt road, scratch our heads, and wonder which way to go.

Should we turn left? Right? Go straight? It seems we don't know what to do . . . but we should. The Bible gives us a map for how to live a life of holiness, and we need to go there for our direction when we're stuck.

God has been clear from the beginning about what He expects of His people: He expects holiness. He expects us to be different. Our relationships should be different. What we watch on TV should be different. The music we listen to, the way we look at sin—it should all be part of our desire to be holy.

There's no room in the Bible for God's people to view sin lightly, and yet we struggle to be set apart. Are you striving toward holiness? Remember, God doesn't expect perfection. He expects surrender. Do your children see you striving to live a life that would please God? Or do they see you doing your best to blend in with the rest of the world? We have a choice to make. Let's choose holiness.

Take Heart!

Here on earth you will have many trials and sorrows.
But take heart, because I have overcome the world.

JOHN 16:33

SUFFERING. WE'RE NOT VERY GOOD AT it, are we? Seems we'll do almost anything to avoid it, and yet, Jesus said that suffering would be part of our lives. Jesus didn't say we would struggle once in a while either. He said we would have *many* trials and sorrows.

He knew how hard this world was going to be. In His infinite wisdom, He laid the groundwork for us—and we need to lay the groundwork for our kids. Jesus showed us how to suffer and not lose heart. Jesus gave us a "theology" of suffering. He taught us how to view God in the middle of the struggle.

So the next time you have an unexpected detour, here are a few things to help you "take heart" and keep your eyes on Jesus:

- Learn to view *worship* as a weapon. Bills seem overwhelming? Up all night with a fussy baby? Transmission went out? Crank up the worship music! God inhabits the praise of His people (see Psalm 22:3).
- Get alone with God to pray and process your circumstances (see Matthew 14:23). Instead of freaking out, take a time-out. Take your requests and fears before the Lord in prayer.
- Remember the promises of God—starting with this one: When we are weak, He is strong. (see 2 Corinthians 12:10). If you feel ill equipped for the challenge you are currently facing, *take heart!* God loves to work in impossible circumstances.

Remember, mom—your children are learning how to handle life's inevitable challenges by watching you! When they see you praising God in the midst of struggle and even sorrow, they are learning what it looks like to praise God in all circumstances.

Do not be discouraged. Take heart! Jesus has overcome the world!

I Was Wrong

If we confess our sins to him, he is faithful and just to
forgive us our sins and to cleanse us from all wickedness.

1 JOHN 1:9

HAVE YOU EVER MADE A WRONG call with your kids? Me too. Several of our kids are grown now—and I am just learning about some of the mistakes I made as a mom.

Sometimes our mistakes are funny. On the occasional night when everyone is home for a meal, the kids like to tell stories around the dinner table. I've become the object of many of them. Some of them are embarrassing! I've been told that I spanked the wrong child, fell asleep during a piano recital, and even left a child at church one night after AWANA. . . . I had been home for an hour before I discovered my "mistake"! (In my defense, I had a two-week-old baby. I'm blaming that one on sleep deprivation.)

Sometimes, our mistakes aren't really mistakes at all; they're the result of sin. When we sin against our children, it can have lasting consequences if left uncorrected. In my thirty years of mothering, I have learned a lot about myself: I can be overly critical and unkind, especially when I'm tired. I have been impatient and even unjust. Knowing I have wounded my child is humbling and heartbreaking— but it can also be a source of healing.

The Lord has used my many moments of failure to teach me an important lesson: when I can humble myself and admit my wrongdoing, there is growth and healing. I am so thankful for forgiveness! I'm thankful for God's forgiveness, and I'm grateful that my children have forgiven my shortcomings also.

Modeling humility for our children is an absolutely essential part of becoming the mothers that God wants us to be. Have you wronged your child? Confess your sin. Telling your child that you were wrong is not a sign of weakness. It's a sign of humility. It lets your child know that you are serious about nurturing your relationship with them. Not only is confession good for the soul, it's setting an example that your children will need throughout their lives.

Have you noticed a pattern of wounding those you love? Confess it to the Lord, and then go make it right. There is healing in seeking forgiveness!

Wisdom Needed!

I will thank the LORD because he is just.

PSALM 7:17

WHEN DAVID SAYS IN PSALM 7 that he can thank God because He is just, he is stating a simple but powerful truth about God. God is perfectly righteous in the way He views us. He shows no partiality (see Acts 10:34). God is also perfectly righteous in His treatment of all He has created. He cares for us perfectly, commanding against the mistreatment of others and executing righteous vengeance against oppressors.

Although we would like to be considered just in the way we shepherd and correct our children, we are often exactly the opposite. At least, I am. I do not care for my children perfectly. In truth, I have corrected them harshly. I am prone to being unkind when I am tired. And as for executing righteous "results" (as we call them in our house), well, let's just say I have missed the mark there too. As our kids have grown into adults, I have heard about several times when I have grounded one child for the sins of another.

The scales of justice aren't always as just as we would like them to be, are they? Why? Because we aren't God, that's why. We can appear to show favoritism to a child because we missed the "look" that started the fight. If we're not careful, we can alienate a child out of a sincere desire to make a right decision. If you have ever misjudged a situation or made a wrong call in trying to get to the bottom of a quarrel in your home, take heart; you're not alone. In truth, we're going to make mistakes as we parent our children.

There are many reasons to praise God for the way He perfectly administers discipline and brings justice to our broken world, but one of my favorites is simply this: God can help us make wise judgments with our children.

The next time you need the wisdom of Solomon to get to the bottom of a situation at home, ask the Lord to help you. Thank Him for His divine wisdom in rendering right judgment—and ask Him to help you do the same. God's Word teaches us that God stands at the ready with the tools we need to judge fairly and see that justice is done.

Who Is Your Foundation?

The LORD rescues the godly; he is their fortress in times of trouble. The LORD helps them, rescuing them from the wicked. He saves them, and they find shelter in him.

PSALM 37:39-40

IN AMERICA, WE LIVE QUITE AN easy lifestyle compared to most of the rest of the world. Many families don't have to "depend" on the Lord for much, as we are generally self-sufficient in our developed country. Most people in our nation have a home to give them shelter and food in the cupboards to eat.

In recent years, though, we have painfully learned what our great-grandparents knew: financial success is not guaranteed. Our country has had seasons of economic instability, with massive job cuts, foreclosed homes, and inflation. While it's easy to see the bad side of this, there is also an upside! Difficult times tend to refocus us on what really matters. For example, when we can't be self-sufficient, we're reminded to go to God in prayer and ask for His help and provision.

The same thing is true of freedom. It's easy to take freedom for granted when we haven't fought, bled, and died for it. Until a few years ago, we were able to enjoy religious freedom and traditional family values. Christianity was generally accepted. Now those values are considered harmful, and we have witnessed some Christians in our country having their religious liberties threatened for abiding by biblical principles.

I remember the day the Supreme Court redefined marriage and struck down the biblical definition *that we know is God's design.* Marriage is God's idea, after all. One man, one woman. Oh, how we struggle when we rebel against God's ways!

These past few years have been heart-revealing for many Christians, I think. I would put myself among them. The Lord has used recent events to show me that I have placed far too much security in my government. My hope is misplaced in any place other than God. This realization was critical for me to realign my heart.

Little did I know what was coming in our country, but it was so good of the Lord to shake me just when I needed it. The Lord is my foundation, and He is never moving—no matter what the circumstances. Of that, we can be sure.

Find Out What Pleases the Lord

Carefully determine what pleases the Lord.

EPHESIANS 5:10

IT'S EASY TO FOCUS ON WHAT displeases the Lord—but did you know that you can please God too? It's amazing, isn't it? We are the created, so insignificant in light of what the Creator has done, and yet God says we have the ability to please Him.

In Ephesians 5:10, the apostle Paul said that we should be thinking about how to please God by carefully determining what that might be. Now, I don't know about you, but it's easy for me to focus myself (and consequently, my children) on what *not* to do rather than what we *can* do to honor and please our Creator.

The Message translation says, "Figure out what will please Christ, and then do it." The best part about knowing that God loves us is that we get to respond to that love and teach our children to do the same. God isn't shy about telling us what pleases Him either. In Psalm 113, we learn that one of the first (and best) ways to please the Lord is to praise Him. Praise is the best response to all that God has done for us, isn't it?

In Psalm 113:5-9, King David lists a few reasons why God is worthy of our praise: "Who can be compared with the LORD our God, who is enthroned on high? He stoops to look down on heaven and on earth. He lifts the poor from the dust and the needy from the garbage dump. He sets them among princes, even the princes of his own people! He gives the childless woman a family, making her a happy mother. Praise the LORD!

I love that David points out the joyful response of a mother who realizes her children are a gift from the Lord. His instruction? Praise! Continual praise is the right response to all that God has done and all that He will do. It's the right response to the gift of our salvation, the right response for our children, our homes—and even creation itself.

As mothers, we set the tone for our homes. Let's let our "tone" be one of enduring praise. God is worthy! There are many ways we can please the Lord. Let's start by being a people of praise.

I Wish I Hadn't Said That

Don't sin by letting anger control you. Think about it overnight and remain silent.

PSALM 4:4

HAVE YOU EVER OPENED YOUR MOUTH and instantly wished you had kept quiet? I have. Come to think of it, as I look back over nearly thirty years of motherhood, my biggest regrets are not things I did or did not do. They're things I said that I wish I could take back. Things said in anger. Things said in hurt. Things said from frustration. Things said from fear. Things said in a moment of exhaustion.

Now, if you're anything like me, I'm guessing that you have been there too. Most of us have had a moment when we let our emotions get the best of us. I call them "MOMents." You know what I mean. They're the things we say when we're at the end of our proverbial rope. It happens—but God says there's a way to keep it from becoming part of the rhythm of our parenting. Are you ready for God's solution? Hang on to your hat, precious mom, because this Holy Spirit gust is gonna blow it right off.

The solution is to be quiet.

Easy to say, harder to do—but like all of God's commands, the peaceful fruit that follows is worth every act of obedience and self-control that you can muster in order to be quiet.

When we let our anger control us, the Bible says we're sinning. God's solution is to walk away before we say something we'll regret. Before our anger boils over. Before our hurt results in heartbreak. Before our frustration causes humiliation. Before fear overshadows the love that's in our heart. Before exhaustion clouds our judgment.

Before any of that—sleep on it. If you're struggling to control your tongue (even if you are justified in your anger), be still. Ask the Lord to show you when to speak, how to speak—and when to be quiet. Our relationships depend on our ability to be wise with our words—even when we're tired.

Rest, precious mom. Sleep on it. God is able to give you the right words at the right time.

Give the Glory to God

"It is beyond my power to do this," Joseph replied.
"But God can tell you what it means and set you at ease."

GENESIS 41:16

IF YOU EVER FEEL OVERWHELMED BY your circumstances, try meandering through Genesis. I promise you'll undergo a change in perspective.

Think you've got sibling issues? My hunch is they pale in comparison to Joseph's sibling struggles. In Genesis 37, we are introduced to Joseph. He was the eleventh son of Jacob, who made no secret of his affection toward Joseph. After all, he was his first son by Rachel, his favorite wife, and was born to Jacob in his old age.

It's a long story, but here's the short version: Joseph's brothers were jealous of him. When their animosity peaked, they decided against murdering him and sold him into slavery instead. If you thought your kids were handling their siblings badly, this should put your mind at ease.

Joseph was bought by a high-ranking Egyptian named Potiphar, and the Bible records that he excelled at his duties. Trouble is, Potiphar's wife had taken note of Joseph also. When he would not sleep with her, she lied to her husband, accusing Joseph of unwanted sexual advances. Potiphar responded by having Joseph put in prison.

While Joseph was in prison, God blessed him with the ability to interpret the dreams of two of his fellow prisoners. Eventually, Pharaoh heard about Joseph's gift and called on him to interpret an unsettling dream. This entire story is a fascinating look at how God uses even humanity's sin for His purposes, but what I want you to see here is how honest Joseph was about the gift God had given him to interpret dreams. He knew where his gifts came from.

In Genesis 46, when Pharaoh asked him to interpret his dream, Joseph immediately conceded that, on his own, he would not be able to do such a great thing. But he didn't stop there—he focused Pharaoh's attention on the *only one who could do such a miraculous thing*: God.

God honored Joseph's humility and gave him the answer that ultimately caused Pharaoh to make him second in command over all of Egypt.

As mothers, we can learn a lot from Joseph's example. When things are going poorly, we are to walk in obedience and humility. When we don't know what to do, we can look to God for direction and encourage others to do the same. God can tell us what the next step should be—we need only listen. Then, as He works in our situation, we are to give the glory to God.

Wisdom over Knowledge

Wisdom will save you from evil people, from those whose words are twisted.

PROVERBS 2:12

As mothers, we are the primary educators of our children. Our job as mothers is all encompassing, isn't it? We teach our children how to take care of their bodies and clean their rooms. We teach them the basic rules of kindness, and hopefully, we model forgiveness and generosity for them. As a homeschool mom, I've spent my days teaching seven children how to read, write, add, subtract, and divide—and many of my friends have been helping their children with homework after school.

Educating our children is a big job with big implications, and while it can be tempting to focus on imparting knowledge, the Bible tells us that knowledge is secondary to wisdom. God's Word tells us that teaching our children wisdom, not knowledge, is what we should be aiming for.

In Proverbs, Solomon talks often about the reality of living in our broken world. One of the realities is that our children will be confronted with evil as they grow. Our children will be lied to by "evil people"—and as parents, it's our job to guard their hearts against such things and to teach our children to recognize "twisted" words when they hear them. The good news, of course, is that there is a way we can inoculate our kids against such evil—and we do so by teaching them wisdom.

If we want our children to live a life of blessing, knowledge by itself is not enough. Wisdom is the standard that God says we should aim for. Wisdom is the ability to see things through a filter of godliness. Wisdom allows us to take the knowledge we have and make right decisions because we are able to tell right from wrong.

Wisdom searches for truth in all things.

Beloved, before you reinforce how important it is for your children to get their math finished and clean their room, be sure they are being trained in righteousness. What are you doing with the time you have been given to teach your children? By God's grace, you will go beyond mere knowledge and train your children in righteousness. That's where blessing and, in fact, safety, are found.

Embracing God's Family Values

The LORD your God, who brought you out of the land of Egypt, is with you!
DEUTERONOMY 20:1

HAVE YOU EVER BEEN AFFECTED BY fear to the point where your body started shaking? If so, you're not alone. Our bodies can be greatly affected by fear. For example, when we're anxious, the amygdala region of the brain responds to any threat (perceived or real) by increasing the production of adrenaline, the "fight-or-flight" hormone.

Adrenaline speeds up the contraction rate of the muscle tissue, getting us ready to fight or flee. If the levels of adrenaline are high enough, they can lead to our muscles twitching uncontrollably, which makes us shake.[4]

I will confess—I have experienced this before in times of confrontation. Sometimes, when my emotions were running high, or I was in a situation that made me feel threatened, my hands or even my voice would shake. The net result? Frustration added to fear.

I find it interesting that God, who created us and knows our bodies and their intricacies, has said repeatedly, "Do not fear." In other words, He doesn't want us to freak out! God values peace over panic. It's part of His DNA, if you will. As part of His DNA, it's something we should embrace, and something we should teach our kids to embrace also.

Listen to what Moses told the Israelites in Deuteronomy 20:1: "When you go out to fight your enemies and you face horses and chariots and an army greater than your own, do not be afraid. The LORD your God, who brought you out of the land of Egypt, is with you!"

We have an opportunity to raise our children to embrace God's high standards and adopt His family values. The Lord of heaven's armies is near, and He still says, "Do not fear." Even when the battle looks overwhelming, His heart is for you. He will not leave or forsake you.

---

4 "Why Do We Shake When We're Nervous or Frightened?" *BBC Science Focus Magazine*, https://www.sciencefocus.com/the-human-body/why-do-we-shake-when-were-nervous-or-frightened/.

When Your Prodigal Returns

He returned home to his father. And while he was still a long way off, his father saw him coming. Filled with love and compassion, he ran to his son, embraced him, and kissed him.

LUKE 15:20

HAVE YOU READ THE STORY OF the prodigal son? It's easy to think this story does not apply unless we are struggling with a child who has walked away from God or left their faith and family.

However, the story has powerful implications for our ordinary interactions as well as the extraordinary. Today, I want you to think about the last time your children sinned against you. It's easy to think of times when our children have frustrated us or let us down. Sometimes we are wounded by the carelessness of a teenager or the willful defiance of a five-year-old.

Every time we interact with our children, we have an opportunity to show them the grace of their loving heavenly Father. When your child sins against you, remember that your response, your reaction, shapes not only how they see you but how they see God. It is always in the father heart of God to strive for reconciliation, and it should be in our heart as well.

The Bible is filled with examples for parents to follow when shepherding our children through times of disobedience and struggle. Notice the attitude of this wonderful father at the sight of his prodigal son coming home. The Bible says that while the son was still "a long way off," his father saw him and was filled with compassion for him! He ran to his son, embraced and kissed him. This is how we should act when our own children apologize, or when our teenager finally realizes the error of their ways, or when our eight-year-old child asks for forgiveness.

Forgiveness should be in the DNA of every Christ-following parent. Remember, God demonstrated His love for us in that while we were yet sinners, He died for us as a ransom and sacrifice for our sin (see Romans 5:8). Does your son know that you love him, regardless of his sin? Does your daughter see a mother who stands ready to forgive, or does she see a mother who does not know how to forgive and move on? Are you struggling to forgive your child today? Ask the Lord to give you His heart and His eyes for your struggling child. When your prodigal comes toward you asking for forgiveness, don't just stand there. Run in their direction. Run with all you have in you—arms open wide, a smile on your face.

That really is what Jesus would do.

Lord, Send the Rain

If you carefully obey the commands I am giving you today, and if you love the LORD your God and serve him with all your heart and soul, then he will send the rains in their proper seasons.
DEUTERONOMY 11:13-14

My HUSBAND AND I MAKE OUR home in the beautiful hills of the Pacific Northwest, just outside Vancouver, Washington. It is a wonderland of sorts, filled with water-falls and hiking trails. Mount Hood is off to the east of us, while Mount St. Helens graces the landscape to the north. Of course, when most people think of the Pacific Northwest, the first thing that comes to mind is . . . you guessed it . . . rain!

It does rain here quite a bit, but for those of us who are used to it, we don't mind. The rain brings a blessing all its own. There is nothing quite like the smell of the earth after a rainstorm. Rain can be a sign of God's blessing.

Years ago, when my husband and I were in a season of great decision, we stood in front of a building where we had hoped to open a homeschool resource center. We were with a dear friend of ours, crying out to God for direction and provision. The rain was coming down in sheets, and the wind was blowing. After we had asked God for direction and given the situation to Him, our friend laid his hands on us and prayed a prayer I will never forget: "Lord, send the rain!"

Of course, the "rain" he was talking about was the blessing of God. He asked the heavens to open up and shower our endeavor with blessing. And that is exactly what happened. Not even two hours later, we received the answer to many years of prayer, and the Lord provided a building that now hosts a wonderful outreach to homeschooling families in our area.

The Bible teaches us that if we carefully obey the commands of the Lord—if we love the Lord our God and serve Him with all our heart and soul—then He will send the rain in its proper season. His rain comes so that we can bring in a harvest of souls for the Kingdom, but it is also for our enjoyment and refreshment.

If you are in the season of frustration right now, look up! God's heart is for you, and His desire is that you would be refreshed and encouraged. So wherever you are right now, whatever you are going through, keep your eyes on the rainmaker. Lord, send the rain!

Keep This in Mind

Keep in mind that I am not talking now to your children, who have never experienced the discipline of the LORD your God or seen his greatness and his strong hand and powerful arm.

DEUTERONOMY 11:2

Do you ever feel like no one is listening to you? Through my seasons of raising our seven children, there have been many times when I thought no one was listening. One of the things I love about the book of Deuteronomy is that Moses is so relatable. In chapter 11, Moses is talking to the Israelites about the blessings that come from following God . . . perhaps not unlike you or me when we try to instruct our children in what can only be considered the "blessings" of obeying their parents! Am I right?

Well, something must've frustrated Moses, since he felt the need to explain himself to the adults in the room by pointing out that he was not talking to the children; he was talking to the adults! I have taken the same approach when giving instructions to all of my children at one time, especially because there were almost twenty years between the oldest and the youngest. Usually, my frustration comes out when I feel like the older ones are not listening, and therefore setting a bad example for the younger ones. Can you relate?

In this case, Moses reminds the people that it is important for them to listen up, because the younger generation had not yet seen how great and powerful God was. It was up to the grown-ups to pass it on to them. Moses was distinguishing between the adults and the children. The grown-ups were those who had seen the amazing works of the Lord as displayed in their rescue from Egypt. They had also experienced the Lord's discipline as they wandered for forty years in the wilderness. It was to these grown-ups that Moses could say, "You have seen the LORD perform all these mighty deeds with your own eyes!" (Deuteronomy 11:7), and as they *remembered* what God had done, they were *reminded* that they were a special and blessed generation of adults, who had been called to pass on the teaching of what they had seen and learned to their children.

Just as it was the job of Old Testament parents to pass on the truths of the Lord in His great love and mercy, it is our job today. God is trying to get our attention when He says, "I'm talking to you, not your children!" The question is, are we listening?

Precious Time Storytime

Jesus told them this story.

LUKE 15:3

"MAMA!" I HEARD THE FAMILIAR SOUND of my littlest one calling from her bedroom.

Is it just me, or do you also have children who turn into thirsty philosophers at bedtime each night? I tried to change my attitude as I walked from the family room to her bedroom.

"What do you want, Sugar?" I asked as I turned on the light.

"Will you tell me a story, Mama?" she asked.

Now, I know some of you are under the illusion that I am some sort of wonder woman in terms of motherhood, so please, allow me to dispel the rumors. I did not want to tell my darling daughter a story that night. I wanted to have a few hours to myself. I was frustrated and tired, weary from a long day of homeschooling and refereeing arguments between my older children. I will confess, I wasn't the nicest mother in that moment, which is why I needed the Lord's help to see my daughter through His eyes.

I love that God understands how tired mothers can get. Jesus must have been worn out by the many demands placed on Him, and yet we often read about how tender He was with children. Jesus knew how to soothe a restless heart through telling stories. I have often imagined how tired He must've been at the end of a long day. After all, I am quite sure that He was in more demand than mothers are! Jesus was followed by adults and children alike, all in need of a special touch that only He could offer.

Over and over in the New Testament, we see that Jesus communicated truth and love through stories. It's a wonderful example for us, isn't it? Your children also need that special touch that only you can offer. So today, I encourage you to keep the book of short stories or chapters near the bedside of your child. Stories are powerful, and you have the opportunity to read life-giving books to your children, starting with the ultimate life-giving book, the Bible. If Jesus could pause to tell a story, so can you.

Be Careful!

Be careful to obey every command I am giving you today, so you may have strength to go in and take over the land you are about to enter.

DEUTERONOMY 11:8

HAVE YOU EVER NOTICED HOW SERIOUSLY God takes obedience? If God takes it seriously, we should too. When the Israelites were about to go into the land that God had promised them, Moses took time to remind them of the importance of obedience.

As a young mother, I did not understand how crucial it was to teach my daughter to respond immediately to my instruction until she ran out into the street on a sunny afternoon. I yelled, "Stop!" But my girl continued to run in the direction of an oncoming car. I had not emphasized how important it was for her to obey me, and in that moment, she almost lost her life because of it.

You can bet that after that, I took training my daughter in obedience very seriously.

Obedience is not something that our culture values today. Everywhere we go, we see examples of and read stories about parents struggling to teach their children to obey. We have been told by the culture that we should be focusing on "friendship" with our children when they are young, but God has a better way. When the Israelites were at the brink of entering the Promised Land, God said, "Be careful to obey."

The Bible says that the reason we are to obey the Lord is so that we can have the strength to do what He is calling us to do. If God says that the way to have strength is through obedience, it must first be modeled by parents as we walk in obedience to the Lord and then passed on to our children through discipline and correction.

Precious mom, part of your role as a mother, a very big part, is to teach your children to be attentive to your voice and obedient to your instruction. Children who are not taught to be obedient to their parents run the risk of a lifetime of suffering. There will be plenty of time to nurture friendship with your children. While they are young, your focus as a mother needs to be on training your children in righteousness.

Obedience is part of a righteous response from a child to their parents. When we teach our child to obey us, we are also showing them how to listen to and obey God.

Be Ready!

Be dressed for service and keep your lamps burning, as though
you were waiting for your master to return from the wedding feast.

LUKE 12:35-36

As a little girl, I loved to listen to my grandmother teach on the book of Revelation. No one was more ready for the Lord to come back than my grandmother! "Are you ready, Heidi?" she would ask. "Are you ready for the Lord to return? He is coming soon!"

Oh, how we need to teach our children this truth. During our lives, we will see hard times with pandemics, natural disasters, lost jobs, and lost friends and loved ones. But we can have hope. As a Christian, my hope is not on this earth. My hope is in heaven and steadied by the fact that this world is not all there is. Jesus taught us to be ready for His return at all times.

This passage out of Luke 12 highlights something that would've been very common and understandable to the people of that time. Back in Jesus' day, a person would dress for service by tucking their flowing outer robe under their belt or sash to be prepared for travel, fighting, or work. Jesus pictures servants waiting for their masters with their lamps aflame (see Luke 12:35-37). When the master finally arrives, we see a reversal of the role between servant and master as the master dresses himself to serve and wait on the servants.[5]

Jesus was highlighting for the disciples the fact that they needed to make themselves ready for His return and be diligent in their service of the Lord, just as the servants were always prepared for their master to return. Jesus says He could come at night or early in the morning, and in this way He stresses the need for vigilance and wakefulness (see Luke 12:38).

But how can we be ready? We can be ready by becoming students of the Word of God and behaving as children of God. We can be ready by seasoning our speech with grace and being careful what we allow ourselves to listen to, watch, and participate in. We can be ready, and we can teach our children to be ready also. He is coming soon!

---

5 Kenneth L. Barker and John R. Kohlenberger III, *The Expositor's Bible Commentary—Abridged Edition: Two-Volume Set* (Grand Rapids: Zondervan Academic, 2019).

Hope

Now I am deeply discouraged, but I will remember [my God].

PSALM 42:6

I AM SO THANKFUL FOR THE PSALMS. I relate to feelings of despair, triumph, and failure. In this psalm, the psalmist takes a good look at how he's feeling and asks questions of himself. Do you ever question what the Lord is allowing in your life? Do you ever feel discouraged? If so, you're not alone. Look at this passage from Psalm 42 starting in verse 6: "Now I am deeply discouraged, but I will remember [my God]—even from distant Mount Hermon, the source of the Jordan, from the land of Mount Mizar. I hear the tumult of the raging seas as your waves and surging tides sweep over me. But each day the Lord pours his unfailing love upon me, and through each night I sing his songs, praying to God who gives me life. . . ."

Maybe you can relate to the psalmist too. Can you hear the tumult of the raging sea? Do you feel as if you might sink beneath the waves and surging tide in your life? If so, the psalms have the answer for you. Notice that when we turn our panic into praise, the result is peace! When doubt seems to be winning, our faith in God sneaks up from behind and triumphs. The psalmist rightly directs our attention to God by saying that God is the one who gives us life. Because our life comes from God, we do not need to wander around in grief, oppressed by our enemies. Even though we may be mocked for our faith by those who do not understand it, alternately, we can praise God because our house is not in this world; it is in the Lord Jesus, our Savior and our God.

When we focus on God and all He has done, and all He is capable of doing, we can turn our worry into worship and our panic into praise. We can become a people of hope—and we can teach our children to be people of hope also.

When the Battle Seems Too Big

When you go out to fight your enemies and you face horses and chariots and an army greater than your own, do not be afraid. The LORD your God, who brought you out of the land of Egypt, is with you!

DEUTERONOMY 20:1

HAVE YOU EVER BEEN OUTNUMBERED? I'm not talking about by your children either, although I can definitely relate to that feeling! No, what I wonder is if you have ever felt like the battle you were facing was beyond your ability to win.

I confess that I often feel this way. It seems that Christian parents are fighting battles on a thousand different fronts. Frankly, they all seem too big to win at times. We are fighting culture's attempts to indoctrinate our children. We are fighting those who would take away our freedom and stifle the voices of Christians. We are fighting to protect our children from media and the machine that is social media. We are fighting a very real tendency to be complacent and lazy in our walk with God. We are fighting our flesh—at least I am. That's for sure.

Sometimes, I confess, my flesh is the victor.

I love reading the Bible when I feel outnumbered! Through the pages of God's Word, my heart is calmed and my fears are put to rest. In studying the men and women of the Bible, I often see myself reflected in their struggles. In Deuteronomy, we become familiar with the story of the nation, precious to God, and yet stubborn and rebellious. You know, like me.

The Bible tells us honestly that we have a very real enemy. His name is Satan, and he is playing for keeps. Charles Spurgeon once said that the fight we are facing is real, real enough that both God and Satan are engaged in it. And yet, God tells us not to be afraid. God, who brought the Israelites out of the land of Egypt, is still at work today. He says that when our enemies outnumber us, when we feel the battle is too big to win, we need only look up and remember that the Lord is on our side.

Precious mom, be still. When you go out to fight the enemy and you face the horses and chariots of social media, disobedient children, and a culture in rebellion against God—be still. The Lord your God is with you! Nothing is too big for Him, and nothing is too hard. You are safe, you are loved—and the battle has already been won.

A Blessing or a Curse? You Choose.

Look, today I am giving you the choice between a blessing and a curse!
You will be blessed if you obey the commands of the LORD your God that
I am giving you today. But you will be cursed if you reject the commands of the
LORD your God and turn away from him and worship gods you have not known before.

DEUTERONOMY 11:26-28

I SPEND QUITE A BIT OF time talking about the spiritual battle we are facing. We talk about it at home with our children, and I talk about it when I speak out on the road. Truth is, God has put a burning passion on my heart to wake up a sleeping church.

The Bible teaches us that God is giving us a choice, and in that choice there are only two outcomes: one a blessing and the other a curse. The Bible says that we will be blessed if we obey the commands of God, or we will be cursed if we reject them. The implications are staggering!

If we reject God's commands in government, the Bible teaches us that we will "groan" under wicked leadership (see Proverbs 29:2). If we reject God's commands regarding marriage, the failure of the marriage is almost certain. If we reject God's laws regarding the raising of our children, the Bible warns that the souls of our children could be lost. If we reject God's commands regarding the church, the church will become apostate, and sadly, we have seen the effects of this in some churches.

Of course, our choice need not be to reject God and suffer. We can choose to obey Him and find blessing! When we choose to obey God in our government, our nation will receive the blessing and covering of God (see Psalm 33:12). When we choose to obey God's Word regarding marriage and sexuality, the result is a blessing far beyond what the world could ever offer in a request for fulfillment and companionship. When we choose to obey God's commands regarding the raising of our children, the Bible says we will be blessed! That kind of joy comes from choosing the ways of God over the ways of this world.

Today, you can make a choice to follow God. The Bible teaches that our children will not depart from the truth when they are old if they are taught it when they are young (see Proverbs 22:6). When we follow Jesus, there is blessing beyond our wildest imaginings. Hope in the midst of heartache—joy in the journey. No matter our circumstances, when we choose God's ways, there is blessing. Praise the Lord!

In Times of Trouble

God is our refuge and strength, always ready to help in times of trouble.
So we will not fear when earthquakes come and the mountains crumble into the sea.
Let the oceans roar and foam. Let the mountains tremble as the waters surge!

PSALM 46:1-3

ON MAY 18, 1980, I REMEMBER exactly where I was. I was standing outside the deck of my family's home in Gresham, Oregon. The deck faced north, offering a beautiful, unobstructed view of Mount St. Helens.

Having grown up in an area with live volcanoes, I was well versed in what to look for in the event of an eruption. For months, we had been warned the volcano was close to erupting. Precautions had been taken and instructions given. A perimeter had been marked in the hopes of preventing people from getting too close and perishing should the mountain erupt.

It was reported that David Johnston, a United States geologist based at the monitoring station six miles away, announced the eruption with his final words, "Vancouver! Vancouver! This is it." [6] Moments later, Johnston was swept away by a lateral blast. His body was never found.

Following the eruption, the cities surrounding Mount St. Helens experienced devastation as I had never seen before. Ash floated through the air in Gresham, penetrating almost everything it touched. For months, we wore masks to protect our lungs and vacuumed ash out of our carpet. Volcanic ash even ruined our car air filters, and we replaced them weekly for a few months.

Incredibly, only fifty-seven people lost their lives that day, but I will never forget the awesome force of nature seen in an active volcano. Scripture says God is even greater than any force we could see in nature! The earth belongs to Him.

It is my prayer that as mothers, we would teach our children that what the Bible says is true. It is such a comfort to know that God is in control of all things. God is our refuge and strength in times of trouble. We do not need to fear when earthquakes come or mountains crumble and fall into the sea. Go ahead, let the oceans roar and foam. Let the mountains tremble and the water surge. I will trust in the Lord of heaven's armies! As children of God, we are watched over by our loving Father in heaven. He can be trusted in times of trouble!

---

6 "Mount St. Helens." In *Environmental Encyclopedia*, edited by Deirdre S. Blanchfield (Detroit, MI: Gale, 2011), https://link.gale.com/apps/doc/CV2644150881/GRNR?u=carl&sid=bookmark-GRNR&xid=f82f3f71.

Nine O'Clock

It was nine o'clock in the morning when they crucified him.

MARK 15:25

I SOMETIMES WONDER WHAT IT MUST'VE been like to be Mary, the mother of Jesus. Especially at Easter, my heart longs to hear her heart—knowing that her child was suffering and being helpless to do anything to stop it.

One of the hardest things I have ever faced as a mother is the suffering of my children. Having seven children gives a mother a whole lot of opportunities to have her heart broken. Years ago, I watched helplessly as my three-year-old son was put into the back of an ambulance. For days, he had been coughing. Having never been around a child with asthma, I did not recognize his cough and shortness of breath as anything other than a common cold. When I finally took him in, I was informed that his oxygen saturation was dangerously low. He was transferred to the children's unit at a hospital in downtown Portland. As I sat in the back of the ambulance, my mind was racing.

Why didn't I call sooner? What could I have done to protect my child? The fear and frustration mixed with guilt were crushing. My heart was so heavy.

I remember watching the sun come up one morning from our room at Oregon Health and Science University. It felt hard to believe that while the rest of the world was getting ready for work, my world had come to a stop. It was nine in the morning, and I had not slept. My heart was with my child. His suffering was almost more than I could take.

Mary must have been in excruciating pain as she watched her child carrying the cross up Golgotha to the place where He would die. I wonder—did she ask herself if she could've done anything to protect Him? She must have felt a pain so heavy her heart was literally breaking.

It was nine o'clock in the morning, and Mary's heart was breaking. The sun was just coming up as our Lord was suffering for our sin. Our world often moves so fast this time of year that we forget the lengths Jesus went to so that we could spend eternity with Him. When I see Mary in heaven, I want to hug her tight. The sacrifice was so great. Stop today, and remember the price that was paid for our salvation. It was greater than we can imagine. *Thank You, Lord. Thank You.*

A Wholehearted Approach to Parenting

Commit yourselves wholeheartedly to these words of mine. Tie them to your hands and wear them on your forehead as reminders. Teach them to your children. Talk about them when you are at home and when you are on the road, when you are going to bed and when you are getting up. . . . so that as long as the sky remains above the earth, you and your children may flourish in the land the LORD swore to give your ancestors.

DEUTERONOMY 11:18-21

CAN YOU IMAGINE PARENTING THE ISRAELITE nation as it exited from Egypt? This was the task that God gave to Moses: to shepherd the people of God from slavery to the Promised Land.

It was no small task either. The Israelites were often rebellious and ungrateful. I am sure that Moses was weary from telling them the same thing over and over again, and yet, out of obedience to God, he did not give up.

Over and over again, we see that Moses took on the heart of a parent toward the Israelite people. In Deuteronomy 11, he emphatically directs them to commit themselves wholeheartedly to his words. So what does it mean to commit wholeheartedly to something?

Merriam-Webster defines *wholehearted* as being "marked by complete earnest commitment: free from all reserve or hesitation." Does this describe your commitment to God? If so, your life should be marked by a passion for following God, right down to the way you shepherd your children. After all, we are modeling what it looks like to follow Jesus for our kids every day! Christian parents should be motivated with a soul-deep passion for seeing their children follow God wholeheartedly. Moses asked the people to commit themselves wholeheartedly to the words he was teaching them about their responsibility as parents. He said we are to teach God's ways to our children, to talk about them when we are at home and when we are not, when we go to bed and when we get up.

Throughout the book of Deuteronomy, Moses went passionately over and over the same ground, and throughout Scripture we see God doing the same thing with His children. Deep in the soul, Moses felt that the entire history of the Israelites hinged on whether or not they would be willing to pass on the truth of God's Word to their children.

He was right, of course. Generations from now, our children will benefit from our decision to train them up in wholehearted devotion to the ways of the Lord Jesus. Don't give up, precious mom! A wholehearted mom is who God wants you to be.

Where Is Your Hope?

Why am I discouraged? Why is my heart so sad? I will put my hope in God! I will praise him again—my Savior and my God!

PSALM 43:5

THE PSALMIST DAVID ASKS THE SAME questions I have asked of myself. Can you relate? Just about the time I think I have got everything figured out, something changes. Maybe there is an upset at work. Maybe it is the questioning of a child who I thought had a better understanding of spiritual things. I go from being content to being discouraged and sad. It can happen in an instant.

We can blame our ever-changing emotions on all kinds of things, can't we? Maybe it's hormones. (Check!) Maybe we've been up all night with a fussy baby. Maybe our teenager has driven us to the brink of what we think we can handle. Maybe that long-standing prayer request has still gone unanswered.

David is reminding us that we are in this thing together and that the solution remains the same. He reminds us, as he reminds himself, that our hope must never be placed in the things of this world. As mothers, we can put all of our eggs, so to speak, in the "motherhood basket" and spend all of our time and energy on our children . . . only to end up sad and disappointed when they let us down or walk away from the truth that we have labored to teach them.

Precious mom, put your hope in the Lord today! Do not put your hope in how your children will turn out, or whether or not you'll have enough money when bills are due. Do not put your hope in things of this world. When we become discouraged or when our hearts are sad, let's take our cues from David and turn to the Lord. He can be trusted with all things. As mothers, when we put our hope in God, we declare that our identity is also found there. When we do this, our attitudes change because our attention has shifted to all that we have to be thankful for instead of what we don't have. Let's praise Him again today, because He is our Savior and our God!

If you know of a mom who is struggling to keep her eyes on Jesus today, pick up your phone and give her a call. Text her, or better yet, drop by her house. Sometimes, helping another mom turn her eyes to Jesus is just the thing we need to keep our own eyes focused there too!

Beware of the Yeast

Meanwhile, the crowds grew until thousands were milling about and stepping on each other. Jesus turned first to his disciples and warned them, "Beware of the yeast of the Pharisees—their hypocrisy. The time is coming when everything that is covered up will be revealed, and all that is secret will be made known to all."

LUKE 12:1-2

As far as I'm concerned, there isn't a smell in my kitchen that can compare to that of freshly baked bread. While I'm sitting here writing from my library, I'm eagerly waiting for some dough to rise. Tonight can't come soon enough!

Now, as everyone who has ever made bread knows, it's impossible to make a decent loaf of bread without yeast. It may seem benign when you scoop it out of a jar from your refrigerator or pour it out of a packet, but yeast is a powerful fungus. In baking, its purpose is to cause a lump of dough to rise into bread. Other types of yeast can even cause a painful infection. When Jesus spoke of yeast, He was aware of its uses and power. In the Bible, yeast is most often used as a symbol of corruption and sin because, just as yeast expands and spreads throughout an entire batch of dough, corruption and sin spread throughout our lives.

Hypocrisy is even more powerful than yeast, since it can contaminate the spiritual integrity of the person engaged in it. In this passage, Jesus is warning His disciples to beware of the "yeast" of the Pharisees, which was their hypocrisy. They said one thing—but did another.

Unfortunately, hypocrisy is rampant in the church. And just like Jesus had serious concerns about the faith of His disciples in the face of such hypocrisy, we must be on the lookout in our own lives. When we teach our children it is ungodly to watch a movie that mocks the Lord Jesus but then we watch movies full of sexual immorality and sin after they have gone to bed, we are guilty of hypocrisy.

Did you notice that Jesus warned His disciples that there would be a time when everything that is covered up will be revealed? I don't know about you, but that makes me tremble. We may be headed for challenges to our faith in the future—and hypocrisy will taint our witness and render us ineffective as ambassadors for the gospel. Do not allow hypocrisy to gain a foothold in your life. Just like yeast, it can rapidly spread throughout your whole family and do tremendous damage to the faith of those who watch you most closely—your children.

True Compassion

When the Lord saw her, his heart overflowed with compassion. "Don't cry!" he said.

LUKE 7:13

ONE OF THE REASONS I LOVE Jesus so much is that He has the heart of His Father in heaven. Growing up, I did not always experience feeling loved by my earthly father. I often felt unloved. Maybe some of you can relate. But when I was very young, I also heard about the love of Jesus, and in Luke 7 we see it clearly.

In verse 11, we see Jesus walking along with His disciples, followed, as always, by a large crowd. As He approaches the village, He notices a funeral procession exiting the village gates. As it turns out, the young man who had died was the only son of a widow. Jesus must have known the pain that she was experiencing. The Bible records that when the Lord Jesus saw her, His heart overflowed with compassion.

Has your heart ever overflowed like that when you saw your own children suffering or in pain? If so, you have had a glimpse into the incredible compassion of God.

As mothers, we would do almost anything for our children when we see that they are suffering. Of course, Jesus eventually went to the Cross because of His love for us, but not before allowing us to see the many different facets of His extraordinary love.

You can see in Jesus' actions how much His heart hurts when we hurt. It can be tempting to want to ignore or minimize the pain of those around us—especially if we did not experience compassion as children—but it's an important part of raising healthy children.

Do our children know that when they hurt, we hurt? Do they know how much our hearts sing when they succeed? If not, we need to change the messages we are sending.

We can learn a lot from Jesus' example. Our children need to know that when they hurt, we hurt. If God can display it, so can we. Compassion should be a hallmark of every Christian mother.

A Lot Like Moses

The LORD said to Moses, "Do not be afraid of him, for I have handed him over to you, along with all his people and his land. Do the same to him as you did to King Sihon of the Amorites, who ruled in Heshbon." And Israel killed King Og, his sons, and all his subjects; not a single survivor remained. Then Israel occupied their land.

NUMBERS 21:34-35

As usual, the Israelites were outnumbered, and the battle seemed lost before it was fought. But as usual, God stepped in and reminded Moses not to be afraid—and what his response to trouble should be. Did you know the original Hebrew title for the book of Numbers was "In the Desert"? Sometimes, I wish Bible translators had kept it, because this phrase lets us know a lot about the content of the book of Numbers. Throughout the book, we find the Israelites surrounded by hostile nations. They marched under the burning sun in a desert filled with snakes, scorpions, and drought.

If you were to visit the Sinai Desert today, you would see why people are still amazed that an entire nation wandered around in the desert for forty years and survived. Our lives as children of God are also marked by periods of rebellion and indifference, not unlike the Israelites. We go through our own deserts, don't we? Oftentimes we find ourselves in the desert because God is testing us. Sometimes, they arise from our own rebellion, or even a simple unwillingness to walk in obedience to God's clear commands.

The major theme, of course—and the reason why the Israelites took forty years to cross a desert that should've taken them two weeks—is simple: they struggled with grumbling and rebellion.

Ouch. I imagine Moses felt like many mothers that I know. Moses had his work cut out for him. Moses was given charge of the people of Israel (not a very fun job, if you ask me)! Like Moses, I have found myself correcting grumbling children who rebel against my instructions.

As a mother, I want to lead my children in a way similar to how Moses led the Israelites. He was not perfect, but he did walk with God. There were many positive qualities in Moses, and I believe that God, who saw Moses' weaknesses as well as his strengths, chose him because He knew he was right for the job. Just like God had to remind Moses not to be afraid, we have opportunities to be reminded today. And just like Moses was right for the job God gave him, you, precious mom, are right for your job too.

Don't Count on Your Warhorse!

Don't count on your warhorse to give you victory—for all its strength, it cannot save you.

PSALM 33:17

THE IMAGERY IN PSALMS IS WONDERFUL. Over and over, Scripture tells us that we are in a very real spiritual battle. Of course, the Israelites had a physical battle to worry about as well as a spiritual one.

The Israelites were very familiar with the weapons of warfare. So when the psalmist reminded them not to count on their warhorses to give them victory, it was imagery that they would clearly understand. The psalmist was reminding the Israelites that as long as they stayed under God's protective rule, they would be both safe and secure.

Listen to how the psalmist goes on to explain where they should put their hope in verses 18 and 19: "The LORD watches over those who fear him, those who rely on his unfailing love. He rescues them from death and keeps them alive in times of famine. We put our hope in the LORD. He is our help and our shield. In him our hearts rejoice, for we trust in his holy name. Let your unfailing love surround us, LORD, for our hope is in you alone."

King David, who is widely considered to be the author of Psalm 33, is going to great lengths to instruct the Israelites as to where they should look for help. David was very familiar with war, and his enemies were great, yet he knew what we need to know today. The Bible teaches us that it is the Lord who is worthy of our trust. He is our help and shield, and because of His great love for us we can greatly rejoice.

What is your warhorse? Where are you placing your trust? What are you counting on to ensure victory today? If our trust is in anything other than the Lord, the Bible says it is misplaced. While people and things will let us down, God never will.

Moms, make sure that your children are watching an example of a mother who does not place her hope in anything but Christ. Don't put your trust in an education system. Do not put your hope in your children's youth pastor or in following the rules. Put your trust in the Lord alone! Ask Him to guide and direct you. When you walk with the Lord, you are safe and secure. It's a promise you can count on.

Where Good Counsel Is Found

The godly offer good counsel; they teach right from wrong.

PSALM 37:30

HAVE YOU EVER NOTICED HOW MANY TIMES the word *godly* is mentioned in the Bible? Godliness is a major theme—this idea of becoming more like Jesus. Sometimes, as Christians, we throw words around, but we do not think about the implications for our everyday lives. If the Bible says we are to be godly, then we should know how to *become* godly, and how to teach our children too.

Godliness, put simply, is respect or reverence for a life of holiness. To be holy means to be set apart. In Psalm 4:3, the Bible says, "The LORD set apart the godly for himself," and in fact, God wants us to become His holy people. A woman who is striving for godliness will be very aware of whatever she allows herself to watch on television or what she listens to. She would be concerned that her speech is honoring to God.

The Bible teaches us that the godly offer good counsel and teach right from wrong—something that is sorely missing in the modern church. This is just one reason why it is so important—so that we might offer good counsel, starting with our children. Do you want to be godly? Start here: get to know the truth as God reveals it in Scripture. In Titus 1:1, Paul talks about a "knowledge of the truth that leads to godliness" (NIV), and in his second letter to the Corinthians he writes of a "godly sorrow . . . that leads to salvation" (2 Corinthians 7:10, NIV).

You can recognize a godly person by their commitment to studying and obeying the Word of God and God's commands in a world that is increasingly hostile to it. Make no mistake—godliness is costly: "Everyone who wants to live a godly life in Christ Jesus will be persecuted" (2 Timothy 3:12, NIV). As Christians, we do not live for the temporary pleasures of this world, but rather for the eternal treasure that is waiting for us in the presence of our Lord Jesus.

As ambassadors of Christ, we want to speak into the lives of our children from a position of godliness. When others ask you for counsel, be sure to seek the Lord. First Timothy 4:7-8 reminds us we are to "train [ourselves] to be godly. For physical training is of some value, but godliness has value for all things, holding promise for both the present life and the life to come."

And that's the best part—while things are passing away, we are training our souls for eternity with Christ.

Stop Grumbling!

We hate this horrible manna!

NUMBERS 21:5

I SURE WISH I DIDN'T HAVE so much in common with the ancient Israelites sometimes! As I read the account of the Israelites moving from slavery to the Promised Land, I must admit, I'm a little ashamed of myself. Like me, the Israelites were prone to complaining. Like me, they had moments of great faith and moments of none at all.

In Numbers 21, we find the Israelites unhappy with where God has put them, even though He has miraculously and beautifully provided for them at every turn along the journey. They are fresh from a victory over Arad, but they soon forget *why* they were victorious—and once again, they begin to see themselves as more important than God.

God was providing for their every need, including making sure they had food to eat every day. At first, the manna God provided was a miraculous answer to prayer, but by Numbers 21, the Israelites had grown weary of the way God had chosen to provide for them.

Can you imagine grumbling to God and telling Him that you hate what He has given you? Something tells me that we can all relate on one level or another.

Oh, how we can learn from their example! The Bible tells us of the people on the road to the Red Sea headed for the land of Edom. But the people grew impatient with the long journey, and they began to speak against God and Moses: "'Why have you brought us out of Egypt to die here in the wilderness?' they complained. 'There is nothing to eat here and nothing to drink. And we hate this horrible manna!'" (Numbers 21:5).

Poor Moses! Imagine how he must've felt. As a mother, I must confess I have been frustrated on more than one occasion by the ungrateful grumbling of my children. Grumbling kids do not make me want to give them what they want. Truth be told, I want to give my grumblers *nothing*.

Grumbling displeases the Lord—whether it is from the Israelites, or me, or my kids. Grumbling demonstrates both a lack of thankfulness and a lack of humility. So stop grumbling!

God Delights in You

The LORD directs the steps of the godly. He delights in every detail of their lives.

PSALM 37:23

As I sit in my study writing today, my heart is full. My two youngest children are playing in the yard with my grandsons—happily running through the sprinkler. Watching them dart in and out of the water and hearing their laughter are some of the best things about the season of life I find myself in.

I have been a mother for thirty years now. The first ten years were all-consuming in terms of physicality and practicality. The all-nighters with babies, the constant training of toddlers, the first tenuous years of homeschooling. In all of it, I found myself delighting in the rare moments when the baby would be asleep or cooing in her carrier, or the kids would be making cookies while I folded laundry—but my favorite memories are moments of sheer delight that had little to do with what my kids were doing and more to do with the fact that they existed at all.

When our babies make their entrance into this world, when we meet our child for the first time, the wonder is all-encompassing. We delight in every detail of their being, from the curve of their noses to that unique little band in their toe. It's all a miracle, and we know it.

It's easy to focus on our children, to pour into them as we train and teach them—and it's easy to forget that, just as we delight in our children, God delights in His. And you, precious mom, *are His.*

The Bible teaches us that God delights in every detail of our lives. I think God looks at us in a very similar way to the way we view our own children. We know that God desires that we walk with Him and that we become like Him, and beyond that, we know that God delights in every detail of our lives as His "dearly loved" children (Ephesians 5:1, NIV).

What a miracle it is to be loved by the God of the universe! Your Creator delights in every detail of your life. You're a miracle too, precious mom, and He knows it.

Do You Trust Him?

The word of the LORD holds true, and we can trust everything he does.

PSALM 33:4

HOW'S YOUR GOD-CONFIDENCE TODAY, PRECIOUS MOM? How's your confidence in knowing that everything that is happening around you is seen by your all-knowing, all-powerful, all-seeing God?

It's easy to say that we trust God when the things around us seem to be going well. It's also easy to forget that our children are imitating us, even in the way that we respond to the challenges of this life. If it's true that we can't pass on what we don't possess, then one thing we need to possess is an unshakable confidence in the sure foundation of God.

The Bible tells us that we can trust everything God does. Why? Because "the word of the LORD holds true" (Psalm 33:4). That means that no matter what happens around us, we can trust in God's heart and in His purposes. Something that my grandmother taught me when I was very little still impacts me today. She said, "Heidi, you either believe that God is good or you don't, and everyone will know what you believe by the way you react to difficulties."

How are you reacting to the circumstances around you today? Do your children see a mom who is rooted and confident in her walk with God and her trust in Him? Or do they see a mom who is worrying and full of fear? My grandma was right—everyone will know what we believe by the way we react to difficulties in our lives. We either trust Him or we don't. If we say we trust Him, let's act like it.

One day, our children will be talking to their children about the way that we handled the difficult circumstances of life. Truth is, they will either be strengthened by our example or they will be sidelined by it.

Today, let's remember that the children God has given us are learning much about what it means to walk with Him from our example. *Father, help us to trust You out loud today!* Today, I pray that our children would see no matter what comes our way, our trust is in the Lord!

Be a Light!

Send out your light and your truth; let them guide me.
Let them lead me to your holy mountain, to the place where you live.

PSALM 43:3

I DON'T KNOW ABOUT YOU, BUT I'm often frustrated with what I see happening in the world around me. I turn on the news, and within fifteen minutes, I want to turn it off and pretend I live in a world that is not sick with sin and groaning because of it.

It's easy to look around and comment about it from a "Christian perspective" on social media. It's easy to be an armchair general in the spiritual battles that are raging around us. What's not so easy is getting off the bench and onto the battlefield. I wonder what would happen if we took the command of Scripture seriously enough to become leaders in the spiritual battle by asking the Lord to show us how to engage in it.

When you study the ministry of Jesus, it is clear that His heart was never that we would sit around and simply talk about what was happening. He wants us to *engage* with those God brings into our lives. Author and speaker Francis Chan rightly pointed out our attitudes with this quote: "Simon says 'pat your head' and we pat our heads. Jesus said 'go and make disciples' and we memorize that verse."

Ouch. He's right, isn't he? It's easy to train our children to be salt and light—but in truth, parents need to be the salt and light before we can ever expect our children to be. How do we get there? David's heart was so plainly seen in Psalm 43 when he asked God to lead him. Before you lead those around you to the holy mountain, to the place where God is, are you asking Him to lead *you* there? You can't effectively lead others without first being led.

What does it mean to "lead" people to the place where they find God? Precious mom, it can start with a simple act of kindness. You can start by asking the mom you meet at the grocery store if you can help her after noticing her struggling with babies and groceries. Often, the person's first introduction to Christ-followers is only what they see in social media. Wouldn't it be amazing if we taught our children to be servants of those around them with the hope of leading them to God?

Father, send out your light—lead me.

He Cares for You

> He cares for you.
>
> **1 PETER 5:7, NIV**

BIG EYES STARED UP AT ME from a warm bath. It had been a rough day. I searched around for some Mr. Bubble while my three-year-old perfected her worn-out cry.

I. was. done.

Done in every way. The laundry was piling up. We had finished dinner, but the dishes were still sitting in the sink. I knew that after I got the toddler to bed, it was likely they would still be sitting there. It seemed like every room in the house was full of clutter. I had spent hours perfecting a wonderful new system for household chores (and I use the word *system* loosely), and no one seemed to care or even try to follow it. And now, to top off my very bad day, I was dealing with a very bad attitude and a little girl who could not remotely comprehend how worn out I was.

As I struggled to find grace for her, tears filled my eyes. "Where is my help?" I complained aloud. "Who cares about the job I am doing?"

Have you ever been there? Have you ever wondered if anyone cared about the job you do to care for your home and family? You know, the things that it seems so often go unnoticed. In moments like this, it comforts me to know that not only does God see me, not only does He notice the little things I do to serve my family, He really does care.

If you stop to think about it, it's amazing. The God of the universe notices me. He notices how tired I am, and how underappreciated I feel. He knows what it's like to be surrounded by people who don't get it, after all. Jesus was in the garden of Gethsemane, exhausted and burdened by all that He knew lay ahead of him . . . and the disciples could not be bothered to even stay awake.

God understands your weariness, beloved. He understands because He created you. He knows your weaknesses even better than you do, and He stands ready to help you right now. Quiet your heart. Let the Lord of heaven and earth saturate you with His love. Something supernatural happens when we allow ourselves to become quieted by the love of Jesus. As mothers, we need to know He cares, and we need to know that He sees us. Today, you can rest in the truth of His Word—He cares for you.

When Friendship Fades

What good fellowship we once enjoyed as we walked together to the house of God.

PSALM 55:14

ONE OF THE DEEPEST HURTS WE can ever experience is betrayal at the hands of a trusted friend—especially a friend who is also a sister in Christ.

It is hard enough to deal with enemies, but an even worse hurt is that of being betrayed by a close friend. When this happens, it is easy to feel we can no longer trust anyone. When our hearts are raw, it is easy to fall into sin. The temptation to gossip, even to slander, is real! After all, we want justice and vindication. If you have ever heard the saying "Hurt people hurt people," then you have a glimpse into the heart of David: "It is not an enemy who taunts me—I could bear that. It is not my foes who so arrogantly insult me—I could have hidden from them. Instead, it is you—my equal, my companion and close friend. What good fellowship we once enjoyed as we walked together to the house of God" (Psalm 55:12-14).

One of the reasons I love this psalm is that David is so relatable. Notice how he hurts because it is not an enemy who has wounded him but a friend. He says he could bear it if it wasn't a friend, but instead, he is left with betrayal and the memories of what he thought would be a lifelong friendship with another believer.

There are many lessons to be learned in a season of betrayal in friendship, but one of the most important lessons I've learned is that in times of hurt and betrayal, I can turn to God for help. David knew that God would never betray him. When he felt that he could no longer trust anyone, David turned to God.

Our children have a front-row seat to many things in our lives, don't they? My children have seen me cry over the loss of a friendship and grieve over injustice—but the most important thing they witness is not the loss itself, but rather, how I deal with that loss. Have you been betrayed by a friend? Is your heart broken today? Turn to God. No one understands betrayal quite like Jesus. Allow Him to soothe your broken heart, and ask Him for wisdom. Even in the midst of your pain, you're teaching your children what it means to walk with God. There is a blessing to be found in running into the arms of Jesus when we are suffering—and teaching our children to do the same.

How to Ruin a Nation

Without wise leadership, a nation falls.

PROVERBS 11:14

As MOTHERS, ONE OF THE MOST important things we can ever teach our children is the importance of having wise leadership in our nation. I grew up in the 1970s, a time of incredible ambivalence toward political things in the church. Not only did we not talk about politics, but we were instructed not to!

It may keep us from awkward conversations, but this ambivalence has led to a lack of understanding about political things. As the church has stepped out of the public discourse, the impact on culture has been devastating. Politics should matter to God's people. At the very least, we should be talking about it. Why? For starters, because the Bible teaches that without wise leadership, nations fall.

Praise the Lord, I was greatly influenced by my grandparents, who taught me the importance of being involved in the culture from a biblical worldview. My grandfather would read newspaper articles to me explaining current events in real time. Grandma was a Bible teacher, and my grandfather was a pastor. They never let their faith keep them from talking about current events and politics. In fact, they believed that their Christianity was central to it! They viewed politics as an opportunity to be salt and light, and I agree with them.

For thirty years, I have been teaching my children the importance of civic responsibility. As often as possible, Jay and I talk to our children about current events in light of Scripture. You see, the Word of God informs every aspect of our lives as believers. This includes participating in the decisions that are being made in our communities. The Bible is very clear about what we should look for in our leaders. If we believe the Bible, then we know it's true that without wise leadership, nations fall.

One sure way to bring a nation to ruin is for Christians to disengage from the political process. It matters who is in authority over us. It matters who sits on the boards of our libraries and our public schools. It matters who we elect to city council, and it matters who our governors are. These people are determining policy, and they will either push righteous agendas or they will promote evil ones. As we get off the bench and onto the battlefield, as we speak up for what we know is true and right, our children are watching. Are you teaching your children about the value of wise and godly leadership? If not, start today.

SHINE

No one lights a lamp and then hides it or puts it under a basket. Instead, a lamp is placed on a stand, where its light can be seen by all who enter the house.

LUKE 11:33

I REMEMBER THE MOMENT THAT I asked Jesus into my heart when I was only four years old. I gave my life to Christ at my grandparents' house. It was bedtime, and my grandmother was kneeling next to the bed after brushing my hair and applying her beloved Mentholatum to my back. It's funny, isn't it, the things we remember!

As a little girl, my heart was wide open. When I realized how much Jesus loves me, I wanted to tell the world. I remember telling my neighbors . . . and the mailman and my teacher. In fact, anyone who would listen to me got to hear about Jesus, because my grandma told me that He wanted me to *shine* for others! Grandma did a good job making me feel important to God.

As a mother, I want my children to feel loved by God. I made a little acrostic (if you know me, then you know how much I love them!) to help you teach your children what it means to SHINE for Jesus.

Stand	**H**elp	**I**mitate (Jesus)	**N**ever give up	**E**ncourage others

The first thing we want to teach our children as followers of Jesus is that they can stand up for Him. As a child, I sang a song that you might be familiar with: *Stand up, stand up for Jesus, ye soldiers of the cross; lift high his royal banner, it must not suffer loss.* Children who are taught to stand are in a better position to do the next thing in my little acrostic—help.

A person who shines for Jesus is a person who helps. It is beautiful to see our children helping others in the name of Jesus, isn't it?

The next thing we want to teach our children starts with us, as most things do: we must imitate Jesus. That means in everything we say and do, we try our best to be like Christ.

The "N" in *shine* is for "Never give up." It's tempting to give up, even as mothers, isn't it? But part of walking with God means learning to persevere even through trials.

Finally, we want to teach our children to encourage other people. Mothers have a tremendous obligation to be the primary encouragers of their children. As we encourage our children, we are teaching them how to be an encouragement to others.

So shine, precious mom! As you shine for Jesus, your children will too.

Good Trees, Good Fruit

A tree is identified by its fruit.

LUKE 6:44

YEARS AGO, WHEN I WAS HOMESCHOOLING six children at one time, I remember feeling very frustrated with a particular child. (Said "child" is now all grown up, so we survived, not to spoil the ending.) As parents, we are always hoping to see the "peaceful fruit of righteousness" (Hebrews 12:11, ESV) in our children. It's the whole goal, isn't it? To see our children begin to bear good fruit?

At any given time in the parenting process, good parents can be found pruning the "tree" that is the heart of their child.

During this particular season in our lives, we had six children, ages fifteen and under. A whole lot of pruning was happening, both in my life and in theirs! For months, my husband and I had been focusing on a character issue with one of our children. The root of the problem was the lack of self-control. We talked about self-control, read stories about self-control, and even memorized the fruits of the Spirit. Nothing seemed to be working. There was no sign of fruit.

One day, while I was sitting at the kitchen table working on a homeschooling assignment, my child was presented with an opportunity to become very angry. (It's amazing how sanctifying it is to have siblings! But anyway, I digress.) I decided to sit this one out and wait to see what my child would do. To my utter amazement, I saw a blossom on my little sapling! I didn't even have to give any instructions! It was amazing, and I could not wait to tell my husband the good news. Our parenting efforts were not in vain after all. There was at least the *promise* of fruit on our young tree.

Really, that's what this is all about, isn't it? The promise of fruit. We teach our children to be Christlike in their character, knowing that all of our efforts, according to the Word, will bear fruit. Now after that, there were many times when I wondered if the blossom I saw was just a mirage, but ultimately, we have seen fruit in the lives of all of our children. Jesus knew what He was talking about when He said a tree would be known by its fruit. If we want our trees to be known for bearing good fruit, we need to keep pruning. It will be worth it. Good fruit is worth the effort.

More Than Enough

Day by day the LORD takes care of the innocent, and they will receive an inheritance that lasts forever. They will not be disgraced in hard times; even in famine they will have more than enough.

PSALM 37:18-19

ONE OF MY DEAREST FRIENDS TOLD me that her husband, who had been a police officer for twenty-five years, was being fired following a vaccine mandate. Her voice shook as she described their situation. They wondered if they would lose their home. They struggled with how to talk to their kids about the changes in the coming months.

This kind of worry was new to my friend. She had been a stay-at-home mom for over fifteen years. They weren't rich by any standard, but they were comfortable. They had always had enough—but now, she was doubting where the provision they needed would come from. She never imagined their family would be in this situation, but God had laid it on her heart months earlier to prepare her children for suffering by teaching them that God is present in every circumstance. She knew her words mattered, and as a result, she and her husband asked the Lord to help them shepherd their children through this challenging season with grace and hope.

In the months that followed the loss of her husband's job, the family learned to trust God in a new, deeper way. God met them in their struggle. He provided through friends and family, and He showed up in ways that were both miraculous and mundane. God never left them. In fact, though the sorrow and anger could have overtaken them, instead, they grew stronger as a family as their faith was put to the test. It wasn't easy, but God was with them.

The bottom line is this: even when we are suffering, God asks us to trust Him. Over and over, the Bible instructs God's children on the goodness and trustworthiness of our Provider. We don't plan for pandemics, or cancer, or the loss of a job. This is why the Word of God becomes even more precious in times of suffering. Before the trial, God tells us He will be there.

Even in famine, God promises that His children will have more than enough. God's heart for us is the heart of the Father to His children. Think of how you feel about your children. That is how God feels about you. And just like you would go to extreme lengths to make sure your children have more than enough, the God of the universe says He will do the same for you.

Rest in this today, beloved. God will provide.

A Bit and a Bridle

The LORD says, "I will guide you along the best pathway for your life. I will advise you and watch over you. Do not be like a senseless horse or mule that needs a bit and bridle to keep it under control."

PSALM 32:8-9

WHEN I WAS A LITTLE GIRL, my parents owned a small farm in a town that sits in the shadow of Mount Hood. Boring, Oregon, was a beautiful place to grow up. On our little farm, we had a miniature donkey whom we named "Patches" because of the white patches on his belly. Now, Patches was delightful to look at. Because he was so small, we were deceived into thinking he was also gentle. He might have been miniature physically, but there was nothing miniature about his personality!

Patches would not, absolutely *would not*, allow us to ride him. Whenever we tried, he would immediately bolt for the barbwire fence and rub himself against it until we were forced to get off. It didn't matter what we tried, he would not be trained, and ultimately his stubbornness made him dangerous. Even the bridle could not keep him under control. Because of his stubborn disposition, eventually, we sold him.

Do you have a stubborn child? Maybe you are the stubborn one? Stubbornness can be a good thing, but notice how the psalmist in today's Scripture passage warns us against refusing to be led. Just like our children need to be led by their parents, we need to be led by the Lord.

The next time you talk to your child about their stubbornness, you can remind them that the Bible teaches us not to be like a mule that requires both a bit and a bridle to keep it under control. Rather than rely on constantly being controlled by human consequences, we need to learn to be controlled by the Holy Spirit.

Of course, the threat of a human consequence is not a bad thing. We discipline our children, generally starting with the threat of a consequence and ending up with an actual one if they continue in disobedience or rebellion. We advise them and watch over them in the same way the Lord advises and watches over us as His children.

This requires that we learn to listen for His still, small voice. Precious mom, remember: we cannot pass on what we don't possess. Are you being controlled by the Holy Spirit today? Or do you still need a bit and bridle?

From the Very Break of Day

The nations are in chaos, and their kingdoms crumble! God's voice thunders, and the earth melts! The LORD of Heaven's Armies is here among us; the God of Israel is our fortress.

PSALM 46:6-7

IN 2020, THE WORLD WAS REELING from the COVID pandemic. It had infected the world, causing fear, panic, and death. At the beginning of the pandemic, we experienced being quarantined in our home for an extended period of time. At first, it was great to spend time with family and focus on getting things done. But as the days wore on and the news of the infection spread, the death toll increased and a feeling of frustration grew.

Our children were asking us questions that we did not have the answers to. Did you feel helpless? I know I did. In those times, just like today, we found refuge in the Bible. God's Word teaches us that we are always seen by our heavenly Father. Nothing that happens takes the Lord by surprise. The Bible says that from the break of day, God will protect His own. Even when the nations are in chaos, the Bible says that the Lord of heaven's armies is here with us.

I love the imagery of the psalmist when he says that God is here from "the very break of day." What that tells me is that from the moment I open my eyes in the morning, God is present. The next time you are in the middle of a crisis, whether it is a personal crisis or an international one, turn your eyes heavenward. God is here among us. He is our fortress. In times of panic, we can be people of peace. This does not mean that we stick our heads in the sand or that we grow callous to suffering or indifferent to struggle. It does not mean that we will not suffer either. In fact, the Bible tells us that we *will* suffer because we live in a fallen world.

The good news, though, is that we do not need to live in a state of fear or panic. In fact, we can be people of peace even in the middle of a pandemic, because we know that our times are in God's hands. The Bible teaches us that our days are ordained for us before we take a single breath. Nothing that happens to us or around us is unseen by our Creator. When we are in Him, when we surrender our lives to His will and His ways, we can rest in the knowledge that nothing can separate us from Him or His love. Make sure that your kids know this truth, precious mom!

Near the Cross of Jesus

Near the cross of Jesus stood his mother, his mother's sister, Mary the wife of Clopas, and Mary Magdalene. When Jesus saw his mother there, and the disciple whom he loved standing nearby, he said to her, "Woman, here is your son," and to the disciple, "Here is your mother." From that time on, this disciple took her into his home.

JOHN 19:25-27

HAVE YOU EVER CONSIDERED THE WAY Jesus took care of His mother? When I was young, a wise woman told me, "Pay attention to the way the man you are dating treats his mother. That is the way he will likely treat you. That is his character."

Look with me at the scene set for us in John 19. Jesus was on the cross, suffering and in unimaginable pain—both physical and spiritual—and yet, He remembered His mother. I would imagine Mary was in such great pain that she could not consider her own future after the death of her son, but Jesus did. Look at how Jesus addressed His mother: He called her "woman." As a mother myself, I see this differently than I did before I had children. Jesus knew that Mary was wracked with pain. Instead of calling her "Mother," which likely would have broken her heart, He used a generic term instead.

Oh, how He cared for her! Come near the cross of Jesus. Picture the Son of God, still speaking with all the tenderness that His humanity displayed. Entering into the suffering of Jesus and His mother gives us a glimpse of the great love God has for us.

See how John was instructed to care for Mary? Jesus must've had incredible trust in this disciple. John must have been both tender and strong. I wonder what it would've been like for Mary to be around men like this. It gives me a renewed appreciation for my husband and my sons. We have an opportunity as mothers to teach our boys that mothers are to be loved, respected, and ultimately, protected. Jesus set the bar pretty high, didn't He? Now that both of my boys are grown, I can tell you this with absolute certainty: nothing beats knowing that they love and protect me.

My husband's mother taught him to value and respect her, and for that, I am grateful. Mothers, teach your sons about this scene from the crucifixion of our Lord Jesus. Even in His greatest hour of suffering, His holiness shone through. His heart to protect and love His mother is beautiful.

Thank you, Jesus, that even in Your dying hour, You were teaching us how to live.

Hiding Place

You are my hiding place; you protect me from trouble. You surround me with songs of victory.
PSALM 32:7

LEAN IN, PRECIOUS MOM. Let's remember what it was like to be little for just a minute. When we take on the heart and perspective of a child, we are near, I believe, to seeing things through the eyes of our heavenly Father.

As I write this, I am listening to one of my favorite songs, "Goodness of God." My heart is quieted as the words wash over me. I love the imagery of God's goodness "running after me." We don't often think of God that way—but oh, He is *just like that.* Even in times of trouble, we can know that He is working all things together for our ultimate good and is surrounding us with songs of victory. He is our hiding place. He wants us to run to Him.

As a child, I made lots of hiding places. I built forts underneath tables and made places in the forest that no one knew about. But the blanket forts were the best. Sometimes, we would make the entire downstairs into a blanket fort. Come to think of it, I can see why it made my mom mad. (It was a whole lot more fun to build them than to clean them up.)

I think children make forts because it gives them a place to hide. When you're hiding, you don't need to think about reality. When you're hiding, you feel safe. Of course, blanket fort "safety" isn't real—it's an illusion. But God says He is our hiding place, and when we lean into Him with a childlike faith, we find a sense of peace and security. We can hide behind our good Father and know that we are safe—hidden from the schemes of the enemy. Can you imagine being covered not by a blanket but by the strong arms of your Creator?

This is a wonderful truth to pass on to our children. The next time you find them playing under a blanket fort, remind them that God shields and protects them. Every detail of our lives matters to our Creator. Our deepest thoughts, greatest insecurities, and unspoken fears are safe with Him, hidden away in His heart—tucked away until we see Him face-to-face.

If you are struggling today, take a page from the psalms and hide in the knowledge that you're loved. Because of the help of God, you can be secure. If you need to hide today, run to the Father in prayer. Read the Bible and be still. You are safe. You are loved. You are His.

A Passion for the City

As he approached Jerusalem and saw the city, he wept over it.

LUKE 19:41, NIV

WHEN WAS THE LAST TIME YOUR heart broke for the spiritual darkness that is so common in cities today?

Jesus had a passion for the city of Jerusalem. He saw the city, and He wept over it. He knew that the citizens' spiritual ignorance was going to bring them suffering. He warned them, saying,

How I wish today that you of all people would understand the way to peace. But now it is too late, and peace is hidden from your eyes. Before long your enemies will build ramparts against your walls and encircle you and close in on you from every side. They will crush you into the ground, and your children with you. Your enemies will not leave a single stone in place, because you did not recognize it when God visited you.

LUKE 19:42-44

Of course, Jesus was speaking with a prophetic voice. Not long after, the Jews were driven out of Jerusalem, and they entered a period of darkness that God had warned them about. Because of their refusal to accept Jesus as their Messiah, God put them in a time-out of sorts and, thankfully, turned His attention to the Gentiles.

His heart, however, remains with His chosen people, the Jews. Like Jesus, we have a message: a warning about sin and a promise of healing. We need to share it!

I wonder, do we share God's heart for people? Where do you live? Where are you raising your children? Jay and I raised our children near the city of Portland, Oregon. We have a passion for seeing revival here in our area—but revival will not come without repentance.

It's easy to live a comfortable life, to barricade ourselves away in our homes and go back and forth from our churches without ever weeping over the spiritual decay in our cities. If we are truly trying to be imitators of God, we will begin by impacting places we live with a life-changing message of the gospel of Jesus Christ.

He Will

The LORD kept his word and did for Sarah exactly what he had promised.

GENESIS 21:1

HAVE YOU BEEN WAITING A LONG time for an answer to prayer? If so, it's time to take a look at the life of a woman who would understand. Sarah was Abraham's wife. She knew about God's promise to her husband—that He would make Abraham into a great nation (Genesis 12:2)—and she spent a lifetime waiting to see that promise fulfilled.

Surely, since the promise included descendants . . . that must have included Sarah! Right? There was a time when Sarah did not know the answer to this question.

Sarah is the first woman named in the faith "hall of fame" in Hebrews 11. I love the story of Sarah, because although she was given an incredible role to play in the lineage of Jesus, she had a whole lot of doubt when it came to whether or not she could trust the promises of God. I absolutely love that the Bible is not filled with perfect people who got it all right. Instead, it is filled with imperfect people who got it mostly, well, wrong.

In Genesis 18, we see Sarah's most well-known attribute: her sense of humor. She had the guts (if that's what you want to call it) to laugh at God's promise of a child. After all, *she* knew better than to expect to get pregnant at the age of ninety. *She* knew.

Except that she didn't. She didn't know that God was going to use her faithlessness to prove a point: when God makes a promise, you can take it to the bank. If God promises you that you will have a child, you will have a child. If God promises that your prayer of salvation will result in a change in your eternal destination, it will. If God promises to remove your sin as far as the east is from the west because you ask Him to forgive you, He will.

Beloved, God is not looking for perfect people. I believe He delights in using imperfect people so that we can know how dependent we are on Him. If you are waiting today for an answer to prayer, keep your eyes fixed on Jesus. We may not always get the answers that *we* want, but we can be assured that God hears our prayers and that He is working things together for our good and for His glory.

Today, if you're waiting and feel a moment of faithlessness come over you, remember Sarah. She had a moment like that too, and yet, God answered her prayers. He will answer yours too.

My Child, Be Discerning

Dear friends, do not believe everyone who claims to speak by the Spirit. You must test them to see if the spirit they have comes from God. For there are many false prophets in the world.

1 JOHN 4:1

DISCERNMENT IS SOMETHING THAT'S SORELY LACKING in most Christian circles today. From entertainment to education, from our politics to our pulpits, the eyes of the children of God have grown dim—starting with parents.

Moms, one of your primary responsibilities is to teach your children to be discerning. To do that, you need to have a right understanding of exactly what discernment is. Charles Spurgeon has been credited with saying, "Discernment is not knowing the difference between right and wrong. It's knowing the difference between right—and *almost right*."

This is exactly what the apostle John was explaining to the baby believers of his time in today's verse. In effect, he was saying, "Eyes open! Truth matters!"

As a mother, I have learned that I must have my own spiritual antennae "way up" in the culture today. I want my kids to discern what is right. I pray my children will be discerning as they grow in wisdom. Oh, how we need to see what God sees! I pray that they will hear the voice of God, who is truth, above all the other voices that will be vying for their hearts and minds.

Remember, we can't give our kids what we don't have. If we want to be discerning, we need to ask God to help us. Discernment does not come naturally to fallen people. We'll need to be drenched in truth if we want to see it. If we desire to have eyes to see through cultural narratives and unwise teaching in our churches, we must ask God to help us. Discernment isn't optional for the Christian. It's imperative.

There are many examples of places where we can lose our way—so allow me to point one out: Does God care about justice? Yes. His Word declares it in Micah 6:8 among other places. But does God's Word define justice the same way the world does? That's dubious. Without the guidance of God's Word, the world's version of justice is steeped in man's wisdom and man's agendas. As Christians, we must be concerned with God's agenda. We know that God's ways are not our ways, and His thoughts are not our thoughts.

A discerning heart sees through trends to truth. Where the world would divide us, the gospel unites us. Teach your children to be discerning. If we want them to walk in the truth, discernment is key.

Is There Hope?

Be strong and take heart, all you who hope in the LORD.

PSALM 31:24, NIV

I COME FROM A BROKEN HOME. Though I am now into my fifties, I still bear the scars, both emotional and physical, left behind by many years of hidden suffering. There were times when I would cry myself to sleep over things that were beyond my control: an angry, abusive father, a home in turmoil—a hidden life. In truth, I rarely felt at peace when I was home.

There were seasons when I felt helpless to do anything about my situation—and that helplessness often led to feelings of utter hopelessness. I wondered if God was really listening, or if He was aware of my situation.

Have you been there too? Abuse is not a prerequisite for feelings of hopelessness. Tender hearts are easily taken captive by all sorts of things, aren't they? A strong-willed child or prodigal adolescent can leave us feeling hopeless in our parenting. Adultery can leave a marriage shattered and hopeless. At times, I have surveyed the landscape of our nation and felt a sense of hopelessness and even despair.

If you're feeling hopeless right now, lean in—because you are on God's heart today.

Sometimes, it feels like God isn't working, but rest assured, dear one, He is. God is always at work. As Christians, our hope is not in an outcome—it's in an Overcomer. It's in the One who keeps His promises and performs miracles. When our trust is in the Lord, we can be strong in the midst of the storm. We can have hope, even in the midst of heartache, knowing that we are never outside of God's watch. His wisdom is available for the asking (see James 1:5-8), and His heart toward us is good (see Jeremiah 29:11).

I am so thankful for God's Word. When all around us is shifting sand, His Word is an anchor for our soul. It's the reason we can be at peace. Because of God's Word, we can know for certain that He is working all things together for our good. God sees you where you are right now in the same way He saw me in my brokenness and struggle as a child. There is hope, but it is available only in God. Cry out to Him. Trust Him. Good things are coming. Don't give up!

Casting Out Fear

Perfect love expels all fear.

1 JOHN 4:18

I'VE NEVER SEEN FEAR LIKE I did starting in March of 2020 with the rise of COVID-19. About three weeks into lockdown, I began to see real fear and uncertainty in my grandsons and youngest daughter. It was impossible to ignore the effects of the virus. As the children saw their playdates canceled and churches closed, the conversation in our home changed. Our youngest daughter, who is naturally intuitive and very tenderhearted, began to obsess over the potential outcomes of the virus. I watched as her brow furrowed. The questions revealed the fear she was dealing with.

"Mama? Where is the virus?" she asked. "Can Grandma get it from me? Is it on my pillow? Or in the car? Why can't we go to church?"

Honestly? I didn't have the answers to her questions. All I knew at the time was that I didn't want her little heart to be taken captive by the spirit of fear. As I prayed with her, peace flooded my heart. I felt a little giggle rising up inside, and I thought, *Laughter!* That's what we needed—a little humor.

The next day, I gave COVID-19 a nickname. I called it "the Rona." Since I could see that her questions would not be easily answered, I began to *cast out* the fear that was beginning to take root in her heart by walking around our house to find where the virus might be hiding.

"Rona? That you?" I queried as I walked from room to room, turning over couch cushions and looking in the freezer, among other places. Within a few moments, she was laughing along with me. The effect? Her fear was muted. We took its voice away as we skipped through the house, laughing and searching together for the Rona. Later that night, we talked about the way God protects us—and that our days are already known to our Creator.

Our Covid conversations continued in the days that followed our initial "search," but I noticed that my daughter was no longer held in the grip of fear. When the fear is cast out, we can hear the gentle voice of our Creator more clearly. He will always say, *"Do not fear."*

As mothers, we have an incredible opportunity to teach our children how to thrive in times of anxiety and fear—always remembering that we can't give what we don't have. Since we can never know what's around the corner, we must lean daily into the One who does. We need to be ready to give an answer for the hope that we have in Christ—starting with our children.

For the Weak and Timid

I came to you in weakness—timid and trembling. And my message and my preaching were very plain. Rather than using clever and persuasive speeches, I relied only on the power of the Holy Spirit. I did this so you would trust not in human wisdom but in the power of God.

1 CORINTHIANS 2:3-5

MOTHERHOOD GOD'S WAY IS DRIVEN BY God's power. I love the way God chooses to use weakness, rather than strength, in the lives of His people. Notice in today's Scripture passage how the apostle Paul held himself up as an example, not of strength but of weakness—and even trembling.

I often look at this passage and think how Paul would teach a new mom to rely on God for wisdom. He would say that weakness is exactly where God wants us to start—but it's not where God wants us to remain. Paul has this amazing way of being rather self-deprecating. I mean, let's think about it! Paul was not known for timidity, or even weakness. He was known for strength, and yet, at least initially, he notes that his message was "very plain." I would never use the phrase "very plain" to describe anything the apostle Paul said. Something tells me that you wouldn't either, which is why this verse is so encouraging!

This is a wonderful way to view the job of motherhood. Do you remember what it was like to see that positive sign on the pregnancy test or hear the news that the baby you'd been praying for would become yours through the miracle of adoption? Truth is, no mother comes into this thing called motherhood with any idea of how it will unfold or change her. We don't know what we're doing—and so we ask God to help us. That's why it's such a miracle!

God has chosen to give us little ones, whether we have experience or not, and He uses us to shape the hearts and minds of young people. What a privilege! So how do we find success? According to Paul, it's found in the power of the Holy Spirit. Are you relying on His power today, precious mom? It's easy to rely upon our own wisdom or self-help books. It's easy to rely on our own mothers for advice, and I thank God for my mom, even today! But at the end of the day, God says not to trust in human wisdom. He says to trust Him for it. When we rely on God, He takes our weakness and replaces it with strength. That's the power of Christ alive in us.

Because of God's Grace

Because of God's grace to me, I have laid the foundation like an expert builder. Now others are building on it. But whoever is building on this foundation must be very careful. For no one can lay any foundation other than the one we already have—Jesus Christ."

1 CORINTHIANS 3:10-11

THE BIBLE TEACHES US THAT WE will be a lot like our parents—and Paul was no exception. The son of Pharisees, Paul (then known as Saul) would have been arrogant and self-assured. The Pharisees were Jewish nationalists who followed the Law of Moses with excruciating precision. He was likely well educated, speaking several of the languages of the people around him, notably Greek and Aramaic, which was the official language of Judea.

Most parents want their children to be well educated to set them up for success—and Saul's family demonstrated that this was a high priority for their son. As an aspiring Pharisee, Saul was well versed in the Scriptures, having studied under a rabbi named Gamaliel. The rabbi, along with Paul's parents, would have taught him that the Greeks were to be hated because they were Gentiles and not the chosen people of God.

Eventually, Saul was well on his way to becoming part of the Sanhedrin (the Jewish version of our Supreme Court), proving he was dedicated to the extremism of the religious Jews. His mission? Ruthlessly pursue and persecute Christians in the name of who he thought God was.

Of course, we don't talk as much about Saul as we do about Paul, do we?

What happened? An encounter with Jesus changed his life (see Acts 9:1-22). As Saul was traveling on the road from Jerusalem to Damascus with evil intent in his heart, a bright light from heaven caused him to fall facedown in the dirt. A voice said, "Saul, Saul, why are you persecuting me?" Stunned, Saul replied, "Who are you, Lord?" Jesus replied, "I am Jesus, the one you are persecuting."

And that was it. From that moment on, Saul's life took on new meaning. His name was changed to Paul, and he began the ministry that continues to this day through the books of the Bible he wrote—because of God's grace.

Mom, if you have a wayward child—or if you did not know to teach your children the ways of the Lord, be still. God is always at work. If God's grace can rescue Saul, His grace can find your child too. Keep praying. Keep trusting. God is always at work. In the end, it won't be something you have done or haven't done. It will be the grace of God.

Who's in Your Child's Village?

Do not be misled: "Bad company corrupts good character."
1 CORINTHIANS 15:53, NIV

HAVE YOU EVER HEARD IT SAID that it takes a village to raise a child? Well, in a broad sense I disagree with this idea. Of course, we need the input of others as we shepherd our children, but Christian parents need to understand two very important truths before they fall asleep at the wheel and let the "village" influence their children.

God will hold *parents*, not a village, responsible for their children. The Bible teaches us that parents are solely responsible for the upbringing of their children, emotionally, physically, and spiritually. In Deuteronomy 6:7-9, we are given very clear instruction about what to do with the commands of God as it relates to teaching our children: "Repeat them again and again to your children. Talk about them when you are at home and when you are on the road, when you are going to bed and when you are getting up. Tie them to your hands and wear them on your forehead as reminders. Write them on the doorposts of your house and on your gates."

In other words, God doesn't give Christian parents any sort of "downtime" when it comes to teaching and modeling righteousness for our children. Christian parents in the modern era have become very used to leaving the spiritual training of their children to youth pastors and teachers—and we are suffering greatly because of it.

The second truth to grasp is the incredible power of the "village" in the lives of our kids. It matters who they walk in relationship with. As today's verse reminds us, "Bad company corrupts good character" (1 Corinthians 15:53, NIV).

Lean in closely, mama, because this is crucial to understand. Your children *will* be influenced, for better or for worse, by the people you allow into their lives. Notice I said "allow." God has made it clear that as mothers and fathers, this is our responsibility. If you have a check in your spirit about a friend, don't ignore it. If you notice your child is being disrespectful or copying the bad behavior of their friends, don't wait. Address it. The people in the village can be good for your child, but they can also be corrupting. Your job is to tell the difference and protect your kids from bad influences.

Making Much of Jesus

After all, who is Apollos? Who is Paul? We are only God's servants through whom you believed the Good News. Each of us did the work the Lord gave us.

1 CORINTHIANS 3:5

HAVE YOU EVER NOTICED HOW SOCIAL media has changed the way we see ourselves and others? We have become a very self-focused culture, even though God's Word teaches us the value of seeing others as more important than ourselves (see Philippians 2:3). We're living in a very "me" focused culture.

But notice how differently Paul looked at his life. If YouTube had been a thing when the disciples were alive, Paul would've been an Internet sensation. After all, everyone knew who Paul was. He wasn't exactly quiet about his conversion from being a Pharisee to being a disciple of Jesus. People knew who he was wherever he went.

In fact, I think that if Paul were alive right now, he probably could have filled a megachurch of his own. My hunch is that there would be many people begging him to start one. Fame is a powerful draw.

Check out how Paul reacted, though, when he realized that the ministry God had given him was turning into an issue of *name recognition* rather than *mission recognition*. Paul chastised the believers who were saying that they were following Apollos's ministry or even Paul's ministry rather than the ministry of Jesus. He reminded them that humility is the mark of a true Christian when he said, "We are only God's servants."

He was committing to making much of Jesus rather than himself.

Paul recognized that each one of us has a special responsibility before the Lord. The moment our mission becomes about the name of a person rather than the name of Jesus, we are missing the mark. Oh, how we need this message right now! God is 100 percent committed to His own glory, and He will not share it with anyone else. We must give credit to the Lord alone, and if we direct our attention to people rather than to God, we are in error. Each of us is responsible for doing the work that the Lord gives us, and when that work is accomplished, we are not to take the credit. We are to give the glory to God. I wonder what the next generation of children would be like if this generation of parents could grasp that simple truth.

Let's make much of Jesus, precious moms, and pray our children will do the same.

A Wise Mother

Though good advice lies deep within the heart, a person with understanding will draw it out.

PROVERBS 20:5

I GREW UP WATCHING TELEVISION TALK shows in the eighties. From Phil Donahue to Oprah Winfrey, cultural advice was abundant. Sally Jessy Raphael had her own brand of "good advice," and as a young teen, I was riveted by her show. My friends and I drank it up. We all listened and watched with bated breath as Sally took to the stage with her cute short hair and her oversized red glasses. She was a ringmaster of sorts, and she paraded people out in front of her audience with problems ranging from the simple to the absurd.

It was a little bit like watching a train wreck in slow motion as we saw husbands confessing to adultery in front of live television audiences, and children left sobbing in the front row as they watched their father announce the name of the woman who had betrayed their family. We couldn't turn away, because in some respects, we know the awful truth about human nature: we all struggle with sin on one level or another. It may not have been adultery, but we can relate to the pain and the struggle.

I think we watched because, secretly, we were hoping that these talk show gurus could offer a solution. The ratings soared, but the solutions never really came. You see, even though human wisdom could be found in abundance on these shows, true healing was never found. That's because healing is found only in Jesus. How we need His wisdom today!

Social media offers solutions in abundance—and our children are being targeted by entertainers now in the same way we were targeted in the eighties. If our children are going to be able to see past the lines and the lies, they will need supernatural assistance.

The Bible says that the fear of the Lord is the beginning of wisdom. If we want to be mothers who will draw wisdom and understanding out of our children, the Bible teaches that we need to find it first in the Word of God. Human wisdom will never be able to address the underlying issues of the problems that we struggle with. When we start with God's wisdom, we can't go wrong.

Who's Behind This?

Satan rose up against Israel and caused David to take a census of the people of Israel.

1 CHRONICLES 21:1

ONE OF THE REASONS I LOVE the study of God's Word so much is that we can learn a tremendous amount from the history of the people of God. The book of 1 Chronicles is an excellent example. If I were to give an overview of 1 and 2 Chronicles, it would be this: obedience brings blessing, but disobedience brings judgment.

I have believed for some time that the United States and indeed the rest of the world is under judgment right now because of our disobedience to God. If we ever wonder, though, who is behind the division, the lack of discernment, and the unwise decisions that many of our leaders make, look no further than 1 Chronicles 21.

The Bible plainly states that it was Satan who rose up against Israel and caused David to pridefully take a census of the people of Israel. Although David's commander Joab warned him that taking a census would cause Israel to sin, the Bible says David chose to take the census anyway.

It's easy for us to look at our children when they disobey and forget that they also have an adversary. When you notice that your children are struggling within, pray for them. When you notice that your children are being disrespectful, disobedient, or unwise in their decisions, point them to the Lord. Show them that they have an adversary who wants to turn their hearts away from God and away from His wisdom.

I know it can feel like it at times, but your adversary is not your child. We are taught that we do not wrestle against flesh and blood, because our adversary is a spiritual one (see Ephesians 6:12). If the devil can tempt someone like David, how much easier would it be for him to tempt our children into sin? Be gracious in your discipline even while you are consistent in it, and always point your children to the truth.

Remember, obedience brings blessing, but disobedience brings judgment. No one knows this better than the enemy of your soul.

A Mother's Dreams

The godly will flourish like palm trees and grow strong like the cedars of Lebanon.

PSALM 92:12

ALL MOTHERS HAVE DREAMS FOR THEIR children. Even before becoming moms, we dream about what our children will be like. We might wonder about the color of their hair or eyes. We may think about what kind of personalities they will have. When a child is born, our dreams expand to what he or she might become in life. We invest in our children's education, we make sure they grow strong physically, and we shepherd them spiritually from the moment they can understand what we are saying. We do all we can to make sure our children are set up to succeed in life.

Dreams are good—and pursuing them is wonderful! Be careful, though, precious mom, not to mistake your dreams for the ones God has for your children. It's easy to insert our desires for our children into the very plans that God has for them without even knowing it. Over the past thirty years, the Lord has been shaping my heart with regard to the dreams I have for my children, just like He is shaping yours. At the end of the day, the most important dream we can ever dream for our children is that they would walk with the Lord—that they would be godly in all they say and do. As a mother, my dream is to see my children walking with the Lord and flourishing in whatever He calls them to be.

Today, ask the Lord for one thing: that your children would grow in righteousness. If our children are walking with the Lord, He will use them mightily in whatever sphere of influence He calls them to. Whether they are doctors, police officers, flight attendants, or teachers, God wants to grow them strong, and they can "flourish like palm trees" in the desert with the Lord as their guide.

Even Me

Since God in his wisdom saw to it that the world would never know him through human wisdom, he has used our foolish preaching to save those who believe.

1 CORINTHIANS 1:21

"HE HAS USED OUR FOOLISH PREACHING to save those who believe." When I read this verse, I raised my hands high and said, "Thank you, Lord! You can use even me!"

The honesty of the apostle Paul resonates with my mother heart, because God knows that we can't do this without His wisdom. Human wisdom will never be enough for the task of motherhood.

When I was twenty-one, my first daughter was born. I had self-help books galore: they were on the nightstands, the coffee tables, even in my diaper bag. I had books on everything from parenting to breastfeeding because I knew that I was woefully unprepared for motherhood. I lacked wisdom, and I lacked experience. Can you relate?

It's funny, though, because even being surrounded by all of those books did not keep me from asking more questions. As my daughter grew, so did my questions. Because I came from a broken home, I felt even more vulnerable to criticism and the prying eyes of mothers who I felt were more equipped and qualified than I was.

Oh, how I needed to turn to God's Word—but instead, I turned to human wisdom. Human wisdom can only go so far. We need God's wisdom!

It's easy in this Internet age to do a quick search when we have a question, isn't it? It doesn't matter what the topic is; we have access to information at our fingertips. But the Bible, ever counter to the culture, reminds us over and over again that God, in His wisdom, knows that our wisdom is only foolishness apart from Him.

This translates into our parenting so beautifully, because God sees us mothers, and He reaches out in love to offer us His wisdom through Jesus Christ. If God can use the "foolish preaching" of the apostle Paul to save an unbelieving world, then surely He can use me to teach and train my children. Even when I make foolish mistakes in mothering, the Lord, who sees my heart, redeems those mistakes. Thank you, Lord! *You can use even me!*

Preparing Our Children for Rejection

The message of the cross is foolish to those who are headed for destruction!
But we who are being saved know it is the very power of God.

1 CORINTHIANS 1:18

ONE OF THE MOST CHALLENGING THINGS I've ever had to do as a mother is to watch my children face rejection and ridicule for their faith.

My children have varying degrees of comfort when it comes to evangelism. One of my sons is particularly amazing at it! I'm telling you, that boy can go onto the streets of downtown Portland and share the gospel of Jesus without so much as a moment's hesitation. He never worries about being rebuffed or made fun of; he is simply bursting at the opportunity to spread the good news of the gospel.

He has the gift of evangelism, and it is plain for everyone to see. However, some of our other children do not have this gift. They are often terrified to talk about their faith, especially given the spiritual climate they face in the Pacific Northwest. I do believe that the Bible teaches that being able to share your faith boldly is a gift, and when it is not your primary gift, it can be very difficult to share the gospel. As mothers, we must be talking about this as our children grow.

One evening in particular, my fourteen-year-old daughter arrived home from an event rather disheartened. She had tried to share her faith, but she was rejected. Tears streamed down her face as she recounted the events of that evening. Of course, as her mother, I wanted to shield her from this kind of rejection and ridicule. I wanted to defend her! But the fact of the matter is that God says that we will be persecuted for our faith. The apostle Paul taught in 1 Corinthians 1 that when we teach and preach the gospel, the world will often see nothing but foolishness. But here's the good news—those who carry the message of the Cross also carry with them the power of God.

As your children grow, they will be rejected for their faith. Though the Word of Faith movement and the prosperity gospel focus on all of the blessings of following God, the apostles' message was quite different. As mothers, one of our primary roles must be to prepare our children for ridicule and rejection because of the message of the gospel—but let's not stop there! Let's remind our kids of the power of God so that when they are persecuted for sharing their faith, they have been trained to turn to Him for help and perseverance.

Where Do You Live?

Those who live in the shelter of the Most High will find rest in the shadow of the Almighty.

PSALM 91:1

I WROTE A GOOD PORTION OF this book during a difficult time for many people. I won't gloss over what it was like. It was very challenging to write a devotional while it felt like the world around me was on fire.

Every morning during that season, the news offered nothing in terms of reassurance. Stories about riots, beatings, and violent clashes between protestors and the police in nearby Portland, Oregon, went on for months and months. Eventually, the violence spread from the inner city to the suburbs, and when it did, I began to truly feel uncomfortable in my own city.

I wondered aloud to myself one day how I could possibly reassure my children that they would be safe and that all would be well if I myself was struggling to live in this truth. Have you ever felt that way? Have things around you upended your heart, along with your sense of security?

I am so thankful that we serve a good, good Father! Psalm 91 promises that "those who live in the shelter of the Most High will find rest in the shadow of the Almighty." So of course, this begs the question, "Where do we live?" To understand what David was trying to say, you have to place yourself in his position. David was no stranger to trials and tribulations. In fact, it seems he spent most of his time running from his enemies. David knew what he was talking about when he reminded us that we need to live in the shelter of the Most High.

God is big. His shadow is even bigger! I love to picture what it must be like to walk protected under the shadow of God. To live in the shelter of God means that we rest in the knowledge that even when it feels the world is upside down around us, God never is. To live in the shelter of the Most High requires that we repeat His promises when the ground beneath our feet shakes and shifts. Living in His shadow means that we can truly rest, knowing that our future is secure. If you need to find rest for your soul, if you need to remember that your soul is safe, held in the arms of God forever, if you need the reassurance for yourself so that you can pass it on to your children and grandchildren, it's time.

It's time to breathe deeply of His peace and find rest in His shadow.

Openly Declare

If you openly declare that Jesus is Lord and believe in your heart that God raised him from the dead, you will be saved. For it is by believing in your heart that you are made right with God, and it is by openly declaring your faith that you are saved.

ROMANS 10:9-10

WHAT ARE YOU PASSIONATE ABOUT? As mothers, we are passionate about our children. I have yet to meet a mother who won't jump at the chance to show me a picture of her family.

Mothers are all too happy to openly declare how beautiful and bright and talented and special their children are. Why do we do this? Love, of course! When our children are born, we cannot wait to share the beautiful masterpiece we have been given. We want the whole world to marvel at our kids right along with us!

It's a strange thing then that we seem to struggle to openly declare the same thing about Jesus Christ. As Christians, we have an incredible thing to proclaim: we have been saved from a life of sin and given the gift of eternity in heaven when this life is over. Years ago, I started a women's conference called Faith That Speaks. The reason I gave it this name is because it has become a passion of mine to encourage women to use their voices to lift high the name of Jesus and proclaim that He alone can save. This is a biblical command!

All throughout Scripture, we are instructed to speak about our faith in the Lord Jesus as passionately as we would speak about our own children. In fact, Paul writes in Romans 10 about the importance of this. He said that if we openly declare Jesus is Lord and believe in our hearts that God raised Him from the dead, we will be saved! I often stop and linger over the first four words of Romans 10:9: "If you openly declare."

Our faith should never be silent faith. It should never be hidden as if it were something we were ashamed of or embarrassed by. God wants us to declare our love for Him wherever we have opportunities to do so. God wants us to give Him glory!

Precious mom, I challenge you today to begin to openly declare your faith in the Lord Jesus. As we declare our faith, we encourage others to do the same, starting with our children. Is your faith a faith that speaks? If not, chances are good that your children will have a silent faith also. Let's learn to "openly declare" that Jesus is Lord! It's a message worth sharing!

God Makes Things Grow

I planted the seed in your hearts, and Apollos watered it, but it was God who made it grow.

1 CORINTHIANS 3:6

ON A BEAUTIFUL FALL DAY, JAY and I were driving up the Columbia River Gorge in an effort to find quiet time alone. It didn't take long for us to start talking about the children, particularly the ones who we're still homeschooling. Things have been busy at the homeschool resource center we founded, and I was feeling the familiar sting of guilt that perhaps I wasn't doing enough for my own children. In a few moments, my mood turned from one of hope and optimism to one of self-loathing and discouragement.

Jay pulled into a little turnout along Interstate 84 and took a deep breath. We have had this conversation many times. "Heidi, why do you always feel you have to carry the responsibility for how everything turns out?" he asked. I don't know the answer, of course. It's just a thing I do . . . an insecurity I have . . . a sin issue I struggle with, even after thirty years of mothering.

We don't like to think of ourselves as sinning when we forget that it is God who makes things grow, but that's what we're really doing. It's almost as if we think we are more powerful than God and that God cannot take our efforts and even our failures and use them for His good and His glory. God, after all, is the Master of working things together for good, isn't He? Paul noted this when he reminded the church in Corinth that though he was planting the seed of the gospel in their hearts and Apollos was watering it, God was the one who ultimately would make it grow.

As Jay and I worked through my frustration and fears about my performance as a mother, he steered my heart back toward truth and away from selfish self-pity. He reminded me that I had forgotten for a moment that it was God who makes things grow.

Every mother needs to lean into this truth daily. Knowing that God is responsible for the outcome allows us to rest in our inability as well as our ability. Our job is to plant seeds into the fertile soil of God's Word and water them with prayer and discipleship every day. As we do, we also commit our children to the care of the One who made them, knowing that at the end of the day and into eternity, it is God who makes things grow.

For this reason, we can rest, knowing our efforts are never in vain.

When Fear Is the Right Response

David was not able to go there to inquire of God, because he was terrified by the drawn sword of the angel of the LORD.

1 CHRONICLES 21:30

I BECAME INTIMATELY ACQUAINTED WITH FEAR at a young age. As I grew older, fear became a taskmaster in my life. It dictated when I would speak to individuals and even *if* I would speak. The spirit of fear made me doubt whether or not I would be a good mother or if I could have discernment in life decisions.

This is an unhealthy fear. Most of the time when we talk about fear, we are talking about the *spirit* of fear that Paul teaches Timothy about in 2 Timothy 1:7. However, there is also a good kind of fear . . . a healthy fear. There is a time for holy fear.

In 1 Chronicles 21, we see a great example of a healthy understanding of the power of God and respect for our small role in His world. David had committed a sin against the Lord by taking a census of the people. When David finally confessed his sin, the Bible records that he was deeply distressed by it and said to God for fear of His righteous judgment, "I am the one who called for the census! I am the one who has sinned and done wrong!" (verse 17). He then went on to ask God not to let His anger fall against His people. After that, the angel of the Lord instructed David to build an altar on the threshing floor of Araunah the Jebusite.

After David bought the land, he built an altar there and sacrificed burnt offerings and peace offerings to the Lord. The Bible records that when David prayed for forgiveness, "the Lord answered him by sending fire from heaven to burn up the offering on the altar" (verse 26). Can you imagine how small that must have made David feel?

When David saw that the Lord had answered his prayer for forgiveness, I can imagine he was grateful beyond words. He had a healthy fear of God. He knew God was just and holy, and his respect for the power of God was evident.

Precious mom, we need to teach our children that God deserves holy respect. When we sin, we must come to God in humility. The next time you have an opportunity, teach your children that God is holy and that He commands and deserves our respect. After all, "the fear of the LORD is the beginning of wisdom" (Proverbs 9:10, NIV).

A Sacrifice of Praise

Giving thanks is a sacrifice that truly honors me.

PSALM 50:23

I USED TO WONDER WHY GOD listed "giving thanks" as a sacrifice in the Bible. It seemed strange to me. After all, when we give thanks, it's because something good has happened, right? Like all of us, I soon learned that life has a way of teaching us things that we don't necessarily want to learn, and as a young mother, I began to learn that giving thanks isn't much of a sacrifice—until you've given thanks in the midst of suffering.

It's easy to offer our thanks to God when things are going well. It's easy to say *thank you* when the finances are in order, when our marriage is doing fine, when our children aren't in a season of rebellion, sickness, or struggle.

As a child and as a teenager, I experienced my fair share of suffering, but I do not recall ever giving thanks in the midst of it. I was more bewildered by the fact that God would allow suffering to come into my life. It never occurred to me to thank Him for it.

Thanking God in the midst of suffering means we thank Him through tears, not because we understand our circumstances, but because we know God is always good and loves us.

I learned we had lost our fourth child during a routine ultrasound as I neared the end of my first trimester. I wasn't ready for this news. I didn't have anyone with me when the ultrasound technician stopped mid-scan and went to find the doctor.

"I'm sorry," the doctor said, "we cannot find a heartbeat." I went straight from the clinic to my husband, who was working in his office at the church. When I shared the stunning news with him, tears filled his eyes as we realized that we had lost what God had so graciously given to us.

As I lay my head on my husband's chest that night, we prayed together as we do almost every night. Only this time, our prayers of thankfulness really were a sacrifice to God. Through our sorrow, we thanked Him for the incredible blessing of being able to have children. We thanked Him for the three children He'd already given us. As we did this, we began to understand just a bit about God's heart for us, as we felt His presence like never before. He is worthy of our praise, dear ones. Especially when our hearts are broken.

The Lord gives, and the Lord takes away. Blessed be the name of the Lord (see Job 1:21).

Siblings

"If the Arameans are too strong for me, then come over and help me," Joab told his brother. "And if the Ammonites are too strong for you, I will help you. Be courageous! Let us fight bravely for our people and the cities of our God. May the LORD's will be done."

1 CHRONICLES 19:12-13

I CAME FROM A BIG FAMILY. For years, we struggled with dysfunction and tried, sometimes successfully and sometimes not, to overcome it. Can you relate? I know some of you are nodding in agreement, and others are thankful that they can't identify.

The Lord is in the business of redeeming things, and He has spent a lifetime showing me how capable of redemption He is. When I got married, I was absolutely certain I did not want a big family. I figured we might have three children, but it was never in our plan to have seven, that's for sure. After all, my mom and dad had seven kids, and it seemed not to be going very well.

However, as the years have gone by, I have come to really appreciate the preciousness of the siblings God has given me. Even more than that, I love watching our adult children interacting with each other, arranging for coffee dates and double dates and birthday parties as they begin to have children of their own.

Siblings are a good thing. I love this story about Joab, an officer in King David's army, as he enters into a battle against the Ammonites in 1 Chronicles 19.

As usual, David was up against more than he could handle, and as one of the elite commanders in his army, Joab saw that the enemy was both in front of and behind his soldiers. In other words, he was in trouble. "If the Arameans are too strong for me, then come over and help me," Joab told his brother. "And if the Ammonites are too strong for you, I will help you."

Now I'm sure there are plenty of spiritual implications we can take away from this story, but as a mother, I immediately thought about how thankful I am for my sisters, who I know always have my back . . . and for my children growing into deepening friendships with their siblings.

This doesn't happen by itself, though. It takes intentional parenting as we help our children work out their "stuff" in the hope that they will one day be each other's biggest fans.

At the end of the day, I want my children to be best friends with each other. This world we live in can be fierce. Battles rage around us every day. Let's be honest: it's nice to know that a sibling has your back.

The Real Enemy

Its walls are patrolled day and night against invaders, but
the real danger is wickedness within the city.

PSALM 55:10

I'M A FAN OF WALLS. God gave Nehemiah instructions to rebuild the wall around Jerusalem. Here in my neck of the woods, we build walls around the things that we want to protect. Many of the new developments in the Vancouver area have fairly significant walls around them.

As helpful as walls can be, David makes a very good point about what ultimately takes down cities. This can also be applied to ourselves and our families. In Psalm 55, he points out that we can patrol our walls in an attempt to guard against invaders, but if we are not fortifying ourselves from the inside out, the danger from the inside will be our ultimate undoing.

Take a moment today to think about the inside of your home. Start with your marriage, and work your way out from there. God's Word tells us that we have an adversary who is actively seeking to destroy families, ministries, cities, and nations. Before you can fight against the schemes of the devil, you must be aware of them. Sometimes, it is easy for us to look outside our home and miss the real danger that is lurking within. Fighting requires an assessment of your family. When was the last time you had a conversation with your children about how they're doing? Are you checking the Internet browser's history on your family's devices? Have you had open and honest conversations about pornography?

We've all heard stories about Christian leaders who have been ousted due to scandal and moral failure in their personal lives. In many cases, it appears that prior to the scandal, they had "everything." The wall looked good on the outside, but there was an enemy within. When we do not guard our hearts, at the very least, we risk losing position and reputation. A man who fails to fortify his heart sets himself up for failure. Sadly, the ramifications may not be fully known for generations.

I want to look back over my family's story and see a legacy, not a tragedy. I do not want someone else to look back at the St. John family as if they were performing an autopsy. The best way to guard against hostile takeover of your family is to fortify it from the inside out.

What Is Wisdom?

God has united you with Christ Jesus. For our benefit God made him to be wisdom itself.
1 CORINTHIANS 1:30

ONE OF THE MOST IMPORTANT THINGS people ever teach their children is where to go for wisdom.

Christian mothers today are facing a lot when it comes to worldviews and ideologies that our children are exposed to on a regular basis. Things we used to consider "neutral" and safe for children have been exposed in recent years as being anything but safe or neutral. While we used to put in a Disney movie and leave our kids to watch it while we cleaned the house, we can no longer do this. We must be on guard against wrong influences and wrong thinking. In short, we must exercise wisdom ourselves before we can hope to pass it on to our children.

Wisdom does not just come to us either. It is something we must seek hard after. The Bible teaches us that true wisdom comes from God and that Jesus is the embodiment of that wisdom (see 1 Corinthians 1:30). As we walk with God and yield to His Holy Spirit, the Bible says we begin to walk in wisdom. This is how we have "the mind of Christ" (1 Corinthians 2:16).

There is a difference between wisdom and knowledge. Wisdom is the ability to apply knowledge to every aspect of our lives. When we read and understand God's Word, we are obtaining knowledge. But when we meditate on His Word, that knowledge brings wisdom. In other words, we learn how to apply the truth of God's Word to our everyday lives.

The culture today is very much like the Greek culture of old. Like the ancient Greeks, we esteem human knowledge over godly wisdom, and the results have been eroding homes, churches, and nations for generations. God's Word is clear: knowledge apart from wisdom is useless. Look at our college campuses and universities today. Knowledge apart from godly wisdom is prone to pride, and the combination is dangerous both emotionally and spiritually.

Knowledge puffs up, but wisdom brings with it the blessing of God.

The Bible teaches us that those who have the wisdom of God will display it in their everyday lives. The first place our children will always look for wisdom is to their parents. Are we being wise? If we are diligently studying the Word of God, asking God for wisdom, and meditating on His Word, God promises that wisdom will be the sure result.

The Cure for Temptation

There he told them, "Pray that you will not give in to temptation."

LUKE 22:40

HAVE YOU EVER BEEN TEMPTED? Temptation, of course, is as old as sin itself, and Jesus understood the cure for temptation. He has a simple solution: *prayer.*

It sounds simple enough, doesn't it? But oh, we are tempted in so many ways! It's easy to think of temptation as something we read about in the movies. Adultery, lust, covetousness, jealousy. So what about the everyday temptations?

Each of us has our own unique set of temptations. I'm guessing you can name your top three without so much as a moment's hesitation—but knowing them isn't enough. The goal here is victory! The goal is to see the temptation, recognize the enemy of our soul, and ask God for His help. Prayer is the key.

I will just be brutally honest and lay it out here for you: one of my biggest temptations is selfishness. There. I said it. I hope you won't think too badly of me. In recent years I have become very protective of personal quiet time. Maybe it was my travel season, maybe it was what felt like an overwhelming workload at times, maybe it's just me getting older. Maybe it's having been a mother for thirty years. But I'll tell you. I can get very, very tired.

When I'm tired, one of my temptations (and believe me, there are others) is to simply withdraw. No, it's not a bad thing to withdraw, but boy, do I need the Lord's help so that I don't cross that oh-so-thin line from self-care to selfishness.

It's easy to do. Thank God, Jesus understands.

I take so much comfort knowing that God isn't up in heaven shaking His fist at me or looking down at my struggle with disdain. Instead, He is reaching down, offering help, and all I need to do is reach back up and take it. If you are struggling with temptation today, reach up. Talk to the Lord in prayer, and let another sister in Christ know about your struggle. We really are stronger together.

He Loves Me

He walked away, about a stone's throw, and knelt down and prayed, "Father, if you are willing, please take this cup of suffering away from me. Yet I want your will to be done, not mine."

LUKE 22:41-42

THE ACCOUNT IN THE GOSPELS OF the days leading up to the crucifixion of Christ is both beautiful and excruciating. Jesus, who knew no sin, gave Himself up for us.

It's obvious by reading today's Scripture that Jesus did not want to suffer. But He went willingly to the Cross because of His love. When I consider the anguish the Father must've felt knowing His son was to suffer through no wrongdoing of His own, my heart is overwhelmed.

He loves me.

I remember the day I knew beyond a shadow of a doubt that Jesus died for my sins and that He loved me. I was sitting in a little Evangelical Free church, listening to a pastor talk about what Jesus went through when He died. As I look at this passage in Luke, my heart is transported back to the hours before Jesus was crucified. I can see my precious Savior, glancing back at His disciples, who couldn't even stay awake—and His heart was nearly overwhelmed because He knew what was about to happen.

He still went to the Cross because He loves me.

One of the things I hope my children remember about their growing up is how much their mother loved the Lord Jesus. I hope they remember the tears that fell down my face as I sang hymns in church with them. I hope they grasp just a little bit of the sacrifice that the Lord made for them because I communicated it well to them.

Jesus went to the Cross because He loves my children.

Today, you have an opportunity to pass on to your children the truth of the sacrifice Jesus made. Don't be afraid to read hard passages of Scripture to them. Don't be afraid to let them feel the hurt and the anguish that our Lord Jesus felt as He considered what was ahead at the Cross.

Maybe, as He did with me, God will use the story of Jesus' suffering to soften the hearts of your children toward the message of the gospel. The gospel should change us. The story of the Cross should impact our brief time on this earth. He loves us. He really does. There is no greater proof than the Cross. Greater love hath no man than this—that a man would lay down His life for those He loves (see John 15:13).

No More of This

When the other disciples saw what was about to happen, they exclaimed, "Lord, should we fight? We brought the swords!" And one of them struck at the high priest's slave, slashing off his right ear. But Jesus said, "No more of this." And he touched the man's ear and healed him.

LUKE 22:49-51

"Stop it!" I yelled. "No more! Everyone, go to your rooms!"

After what felt like hours of breaking up fights between bickering children, I had reached my breaking point. What little patience I thought I might have left disappeared in a moment of anger and disappointment after watching my children continue to fight and argue.

Within moments of my instruction, the excuses from my children came pouring in—but it was frustrating to me that not one of my kids seemed to care what my day had been like. No one wondered what stress I was under or asked to pray for me. My frustration mounted.

It'd been a long day. Have you ever had a day like that? You know, the kind that you just wish you could scratch off the calendar and start over with a clean slate? This was definitely one of those days for me. I needed a do-over more than french fries need ketchup.

It's comforting to know that Jesus had days like this too. In Luke 22, we find Jesus, moments after being betrayed by someone who pretended to love Him, parenting His disciples. I'm sure the disciples were frustrated and even frightened by what they saw happening to their Lord, and they responded in an act of human frustration by fighting back.

Watch how Jesus steps into the situation. Though I'm sure He was weary and struggling Himself, He simply said, "No more of this." But our beautiful Lord didn't stop there. He touched the ear of the man who had been wounded, the man who was His sworn enemy, and healed him.

The stress I was under as I was trying to referee fights between my own children that day was nothing in comparison to what the Lord must have been carrying—but Jesus saw beyond His own circumstances and ministered to His followers. Oh, how we can learn from our precious Savior.

If you are weary of parenting today, if you are tired of refereeing your children, ask the Lord to help you have His perspective—and see what you can do to bring calm and healing to the situation around you. What would the Lord have you bring a healing touch to today?

Forgiveness Brings Joy

Oh, what joy for those whose disobedience is forgiven, whose sin is put out of sight!
PSALM 32:1

Do you remember the moment that you first knew your sins had been forgiven? Do you remember the peace that flooded your soul when you realized that God had forgiven you and put your sins as far away from Him as the east is from the west? What was the result of this understanding? My hunch is that it was joy. As a mother, I have observed this same thing in my children. When they know for certain that their transgression is forgiven, there is joy. This usually comes after a consequence and a hug, doesn't it?

In the Bible, we read about the importance of forgiveness. Over and over again, God tells us that we need to seek and give forgiveness. It is a hallmark of every successful human relationship.

In the Psalms, we learn exactly why it is so important to forgive our children. We have joy when our disobedience is forgiven because we know that the debt has been paid. We no longer carry the burden of guilt. When we forgive our children, they experience the same joy and freedom from guilt.

Today, as you interact with your children, chances are pretty good that there will be something that needs to be forgiven. Perhaps you will need to ask for forgiveness . . . and it is almost a certainty that your child will need to seek forgiveness. Asking for forgiveness does not come naturally. Children need to be taught that this is an important step in restoring trust and healing in relationships. This may happen with siblings, cousins, friends, and even parents. At the end of the day, God has given you the responsibility for teaching your child the importance of seeking forgiveness.

When your child comes to you and asks for forgiveness, don't forget to let them know that they are forgiven! Make sure that you let your child know that you will not bring their sin up again and that you will put it out of sight. It's also a great opportunity to remind your child they have also been forgiven by their heavenly Father. He forgives us when we ask for it. Shepherding a child through the process of asking for forgiveness is a wonderful opportunity to share the gospel with them.

What the Bible promises will always be true: when our disobedience is put "out of sight," the result is joy!

But I am trusting you, O Lᴏʀᴅ, saying, "You are my God!"

PSALM 31:14

I ʜᴀᴠᴇ ᴀʟᴡᴀʏꜱ ᴛʀɪᴇᴅ ᴛᴏ ʜᴇʟᴘ my kids refrain from using the word *but*. I'm not talking about the body part here. I'm talking about the conjunction. (That's my homeschool mom coming out right there.)

But, mom . . . you promised! But I don't want to go to bed. But it wasn't my fault!

As a mom, I've used this word too . . . especially when I'm wrestling through something with the Lord.

But, Lord, it wasn't supposed to be this way. But I never got to say good-bye.

King David used this word also. Let's take a look at the context of it from Psalm 31:9-13: "Have mercy on me, Lᴏʀᴅ, for I am in distress. Tears blur my eyes. My body and soul are withering away. I am dying from grief; my years are shortened by sadness. Sin has drained my strength; I am wasting away from within. I am scorned by all my enemies and despised by my neighbors—even my friends are afraid to come near me. When they see me on the street, they run the other way. I am ignored as if I were dead, as if I were a broken pot. I have heard the many rumors about me, and I am surrounded by terror. My enemies conspire against me, plotting to take my life."

As I read these words, my heart goes out to David. I too have felt like I might die from grief. I can relate when he says that sin has strained his strength, and I know the pain of feeling rejected by someone who I thought was my friend. All of these things shine a light on David's emotions when he used the word *but*. Look at what happens in verse 14: "But I am trusting you, O Lᴏʀᴅ, saying, 'You are my God!'"

David used this word to remind himself that no matter his circumstances, his job was to trust the Lord and to serve Him. Today, as you encounter situations that you may not have planned for, take a lesson from King David, and use this word to remind yourself to keep trusting God, no matter what.

Any Day Now

Don't let him find you sleeping when he arrives without warning.
I say to you what I say to everyone: "Watch for him!"

MARK 13:36-37

WHEN WAS THE LAST TIME YOU talked to your children about the second coming of the Lord? We are living, I believe, in incredible times, and they are times for us to be watchful. This is an amazing time to be a Christian!

As a young girl, I grew up listening to my grandmother teach on the book of Revelation. Grandma was absolutely thrilled by the idea that she might live to see the return of her Lord. I'm always telling my own children that if she were still alive today, I can imagine she would be sitting out on the front porch in a lawn chair, a big glass of lemonade in her hand, eyes to the heavens, listening for the sound of the trumpet.

"Any day now," she would say. "The Lord's return is near!" Grandma's enthusiasm and readiness to see the Lord come back impacted my life in a powerful way. The truth is, Scripture reminds us over and over again that we are not to be found sleeping when the Lord arrives. He wants us to be watching for His return!

Sometimes I meet parents who are reticent to talk about the end times with their children, but it is not something to be afraid of. It is something to get excited about! We are living in a time when many of the prophecies in the Bible have already been fulfilled, and we are only waiting for a few more before we will see the heavens part. The Lord is coming back for His church!

When I began to study the book of Revelation with the women of MomStrong International, it was thrilling to watch as they began to get an understanding of what it should be like to live at the time when the Lord returns. As you teach your children to be watching for the Lord, remember the importance of walking with Him. When Mark said that we are not to be found sleeping when Jesus arrives, he meant that we are to be found walking in right relationship, *intentionally*, with the Lord.

This means that we study His Word and seek Him in prayer daily. Walking with the Lord is an exciting way to live, and soon, it will be even more exciting as we see Him face-to-face.

Partnering with God in Prayer

The LORD frustrates the plans of the nations and thwarts all their schemes. But the LORD's plans stand firm forever; his intentions can never be shaken.

PSALM 33:10-11

DO YOU EVER WATCH WHAT'S HAPPENING around you and feel overwhelmed or frustrated? I sure do. I am a "getter doner," as my grandma would say. My nature has always been to do. I am a problem solver who likes to be a part of creating solutions for things around me that seem to be struggling.

It's all well and good when everything around me appears to be within my control. For example, when I noticed that homeschool moms in my area needed support, my husband and I rallied our community together and started a homeschool co-op.

Sure, it took a lot of work, but we saw that it was possible. This was something that was within our control, something we could actively participate in.

But what about the impossible? What happens when we look around us and the situations that we face seem too big or too complicated? What happens when we are helpless to do anything about decisions that are being made that will impact our families? Do we fret? Or do we pray? I'll admit—for me, it's more natural to worry! Can you relate?

If you are frustrated today by what's happening around you, take it to the Lord in prayer. As mothers, we have an awesome responsibility to pass on not only our faith but the confidence we have in the plans that God establishes. We do not need to live in fear, and we do not need to be afraid, because the Lord promises us that He watches over His own and that His plans will stand firm forever. In Jeremiah 29:11, we read that His plans for us are good. So today, don't let your heart be troubled by what you see happening around you. Look to the heavens, ask the Lord to remind you of His plans, and then pass that reminder on to your children.

The intentions of the Lord can never be shaken, and that's good, because we can trust Him. Our role is to *participate and partner with God in prayer. Not our will, but His, be done!*

Lavish Love

How great is the goodness you have stored up for those who fear you. You lavish it on those who come to you for protection, blessing them before the watching world.

PSALM 31:19

ONE OF THE THINGS I HAVE always tried to do as a homeschooling mother is to instill in my children a sense of wonder about the world around them. From the time they're old enough to take a walk through the woods here at our home in the Pacific Northwest to when they graduate and go out on their own, I want them to see and appreciate the handiwork of God all around them.

The Bible teaches us that if we don't give God glory, the rocks will do it for us—in fact, evidence of the creativity and goodness of God in creation is all around! In Psalm 31, David recalls the amazing love of God, noting He "stores up" His goodness for those who fear Him.

In fact, he goes so far as to use a word that we do not normally use in our culture today to describe exactly what His goodness does. David said that God "lavishes" His goodness on those who look to Him for protection. I love this—especially when I am aware of my total need for His protection and provision. God says, in effect, "Don't worry! I got you!"

Lavish is quite a word! In fact, I looked it up for you in Merriam-Webster:

lavish *verb*
to expend or bestow with profusion

Wow! Now *this* is a love I want to tell my children about! This kind of love is nothing short of extraordinary. This kind of love is otherworldly. This kind of love is not like any kind of love we could ever give on our own, but God doesn't stop there. He says that He blesses His own before the entire world!

You see, God loves us in the same way that we love our own children—only better.

His love isn't hindered by a bad day or a misunderstanding or a bad attitude. His love is a lavish kind of love, and He longs to lavish it on us, His kids.

When was the last time you stopped to talk to your children about the incredible love of God?

> When they came near the camp, Moses saw the calf and the dancing, and he burned with anger. He threw the stone tablets to the ground, smashing them at the foot of the mountain. He took the calf they had made and burned it. Then he ground it into powder, threw it into the water, and forced the people to drink it.
>
> EXODUS 32:19-20

SOMETIMES, I RELATE TO MOSES MORE than I would like to admit. As I read about the children of Israel, I'm finding it easier to understand why God repeatedly referred to them as children. I'm sure that Moses loved them; after all, they were "his people." But let's be real. They were also disobedient, disrespectful, and even wicked at times! It seems to me that Moses spent most of his time parenting the children of Israel!

In Exodus 32, we find Moses coming down off of Mount Sinai after receiving the Ten Commandments. Talk about a "mountaintop" experience! I can imagine that he was excited to share with the Israelites all that he had learned, only to be confronted by their sin and disobedience immediately upon his return. This reminds me of a women's conference that I attended quite a long time ago. I felt so rested after the event, and I had a new vision for motherhood. I came home with such high hopes, but the first thing I encountered was . . . let's just say it wasn't awesome. #Relatable.

Have you ever been so frustrated with your children that you wanted them to "drink from the cup" they poured for themselves? Have you ever lost your temper? You're not alone! Moses would be nodding his head right along with you.

Sometimes, we are justified in losing our temper. And honestly? I think it's good for our children to see the anguish in our eyes and hear the frustration in our voices from time to time. It comforts me to know that Moses, even though he had been appointed by God to lead the children of Israel to the Promised Land, had moments of frustration.

Ultimately, however, he did not stay in that place.

Just like you, Moses got over it. Just like you, he kept on going, kept on forgiving, kept on listening for instruction from the Lord, and kept on shepherding the Israelites. If you're frustrated today, take a moment to talk to the Lord about it. Maybe it's a good idea to call a friend, take a break so that you can hit the reset button, and start again tomorrow. Frustration does not need to lead to failure.

Just Stand Still

Moses told the people, "Don't be afraid. Just stand still and watch the LORD rescue you today. The Egyptians you see today will never be seen again."

EXODUS 14:13

MOSES WAS THE CHILDREN OF ISRAEL'S biggest encourager. He was constantly reminding the children of Israel who they were, where they had come from, where they were going, and whose they were. You know, kind of like what you are doing with your own children right now.

In the beginning of Exodus 14, you will see that Moses was facing a very big problem. With the help of God, he had rescued the Israelites from the hand of Pharaoh and out of slavery, only to come up against what felt like an impossible barrier: the Red Sea.

As usual, the Israelites began to complain and display an incredible lack of faith. Moses could throw his hands up in the air and leave the whining, complaining, immature Israelites to figure it out for themselves, or he could continue to be the leader God had called him to be.

I often wonder what it must've been like to see Moses when he was alone with God. I picture him frustrated, weary, and sometimes even afraid as he accepted the challenge God had given him.

In this case, God must've given Moses extraordinary faith, because he should've been afraid. Instead, he was filled with courage because of God, and though the Egyptian army was closing in on them, he spoke with confidence: "Don't be afraid. Just stand still and watch the LORD rescue you today. The Egyptians you see today will never be seen again" (Exodus 14:13).

Of course, you know the rest of the story. God parted the Red Sea and did the unimaginable—the people of God walked across the seafloor on dry land. And the words that Moses had spoken to the people of Israel came true before their eyes. The Egyptians who were chasing the Israelites that day were never seen again.

Precious mom, your job is to impart this kind of faith to your children. Against all odds, and sometimes in the middle of what feels like an unwinnable situation, we are called to point the eyes of our children heavenward and remind them that God is the one who rescues.

Our children need their parents to lead them on the journey of trusting God more than ever before. Think about the situation you're facing today. Are you pointing your children to God with confidence? God can be trusted! We just need to stand still and watch Him work.

Inheritance and Prosperity

Who are those who fear the LORD? He will show them the path they should choose. They will live in prosperity, and their children will inherit the land.

PSALM 25:12-13

HOW DO YOU DEFINE PROSPERITY? For generations now, the church has confused earthly prosperity with spiritual prosperity. This is an error that we must correct in this generation. You see, God does not view prosperity the way we do. He has an eternal perspective. When I was little, my grandparents used to try and explain the inheritance I could look forward to as a child of God. They were so wise! It wasn't an earthly inheritance that made them so excited. It wasn't about money. It was about a blessing that can only be found as we serve and obey the Lord.

The Bible teaches us that there is a right path and a wrong path. One leads to life, the other to death. One leads to blessing, the other to destruction. One leads to prosperity—but not the kind that we have heard about in modern churches. No, this prosperity is much better. It will last long after the moths have eaten our earthly possessions.

In Psalm 25, the psalmist teaches us that when we fear the Lord, he shows us the path of blessing. This is the inheritance we want for our children, isn't it? Any other kind of inheritance doesn't last very long. We might be able to pass along our earthly possessions to our children, but unless they walk in right relationship with the Lord, the Bible teaches that this is just a temporary blessing. Money comes and goes, but the "prosperity" of God extends far beyond anything money can buy. He offers peace in the midst of panic, hope in our heartache, and security for our souls. Because of Jesus, we can know that our inheritance is to be sons and daughters of the King of Kings!

This is the way of true blessing and godly prosperity. As you train your children today, visualize the path that you are on. Is it a path that you would want your children to follow? Is it the path of a godly inheritance? If not, turn around! Let's secure an inheritance of eternal blessing for our children by walking along the right path and leading them along that path also.

A blessing that can never be lost is waiting for us!

Don't Even Think about It!

Don't even think about it; don't go that way. Turn away and keep moving.

PROVERBS 4:15

SOLOMON KNEW A THING OR TWO about raising children. One could argue that he had done it well but had also failed at times. For all his wisdom, Solomon struggled to put his own advice into practice. He was the first "do as I say, not as I do" sort of parent.

Have you been this way too? I can hear the urgency in his tone as he penned this message from Proverbs 4:10-15: "My child, listen to me and do as I say, and you will have a long, good life. I will teach you wisdom's ways and lead you in straight paths. When you walk, you won't be held back; when you run, you won't stumble. Take hold of my instructions; don't let them go. Guard them, for they are the key to life. Don't do as the wicked do, and don't follow the path of evildoers. Don't even think about it; don't go that way. Turn away and keep moving."

Can you feel the sense of urgency too? After all, this guy knew what he was talking about. Can you imagine what it must've been like to listen to him dish out advice? Though, for all of Solomon's wisdom, my hunch is that his children looked at him in the same way my children look at me.

Maybe that's why he so emphatically said, "My child, listen to me" and "take hold of my instructions." Solomon knew he had only so much time to impart wisdom to his children. It is very clear that he wanted his words to make an impact.

Today, I want to impress upon you a sense of urgency as you train your own children in righteousness. Take a page out of Solomon's parenting playbook. You might even want to quote him—especially when it comes to staying away from wicked influences. If you see your child tempted to follow the path of evildoers, it's time to warn them not to even "think about" going that way.

As parents, we have a sacred responsibility to remind our children of the blessings that will come when they follow God and the perils that lie ahead if they don't.

An Example Worth Following

What do you want me to do for you?

MARK 10:51

OUR CHILDREN ARE LEARNING A LOT about how to talk with God by the way that we interact with the Lord in prayer. It can be easy to think that flowery words or manipulative speech are required when we are speaking to God, but God knows our hearts. He knows what we need before we ask, though we sometimes forget.

In Scripture, we can see how Jesus communicated with people. In Mark 10, we see a beautiful exchange between Jesus and Bartimaeus, a blind beggar who was sitting by the side of the road that Jesus was traveling down. Bartimaeus began to shout at Jesus in an effort to get His attention, asking the Lord to have mercy on him.

When Jesus saw him, He already knew what the problem was, but notice in today's verse how He directly asked what the blind man wanted. From this brief exchange, it's clear—Jesus' heart is always to heal. He saw the faith that Bartimaeus had, and He rewarded that faith without a moment's hesitation. The results? After his healing, Bartimaeus began to follow Jesus.

Isn't that what we want for our children? To feel free enough to cry out to Jesus and then to follow Him like Bartimaeus? The question we need to ask is always, "Am I setting the kind of example that my children will want to follow?"

My husband often recalls that one of the most impactful memories from his childhood is of listening to his mother talk to God. Every morning, Jay would find her sitting by the window in Big Lake, Washington, with her Bible, having a conversation with the Lord Jesus. Jay heard many of those conversations in the early morning hours. He noted that his mom's talks with God were straightforward and simple. I believe they're the kind that God loves to hear.

What a precious example she set. Because of his mom's example, Jay is doing the same thing in our home for our children. In thirty-one years of marriage, I have rarely seen a morning when Jay is not reading his Bible, ready to talk with the Lord.

Though you may not realize it right now, I promise, your children are learning how to talk with God by watching how you do it. Let's set an example worth following.

If It Breaks God's Heart

If anyone takes a human life, that person's life will also be taken by
human hands. For God made human beings in his own image.

GENESIS 9:6

I AM UNABASHEDLY PRO-LIFE. Over the seasons of my life, the passion God has
given me for the unborn has taken me to pro-life rallies; to abortion mills where I
can stand, pray, and counsel; and to pro-life speaking engagements. This is a passion that both my husband and I have endeavored to pass on to our children. Why?
Because we want our children to value what God values. This is one area where we
can work to align our hearts with God's heart. In other words, if it breaks God's
heart, it should break ours too.

Heartbreak translates into many areas of life, not just into the pro-life movement, and so the question should always be, "Lord, what do you want me to do?"

As the mother of seven mostly grown children and (currently) three precious
grandchildren, I am always interested in ways that I can be an example of action
rather than apathy when it comes to the suffering of others.

Remember that your children will care about what you care about. What has
God put on your heart? What things has He asked you to do? Has He asked you
to defend the unborn, become a foster parent, or fight sex trafficking? Whatever it
is you are passionate about, do it with all your heart, all your soul, all your mind,
and all your strength, remembering that it is the Lord who gives us our passions
in the first place.

In our home, we do not talk about protecting the unborn as if it were someone
else's responsibility—we take responsibility. Today, think about your family and
the passions God has given you. What can you do now to pursue those passions?
If you have a young family, it may look simple compared to what you'll be able to
do five years from now. If your children are older, consider what they can do to
further the ministry God has put on their hearts. Even if your children do not go
into the same sphere of influence God has called you to, they will undoubtedly be
influenced by your passion and your obedience.

A Clear Distinction

I will make a clear distinction between my people and your people.

EXODUS 8:23

I HOPE THAT YOU ARE REGULARLY reading the Bible with your children, precious mom. God's Word is replete with stories and examples of God's faithfulness and mercy, but it also shows us that God is a God of justice. We see His anger at sin and His plan for how to be victorious over it. Why? So that we would know Him and follow Him! He is not hidden from us. He has revealed Himself so we can know how to follow His instructions and share His plan of redemption with the world. We are His representatives!

In Exodus 8, we find the children of Israel in the midst of the plagues that God sent to Egypt because of Pharaoh's refusal to let His people go. In verse 23, they are about to begin experiencing the fourth plague: flies. Remember, Moses was trying to bring Pharaoh in line with God's instruction. Obviously, it was not working. Pharaoh did not soften his heart toward the children of Israel.

In today's verse, notice that God says specifically He will make it clear that there is a huge difference between the children of Israel and the Egyptians. God wanted Pharaoh to know that there was something special about the Israelites. They were God's own—they did not belong to a king of Egypt. Pharaoh refused to recognize this, so the plagues continued.

We are also "God's own."

My heart aches for the lack of distinction we see in the world today between God's blood-bought believers and the world. It is not God's heart that we would blend in and be like the world. Rather, God sees His people as distinct from the world. He wants us to stand out. He wants us to be set apart for His glory and His purposes.

Today, as you shepherd your precious children, remind them of this. It can be tempting to try to blend into the world when it comes to just about every topic, but God has made it very clear that this is not what He wants for His children. When the world looks at us, they should see a clear distinction, something that makes us stand out from the crowd. That something is Jesus.

Are you set apart? Would your children say that their family has made a *clear distinction* between the ways of the world and God? If not, it's time to earnestly seek the Lord for direction. Today is a good day to start!

Just Stop

The Lord replied, "I will personally go with you, Moses, and I will give you rest—everything will be fine for you."

EXODUS 33:14

I TOOK A BREAK OUTSIDE THE OTHER DAY, after what felt like a straight week of fighting spiritual battles. Sitting on my back deck, I took in the scenery and breathed deeply. We are surrounded by forest on most sides of our home, and when the sun shines through the trees, and the birds sing, and I have a steaming cup of tea in my hands, there's no place I would rather be.

Occasionally, though, even the beautiful surroundings that I call home don't offer the protection from the struggles of this world that my heart craves. For a variety of reasons, my heart was heavy. I needed to rest, and I knew it.

The trouble was that I could not give myself permission to just *stop*.

As mothers, we don't often take the rest that we need. Notice I didn't say "get" the rest we need. That goes without saying! But taking rest when it's offered and ignoring the signs that we need to stop and be still . . . well, that's usually not the fault of others.

I know I am guilty of this. There've been many times throughout my career as a mother when I should've just called it a day, but instead, I turned into "that mom." You know the one I'm talking about: the one who acts like a martyr because it just seems like the thing to do.

I'm older now. These days, when I feel the strain of the world around me closing in, when I can feel myself responding to situations in a way that does not bring encouragement to those around me, I know it's time to take a break.

I think that God understands it when we need to take a break. Even Moses needed a break from time to time! And when he did, God responded graciously to him. Rather than speak harshly or wonder why Moses couldn't toughen up and keep going, the Lord gently encouraged him, promising to give him rest.

God's promise alone is wonderful, but the best thing He said to Moses in today's passage was to remind him that in the end, everything was going to be fine. Sure, we can keep going beyond what makes sense, but today, let's hear the gentle voice of the shepherd of our soul and *just stop*. Whatever it is, we will handle it better when we've rested and have drunk deeply of the many blessings God has given us.

Suffering Well

Of course, you get no credit for being patient if you are beaten for doing wrong. But if you suffer for doing good and endure it patiently, God is pleased with you.

1 PETER 2:20

PETER IS SUCH A RELATABLE BELIEVER. He spent his entire life focused on knowing the right way to live as a devoted Jew and following the Law. However, his life didn't go as he planned. Is your life going as you planned? The good news for Peter, of course, was that he finally met the One he had been studying his entire lifetime. From then on, we see Peter striving—sometimes impetuously, sometimes fearfully, sometimes getting caught by previous ways of "what was right"—to follow Jesus. I do that too. Do you?

After all, isn't that our goal as Christian mothers? To follow Jesus and to train our children to follow Him? We need to have a theology for suffering. We are going to encounter suffering. The question is, will we suffer well?

Peter understood the times he was living in. He wrote his letters to a group of Christians who were struggling. These members of the early church were familiar with persecution. Many of them had heard Peter preaching. He preached in a way that resonated with them.

In speaking to the Jews and the Gentiles (non-Jews), Peter referred to them as "foreigners" (1 Peter 1:1). He knew that they were feeling the beginnings of *intense scrutiny* as they lived their lives in such a way that their neighbors noticed a stark difference between these "Jesus people" and the rest of the culture.

As they entered the final years of Nero's reign, Peter focused his attention on preparing the young Christians to face persecution. Though he had not yet been arrested, the writing was on the wall. Peter knew his time was short, so he didn't mince words. You see, many of the Christians of Peter's time had left their first love and had given themselves over to idol worship and false gods. It was Peter's calling to awaken a sleeping church and prepare them for persecution.

We are living in a tumultuous time and a real time of shifting for the church. Like Peter, let's prepare our children to live a life that pleases the Lord, even if they encounter suffering.

Peter is calling us to endure for the *sake of the gospel* and to keep our eyes on the goal: to never lose sight of eternity. Persevere, precious mom! And teach your children to do the same. The Lord's return is near!

A Surprising Sin

There are six things the LORD hates—no, seven things he detests: haughty eyes, a lying tongue, hands that kill the innocent, a heart that plots evil, feet that race to do wrong, a false witness who pours out lies, a person who sows discord in a family.

PROVERBS 6:16-19

LOOK CLOSELY AT THE LIST OF things that God hates in today's Scripture passage. The first few things on this list are things we would expect: pride, a lying tongue, hands that would kill the innocent, a heart that plots evil. Of course, God doesn't love it when we bear false witness about each other, but the last thing—sowing discord in a family—doesn't get much airtime right now.

Does it surprise you that the Lord includes sowing discord in a family in a list with murder and a heart that plots evil? It is such a wonderful insight into the heart of God! God's heart beats for families. After all, the family was His good idea. God has instituted the family as a way to bring glory to Him, so it shouldn't be any wonder that He hates it when a purposeful attempt at sowing discord affects a family unit.

Think about the things that you have struggled with in your family over the years. It could be your family of origin, or it could be the family that you are currently raising. Either way, God does not want us to be people who sow discord into families. Especially our own!

Over the years, there's been a fair amount of drama in my family. We've had our ups and downs, and as I have grown older, I have come to really appreciate it when family members go out of their way to ensure peace rather than division. Sure, we will not always agree, and sometimes the disagreements are severe enough to cause separation. But this should not be the norm. It should be the exception. Whenever possible, we should strive to live at peace with one another and teach our children how to do the same. Remember, our children are taking into their own families the things that they learn about family life from their parents, aunts, uncles, and grandparents.

It's easy to make excuses for why we fight and argue. Think with me for just a minute about the little things we do that sow seeds of division. Gossip, backstabbing, thinking the worst rather than the best about a sibling, a stepparent, or parents . . . just for starters. None of these things honor God. Today, let's honor Him by being people of peace, starting in our own families.

Lord, I Am Coming

My heart has heard you say, "Come and talk with me." And
my heart responds, "LORD, I am coming."

PSALM 27:8

WHEN WAS THE LAST TIME YOU heard the still, small voice of your Savior beckoning you to come and talk with Him? I have to admit, in times of stress and struggle, I find it more difficult to hear His voice. I have to be still. I have to be listening.

When all of our children were young, there were seasons when I could not hear His voice unless I was totally dedicated to it. When I was up all night with a newborn, or in a demanding season of shepherding a willful adolescent, I didn't always hear Him call me. But as I grew older, He made it clear that He always was calling. It wasn't that the Lord didn't want to spend time with me; it was that I was too busy to hear His voice.

As I read today's verse from Psalms, my heart beat in time with the author's. As a woman who has walked with the Lord for a long time, I know beyond a shadow of a doubt that God's heart is always that I bring my burdens to Him and leave them there. It really is my flesh that picks up my burdens every day and carries them alone. I fall into bed at the end of the day weary and wondering why I didn't take time to respond to the gentle voice of God as He waited for me.

Come talk with Me.

Oh, how He loves me! Oh, how He loves you! God's heart is never that we would carry the burdens of this world on our own. On the contrary! His heart is to help us. I want my children to look back on their time in our home and someday be able to say with confidence that I was a mother who was always listening for the voice of the Lord. I want them to see that my heart is not only to listen, but to respond.

Lord, I am coming.

I am so thankful that the Lord of heaven and earth wants to take time to talk to me. I'm so grateful that it matters to Him when I am weary and when I am rejoicing. I pray it will always be my heart to want to spend time with Him also.

Is this your prayer today too?

To See Only Jesus

Suddenly, when they looked around, Moses and Elijah were gone, and they saw only Jesus with them.

MARK 9:8

HAVE YOU EVER HAD A MOUNTAINTOP EXPERIENCE? Peter, James, and John definitely had one. Jesus, after telling His disciples that He would suffer, be killed, and then be raised again to life, took Peter, James, and John up a mountain to pray. While Jesus was praying, the Bible records that "his face was transformed, and his clothes became dazzling white" (Luke 9:29). This is known as the Transfiguration. As if that weren't enough, Moses and Elijah appeared and began talking with Jesus (see Luke 9:30). Can you imagine how frightening this would have been?

Peter, one of my favorite figures of all Scripture, clumsily offered to put up shelters for the three of them as memorials. As Peter was expressing his desire to honor Jesus, Moses, and Elijah, a cloud enveloped them and a voice from the cloud said, "This is my dearly loved Son. Listen to him" (Mark 9:7).

Immediately after that, the Bible records that *all Peter, James, and John could see was Jesus.*

Witnessing the Transfiguration of Christ was a precious opportunity for those closest to Jesus. It gave them a chance to get a better idea of who He was. Right before their eyes, Jesus experienced an incredible change in His appearance, which allowed the disciples to behold His glory. Remember that they had only known Him in human form until that point. After the Transfiguration, they had a better idea of who they had been spending so much time with, though they probably could not fully comprehend it.

It can be so easy to focus on things that take our attention away from God. Life is full of distractions. Sometimes we're too busy to think about God and who He really is. Other times, we're so focused on worrying that we forget He is there with us. The good news is that Jesus is coming again, and one day, we will be home with Him face-to-face. Until that time, let our prayer be to see only Jesus. When we do this, our vision becomes clearer when we keep our eyes on Him.

Confused

"God made them male and female" from the beginning of creation.

MARK 10:6

MORE THAN EVER BEFORE IN HUMAN HISTORY, we can see our children are being targeted by the culture. They're being lied to on a scale of epidemic proportions, starting with pop culture, which has infiltrated every aspect of our children's world. From education to entertainment, the world is seeking to influence the hearts and minds of our kids. The result? We are seeing mass confusion among our young people today. This is not an accident. It is intentional.

So what can we do? Since we mothers are on the front lines of this battle for the hearts and minds of our children, the first thing we need to know is the Truth. Truth is not an abstract idea. It is not subjective. The Bible teaches us a truth that is found in the work and person of Jesus Christ: "Jesus told him, 'I am the way, the truth, and the life. No one can come to the Father except through Me'" (John 14:6).

Jesus is truth—and His Word is the way to know the Truth.

For example, there is a lot of confusion regarding gender and sexuality. But we don't have to fall victim to the world's lies. A study of the Bible clears up the confusion immediately. The Bible says that we have been made in the image of God (see Genesis 1:27) and that God has made us male and female, from the beginning of creation (Mark 10:6). Though we may face ridicule from others for believing this truth, it is important to impress it upon the hearts of our children from the time they're very young.

The Bible says that God is not the author of confusion (see 1 Corinthians 14:33), so wherever you see it, you will know it is not from God. Are your kids asking tough questions? Take them to the Bible. Are the questions making you feel uncomfortable? Answer them anyway. Do you feel ill-equipped to take on the lies around you? Straighten your crown! You are a daughter of the King, and you have been given the mind of Christ! According to the Bible, you have been given everything you need in the Word of God to answer the tough questions this generation is asking.

The intentional onslaught of evil that's alive and well in our culture today can be overcome only by an intentional counterattack of truth. Are you ready? Know the Word of God!

People > Possessions

Store your treasures in heaven, where moths and rust cannot destroy, and thieves do not break in and steal. Wherever your treasure is, there the desires of your heart will also be.
MATTHEW 6:20-21

"But, Mom! It was just a mistake!" my daughter said. I looked at my little brown-eyed beauty. She was holding what was left of my broken Mary Engelbreit teapot. It was a gift from a bygone life season. I rarely used it for tea. It was a reminder of a precious friend and a season I cherish.

Anyone who knows me well knows that I am not a very sentimental person. Like my mom and my grandmother, I don't keep many things beyond what seems reasonable to me.

"I'm sorry, Mama," my daughter said. I looked at her, aware that my response to her confession was going to make or break this moment for her. I hugged her tight. "It's okay," I said. "I like you more, anyway." She cleaned up the mess, and I cringed just a little when she put the last piece into the trash.

Over the course of my life, I have been the owner of just a few things that I would consider precious: a bracelet that my grandmother gave me comes to mind. I lost it in the excitement of a DeGarmo and Key concert in 1986. In 1989, my husband gave me a necklace that is woefully out of style today, but I could never part with it. That necklace transports me to the beginning of our life together. I love it. Actually, as I'm sitting here writing my way down memory lane, it occurs to me that the teapot was one of the handful of things I would consider a keepsake.

My children, and more recently my grandchildren, remind me that nothing in this life lasts. Jesus tells us not to work so hard at protecting our earthly possessions. Instead, He urges us to make an eternal investment (see Matthew 6:20-21). How do we do that? One way is by loving our families well. We do that by leading our children to the heart of the One who made and loves them, and by setting our hearts not on things here, but on things above.

Truth is, that teapot, my necklace, and even that bracelet from my grandma aren't necessary to my life. The memories they represent and the people who gave them to me are more important. Let's pray today that the Lord will help us keep our eyes on the most precious part of life—and invest in it. People will always matter more than possessions.

A Big Mistake

Jesus replied, "Your mistake is that you don't know the
Scriptures, and you don't know the power of God."

MARK 12:24

IN 2017, MY NEPHEW BOBBY SUFFERED a broken neck after being hit by a car near Gresham, Oregon. The weeks and months that followed changed his life forever. In fact, I think it changed all of our lives. Until that point, we had not begged for a life. We had not felt the cool breath of death upon our family. The initial diagnosis was a devastating one; we were told that Bobby would likely never wake up from the coma that he was in, and if he did, he would most certainly be a quadriplegic.

I could write an entire book on the events that took place around his accident. I could talk about the culture of death that we live in and the fact that many in the medical community in Portland, Oregon, advised my sister to end Bobby's life due to what they determined would be a low "quality of life."

You see, they made a big mistake when they determined the value of my nephew's life. Their mistake? They didn't know the Scriptures and based their decisions on their own wisdom and understanding—and they definitely didn't know the power of God.

In Mark 12, Jesus corrected (yet again) the Sadducees, who, for all their head knowledge of the law and prophets, did not know the Word (Jesus) or the power of God. It is God's heart that we would not be like the Sadducees. He wants us to truly know Him.

In the months that followed the accident, I came to see prayer in a whole new way. I saw the Lord breathe new life into a broken body. I saw miracles. I saw the power of God—in more ways than the physical healing of Bobby—as I watched my sister begin to learn what it truly meant to surrender her child to God's will and entrust him into God's hands. God truly is a multitasking, miracle-working God!

As Christians, we are called to view the world through the lens of what we know to be true about God. Jesus wants us to know His Word, and He wants us to experience His power. Don't wait until you are in a life-and-death situation to know the Word of God, precious mom, and pass on the Truth to your children!

Pay It Forward

Encourage each other and build each other up.

1 THESSALONIANS 5:11

SOMETIMES, MOTHERHOOD CAN FEEL LIKE A competitive sport. I'd like to blame it on Pinterest, but the competition between mothers has been around, I would imagine, for thousands of years. It might be funny to be able to eavesdrop on the conversations that mothers had in Jesus' time. I bet they talked a lot about how amazing their kids were while they were sharing a new recipe for hummus and talking about who harvested the best batch of wheat that season.

Somewhere inside of each one of us, we want to be seen as valuable. We all want to have something to contribute to the community. Mothers are no exception.

There's no such thing as "just a mom." Moms are amazing. Over the years, I have met some awesome moms. Some of my mom friends have had a dozen kids, some of them have adopted sibling groups from foster care, some have worked with special needs children, and some of them have started their own businesses. I know women who are entrepreneurs, authors, speakers, and even inventors. All of these women are incredible.

But you know what? The women who are the most amazing are the ones who encourage other people before promoting themselves.

Moms, we need to rejoice in the giftings of other mothers. We need to spur them on and encourage them without fear of being one-upped or overshadowed by someone else. There will always be the better homeschooling mom, a more financially savvy mother, a mom who is better at fixing healthy foods, and a mom who is thriftier. Instead of becoming jealous, let's be sure to be like David and ask the Lord to help us see more clearly into the motives of our own hearts (see Psalm 26:2). When we're clear about our own motives, we can see our actions more clearly. We don't have to prove anything to anyone, but we do need to encourage and build one another up. The mom you encourage today will be the one who encourages another tomorrow.

With God, Everything Is Possible

The disciples were astounded. "Then who in the world can be saved?" they asked.

MARK 10:26

THE STORY OF JESUS' ENCOUNTER WITH a rich man offers us an incredible insight into the heart of human beings.

Let's look at Mark 10:17-20: "As Jesus was starting out on his way to Jerusalem, a man came running up to him, knelt down, and asked, 'Good Teacher, what must I do to inherit eternal life?' 'Why do you call me good?' Jesus asked. 'Only God is truly good. But to answer your question, you know the commandments: "You must not murder. You must not commit adultery. You must not steal. You must not testify falsely. You must not cheat anyone. Honor your father and mother."' 'Teacher,' the man replied, 'I've obeyed all these commandments since I was young.'

The man gave the right answer, but Jesus knew his heart. Jesus knew his struggle, and still He genuinely loved him: "Looking at the man, Jesus felt genuine love for him. 'There is still one thing you haven't done,' he told him. 'Go and sell all your possessions and give the money to the poor, and you will have treasure in heaven. Then come, follow me.' At this the man's face fell, and he went away sad, for he had many possessions" (Mark 10:21-22).

It's such a sad outcome for this man—but there is much to glean for our own lives. This man's struggle was caused by money, but we all struggle with something. Notice how the disciples reacted when Jesus pointed out the truth: "Jesus looked around and said to his disciples, 'How hard it is for the rich to enter the Kingdom of God!' This amazed them. But Jesus said again, 'Dear children, it is very hard to enter the Kingdom of God. In fact, it is easier for a camel to go through the eye of a needle than for a rich person to enter the Kingdom of God!' The disciples were astounded. 'Then who in the world can be saved?' they asked" (Mark 10:23-26).

When the disciples heard what Jesus said, they rightly thought of their own inward struggles. They were absolutely right to ask Jesus *who in the world can be saved*, in light of their own sin and selfishness. Jesus answered by famously saying, "Humanly speaking, it is impossible. But not with God. Everything is possible with God" (Mark 10:27).

Isn't that encouraging? Whatever your struggle is today, God can help you overcome it. Whatever your children are struggling with, let them know that with God, everything is possible.

Have Faith!

"What do you mean, 'If I can'?" Jesus asked. "Anything is possible if a person believes."
MARK 9:23

IN MARK 9, WE READ THE account of a young boy who was possessed by a demon. The crowds following Jesus had heard about His power. Rumors swirled about who He was. One man in the crowd, a father, saw an opportunity to speak to Jesus, and he took it: "Teacher, I brought my son so you could heal him. He is possessed by an evil spirit that won't let him talk. And whenever this spirit seizes him, it throws him violently to the ground. Then he foams at the mouth and grinds his teeth and becomes rigid. So I asked your disciples to cast out the evil spirit, but they couldn't do it" (Mark 9:17-18).

As we continue reading the passage, you might be surprised by Jesus's response: "Jesus said to them, 'You faithless people! How long must I be with you? How long must I put up with you? Bring the boy to me'" (Mark 9:19).

Can you hear the frustration in His voice? The unbelief of the disciples and the lack of understanding from the crowd grieved the Lord Jesus. After all this time, the disciples still struggled to understand what Jesus was trying to accomplish. The faith of the father seemed too weak. Faith matters to God. Let's keep reading. The Bible says, "So they brought the boy. But when the evil spirit saw Jesus, it threw the child into a violent convulsion, and he fell to the ground, writhing and foaming at the mouth. 'How long has this been happening?' Jesus asked the boy's father. He replied, 'Since he was a little boy. The spirit often throws him into the fire or into water, trying to kill him. Have mercy on us and help us, if you can.' 'What do you mean, "If I can"?' Jesus asked. 'Anything is possible if a person believes.' The father instantly cried out, 'I do believe, but help me overcome my unbelief!'" (Mark 9:20-24).

I love the honesty that this father displayed with his lack of faith. We can all relate to him, can't we? There is much to be learned from Jesus in the situation. He does not want us to question His ability. Healing depends on the power of God—not how much faith we have—but faith is important! Today, when you face your own lack of belief, remember how loved you are and how powerful your heavenly Father is. Have faith! Anything is possible with God!

Tell Everyone

Give thanks to the LORD and proclaim his greatness. Let
the whole world know what he has done.

PSALM 105:1

HAVE YOU EVER MET SOMEONE WITH the gift of evangelism? You know the kind of person I'm talking about: they can't be quiet about what God has done. The Bible teaches us that it pleases the Lord when we tell others about Him!

Several years ago, I had a conversation with one of my adult daughters as we sat around the family room after dinner. We were talking about reasons why it's so hard and sometimes frightening to share our faith. The number one fear that most people have is a fear of rejection. We can see this fear on full display in virtually every area of life, starting when we are very little. We'll do almost anything to avoid being singled out and ostracized—but if we're honest, we also struggle because, on some level, we're embarrassed. It goes back to the fear of rejection, doesn't it? Savannah noted what the apostle Paul said in Romans 1:16: "I am not ashamed of this Good News about Christ. It is the power of God at work, saving everyone who believes."

Isn't it something that the adversary would use our fear of rejection to keep us from sharing the good news about the One who can save us from ultimate rejection? The ultimate rejection, of course, is what happens when we die without ever asking Christ into our lives. Jesus Christ came and died so we could be set free from the consequences of our sin—eternal separation from God.

One of the things my grandmother taught me was the importance of sharing my faith. She was bold about her relationship with God. She wasn't ashamed—and she passed that boldness on to me. She lived it as an ambassador of God's Kingdom. It didn't matter if we were taking the bus into downtown Portland or conversing with the mailman, my grandmother was interested in sharing the gospel.

She told everyone about Jesus, and now, I am endeavoring to do the same thing.

Mama, your children are watching how you share your faith. Do they see a mother who cannot wait to share the hope of Jesus with those around her? Or do they see someone who is ashamed of the gospel? If we want our children to "let the whole world know" about Jesus, they need to see us sharing it as if it was the best news in the world. Because it is.

It's a Great Day for Hope!

Be strong and courageous, all you who put your hope in the LORD!

PSALM 31:24

I WILL NEVER FORGET THE SEASON when Barack Obama was running for president of the United States. My hunch is that you will never forget it either. His slogans are still with us today.

"Hope" and "Change."

It worked, of course. After all, who doesn't want hope and change? We are a people in dire need of hope! Here's the thing, though, precious mom: we need to tell our children the truth about hope. It isn't something we can get from a politician or even a pastor. We don't have hope because of a policy or a medical procedure. Hope isn't something that we manufacture. As Christians, we have hope because of Jesus.

Praise the Lord! We can have hope no matter what our circumstances are because we know that ultimately we are safe in the arms of the Lord. When the Bible tells us to be strong and courageous, it is because our hope is in the Lord. In Psalm 31:21-22, David echoes the feelings of many of us right now: "Praise the LORD, for he has shown me the wonders of his unfailing love. He kept me safe when my city was under attack. In panic I cried out, 'I am cut off from the LORD!' But you heard my cry for mercy and answered my call for help."

This is the reason that we can have hope, and even in the midst of trouble! We have hope because God shows us the wonders of His unfailing love. He hears our prayers, and He answers them. We can be strong and courageous, in every circumstance, because our hope is in the Lord. Aren't you glad? This is such good news! It means that no matter what is going on around us, we have hope because of Jesus.

This is such an important truth to pass on to our children. Before we fall for cleverly crafted slogans or man-made promises, let's find our hope in the One who always keeps His promises and teach our precious children to do the same.

Mothers Need a Teacher Too

Teach me how to live, O LORD. Lead me along the right path, for my enemies are waiting for me.

PSALM 27:11

Do you remember the very first time you held your child in your arms? Do you remember the weight of responsibility and the incredible love that you felt? Of course you do.

I remember feeling overwhelmed at the thought that the hospital staff would let me take home this nine-pound human being. I mean, let's be honest—I didn't know what I was doing! Truly, I was just making it up as I went along. Come to think of it, I'm still doing that in many respects.

Most of my seven children are grown now. They are getting married and having children of their own, and I am navigating yet another season of motherhood that I feel unprepared for. Motherhood is humbling at every stage and in every season. The challenge I am facing now is how to let my children leave. It is both heartbreaking and exhilarating, and I find I am leaning into the Lord to teach me how to live in this season of life.

David modeled so well what it looks like to depend on the Lord. And we mothers need the Lord to teach us too. One of the beautiful things about being a Christian is that you don't have to have it all together. You don't need to know the answers. You simply need to know the One who does. When you know how much you need wisdom and direction, you're in a place to receive it. The Bible holds the keys to this kind of growth. In every season of motherhood, in every stage of life, we need to be led along the right path, and the Bible will show us the way.

David was keenly aware that He had enemies who would take his life without a moment's hesitation. We may not feel that our lives are in danger in the same way, but we must never forget that we have a very real enemy who would love to see us trip up and fall off the path that God has put before us.

No matter what season of motherhood you're in right now, whether you are starting out with the feeling of being overwhelmed by the responsibility and love that new motherhood brings with it or your children are leaving the nest and beginning lives of their own, you have a Teacher. God wants to show you how to navigate each season that you are in with wisdom and love.

Today, let your heart's desire be to be taught by the Lord.

Does Your Faith Speak?

I stand on solid ground, and I will publicly praise the LORD.

PSALM 26:12

ONE OF THE THEMES OF MY life has been learning how to publicly proclaim my faith. My women's conference, Faith That Speaks, reaches thousands of women every year with one goal in mind: to stir their faith to action. Do we love the Lord? If so, our faith should never be silent. Our faith should be a faith that speaks.

As a mother, I want my children to know that their faith should permeate every aspect of their lives. Our faith should speak into every sphere of influence God gives us.

Unlike the unbelieving world, as Christians, we stand on solid ground. We can offer hope and wisdom because of Jesus. Do you believe this? If so, we should be incorporating our bold defense of Scripture into all aspects of our lives. Our faith should influence medicine, education, politics, the law, and even our local libraries.

The more I study God's heart, and the more I read His Word, the more I want to teach my children the importance of publicly acknowledging and praising the Lord. God is resolutely committed to His own glory. Jesus said that if we don't give Him glory, even the rocks will cry out! (see Luke 19:40).

Are we giving Him glory for everyone to see?

With all my heart, I believe that one of the reasons we are struggling so much in the world right now is that Christians have removed themselves from the public square. We bought the lie of separation of church and state and have become apathetic and even cowardly in our public acknowledgment of Jesus Christ. Today, I am praying that this generation of mothers would be on the front lines. We need to bring our faith back into the public square again.

In a world that is built on shifting sand, we stand on solid ground. Let's shout it from the rooftops! Let's give our faith more than a quiet nod. Let's give it a voice. The world is watching—and the whole world needs Jesus.

Little Things Matter to God

Look at the birds of the air: they neither sow nor reap nor gather into barns, and yet your heavenly Father feeds them. Are you not of more value than they?

MATTHEW 6:26, ESV

HAVE YOU EVER LOST SOMETHING PRECIOUS? After raising seven children and having four grandkids racing through my house on a regular basis, I've learned to hold on to things loosely. I went from being upset when my things would get broken or lost to somehow saying, "What's that, honey? You broke my favorite teapot? It's okay, I have pictures. Let's clean up together."

Turns out that people are much more precious than things. But still, there are some objects that hold a special place in our hearts. For me, it's the first love note I received from my husband (which is yellowed and faded now). Another is my grandmother's diamond ring. I have always taken great care not to misplace this precious heirloom. It holds tremendous meaning for me.

One day, I was at an event and happened to look down at my ring. To my horror, the center diamond was missing. I stared in stunned disbelief and dissolved into tears. Frantically, I searched my purse and the floor mats of my car, but soon I gave up. After all, with the busy pace of my life and the dozens of places I had just been with that ring, how could I ever find it again? It was so small that it would be like finding a needle in a haystack. It would take a miracle.

Within a few minutes of realizing the diamond was missing, some friends approached me to pray. We asked God to restore my grandmother's diamond to me—but beyond that, through our prayer, I was reminded that God does indeed see the little things. No matter if it's your missing ring or your child's favorite stuffed animal that's lost, it's worth taking to the Lord in prayer.

Almost exactly a month later, I noticed a little sparkle in the bottom of my purse as I was fishing around for lip balm. Hesitantly, I reached in and held my breath as I took out a tiny stone. I showed it to my friends Steve and Jane. "Do you think this is my missing diamond?"

"Well, kid," Steve said, "It looks like God heard your prayer. This is definitely a diamond!"

And while finding the diamond was a tremendous gift, the best gift of all was hearing my children talking about how God heard and answered our prayers. His eye is on the sparrow, mama. Nothing is too small to take to Him in prayer.

Because of Who He Is

It was I who rescued you from the land of Egypt, that I might be your God. I am the LORD.
LEVITICUS 22:33

FOR MOST OF MY LIFE, I read Leviticus with a bored and irritated attitude: *the law blah blah blah . . . genealogies blah blah blah . . . rules for priests blah blah blah.* Have you felt that way?

Let's look at a message that mothers can take away from this summary of God's instruction to the Israelite priests in Leviticus 22:31-32: "You must faithfully keep all my commands by putting them into practice, for I am the LORD. Do not bring shame on my holy name, for I will display my holiness among the people of Israel. I am the LORD who makes you holy."

As I read this, I was reminded of something very precious: I am a spiritual example and teacher to my children—and God takes my role seriously. He views mothers as His representatives. Leviticus contains a lot of rules and regulations that are no longer in place because of the death and resurrection of Jesus—we have been set free from the law—but it's important that we understand how serious God is about our living in a way that honors Him!

God commanded Israel to honor him for one reason: He is God. Our lives should bring Him glory because of who He is: the Creator and Sustainer of all. We must teach our children to honor Him as such.

God wants us to live a holy life (in other words, to be a set-apart people) for the sake of His name. When we as Christians act shamefully (on social media, at work, at church, and even at home!), we do more than bring dishonor to our own name—we bring shame on the Lord's name.

We are to live as He commands. God is working to make us more like His Son, Jesus! When we talk to our children about the importance of obedience, it's important to remind them (and ourselves) that as long as we live on this earth, we will struggle with sin. The *good news* is that with the help of God, we can overcome it!

Lastly, we are to keep His commandments because of what He has done ("It was I who rescued you"). When was the last time we talked with our children about all of the things that God has done? Today's a good day to write down all the things that God has done for you, starting with the day you became a Christian. We have so much to thank Him for!

Because of Your Faith

He touched their eyes and said, "Because of your faith, it will happen."

MATTHEW 9:29

CAN YOU IMAGINE WHAT IT WOULD have been like to follow Jesus (literally) as He moved in crowds of people? In Matthew 9, we get a wonderful glimpse into His mission and ministry. The entire chapter is a wonderful window into the heart of Jesus. He wants us to believe in Him, to trust Him, and to teach our children to trust Him too.

Jesus' love for people is so evident as He interacts with the sick and the suffering. At the beginning of Matthew 9, we see Jesus interacting with a paralyzed man who had been brought to Him. He says, "Be encouraged, my child! Your sins are forgiven!" (verse 2). As usual, Jesus had His detractors. Even as they criticized Him, He told the paralyzed man, "Stand up, pick up your mat, and go home!" (verse 6).

Can you imagine the joy that man must have experienced? From paralyzed to walking! The Bible records that he literally "jumped up and went home" (verse 7). God's heart is always to heal. That's why Jesus came into the world—to bring eternal healing.

Later on in the chapter, we read about another healing: a woman who knew that if she could just touch the robe of Jesus, she would be healed. Again, Jesus told her to be encouraged and reminded her that it was her faith that made her well (see Matthew 9:20-22).

Her faith! But He wasn't done yet: "Two blind men followed along behind him, shouting, 'Son of David, have mercy on us!' They went right into the house where he was staying, and Jesus asked them, 'Do you believe I can make you see?' 'Yes, Lord,' they told him, 'we do.' Then he touched their eyes and said, '*Because of your faith*, it will happen.' Then their eyes were opened, and they could see!" (Matthew 9:27-30, emphasis added).

"Because of your faith." What are you trusting God for today? Does your marriage need healing? Do you have a prodigal child? Is there a relationship in your life that seems beyond repair? Take these things to the Lord in prayer *with faith*. God honors faith. God can do it!

But First, Forgive

When you are praying, first forgive anyone you are holding a grudge against, so that your Father in heaven will forgive your sins, too.

MARK 11:25

HAVE YOU EVER STRUGGLED TO FORGIVE SOMEONE? I have. Sometimes, forgiveness means accepting an apology you will never hear. Sometimes, it means going to a person who has wounded you and doing the hard work of reconciliation. Forgiveness is essential to walking in victory in this world.

Remember, before we can teach forgiveness, we need to model it. Our children are not listening to us all the time, but I promise you, they are watching! Children can tell when their parents are walking in unforgiveness. Maybe it's a phone call that they overheard or a conversation that they witnessed. Maybe it's a little side remark that we made about a person from church. Remember, we can't pass on what we don't possess. Unforgiveness tears relationships apart and robs us of peace.

The Bible teaches us that forgiveness is not an option—it is a command. Forgiveness is such a big deal to God that the Bible teaches us a lack of forgiveness can hinder our prayers. Did you catch that? *Hinder our prayers!*

I spent nearly twenty years as a pastor's wife, and the truth is this: the place that I have seen the most unforgiveness on display is in the church. This is disheartening, but it's a great opportunity for us to change this for the next generation. We need to turn this around, mamas! Our kids are watching us. It matters how we talk about the person who offended us. It matters that we do not constantly bring old grievances up after they have been dealt with. If someone comes up to you and wants to bring up an offense, your job is to respond in a godly way.

If you know that you have unforgiveness in your heart, take a moment to confess it to the Lord. Pray for the person that you are struggling to forgive, and ask the Lord to help you let go of any bitterness you are still carrying. If we want our children to walk in the freedom that forgiveness offers, we must make sure we are not captives of unforgiveness ourselves.

Genuine Love

> Looking at the man, Jesus felt genuine love for him.
>
> **MARK 10:21**

IF YOUR CHILDREN WERE TO ASK you the definition of genuine love, what would you say?

Our culture has pretty mixed-up ideas about love. The entertainment industry has reduced love to little more than a feeling that can come and go, or worse, a physical encounter that carries no commitment with it.

Even the church is confused about what genuine love looks like. Rather than focus on the gospel and on the saving message of Jesus, many churches today have, in the name of love, begun advocating for things that are clearly in opposition to God's Word.

Really, if we want to teach our children what genuine love looks like, we need look no further than Jesus Himself. Jesus was known for His love of people from all social backgrounds and stages of life. He had an affinity for little children, and He often went out of His way to pay attention to them. Jesus visited the lepers and hung out with tax collectors and prostitutes.

He wasn't in it for Himself; He was motivated by an incredible kind of love. His concern was always for the part of us that will live on after our earthly bodies die. Jesus is after our hearts. Jesus, in an act of true and genuine love, willingly gave Himself up and was crucified on our behalf.

In Mark 10, we read the story of Jesus and a rich man. The Bible records that when Jesus saw him, He felt "genuine love" for him. I can picture the look of kind concern on Jesus' face as He tried to explain why this man must sell his possessions and instead store up treasure in heaven. Though Jesus gave him an opportunity, in the end, the man wasn't willing to leave his riches to follow Jesus.

One of the interesting things about Jesus is that He always knew what genuine love looked like for the people He was with. Jesus showed this man genuine love by telling him the truth, even though the man rejected it.

Today as you shepherd your children, ask the Lord to help you see the unique needs of each of them, and then ask Him to show you how you can meet their needs. Walk out the message of the gospel, precious mom! This is modeling genuine love.

Precious Partnership

You led your people along that road like a flock of sheep,
with Moses and Aaron as their shepherds.

PSALM 77:20

HAVE YOU EVER WONDERED WHAT TRUE friendship might look like? The older I get, the more I appreciate friends who have been in my life for a long time. True, abiding friendship is rare. Friendship is work—but the rewards are worth it!

God has created us for relationship, and God uses our friends to bring out the best in us. Sometimes, God brings people into our lives who complement us perfectly and help us achieve things we could never achieve on our own. I call these kinds of friendships "precious partnerships."

Moses and Aaron had perhaps one of the greatest partnerships in history. God used them to do amazing things. Moses and Aaron were very different from each other, a reminder that we don't need friends who think exactly like we do or who have our same strengths.

For example, Moses was afraid to speak publicly. Seeing this, God appointed Aaron as his speaker and supporter. Aaron was an incredible gift to Moses and supported him through many challenging circumstances. Together, Moses and Aaron worked in obedience to God to accomplish one of the most amazing rescues in all of history—they freed the Israelites from slavery in Egypt. Their partnership was legendary, and they are mentioned throughout the Bible as having been used mightily by God.

We mothers need good friends, don't we? Over the years, I have been blessed by the friendship of many women. Some of them have only been in my life for a season, while others have remained for decades. Sometimes, friendships end painfully. It can be difficult to put yourself out there and try again, but when you finally find that lifelong friend, I promise, the reward will be worth it.

Today, take a moment to thank God for the friendships in your life. As I reflect on the precious partnerships that God has blessed me with, my heart is filled with joy. I pray my own children will be blessed by wonderful friendships in their lives too.

Check Your Heart

Put me on trial, LORD, and cross-examine me. Test my motives and my heart.

PSALM 26:2

MOTIVE.

It's a hard thing to get at in my own life, let alone in the hearts of my children. Sometimes, I don't even know my own motives until I feel the sting of rejection or a check in my spirit.

- I don't really have the time or energy to volunteer right now. Maybe my motive wasn't to do that thing I signed up for—maybe it was to be liked.
- As I probed my heart, I had to confess that I really did hope the moms at the co-op would like me. It did seem a little selfish—maybe my motive was more self-promotion than I would be inclined to admit.
- I probably spent more time staging that picture of my Bible and open notebook in the sunlight than I did in reading the Bible today—maybe my motive for Bible study today was to get a good response on social media. (Ouch!)
- Maybe my motive for _____ was _____.

Oh, how we need to have a heart like David. In Psalm 26, he set an example for all of us when he asked the Lord to cross-examine his heart in order to test his motives. It's amazing what happens when the Holy Spirit shines the light of truth into the quiet places of our hearts. When our hearts are pure, the result is pure.

Today is a good day to teach your children the importance of asking God to reveal our motives. For example, if we give to the church simply to get a tax write-off, it's a wrong motive. A motive like that does not please the Lord. And honestly? It taints the gift and casts a shadow on the giver.

If you feel a check in your spirit about your motives, don't ignore it. Come before the Lord in prayer and ask Him to search your heart like He did David's. What you see may be painful, but it will give you an opportunity to bring your heart and your motives into alignment with God's own heart.

Praise > Panic

You will hear of wars and threats of wars, but don't panic.

MARK 13:7

IT SEEMS THERE'S A LOT TO be worried about in the world right now. How can we teach our children to be at peace in a world full of panic and fear? The answer is both simple and profound.

The answer is praise.

As many of my readers know, I was diagnosed with a panic disorder in my early twenties. Years of hidden physical and emotional abuse caught up with me just as I was preparing for motherhood. PTSD is not much fun. My childhood had set me up for years of private pain and a struggle with the spirit of fear, but God stood ready to bring hope and healing to my broken heart.

Praise the Lord, He has been so faithful! For the most part, I don't suffer from anxiety today. Sure, it rears its ugly head now and again, but I no longer live in the state of panic that I did for so many years. This didn't happen by itself. One thing the Lord showed me is something I have tried to pass on to my children: the power of praise.

Praise really is the best antidote to panic. Have you ever noticed that when you sing to the Lord, your heart becomes focused on Him? I believe this is by design. God loves it when you give Him praise, so it makes sense that as you praise God, the things of this earth really do, in the words of the old hymn, "grow strangely dim."

Honestly? If you struggle with anxiety, panic, and fear, it is likely that your children will inherit this struggle too. Part of our job as mothers is to give our children tools in their emotional and spiritual toolbelt so that they can handle the things life throws at them. Today, make sure they know about the gift of praise. The next time you feel the panic rise inside of you, turn up the praise music, lift your hands to the heavens, and dance around the living room like no one except God Himself is watching. Then, see what happens as the spirit of the living God replaces your fear with His perfect peace.

Praise really is the antidote to panic.

When Friendships End

Their disagreement was so sharp that they separated. Barnabas took John Mark with him and sailed for Cyprus.

ACTS 15:39

SANDY MILLAR, A RETIRED ANGLICAN BISHOP from the Province of Uganda, often says, "The calling is divine; but the relationships are human!" I agree.

Relationships can be hard. Really hard.

Ever since Adam and Eve got kicked out of the Garden of Eden, it seems that we've been struggling to get along. Over the years, I have found myself on both the giving and the receiving end of sharp disagreements with friends. It comforts me to know that I'm not alone, though—even the most sincere Christians sometimes need to part ways. I think this is why God made sure to include this short account of Paul and Barnabas's separation.

It's impossible to know exactly why Paul was so dead set against Barnabas taking John Mark along, but the bottom line is that Paul didn't trust him. Where there's no trust, there can be no real relationship either.

We have all felt the sting of the end of a friendship—but mom, let me tell you, you can have a positive impact on your kids by showing them the *right way* to disengage from a friendship.

The thing to note here is the absolute *lack of drama* that you see in this account of Paul and Barnabas's separation. No gossip. No long-drawn-out arguments. I don't see that they called the rest of the disciples into the disagreement. When they realized that the situation was unworkable, they parted ways.

After they parted, it doesn't appear that the disagreement slowed down their calling either. Paul chose Silas, and before he left, the believers there prayed over him and entrusted him to God. His ministry continued.

We can learn a lot from Paul and Barnabas. Let's teach our children the importance of handling disagreements in a godly way. If a friendship must end, we should do our best to honor God in the separating. When we do this, our children learn to be better disciples of the Lord Jesus.

When friendships end, your ministry doesn't need to. Whenever possible, part in the spirit of Christ. You never know what God will do!

No Time for Bitterness

You have turned my mourning into joyful dancing. You have taken away my clothes of mourning and clothed me with joy, that I might sing praises to you and not be silent.

PSALM 30:11-12

IN A SORT OF MODERN-DAY RELIVING of Paul's imprisonment, Cuban pastor Noble Alexander served over twenty-two years in a Cuban prison, where he endured starvation, hard labor, and lengthy periods in solitary confinement.

Why? After serving three years in pastoral ministry, Alexander preached on the origin of sin. That March 20, 1962, sermon turned his world upside down.

Convinced that Alexander's sermon was an attack on Communist leader Fidel Castro, government security forces ambushed the twenty-eight-year-old pastor and arrested him. Soon Alexander was tried and convicted of conspiring to assassinate Castro. He then spent more than two decades of his life in a Cuban prison. Not long after his conviction, Alexander's wife, Yraida, divorced her young husband and chose to marry a Communist leader.

Despite being wrongly accused, illegally imprisoned, and betrayed by his wife, Alexander stood firm in his faith. He continuously praised God. He was secretly ordained in prison in 1979 by another of Castro's political prisoners, Pastor Pedro de Armas.

Pastor Alexander was in his fifties when he was eventually liberated from prison and flown to Washington, DC, on June 26, 1984, thanks to the work of a network of Christians in the United States. Instead of being angry at what had happened to him, Alexander began a ministry in the United States. God blessed him with a new wife and a powerful ministry. His mourning truly was turned to dancing.

Before his passing in 2002, Alexander wrote, "In spite of the painful reflections and memories, I have no time for bitterness. My life is filled with too much happiness, too many loving, caring people to allow myself to be devoured by the cancer of hate. I rejoice. I sing. I laugh. I celebrate, because I know that my God reigns supreme over all the forces of evil and destruction Satan has ever devised. And best of all—my God reigns supreme in me!"[7]

We can learn so much from this giant of the faith! He remained focused on the eternal God he served rather than his temporary circumstances. Moms, lean into this truth right now. We don't know what is ahead of us, but God does. Wherever life takes us, God will be there.

---

7 Quote found at persecutionblog.com/2007/06/extreme_devotio.html.

Good Roots, Good Fruit

A tree is identified by its fruit. If a tree is good, its fruit will be good. If a tree is bad, its fruit will be bad.

MATTHEW 12:33

As a mother, I like to think of myself as a bit of an arborist. Arborists are basically tree doctors. I'm basically a kid doctor, right? Anyway. Arborists are awesome. They'll come in and inspect your tree, let you know if it needs to be pruned, and suggest things that will help you keep your tree healthy. A good arborist also knows when it's time to cut a tree down.

Several years ago, we hired a friend of ours to come out and inspect the trees in our yard. We live in a little bit of the forest, and every once in a while, strong winds will come through. Healthy trees can survive the storms. Unhealthy trees cannot. The trees on our property are hundreds of feet tall. If one of them were to fall, it could hit our house. Needless to say, we keep an eye on the health of our trees.

The same thing holds true for our fruit trees. Jay's mom planted several fruit trees, which are just now beginning to bear fruit. Unfortunately, not all of the fruit has been good. One of our fruit trees got an infection, and eventually, we had to take it out so that the infection didn't spread to the other trees.

Jesus correctly pointed out the parallels between human beings and fruit trees in Matthew 12. A tree really is identified by its fruit.

Good moms are arborists, and I have learned a lot from tending to my trees . . . and my kiddos.

Healthy trees need pruning. Healthy children need pruning also. Notice a bad attitude? It's time for some loving pruning! Watch for any sign of infection. Healthy trees need good soil. So do healthy children. The "soil" a healthy child needs is the rich soil of the Bible. Water daily with prayer, and then watch for good fruit. It may take time, but keep at it! Good things are coming.

The Way Out

When you are tempted, he will show you a way out so that you can endure.

1 CORINTHIANS 10:13

THERE IS A GIANT HORNET STUCK in my window right now. As I type this, I can hear it—frantically buzzing in the window, trying to escape into the yard. Occasionally, he seems to reevaluate his approach, and his buzzing stops—but within a minute or two, it starts up again, more frantic than before. He flies from side to side, always looking through the glass, never knowing he is doomed unless he turns and flies toward an open door rather than continuing to plow into a window that can never open.

Now don't get me wrong. I *hate* hornets, but I have tried to let this guy out of my dining room twice. I opened the windows closest to him and stood back. Nope. He seems to like his frantic, futile buzzing. Even though there are ways out, he is stuck because he can't allow himself to fly another direction.

He doesn't know that the other direction offers a way out.

I have to laugh at how often I am like that stupid hornet. How many times have I kept using the same, failing technique with one of my kids, only to be disappointed with the result? I know it's not going to work, and the effort it will take me to try a different approach keeps me from succeeding.

Come to think of it, the Bible teaches us about open doors too. In 1 Corinthians 10:13, God says He will provide a way out when we are tempted by sin—but boy, is it easy to ignore the way out and fly right back into the situation that ensures our failure.

Today, when you're tempted to keep flying headlong into a closed window, ask the Lord for the grace to make a course correction. In so doing, you will learn how to offer a course correction for your children. God is always there, ready to show us the way out. All we need to do is look up and follow Him.

Good News for Hard Days

"Am I only a God nearby," declares the LORD, "and not a God far away?"

JEREMIAH 23:23, NIV

SOMETIMES, THE BURDENS OF THIS WORLD are too heavy. Sometimes, the hard really does feel *too hard*.

As mothers, we are fixers, aren't we? We want to fix "all the things," as my youngest daughter would say. As I write this, the world is in chaos, and though I desperately want to fix it, I know it is beyond my ability. I can't even begin to fix it. The result? I feel helpless, and my heart is heavy. Do you feel that way too? There is a lot of brokenness in our world right now. I don't know a person who has not been affected by it.

Oh, how the world groans under the weight of sin.

Every day, it's increasingly clear how much we need Jesus! Our weary hearts need to feel His presence. Our minds need to know His truth, and our bodies need the kind of rest that only He can provide.

Praise the Lord, He *knows* this about our human hearts.

God is present in every circumstance. He never sleeps. He's on duty 24-7.

In Jeremiah 23:23, we read a warning to the false prophets. The message? They cannot hide from God. The warning was meant to terrify these wicked men—but to the one who longs to be near to the Lord, they are a great comfort. To the brokenhearted and weary, to the overwhelmed and afraid, God says, "I am near."

Jesus Christ is as near in one place as in another, precious one, and He's near to our children too. No matter what we are facing, God is near. He is a present help in times of trouble (see Psalm 46:1); He hears our cries and binds up our wounds (see Psalm 147:3). He is near to give us assistance when we are struggling, and to carry us when we feel we cannot continue on.

If your hard feels too hard today, look up. God is near. This is good news for those of us who have come to the end of ourselves, isn't it? He is near.

If you've reached the end of your own strength today, look to Jesus. He is near.

When the Warrior Needs to Rest

My flesh and my heart may fail, but God is the strength of my heart and my portion forever.

PSALM 73:26, NIV

DO YOU EVER FEEL LIKE YOUR flesh and your heart might fail? You're not alone. The psalmist David would have been nodding his head in agreement with you. He was a king and a warrior who knew how to put his struggles out there for the world to see.

As mothers, we are often weary. Pregnancy. Sleepless nights. Sick children. Grumpy teens. Dirty dishes. Most days seem to be a repeat of the day before, but with the occasional trip to the ER or the realization that we're out of milk just when we need it. It's no wonder we're tired!

Of course, the good news is that God understands. He uses even our weakness when we offer it to Him, and David was a perfect example. David was honest about his struggles. He acknowledged that his flesh couldn't be counted on—but God always could be. It's part of why we love the Psalms so much!

In 1984, CCM artist Twila Paris released the song "The Warrior Is a Child." She was only twenty-two at the time, but the lyrics offered refreshingly honest insight that many battle-weary warriors could relate to: "Lately I've been winning battles left and right / But even winners can get wounded in the fight / People say that I'm amazing / Strong beyond my years / But they don't see inside of me / I'm hiding all the tears / They don't know that I go running home when I fall down / They don't know who picks me up when no one is around / I drop my sword and cry for just a while / 'Cause deep inside this armor / The warrior is a child."

I can almost see King David listening to this song in heaven, nodding his head and wondering why God gave the lyrics to Twila instead of him!

From the outside, you might look like you've got it all figured out—but deep inside, we all have fears, insecurities, and heartache. And that's okay.

Like David, Twila acknowledged her failings and weaknesses—but she didn't stay there. She acknowledged that she went "running home" when the sword became too heavy to carry. Like David, she knew that her heavenly Father would welcome her and offer her rest.

If you need to drop your sword for a while, it's okay. The One who made you and knows you best is waiting with open arms. After all, you're *His* child.

Born for This

Who knows if perhaps you were made queen for just such a time as this?

ESTHER 4:14

THANKS TO SIN, THE WORLD IS a dark place. Political unrest. Natural disasters. Government brutality. Religious persecution. Economic instability. It's okay to be honest about the world that our children are being born into, as long as we keep in mind one thing: just like Esther, Daniel, David, Ruth—our children were born for this time in history.

The sovereign God of the universe knew that we would be here right now. God chose you in the same way He is choosing your children, and He will provide for you and your children in the same way He provides for the birds of the air.

As a mother of seven, I must choose every day to release my children to the unique purpose God has created them for. I hate to see them hurt, and God, who is our Father, knows this feeling better than anyone. After all, He sent His only Son into this world to be the sacrifice for our sin.

The war is real—but remember, the victory will belong to God. He's not up in heaven wondering if He should've picked another mom. He chose you for this. So don't feel afraid for your children because the world is changing so quickly; instead, raise them up to know the power that is available to them as children of the living God.

Teach them that they are not an accident of nature but rather that they were created on purpose *with* a purpose. They were literally born for this battle. Raise them up in the nurture of the Word, and arm them with the authority that comes from knowing it. Remind them that with God, all things are possible. Tell them about the courageous men and women of the Bible who faced great danger and trouble by accessing the power of the living God.

Our children are today's Deborahs and Daniels. Be honored that God chose you to raise them up as servants of the Most High God, and then release them to walk out God's plan for their lives with confidence.

They were born for this—and so were we.

The Wonder Years

Children are a gift from the LORD; they are a reward from him.
PSALM 127:3

I'VE BEEN SPEAKING TO HOMESCHOOL MOMS for nearly two decades now. When I started speaking to other homeschool moms, I was very much in the throes of my own motherhood journey. I had a new high schooler and a new baby.

When a mom asked me what it was like to have very young children, I casually remarked, "I love the young years—they are the 'wonder years'!" The room erupted in laughter as I went on to explain why: when our kids are young, it's a time to instill a *sense of wonder* in them. Our children come to us with a natural sense of curiosity about the world around them. As mothers, we should respond to this by pointing out the wonders of creation—insects, the stars and moon, animals, plants.

God's creation is a miracle—from the tiniest atom to the largest planet in our solar system. Think about it, mom! We have birds that talk and plants that eat insects! God's creativity knows no bounds. It truly is a wonder! The question is, do our kids see it that way?

The Bible teaches us that our children are a gift from God. They are a reward—and we get to enjoy them. What a privilege! When was the last time you saw your purpose to instill a sense of wonder in your children? When was the last time you marveled at the design on a spider (okay, that might be asking too much) or looked at the details of a flower through a microscope? The fingerprints of God are everywhere.

The wonder years are full of opportunities to build a strong foundation for a love of God's creation that will last a lifetime for your children. Investing in your children is worth it, busy moms! Get outside. Study God's world together, and watch your children grow to appreciate that they are part of God's amazing creation, right down to the color of their eyes.

As your children get older, you can continue to remind them of the awesome creativity and power of God by simply noticing it yourself. When was the last time you modeled the wonder of King David or Solomon? At every age, your kids are watching. God is the God of awestruck wonder, isn't He? Let's praise Him for it!

Sleepy Visits with God

He will gently lead the mother sheep with their young.

ISAIAH 40:11

Have you ever fallen asleep while you were praying? Be honest—no one's watching but the One who knows that the answer is probably yes.

I confess, when I was a very young mother, I fell asleep praying many times. I even fell asleep reading my Bible! Sometimes I would try to read the Bible when I was nursing an infant, and if the baby fell asleep, I did too. Occasionally I would startle awake and instantly feel the need to apologize to the Lord. The guilt was real! Surely the Lord saw me as one of the disciples in the Garden of Gethsemane—the ones who could not stay awake as Jesus was waiting to be arrested!

But is this really what our heavenly Father wants us to think about Him? I don't think so. In Isaiah, we see that our Lord wants to "gently lead" those of us who have children. This is the heart of the Good Shepherd, and He has a true father's heart.

Some years ago, through a conversation with a seasoned mom, the Lord gently opened my eyes to how He sees me when I pray to Him and doze off, or when I fall asleep reading His precious book. He feels the same way about me that I do about my own children. In fact, He loves us moms even more than we love our own children! Can you even fathom that kind of love?

How do you feel when your precious child feels so comfortable, so safe, and so loved that they fall asleep in your lap? Are you angry? Of course not. The fact that our kids feel safe enough to rest completely tells us that we are loving them well.

In fact, I love it when my kids fall asleep on my lap. Most of my kids are grown now, but my grands are starting to fall asleep in my lap. Sometimes, I don't make it to the end of the story before I feel that familiar weight of slumber setting in. They feel safe. They know I love them.

The next time you have a sleepy visit with God, know that He is glad you feel safe in His arms too. After all, you're *His child.* He loves you, precious mom.

It's Who He Is

The LORD is good; his steadfast love endures forever, and his faithfulness to all generations.

PSALM 100:5, ESV

FEW VERSES CONTAIN A MORE PROFOUND truth or a more powerful promise than Psalm 100:5.

It begins with a thunderous, glorious declaration that supersedes all of the enemy's lies, all of this world's sinister whispers, and all of our own doubts: "The LORD is good!" Those four words resonate within my heart every single morning when I wake up. They should be ever present in your heart too. These words are the reason Horatio Spafford could write "It Is Well with My Soul" in 1873 following the loss of all four of his daughters when the ship they were on sank in the Atlantic Ocean.

Despite all that he had suffered, Spafford clung to this simple, eternal truth: the Lord is good. That fact alone can provide peace in the midst of unimaginable tragedy. Do you know that the Lord is good? Do you know it deep in your "knower," where it can never be shaken? In those four words is the hope that meets us at the end of the darkest hallways of this passing life.

But that's not all. This good Lord's love will endure forever. Forever—not just when we're good. Not just when we seek forgiveness. Not just when we're living a life pleasing to Him. His love endures forever, and it is steady. Unshakable. Unmovable. Never changing. There is seldom a day when I don't think about this truth. I can't count on myself to consistently do the right thing. I battle constantly with my flesh. Can you relate? My love ebbs and flows, conditional at times and far away at other times. But the love of our good Lord never wavers. Circumstances don't change it. It endures forever.

Finally, God's faithfulness is to *all* generations. From Adam to Noah to Abraham to David to Jesus to you. Moreover, his faithfulness extends to our children, our grandchildren, and to every generation yet to come. We can entrust our lives and the lives of those we love to the steadfast, good, enduring love and faithfulness of this incredible God.

Meditate on this simple verse today. Ponder these three profound truths and let your soul soak in them. The Lord is good. His love is steady and goes on forever. He is faithful to every generation—past, present, and those yet to come. That's you, your children, their children, and their children's children. What an awesome thing to know that this kind of love is available to us! It's not that we deserve it. It's simply who He is.

Heal Our Land

> If my people, who are called by my name, will humble themselves and pray and seek my face and turn from their wicked ways, then I will hear from heaven, and I will forgive their sin and will heal their land.
>
> **2 CHRONICLES 7:14,** NIV

You're holding a book in your hands that was written during 2020 and 2021. It was a dark time for the United States and for the world, quite frankly. As I wrote this book, I wanted so much to encourage you, but honestly? There were months I struggled to come up with anything that felt encouraging. Have you been there too?

Many times, I found myself on my knees asking God to give me *anything* to encourage you, and all I heard in response was "Ask them to pray."

We have so much to pray about, don't we? Often, our first response to trouble or heartache is to phone a friend or to fret (or in my case, to purge my house). But I wonder—what are we teaching our kids when prayer is a last resort rather than a first? John 14:1 says, "Don't let your hearts be troubled. Trust in God, and trust also in Me." What should we teach our kids to pray when our hearts are troubled about the world around us?

We should teach our kids to pray . . .

- that God's people would return to God's Word and God's way.
- that we would not be ruled by the spirit of fear, but that we would stand in the knowledge that God has given us "a spirit of power and of love and of a sound mind" as the Bible teaches in 2 Timothy 1:7 (KJV).
- that our hearts would be at peace, no matter the storms we are facing.

Precious ones, God is aware of everything that we're going through. He is listening—and He wants us to pray! Pray with your family today. Lay it all out there.

The nations need the healing touch of God.

Father, heal our land. Bring us back to You.

Leading in Times of Fear

Even when I walk through the darkest valley, I will not be afraid, for you are close beside me.
PSALM 23:4

RECENTLY, MY FAMILY ENJOYED DINNER AT the home of a local pastor and his wife. We sat around his living room for hours, remembering what it was like in April of 2020, when he opened the doors of his church again. As the shepherds of their flock in Vancouver, Washington, Bill and Talia Henry were processing a lot. How could they encourage their people through a season of fear?

As mothers, we are also shepherds. When times of fear surround us, God calls us to lead our children by example. A cursory read-through of the Bible clearly shows that courage is a trait God honors. But what does it look like? The Henrys led by example when they opened their church's doors in spite of the fear surrounding the pandemic. They shared hope and healing with their church family. As a result, the church was strengthened and encouraged.

Courage is best displayed when we refuse to be overcome by fear. I once heard fear described by this acronym: **F**alse **E**vidence **A**ppearing **R**eal.

Fear, like all things from the devil, is a liar. When fear determines our decisions, we need to check in with the Lord and ask for wisdom. Psalm 23 reminds us that He is "close beside" us, even through our darkest valleys. Jesus understands our fear.

Was Jesus ever afraid? Yes, He was. In the Garden of Gethsemane, Jesus was afraid of what lay ahead of Him. He knew He was about to suffer a terrible injustice. Yet, He knew that His Father would be with Him, even through the agony that awaited Him at the Cross.

Our children are watching the example we are setting for them in the midst of all of the turmoil and uncertainty in our world.

Today, let's pray against the spirit of fear, both in our lives and in the lives of our children. Let's ask God to give courage to Christian leaders and pastors. Let's ask God to embolden us to lay hands on the sick and the suffering without fear, and to anoint with oil the heads of those who are desperate for healing, whether it is spiritual, emotional, or physical.

The Bible says our days have been ordained for us. Our timetable has been determined by our Creator. This is not an excuse to act foolishly, but rather, it is permission to live out our call to ministry courageously.

Our children are going to model their behavior after us. Are we leading well?

I'm Sorry

Therefore, since we are surrounded by such a huge crowd of witnesses to the life of faith, let us strip off every weight that slows us down, especially the sin that so easily trips us up.

HEBREWS 12:1

IN MOTHERHOOD, TESTS OF OUR EMOTIONAL and spiritual maturity seem to happen daily. I remember a specific time I failed one such test and lost my temper. The frustration and anger had been building inside for days. I felt like the kids weren't listening to my instructions. Rather than communicate my frustration maturely, I was short with them.

Finally, after what seemed the millionth time of asking the kids to clean up, I launched into full "martyr mom" mode. To my embarrassment, words no good mother would say tumbled out: "You *never* listen to me! I'm sick of you! Just go away!" I'm sure there was more—but you get the idea. That "cloud of witnesses" my husband and I had created in harmony with a holy God stared blankly at me, dumbfounded their mother could sink to such a level. Hot tears ran down my face, a mixture of shame and embarrassment. *How had it come to this?* Here I was, wounding the people I love most in this world over a sink full of dirty dishes!

"What is wrong with me?" I asked myself out loud.

"I'm sorry, kids," I said quietly. "Mama needs a minute. I'll be right back."

As I retreated to my bedroom, Hebrews 12:1 came to my mind. The apostle Paul got it right. Sin really does trip us up. We can be justified in our anger, but that doesn't excuse sin. Motherhood can be challenging, but God wants us to grow as we go!

We need to walk closely with the Lord, seeing Him as our friend and counselor. When stress builds, we have an advocate in the Holy Spirit. As I prayed, the Lord began to replace frustration with a profound sense of *acceptance*. I needed to accept that I was in the midst of training my children to obey, with the hope that at some point, they would be obedient. I was teaching them to cook, clean, and make their beds, knowing one day they would be blessed by these skills.

It's been years since that particular failure. There have been many more since then, but that "cloud of witnesses" and the tests motherhood provides are now my favorite testimony. My children make their beds now. They're teaching their own children to be obedient—and they remember that I was able to say, "I'm sorry."

Hang in there, precious mom—the testimony will be worth the test.

Especially Now

Let us not neglect our meeting together, as some people do, but encourage one another, especially now that the day of his return is drawing near.

HEBREWS 10:25

BEFORE I WAS AN AUTHOR, SPEAKER, or congressional candidate, I was a worship pastor's wife for nearly twenty years.. We often tell people that we "cut our teeth" for what God was calling us to do by working in churches. I will always have a love for the body of Christ. The church is meant to be a gift!

Although Jay is no longer pastoring full-time, we are still working in ministry together. God has called us to encourage His people to stay the course and to run the race with endurance. In the nearly two years that it took me to compile this devotional, this challenge has been immense. The world has shifted. Something happened in 2020 that shook our world, our families, and the church to its core.

In 2020, we learned the value of meeting together. We were created for relationship, first with the One who made us and loves us and then with one another. The apostle Paul knew that at some point, we would take the ability to meet in person for granted, so he warned us not to grow complacent about it: "Let us not neglect our meeting together, as some people do, but encourage one another, especially now that the day of his return is drawing near" (Hebrews 10:25).

Do you see the day of His return "drawing near"? I know you do. The church is not just a building, and yes, we can worship online, but we need to remain close in person, and our children need to see us *gathering* together. We need each other, especially now. There's encouragement to be found when we hold hands, laugh, cry, and pray together. Paul was right. We must not forsake gathering together.

Online church is a great stopgap if you're sick or unable to attend a local body of Christ. But don't let it become "normal" to your kids. They need to see that as Christians, we do not forsake gathering.

Especially now.

Be Present

> Be careful how you live. Don't live like fools, but like those who are wise. Make the most of every opportunity in these evil days. Don't act thoughtlessly, but understand what the Lord wants you to do.
>
> **EPHESIANS 5:15-17**

NEARLY TWENTY YEARS AGO, I BEFRIENDED a mom who constantly complained about what she perceived as a "missed opportunity" to be doing something more meaningful than staying home with her young boys.

"I hate it here," she said, as she pointed to her minivan. "I feel stuck. One day, I'm going to get a real job. I worry that my life is passing me by."

She was right, of course. Life *was* passing her by. She *was* missing an opportunity. She just didn't realize that the opportunity she was missing was right in front of her: the opportunity to build a lifelong relationship with her boys. Sadly, in her desire to do something "big," she was unable to be present for her boys and enjoy being their mom.

It's easy to miss the point when we're with our kids every. single. day. It's easy to whine about how we want "me time" and how frustrating it is to always be communicating on a third-grade level. But we can look to Jesus, who knew the value of being present.

Does this sound vaguely familiar? If so, you're not alone. But moms, we've got to get this right.

It's hard to be present today, isn't it? Social media and our instant access to distractions have made this a difficult sell.

Being present is challenging with all the distractions of the modern world—but we must learn to be present so we don't end up missing out on the most valuable moments we have in this world: the moments God gives us with our kids.

It's easier to lose ourselves in scrolling social media on our phones than it is to engage with our kids—but we won't get another chance at raising our children.

Being present is a rigorous demand. It's never easy. It requires that we become truly aware. If we want our kids to remember that we were present in their growing up, we need to clear the clutter from our lives and ask God to help us to be truly "careful" how we live. The time goes by fast!

He Hears

This is the confidence we have in approaching God: that if we ask anything according to his will, he hears us.

1 JOHN 5:14, NIV

HAVE YOU EVER MET A TRUE intercessor whose heart is always in prayer mode? While prayer might be the second thing I think to do in times of crisis, an intercessor thinks of it first. My grandmother was one. How I miss her! No problem was too small. She would stop what she was doing and begin to talk to God.

My friend Collette is the same way. When I text her, peace floods my soul because I know the situation will be covered in prayer. In today's Scripture, John says we can have *confidence* in approaching God, and when we pray according to God's will, He hears us.

Can you imagine it!? The Lord of the universe *hears us when we pray.* What an incredible privilege it is to be able to bring our fears, hopes, concerns, and praise before the Lord in prayer. I hope someday my own children and grandchildren will remember that I too was a woman of prayer. I hope you don't mind, but today, instead of my usual devotion, I'd like to pray with you.

Lord Jesus, We come before You today with one voice to say that we love You. Thank You for dying for us. Thank You for saving us. Thank You that nothing that is happening around us right now is escaping Your sight. You are El Roi, the God who sees. Father, today we ask that Your spirit would blaze brightly in our hearts! Help us to shine for You—first for our children and then for others to see. May our lives bring You glory.

Give us courage, God. Soften our hearts to hear Your still, small voice. Give us hearts like David. Search us to see if there is anything in our lives that grieves You, and help us get rid of it.

Forgive our complacency about so many things that are plaguing our nation and our world. Bring our hearts back into alignment with Yours. Break our hearts for what breaks Yours, and send us out as Your ambassadors. Give us opportunities to bring hope and healing to those we meet. Help me to love my family well today. Help me to be patient and kind. Give me joy.

Bring revival, Lord. Let it start with me, with my family, in my home. Help me be the woman you have created me to be in every relationship I have. Thank You for listening—thank You that you hear me.

In Jesus' name, Amen.

Every Moment

You saw me before I was born. Every day of my life was recorded in your book. Every moment was laid out before a single day had passed.

PSALM 139:16

A FRIEND ONCE CALLED ME "CAPTAIN ANXIETY" because, she said, I was "able to leap to the worst conclusion in a single bound."

Me? Okay, yes. She knew me well. Becoming a mom heightened this for me. Suddenly I wasn't just worried about myself—I was worried about a tiny person who was totally dependent on me for every little thing! I'll never forget the first broken bone or the time I lost my son in a hotel after he jumped out of my arms and onto an elevator going I didn't know where. My sixth child has life-threatening allergies. When my youngest broke her arm in two places, I don't know who hurt more—Saylor or her mama.

Those heartstrings are strong, aren't they?

Just about the time we mature enough in our walk with God to realize that He is our source of strength, wisdom, protection, and provision, we have children. Aaaaand it's a whole new ballgame.

Suddenly, we're worried about another human being. A person who, like all humans, could suffer injury, disease, rejection, or heartbreak. And we want to protect them from all these things, but of course we can't.

By the way, this doesn't stop just because the kids grow up. In some respects, it gets harder. (Hey, don't shoot the messenger!)

Here's where we need to believe the truth of God's Word to the core of our being.

Precious mom, lean in. I'm going to gently speak truth to your mama heart. Here it is: *your days . . . and the days of your children . . . have already been ordained by God.* This precious truth from God's Word means that we do not have to worry. Our lives, and the lives of our kids, are in His hands.

This is not a license to be reckless. Rather, it's reason to rest.

Stop worrying. Breathe. Enjoy every moment, and trust God for the future. Whatever is ahead, His grace will meet you there.

Commanded to Be Courageous

Have I not commanded you? Be strong and courageous. Do not be afraid; do not be discouraged, for the LORD your God will be with you wherever you go.

JOSHUA 1:9, NIV

WHEN WAS THE LAST TIME YOU talked about courage with your kids? Do they know what it means?

courage *noun*
the ability to do something that frightens one

My grandmother was a spitfire. I'll never forget her response to me when I was hesitating to try out for a play in elementary school. She said, "Heidi, you can do anything God is calling you to do—but you might have to do it afraid!" What she was teaching me was that fear was not something that should keep me from stepping out beyond my comfort zone.

Second Timothy 1:7 tells us that "God has not given us a spirit of fear."

Did you catch that? God has *not* given us a spirit of fear. Fear does not come from God. God offers us peace when the world is prone to panic. Do your kids know that down deep in their own hearts? Because they *need* to know—and you're the one God has called to teach them.

One way Christians can discern things that are happening around them is to watch how people are behaving. Fear has a way of clouding our judgment and keeping us from moving forward in situations that cause our hearts to tremble. But as God's people, we need to do better. We must be of sound mind, asking God for wisdom. He is with us, ready to help.

There is, of course, a "healthy" kind of fear. When we teach our children not to touch a hot stove for fear of getting burned, that's healthy. Once we understand that unhealthy fear is not from God, we can identify how we should respond to it.

Courage is doing what you know you're supposed to, even in the face of fear. It's pushing through and stepping up to the piano for your first recital. It's getting on the track team and running your first race. It's speaking the truth even though your voice is shaking. It's refusing to participate in something you know to be wrong, even though the consequences may be dire.

For the Christian, courage is not optional. It's required. God commands it. In exchange, God offers peace in the midst of panic and wisdom when we feel overcome with worry.

Be strong and courageous, mom! God is at your side!

The Great Pretender

Stay alert! Watch out for your great enemy, the devil. He prowls
around like a roaring lion, looking for someone to devour.

1 PETER 5:8

PAUL WASN'T KNOWN FOR SUGARCOATING OR PANDERING. While we tend to focus
on people as the source of our frustration, Paul knew the spiritual battle was the
one we need to keep our eyes on. Check out his clear admonition from Ephesians:
"Our struggle is not against flesh and blood, but against the rulers, against the
authorities, against the powers of this dark world and against the spiritual forces
of evil in the heavenly realms" (Ephesians 6:12, NIV).

Even though we have been warned, our human hearts want to blame what we
see with our eyes. Mom, lean in, because if we fail to understand this truth, we will
not be able to prepare our children to walk in it. We are absolutely in a war. It's a
war with an invisible enemy—the *adversary of your soul.*

Peter warned Christians about this a long time ago: "Stay alert! Watch out
for your great enemy, the devil. He prowls around *like* a roaring lion, looking for
someone to devour" (1 Peter 5:8, emphasis added).

If you knew there was an actual lion prowling about in your backyard, you
would be looking for even the smallest indication that he was nearby. You would
train your children to have their eyes wide open, to discern even the quietest
sounds he might make. Why? To defend yourself and your loved ones against being
devoured by the beast.

But here's something else: notice that Peter shared something very valuable
about our adversary. He is *not* a lion. He is only acting like one. Yes, he is seeking
someone to devour, but he is not the lion he wants us to believe he is. Satan is
only disguised as a lion—but you serve the Lion of Judah! Ultimately, He will be
victorious.

Satan is the great pretender. Everything he does is meant to deceive and
frighten you. He's hoping to scare you into forgetting who the real enemy and the
ultimate Victor really are. Rather than letting this pretender frighten you, put on
the full armor of God and use the weapons of prayer and worship as your primary
defense against the schemes of the devil.

You're on the winning side!

Come Away

Come to me, all you who are weary and burdened, and I will give you rest.

MATTHEW 11:28, NIV

It's been a busy season for my family. A run for Congress, an explosion of enrollments in the homeschool center, children to homeschool, college students to support, grandbabies to love on, dinner to make, a husband who needs me. Don't get me wrong, I love "all the things," as my daughter would say, but sometimes . . . sometimes you just need to take a break to refocus.

Jay had been asking me for weeks to take a night to just get away, but things always felt too pressing. I always had an excuse for why I needed to be home—which basically meant I kept working.

Last night, my husband finally convinced me, and we stole away to the Oregon coast. This morning, I'm sitting in a hotel room that we really can't afford, drinking deeply of the sound of the ocean and the smell of the salt air. I'm so glad to be here. I can feel my soul coming back to life.

Seagulls are fighting over a crab who seems to have met a rather unfortunate end. A dad is teaching his son to fly a kite. I can't help but smile as my eyes take in the beauty around me. Today I think I'm happier than the bird with a french fry who is staring at me from the balcony.

Yep. As usual, my husband was right. We needed this little overnighter. We needed to rest.

There's just something about being close to nature that soothes the spirit and refreshes the soul. Creation really does speak of the Creator. When I can remove the distractions, I can hear His still, small voice so much more clearly.

Why is it so hard for us to rest? Jay and I have been married for more than thirty-three years, and still we have to force ourselves to take a break. Moms are like this too, I think. How many times have you pushed yourself to the breaking point instead of taking a break?

A tired mom is much more likely to feel overwhelmed and lose perspective.

Jesus told us to come to Him and find rest. He knew we would need rest—so give yourself permission to take a break today, mom. Spend time with the One who made you. Enjoy His creation if you can.

All the other things can wait. Come away and be refreshed.

Choose Forgiveness

Make allowance for each other's faults, and forgive anyone who offends you. Remember, the Lord forgave you, so you must forgive others.

COLOSSIANS 3:13

ARE YOU SOMEONE WHO FINDS IT easy to forgive, or do you tend to hold a grudge? Is it easy for you to forgive unbelievers but not believers? Forgiving close friends and family can be the most difficult of all. The Word doesn't give us any loopholes for people we get to skip, even though in our flesh that sounds like a nice option!

Colossians 3 tells us to "make allowance for each other's faults." In my life, that means giving people the grace to behave as imperfect humans. Plan for it. Expect it.

Many small offenses in our lives can grow to be large grudges. When a friend says something that is offensive to me, I can choose to believe the worst about her and assume that she intentionally hurt me. I can hold a grudge, being sure about her intent to be rude. I can keep distance between us and guard myself against her, building a wall to be sure it never happens again. But the Bible tells us to take a different approach: "Most important of all, continue to show deep love for each other, for love covers a multitude of sins" (1 Peter 4:8).

Instead of believing the worst, I can take those thoughts captive (see 2 Corinthians 10:5) and consciously choose to believe the best about her, allowing for the possibility that she didn't intend to offend me at all. I can consider that her heart toward me is good, and that she may not even realize she came across the way she did. I can consider the possibility that she is hurting in a way I might not even know or be able to imagine. I can choose to forgive her, as Christ forgives me. I can show deep love for her.

In making a choice to forgive, I'm choosing to be gracious and loving, as Christ is to me. Taking it one step further, I can acknowledge that sometimes I offend people by accident, and I am thankful for their grace toward me as well.

It pleases our Father when we love others as He loves us, and choosing to forgive is one of the most tangible ways we can do this.

The Heart of the Matter

Fathers, do not provoke your children to anger by the way you treat them. Rather, bring them up with the discipline and instruction that comes from the Lord.

EPHESIANS 6:4

FOR YEARS I THOUGHT TODAY'S VERSE was talking about yelling at my kids or being impatient with them—committing active sinful behaviors directed at them. Obviously, I had my days, but generally I felt like I was doing fairly well.

Then I realized I was missing an entirely different application of this verse.

I had a nine-year-old who was acting out in very frustrating ways for a few weeks, and I was feeling stuck because I couldn't figure out the root of it.

I asked the Lord for wisdom, and He made it beautifully clear why we were having trouble. I wasn't exasperating my son by behaving sinfully toward him, but I was completely missing something he needed from me, and that was the root of the problem.

He was a kid who needed structure in his schoolwork. (Where are my checklist moms?) He needed to know our family plans. He needed to know what was expected of him so he could feel secure and take the initiative to move forward on a daily basis. I realized it had been a few weeks since I had written a list for his schoolwork and chores, so I got it done that day! And my happy kiddo came right back.

As moms, it's our job to have our finger on the pulse of the house and adjust as necessary. If our kids are cranky and disobedient, is it because our schedule is so busy that bedtimes have been pushed later and later until we're all bleary eyed and short tempered? Are we eating junk because we haven't been home to cook a healthy meal? Are the kids fighting because they've had too much unsupervised time with friends? Are we neglecting our children because we are spending too much time on our phones? It's our job to know our children's needs and adjust our expectations as they grow.

God will give wisdom as we ask for it. Ask Him today to help you care for the unique needs of your family members!

Devoted to Prayer

Devote yourselves to prayer, being watchful and thankful.

COLOSSIANS 4:2, NIV

I'LL NEVER FORGET MY FIRST POSITIVE PREGNANCY TEST. I was completely unprepared for the wave of emotions. From that moment, something inside me changed. My prayer life deepened, because I was praying for my unborn baby too. Oh, the dreams I had for this beautiful new little girl!

What dreams do you have for your children, mama? It's tempting to think we know what's best—but the question must always be "What does God want?" The only way to know the answer is to spend time in prayer. Paul said that we should "devote ourselves" to prayer.

I've often asked the Lord to help me see little seeds of God-given talent in our kids. Once I identified them, my requests changed. I need His wisdom as I water those seeds through prayer.

Is your child struggling with a challenge? Ask God about it. Is your child journeying down a dangerous path? Take it to the Lord in prayer. As children get older, our prayers change as we pray about problems too big for them to handle by themselves, or heartbreak our kisses can't fix.

Today, let's pray that the Holy Spirit will give us wisdom to counsel and encourage, so that our children can grow and eventually take flight for God's purposes.

When we see prayer as our opportunity to collaborate with God—to communicate with Him and seek His heart and His will—it changes things. When we pray, we can speak to God honestly. Our prayers make our requests known to God (see Philippians 4:6). Paul tells us in 1 Thessalonians 5:16-17 that we are to pray without ceasing. This means our prayers don't need to be formal and stiff, but an ongoing conversation we have throughout the day about everything that we're concerned with, worried about, or thankful for. God is interested in all of it.

Have you spent time listening with an open heart to the Holy Spirit about God's plan for your kids? If so, you may have already felt that gentle nudge to do more listening and less talking when it comes to the plans God has for your children. Prayer is the solution!

A mother who is devoted to prayer is a powerful force for good in the lives of her children—because she has humbly partnered with the Lord of heaven's armies on their behalf. There can be no more powerful combination in the lives of our kids. And while it can be a difficult thing to yield my plans for His, the results are always better. His ways are not our ways . . . they're better.

Called to Peace

Let the peace of Christ rule in your hearts, since as members
of one body you were called to peace.

COLOSSIANS 3:15, NIV

MORNING IS A GOOD TIME TO PRAY. Before my heart can take on the heaviness of the world, I need to hear from the Lord. After all, mothers set the tone at home—and we know how important that is! In a world full of turmoil, I want my home to be a place where my family can find respite, joy, and safety. But it's easy to let the cares of the world steal my joy and peace at home.

The Bible teaches us that we should be people who strive for peace. I am not a person who sees things in shades of gray. I am an exhorter. But exhorters have a huge weakness—we can struggle with how to be peacemakers. In Matthew 5, Jesus speaks of peacemakers as those who identify with God's family—those who are called children of the Lord (verse 9). As God's children, we should be men and women who pursue, and model, peace.

As Christians, we should be a unifying voice, not a divisive one. This does *not* mean that we bury the truth or refuse to say hard things when they need to be said. It means that whenever possible, we speak graciously to—and about—others, starting at home. It's easy to focus on the turmoil around us, but that's not God's heart for His people. As those who are shepherding the young, how might we be a force for healing and hope?

Jesus said, "*Blessed* are the peacemakers" (Matthew 5:9, emphasis added). I don't know about you, but I want the blessing of God.

Let's find that blessing today as we ask God how to bring peace into our homes and communities:

Father, forgive me for the times that I fall victim to the devil's narrative and sow seeds of frustration rather than faith. Help me to be a peacemaker today—to love a little deeper, to listen a little longer, and to give the best of me . . . not the rest of me . . . to the ones You have entrusted to my care.

Help me to be the wife, the mother, and the friend You have asked me to be, even in the midst of this crazy, upside-down world I'm living in. Give me Your words, not mine. Give me the grace to be a peacemaker.

Teach me how to speak the truth in times of trial in such a way that You are seen.

In the matchless, powerful, and beautiful name of Jesus, Amen.

Recalculating the Heart

Do all things without grumbling or disputing.

PHILIPPIANS 2:14, ESV

"RECALCULATING!" THIS IS THE WORD MY GPS seems to use more than any other word in its vocabulary. To "recalculate" means an adjustment is necessary to the route. When I hear the word, I know that I've missed a turn. If I'm not paying attention, often it's the difference between a quick turnaround and a twenty-minute delay or a missed appointment.

Warnings are there for a reason. My GPS has a job—it's to get me to my destination on time and to help me avoid traffic jams. (That's my favorite feature, by the way.)

Relationships have similar warnings. Our kids may not say, "Recalculating," but we can certainly sense when it's time, can't we? Bad attitudes, short answers, and disobedience are a few of the warning signs. Just like my GPS has a job, we have a job too! Our job is to pay close attention to the hearts of our children, so that we know when it's time to offer up our own "recalculation."

Paul said, "Do *all things* without grumbling or disputing" (emphasis added). Not some things. You shouldn't hold your child up to an impossible standard, but when you notice that they are grumbling and complaining, address it. These are heart issues that, if allowed to go unchecked, will carry over into adulthood. You are your child's GPS. Steer them in the right direction!

Ignoring the signs that a heart recalculation is necessary can have a lasting and devastating impact. Many parents ignore the warning signs until it's too late. It's much easier to help a five-year-old adjust their attitude than a fifteen-year-old.

Sometimes, we know a recalculation is necessary, but we ignore it because we want the problem to fix itself. This rarely happens. Precious mom, your role is to train your child up in the ways of the Lord and to make sure they know what the Lord expects of them.

As our kids grow into adulthood, they should know the familiar voice of the Holy Spirit. He is the one who does the recalculating for the rest of their lives. Give your kids a firm foundation, sweet mom. Don't ignore the warning signs. Pay attention to the hearts of your children.

Solace in Suffering

He went on a little farther and bowed with his face to the ground, praying, "My Father! If it is possible, let this cup of suffering be taken away from me. Yet I want your will to be done, not mine."

MATTHEW 26:39

WHEN JESUS WAS IN THE GARDEN OF GETHSEMANE, shortly before He would be arrested and eventually put to death on the cross, He asked His Father to take away the cup of suffering that He was about to endure. But God knew that Jesus' death on the cross was the only way for His story of redemption to be written. So Jesus bore up under the sin of the world, suffered in all of His humanness, and died to save us.

I have been through some tremendous suffering in my years. I've been wounded by some of the people closest to me—the ones you'd expect to have your back for your entire life. While I know that my suffering was nothing compared to what Jesus went through for us, when I ask God for an end to the pain and don't receive relief, it gives me hope to know that Jesus also asked for another way and was denied His request. He knew what it was like to be told no by our heavenly Father, yet He still had an unshakable trust in Him to move forward with His Father's will.

The King of the Universe knows what is best for me and for His glory. He knows how much it hurts. He knows I would prefer another way sometimes, but He knows what circumstances to allow in my life to prune and shape me to give glory to Him. He sees the bigger picture that I can't, and I know I can trust Him.

When you are being told no and walking a road of suffering on this earth, know that your Creator knows your deepest desires. He knows your pain, and He has left you the Holy Spirit as a helper to give you courage as you bear up under your "no." And as alone as you feel, remember that Jesus walked the same road. You can keep walking, sister. You are not alone.

No Squawking!

May these words of my mouth and this meditation of my heart be
pleasing in your sight, LORD, my Rock and my Redeemer.

PSALM 19:14, NIV

A BIRD WOKE ME UP AT five thirty this morning. It wasn't the sweet, musical kind either. It was a squawker. Right outside my window. *SQUAWK!!!!! SQUAWK!!!!* This went on for half an hour. Our family is staying on the Oregon coast right now, so I've been sleeping with the window open. You know, to hear the ocean—not a squawking alarm courtesy of a sent-from-the-devil bird.

I could've handled being awoken by a sweet chirp, even if it was an hour before I wanted to get up, but the squawk? No thanks. There's a whole lot of squawking going on in the world right now, isn't there? A whole lotta yucky, aggravating noise. It kinda puts you in a bad mood, but then I think of myself. I can be like that bird, if I'm not careful.

Paul understood a noisy culture. He was trying to wake up the church in Corinth, as they had become a sin-riddled, complacent bunch of Christian "squawkers."

In 1 Corinthians 13:1, Paul reminded the church of an important truth: "If I speak in the tongues of men or of angels, but do not have love, I am only a resounding gong or a clanging cymbal" (NIV). In other words, no one will want to listen to our words if they are said without any love. This includes our children. Ouch! When we speak, especially now, our words must carry a message of truth *and* love.

I have observed the church as it has sacrificed truth on the altar of misguided mercy, which is not love. Love tells the truth—and I pray today that our words would be seasoned with love. The hard truth is easier to hear when love is there.

Sometimes, of course, even when we do our best and our words are seasoned with love and full of truth, they are rejected. Jesus knew this well. His words were the best kind, and what did He get for the message He brought? He was killed by an angry mob whose sin had clouded their minds. He brought the message anyway.

Today could present us with a thousand opportunities to sow division and discord. Today, we have a chance to love people well. Let's handle whatever comes today with love.

No squawking!

When There Is Nothing Left

Even though the fig trees have no blossoms, and there are no grapes on the vines; even though the olive crop fails, and the fields lie empty and barren; even though the flocks die in the fields, and the cattle barns are empty, yet I will rejoice in the LORD! I will be joyful in the God of my salvation!

HABAKKUK 3:17-18

DO YOU EVER FEEL LIKE EVERYTHING is going against you? Does it seem like the unjust are winning, liars are ahead, the enemy seems to be running circles around the good guys? You're not alone.

Habakkuk is an often-missed book in our studies, yet it is so rich in foundational truth. Pastor Chuck Swindoll noted that "the book of Habakkuk pictures a frustrated prophet, much like Jonah, though Habakkuk channeled his frustration into prayers and eventually praise to God, rather than trying to run from the Lord as Jonah did."

Swindoll also notes that "the book of Habakkuk offers us a picture of a prideful people being humbled, while the righteous lived by faith in God (2:4). It reminds us that while God may seem silent and uninvolved in our world, He always has a plan."[8]

Maybe at your job you are persecuted for standing up for Christ. Maybe your spouse doesn't know the Lord, which makes every day difficult as you try to raise children in an unequally yoked marriage. Maybe you grew up in a dysfunctional home and can't figure out how a loving, all-powerful God allowed it. Maybe all of those are true for you.

At the end of the day, our faith is built on a deep gut-level knowing that the God of the Universe knows what to allow in our lives so we live in desperation for Him. Fully trusting Him for your life means that you can say, "I know that I know that my Creator knows what is best—for my sake and God's glory." When you settle here, each day has an entirely new excitement as the question "Why?" is removed from your thought process and replaced with a surety that God allowed it because He knew it would draw you to Him and you would use it for His glory.

Habakkuk understood that God had a plan that was ultimately for his good. When all I have is truly nothing, by God's grace, I can echo the words of this suffering prophet: "I will rejoice in the LORD! I will be joyful in the God of my salvation!" (Habakkuk 3:18).

Have faith, sister. You were made for His glory.

---

[8] "Habakkuk," *Insight for Living Ministries,* https://www.insight.org/resources/bible/the-minor-prophets/habakkuk.

Be Strong and Courageous

David also said to Solomon his son, "Be strong and courageous, and do the work. Do not be afraid or discouraged, for the LORD God, my God, is with you. He will not fail you or forsake you until all the work for the service of the temple of the LORD is finished."

1 CHRONICLES 28:20, NIV

BILLY GRAHAM SAID, "WHEN A BRAVE man takes a stand, the spines of others are often stiffened." Boy, do we need some bravery right now from godly men and women. We can't pass on what we don't possess, so if we don't possess courage, well, you get the idea. One of these days, our kids will be leading. Our time will be over. Our race will have been run.

In today's passage David echoes God's exhortation to Joshua before he led the people of God into the Promised Land (see Joshua 1:5-7). Throughout the Bible, we see similar instructions passed down from one leader to the next, one generation to the next. It's your generation now, mom. This is your time to lead with courage. The baton that Moses passed to Joshua has been passed on to you. The question is, will you run with it? It will require courage to run this race.

We've got a massive sin problem, and it's going to take courage to look it in the face and deal with it. We've got sin in our churches. We accept things that God clearly has condemned. We have quietly allowed the egregious act of abortion to take the lives of millions of our most innocent. These things have happened on our watch.

We are now God's chosen. We have been chosen by God to build His church. We can look at this Old Testament example that was written for our instruction, our endurance, our encouragement, and our hope, and consider *how* we are to go about the work that God has chosen us to do for such a time as this. If we are going to stand for righteousness, and if we are to train our children to do the same thing, we have to have the courage today.

Christians have an opportunity to demonstrate the kind of courage that comes from God right now. Courage that comes from God is the courage to obey—for *His* glory, not for ours.

It's going to take courage to set things right, but with God, all things are possible. What is God asking you to do right now that will require courage? How can you demonstrate righteous courage for your family and for those who are watching you?

Not sure? Ask. He'll show you.

So the World Will Know

I am praying not only for these disciples but also for all who will ever believe in me through their message. I pray that they will all be one, just as you and I are one—as you are in me, Father, and I am in you. And may they be in us so that the world will believe you sent me. I have given them the glory you gave me, so they may be one as we are one. I am in them and you are in me. May they experience such perfect unity that the world will know that you sent me and that you love them as much as you love me.

JOHN 17:20-23

RIGHT BEFORE JESUS WAS BETRAYED, He spent time in the Garden of Gethsemane alone, praying. We are privileged to read His prayer in John 17. It's one of my favorite passages in the Bible because we get to see so clearly God's specific heart for us.

In the passage, Jesus is praying not only for His disciples (we know this from verses 6 to 19), but for those "who . . . believe in me through their message" (verse 20). That's us! The disciples were the people who continued to share the story of Christ on this earth, and generations later, we are the beneficiaries.

There is one phrase we see repeatedly in this passage. Jesus asks the Father that "they will all be one" (verse 21) and that "they may be one as we are one" (verse 22). Why? So "the world will know you sent me and that you love them as much as you love me" (verse 23).

The cry of Jesus' heart as He was about to be betrayed, tortured, and crucified was that His people would be one so the world would know the love of His Father. Are we sharing this message with our children? Or are we reflecting brokenness around us rather than God's heart?

With all the division in the global church today, we would do well to refocus on Jesus' prayer from John 17. If every Christian asked the Lord each day, "Let me be one with every brother and sister in Christ, so the world will know how much You love them," what an impact we could have on the lost world! Petty arguments would be no more, forgiveness would be second nature, grace and mercy would define our relationships.

This unity can start with you, in your family, your circle of friends, your Bible Study, your church.

May we all be completely one!

Personal Responsibility

He answered, "You shall love the Lord your God with all your heart and with all your soul and with all your strength and with all your mind, and your neighbor as yourself."

LUKE 10:27, ESV

IN LUKE 10:27, JESUS TELLS IT LIKE IT IS: each of us is individually responsible for loving God and our neighbors. We are expected to take personal responsibility. (This is a message I can get behind!)

No matter what we're facing, we're all writing a story. We're writing the story of our lives, and one day, other people are going to be telling it for us. Long after the breath has left our body, the effects of how we lived, and how we responded to life's challenges, will continue.

How will we respond to the events in the news and in our families? Will we choose to harbor bitterness? Or will we take responsibility to work toward healing? Will we sit on the sidelines? Or will we stand up and help?

Before I was born, my grandma was in a car accident. She literally went through the front windshield. The trauma was severe, and she was in the hospital for a very long time. I asked her about it once, and she simply said, "I thought it was my time, but here I am. Guess God has more for me to do!"

Grandma wasn't bitter. She knew she alone could determine how she responded to her circumstances, and so she took responsibility for her response to the accident.

No talk of suing the car manufacturer. Not a word about how much she suffered. No anger at the injustice of her situation, the permanent pain she lived with afterward, or the person who ran a stop sign and hit her at fifty miles per hour.

She had a bigger picture in mind. She knew her life was telling a story, and she wanted that story, the story that I would retell someday, to be about a woman who lived a life we would be proud of. She knew her decisions and her actions in the face of trials were *her responsibility*, not someone else's.

Her character was revealed through crisis.

And our character is too.

Sympathy

Sympathize with each other.

1 PETER 3:8

HAVE YOU EVER HAD TROUBLE SYMPATHIZING with others? I have. I am not always good at the "feeling" part of motherhood. To sympathize means that you are aware of what others are feeling and share in their suffering.

I'll never forget the time (and to be sure, this was a low point for me) when I barked at my grumpy toddler only to find out later that she had a double ear infection. Talk about a bad mom moment.

There are many things we do to keep harmony and unity in our homes. When we sympathize with others, we are trying to understand what they are going through. To do that, we need to get good at asking questions.

What made my husband snap at me? Is something I don't know about going on? Is he tired?

Why is my toddler frustrated? Is he getting enough sleep? Has his diet changed? Could he be sick?

Why is my teen moody? How are her friendships? Grades? Hormones?

To be sympathetic means to truly enter into another person's life, to share their emotions and experiences. This might look like sharing in your child's excitement over being in the school play or grieving with your child over a lost friendship.

Romans 12:15 says, "Rejoice with those who rejoice, and weep with those who weep" (NASB). What would happen if we taught our children to relate to their siblings this way? What if we taught them to seek to understand their family members, figure out what they're experiencing, and then celebrate or sympathize with them?

The next time you are struggling to understand your spouse or your children, try to put yourself in their shoes before you try to "fix it."

Sometimes, just entering into your child's struggle and letting them know you care is enough. Not sure how to do that? Ask the Lord. He'll show you!

Developing Maturity

When troubles of any kind come your way, consider it an opportunity for great joy. For you know that when your faith is tested, your endurance has a chance to grow. So let it grow, for when your endurance is fully developed, you will be perfect and complete, needing nothing. If you need wisdom, ask our generous God, and he will give it to you. He will not rebuke you for asking.

JAMES 1:2-5

HAVE YOU EVER WANTED TO STOP ADULTING? I have. I'll be honest, my first response when I'm in a trouble spot in my life is not to stop and consider it joy.

It's much easier to crawl into bed and pull the covers over my head, complain to my closest friends, and feel sorry for myself. But that doesn't really do anything to solve the problem or endure the trial. As I mature, I do recognize that learning to survive the trial and walk *through* it rather than avoid it develops maturity in me, which makes the next trial easier to endure.

Remember, you can't pass on what you don't possess. This includes maturity. I've been amazed at my ability to be totally immature in front of my children. God continues to be patient with me as I grow in Him. *Lord, I want to be more mature than I was yesterday.*

God is growing us up in so many ways through mothering. As I've grown, I've learned to depend on the first part of James 1:5: "If you need wisdom, ask our generous God, and he will give it to you." I picture it like a gift sitting on a shelf, ready for us to access it freely—if we would only ask.

This asking thing, however, requires maturity. When we grow, we see our need for wisdom!

Proverbs 9:10 tells us that the "fear of the LORD is the foundation of wisdom." So that fear is a humble reverence for Him, and the natural response is a need for Him. Then as we trust God to give wisdom as He promises, we apply the wisdom He gives as we walk through these troubles that are sure to come. Our faith is tested, and over the years, our endurance grows and fully develops.

What hope is offered there in a simple action of us humbling ourselves and asking our generous God for wisdom!

Say So!

Let the redeemed of the LORD say so.

PSALM 107:2, ESV

OUR WORLD IS ASKING QUESTIONS RIGHT now that up until very recently would have been considered absurd. We are openly debating whether or not men can get pregnant and give birth. We're allowing boys into girls' locker rooms and onto girls' sports teams. How did we get here? Simple. We got here by uninviting God from our nation.

Instead of keeping God and His will for us first, we placed our love of self and our own desires above all other things. Instead of seeking unity in Christ, we invited the spirit of division. We did it—and the only way to wrestle free from the enemy's grasp is to repent of our sins and then to speak truth and life to each other.

We need to invite God back into our nation, into our schools, into our government, and yes, into our churches. Worldly wisdom won't fix this. We need the forgiveness of God and His wisdom.

So here's some truth and life I want to speak to you today:

We may see only our differences and be drawn to division and taking sides for every topic, but we have one very important thing in common: we are all members of the human race—created in the image of our Creator. We are all sinners in need of a Savior. And He is *weeping* at what we are doing to each other.

I speak the truth because I am compelled to speak it. I'm compelled because I know the power of forgiveness. God rescued me. Did you know that? He took Heidi, a girl who was born into pain and generational abuse, and lifted me out of a pit. Me! Nothing I did could save me from my suffering—but God could. He did.

He's the chain-breaker. He's the way-maker. There is no other way to get out of this mess than to turn to Him.

I've read to the end of the book. As Christians, we already know how it turns out. God's love and forgiveness win in the end.

In the meantime, I'll keep speaking truth into a world steeped in lies. I know who I am. I am redeemed.

If you know Him, speak out. Share the truth of God's love and redeeming grace with everyone. The world needs to hear it.

Self-Control Pleases God

God is working in you, giving you the desire and the power to do what pleases him. Do everything without complaining and arguing, so that no one can criticize you. Live clean, innocent lives as children of God, shining like bright lights in a world full of crooked and perverse people.

PHILIPPIANS 2:13-15

IN OUR CULTURE TODAY, IT IS almost normal to explore your sexuality as a teenager, cheat on your spouse, fudge on your taxes, use someone else's Netflix login, grumble and complain about anything that doesn't go your way, air your dirty laundry on social media, gossip about your friend when they frustrate you, and so much more. We expect these things of unbelievers. But Christians should live according to a higher standard.

God has given us the Holy Spirit to be a helper as we walk through these days on earth. Ask the Lord to alert you before you act in an ungodly manner—He will do it. I've been asking Him for years for help in this way! Then when you hear the voice of the Holy Spirit, it's up to you to act on that prompting with self-control.

Frankly, the bar is set fairly low at the moment, as we compare ourselves to a "world full of crooked and perverse people," but what an opportunity we have to shine like stars in the universe as we are set apart in each and every one of our actions. Politely handle a customer service frustration even when the company is in the wrong. Honor your spouse even when he is short tempered. Control your tongue even when you are tempted to curse. Choose not to friend that old flame on Facebook, even if it seems harmless. Speak cheerful words that are life giving to those around you even when you are spent.

As Paul reminds us in Philippians, "God is working in you, giving you the desire and the power to do what pleases him."

We are not alone, because the Holy Spirit will make us capable of living differently when we walk with Him!

Altar of Remembrance

Joshua said to the Israelites, "In the future your children will ask, 'What do these stones mean?' Then you can tell them, 'This is where the Israelites crossed the Jordan on dry ground.' For the LORD your God dried up the river right before your eyes, and he kept it dry until you were all across, just as he did at the Red Sea when he dried it up until we had all crossed over. He did this so all the nations of the earth might know that the LORD's hand is powerful, and so you might fear the LORD your God forever."

JOSHUA 4:21-24

As MOMS, I THINK IT'S DIFFICULT to be vulnerable with our children when we're walking through hard times. Of course, when they are little, it's not appropriate to share what might be stressful for them, and then as they get older, we are in the habit of bearing our troubles alone or wrongly thinking we need to be stoic for everyone else who counts on us.

As I read today's passage from Joshua, I am reminded that I need to be purposeful about sharing the work the Lord has done—which I can't do if I am not willing to be vulnerable and share the hardship with my family.

I encourage you to read all of Joshua 4 and choose as a family a way to make an altar of remembrance like the Israelites did. Maybe you can get a collection of small rocks and write on them with permanent markers the miracles the Lord has done in your family, then display them in a bowl on the hearth or dining room table.

My family's list would include things like the day the Lord gave me an opportunity to earn five dollars when we desperately needed it, a specific answer to prayer in a new employment situation, a miracle in a medical situation, or the like. Your children may have answers you might not even know about, but what an opportunity for them to begin to "know that the Lord's hand is powerful, and so [they] might fear the LORD [their] God forever."

Start writing your list with your family today, precious mom. Remember that the Lord is so faithful.

Fixing Your Thoughts

Now, dear brothers and sisters, one final thing. Fix your thoughts on what
is true, and honorable, and right, and pure, and lovely, and admirable.
Think about things that are excellent and worthy of praise.

PHILIPPIANS 4:8

AS PAUL WRAPS UP HIS LETTER to the Philippians, he encourages them to control
their thoughts. I suppose nineteen hundred years ago they must have struggled
with some of the same things we do. I'm not sure whether that's encouraging or
not!

Our thoughts can make or break every waking moment of the day, right?
Before I'm even out of bed in the morning, I can spiral into frustration and chest-
tightening anxiety at the first sound of a text that hits my phone on the nightstand.
I hear kids fighting over the shower, and the last thing I'm thinking is anything
pure. Then I get up, and by the time I stumble into the bathroom, "admirable" is
out the window and "lovely" never even made it to the table.

But when I "fix" my thoughts, I choose to address each one and put it in its
rightful place. Is it true that the to-do list is going to crush me today or that I really
can't feed my kids fourteen times? Or am I just overwhelmed by it? If I'm honest,
it's just overwhelming, so I choose to stop thinking those thoughts and choose to
think instead that the Lord has given me these gifts of little people and that I will,
most likely, survive this day.

Is it honorable to be critical of my husband and short-tempered with my tween
even if it stays in my head? Or is it honorable to consciously replace those thoughts
with grace and understanding toward the people in my home?

The exercise of taking your thoughts captive (see 2 Corinthians 10:5) has far-
reaching effects. Not only are you choosing to think godly thoughts, but as your
thought life improves, so will your countenance, speech, and behavior. You will
sleep more restfully, you will lower your stress level, your eyes will shine brightly.
Most importantly, you will begin to speak life and offer the hope of Christ to those
around you.

But God Remains

My health may fail, and my spirit may grow weak, but God remains the strength of my heart; he is mine forever.

PSALM 73:26

LAST NIGHT, I WENT TO BED whispering a simple prayer: *"God, help us."*

I tossed and turned as I struggled to fall asleep. Like many of you, I was trying to let go of the images of the day. Images of the suffering and loss in a troubled part of the world that were burned into my mind. I wanted to help—but the reality was that I was helpless.

People with spiritual eyes see what's going on. We know where the suffering originates from. We know the struggle is spiritual at its roots. Spiritual problems need spiritual solutions. Paul reminded us in Ephesians 6:12 that we are not fighting flesh and blood—but an adversary as old as time itself.

Satan wants us distracted by temporal things. He wants us to hate each other. He hopes we'll try to fix our problems from a position of worldly strength. He is banking on us grasping for worldly wisdom because he knows this problem needs more than what the wisest, most culturally aware person will have to offer.

If we keep looking to human wisdom for the answer, we may win a skirmish here and there, but we'll lose the big battle—the battle for our souls. Yes. We'll lose—unless God intervenes. We need a move of God! "God, please help," was the last thing I said as sleep finally found me.

I am so thankful for God's promise of new morning mercies (see Lamentations 3:22-23). Today as I woke, the Lord reminded me of a precious promise: nothing is too hard for Him. In Jeremiah 32:27, God says, "I am the LORD, the God of all the peoples of the world. Is anything too hard for me?"

Anything. This means nothing is too hard for Him. Nothing. Not riots. Not lawless leaders. Not evil intent. Not misguided officials. God is our hope. For as much as we want to love people and nations, we must remember that God loves them more.

God's love is fierce. So is His justice. He sees what's happening. As I have said many times, this nation, and our world, are ripe for judgment—but they are also ripe for revival.

Let's pray for revival today—and every day. Our flesh may fail, but God never will.

Our hope is in Him—He remains!

Who Is on the Lord's Side?

Moses stood in the gate of the camp and said, "Who is on the LORD's side? Come to me." And all the sons of Levi gathered around him.

EXODUS 32:26, ESV

"WHO IS ON THE LORD'S SIDE?" I woke with the tune from the old hymn playing in my heart this morning, and so I looked up the lyrics. Google them, and you'll see a definite connection to what is happening in our world today.

Here is verse four: "Fierce may be the conflict, strong may be the foe, But the King's own army none can overthrow; 'Round His standard ranging, vict'ry is secure, For His truth unchanging makes the triumph sure. Joyfully enlisting, by Thy grace divine, We are on the Lord's side—Savior, we are Thine!"

The hymn refers to a passage in the Bible. In Exodus 32, we read the story of one of the most famous interactions between Moses and the Israelites.

The people had become restless as they waited for Moses to come down from Mount Sinai, where God was giving him the Ten Commandments. It had been a while. Eventually, they started to fear Moses would never return, so they asked Aaron, who was a weak leader, to make them other gods to worship. Sadly, Aaron gave them their wish. Aaron's actions showed that he feared people more than God.

We need to keep our eyes on the "Aarons." It's the "Aarons" that the church needs to watch out for. The church today has grown weary as it waits for the return of the Lord. Can you feel it?

We are living in the same kind of atmosphere that Moses found when he came down off that mountain—weariness is everywhere. We have been playing church for a long time in this nation, and our current struggle has highlighted this as nothing else could have.

The question must be asked again: "Who is on the Lord's side?"

When we are on the Lord's side, our lives, our families, and our churches reflect it.

God's people should never be characterized by fear or indifference, but by courage and wisdom.

He Rides on the Clouds

Sing to God, sing in praise of his name, extol him who rides on the clouds; rejoice before him—his name is the LORD.

PSALM 68:4, NIV

IN 2017, MY SEVENTEEN-YEAR-OLD NEPHEW WAS in a devastating car accident. The impact broke his neck and back. Doctors said he would never walk again. They said he was a "vegetable." They said we should "pull the plug" because his life would not have meaning.

They never factored in the Healer. The Healer rides on the clouds. He is beyond our understanding. We praised Him for what we believed He could do, even before it was done.

Where the wisdom and understanding of man ends, God's has just begun. Today, my nephew is a high school graduate who is walking and talking and praising the Lord. When God heals, the healing is real and lasting. What He did for my nephew, He can do for this country and for a world in desperate need of healing.

God was with us in the hospital as my nephew clung to life in the ICU, and He's here today as our nation seems to be on spiritual life support. Let's pray together with one voice today—entering His courts with praise and asking God to heal our land. Let's praise Him for what He can do! Let's let our faith speak loudly and boldly for the world to hear.

God was in the ICU, and He's in the White House too. He's on the streets of our cities. He's everywhere. He sees everything, and He is able to heal our nation and forgive our sins. Let's seek Him in prayer:

Father, thank You. Thank You for physical and spiritual healing, for miracles, for mercy, and for forgiveness. We praise You for who You are and what You have done—and we praise You for what You will do. You are worthy of our praise.

Even though we are often frustrated and tend to worry about what is happening around us, help us today to turn off the noise of the world so that we can listen to Your still, small voice.

We love You. Help us to live like it. Come soon, Lord! We can't wait to see You!

Gather your children and sing His praises today! It's time to turn our worry into worship.

Finish Strong

You should finish what you started. Let the eagerness you showed in the beginning
be matched now by your giving. Give in proportion to what you have.

2 CORINTHIANS 8:11

HAVE YOU EVER STRUGGLED TO FINISH a project with the same enthusiasm you had
when you began it? I can think of many things like this. I have a box of unfinished
craft projects. I bought a subscription to a cooking club one time, thinking I would
have the time to cook these exotic meals, only to stop trying at month three. Then
there was the tree house. Sigh.

Anyone can start something, can't they? But it takes dedication and perseverance to finish strong. Parenting is like this. My oldest and youngest are nearly
twenty years apart. I must confess—especially in the area of homeschooling—I
have struggled to finish well with my beautiful youngest daughter. The wonderful
lessons that were so new and exciting with my oldest three seem to have lost their
luster now that I've taught the concept over and over.

Our kids need us to stay in there for the long haul, and in order to do that, we
need to rely on the strength that comes from God. It doesn't mean that we keep
doing the same thing but rather that we have the same heart for our first child as for
our last. It means that we ask God to give us fresh perspective.

If you're struggling to finish strong, don't be too hard on yourself; finishing
strong is hard for most of us. It took the church at Corinth over a year to finish a
fundraising campaign they had committed to, and in 2 Corinthians 8, Paul took
them to task for it.

Notice that Paul's focus was on their attitude, not on the project itself. He
wanted more than mere completion; he wanted them to be eager at the end like
they were at the beginning. Paul even says that attitude matters more than the
amount. The heart attitude of willingness, not the amount, makes the gift acceptable to God.

The same thing is true for relationships. Let's finish strong with our kids. I
want my youngest ones to see the same enthusiasm as my older ones did—even if
our lives have changed and we're just a *bit* older. Finish strong!

Paul's admonition to the Christians of Corinth is useful today, isn't it? Let
the eagerness you showed in the beginning of parenting be matched now by your
commitment

You'll be glad you stayed strong until the end, and so will your kids!

Unexpected Encounters

Don't forget to show hospitality to strangers, for some who have done this have entertained angels without realizing it!

HEBREWS 13:2

IT'S NOT EVERY DAY YOU MEET a random stranger who may be an angel, but when you do, you remember it. I had such an encounter one hot, steamy Alabama night. Our family had embarked on the adventure of a lifetime: a cross-country trip that had me speaking about education in churches around the United States. Over and over, God had been providing for our journey.

After speaking to approximately thirty-five parents, I wearily headed back to our RV with two of our children. In the corner of the lot was a rather beat-up old Volkswagen. As we walked, a woman got out of it and came toward us. I hesitated. Her clothes were dirty, her hair unkempt.

"Are you Heidi?" she asked.

"Kids, stay behind me," I quietly cautioned. I answered that yes, I was Heidi, and as I did, she reached into her pocket and handed me what appeared to be a dollar. As she did, she echoed the same exact words that I had been hearing for months from strangers all across the country.

"The Lord loves you, and He is so proud of you. The Lord will be with you wherever you go. He will never leave you or forsake you. Keep going!"

"Thank you," I said, humbled by her kindness. "Thank you." Tears were streaming down my face because as soon as she said those words, I knew that I was not holding a dollar in my hand. You see, this wasn't the first time we had heard those words. This had happened over and over.

"Mom!!!" Summer said. "Look! I bet it's a hundred-dollar bill!!!" Of course, she was right. After all, she had seen this happen before too. When I looked up, the woman was gone. As quickly as she had arrived, she left—but we were changed. God sent a message loud and clear: He knows what we need. That night, we were at the end of ourselves. Our kids had been cranky and disobedient, and our money was running low. We were beginning to doubt, again, whether we had really heard the Lord.

God knew we needed a special reminder that we were on the path He had chosen. He is rarely early, but never late. In our years of humble travel, Christians have given us lodging, food, and encouragement. And sometimes, angels have shown up in dark, steamy parking lots and become part of facilitating our mission. Look for Him everywhere, my friend. He is always at work.

This Is My Dearly Loved Son

A voice from heaven said, "This is my dearly loved Son, who brings me great joy."

MATTHEW 3:17

ACCORDING TO AUTHOR GARY CHAPMAN, THERE are five love languages. Our "love language" describes how we prefer to receive love from others. People can show their love for us in the following ways:

Words of Affirmation: saying supportive things

Quality Time: spending meaningful time

Receiving Gifts: giving gifts that say, "I'm thinking about you!"

Acts of Service: doing helpful things

Physical Touch: giving hugs and back rubs (these would be your "lap lander" children)

Some of these are easier for me than others. I am an "acts of service" person. You want to show me that you care? Help me clean the kitchen. Really! It's my favorite!

Each of us differs in the ways that we receive love. But as moms, we've got a big job: to learn how each of our children receive love.

Jesus, who lived a perfect life, exhibited all of these love "languages." We have seen Him spending quality time with His disciples, washing their feet, receiving the gift of expensive perfume, and laying hands on the sick. What an example He set for us with regard to how we should treat others!

His heavenly Father loved Him uniquely and perfectly also. Notice that God spoke in the affirmative of Jesus, saying, "This is my dearly loved Son, who brings me great joy."

If Jesus needed encouragement from His Father, how much more do our children need to hear about our love for them? This word from the Father must have greatly encouraged Jesus at the very outset of His earthly ministry. God has always been and always will be "well pleased" with His Son, and He told Him so, in front of witnesses!

When was the last time you looked at your son or daughter and praised them? When was the last time they knew their very existence brought you joy? If it's been a while, today is a good day to affirm your love for your family. If God knew Jesus needed it, we have much to learn.

Today, let's love our people well.

Learning to Love Like Jesus

Love is patient and kind; love does not envy or boast; it is not arrogant or rude. It does not insist on its own way; it is not irritable or resentful; it does not rejoice at wrongdoing, but rejoices with the truth. Love bears all things, believes all things, hopes all things, endures all things.

1 CORINTHIANS 13:4-7, ESV

As I WAS READING OVER THIS familiar passage one day, it seemed like the Lord gave me a new insight. We all know that love is defined as being patient and kind and never envious, boastful, arrogant, or rude. Love never insists on its own way and is not irritable or resentful. Love never rejoices in wrongdoing but instead rejoices in the truth. Love bears all things, believes all things, hopes all things, and endures all things.

But as I was reading, 1 Corinthians 13 took on new meaning for me. I felt as if the Lord challenged me to try inserting that definition of love into other passages that use the word *love*. Try it and see what you think. What would it mean, for instance, if you inserted that extended definition of love into John 15:12? "Love each other in the same way I have loved you" would look like loving each other with patience and kindness, without insisting on our own way or being irritable or resentful.

John 3:16 tells us how God loved us: "He gave his one and only Son, so that everyone who believes in him will not perish but have eternal life."

God loved the world with patience and kindness. He was never resentful. He bore all things, and He endured all things. That's a big kind of love—and it was for the whole world!

Want to really be stretched? Try Matthew 5:44: "I say, love your enemies! Pray for those who persecute you!"

Boy, this is a hard one. How are we to love our enemies? We shouldn't become resentful. We should be patient and kind in dealing with them. We are called to *pray* for those who persecute us! Wow.

The Lord will help us to love others the way He loves us . . . even our enemies.

Committed

Commit everything you do to the LORD. Trust him, and he will help you.

PSALM 37:5

HAVE YOU EVER READ *CHARLOTTE'S WEB* with your kids? Growing up, I loved that story about Charlotte the spider and her commitment to help her friend, Wilbur the pig, and our kids have loved it too. It's a chance to see life from a perspective we may not otherwise consider.

Perhaps you've heard the joke about the conversation between the chicken and the pig. They were discussing their respective contributions to a wonderful, stick-to-your-ribs country breakfast. The pig rightly observed that the chicken only made a small "donation," while the pig literally gave everything. He was totally committed to that breakfast.

Psalm 37:5 exhorts us to *commit* our way to the Lord, and He promises He will help us. What does it mean to "commit" our ways to the Lord? The homeschool mom in me likes to go to Merriam-Webster for clarity:

commit *transitive verb*
to carry into action deliberately

To carry into action deliberately. That sure puts a light on what the Lord wants, doesn't it? Are you committed to God's ways? Or are you just willing to make a small donation from your life? Do you wonder why the Lord hasn't given you the desires of your heart?

The church is filled with people who make minimal donations or contributions to the Kingdom. They drop a check in the collection plate, and they volunteer to work in the nursery one Sunday each month. Most churches couldn't continue to operate without those kinds of members. But what would total commitment to God's Kingdom look like? How would our churches be different?

What would our lives look like if we were fully committed to living in accordance with God's ways? In our marriages? In our finances? In our times of prayer and worship? In how we serve the least among us? If we were truly willing to "commit" our way to the Lord, would He give us the desires of our heart?

Or perhaps—the desires of our heart would change to align with His will in our life.

In Due Season

Let's not get tired of doing what is good. At just the right time
we will reap a harvest of blessing if we don't give up.

GALATIANS 6:9

MY MOM'S FAMILY CAME FROM FAIRBURY, NEBRASKA. I had the privilege of going there some years ago to see the train station that my grandparents used to meet at. Unlike the Pacific Northwest, Nebraska is truly farm country—corn as far as the eye can see in every direction. It's fascinating to learn a little about farming, and these people have a wealth of knowledge to share!

In the twenty-first century, not many of us know much about sowing and harvesting. But in Galatians 6, Paul was talking to people who understood the times and the seasons. His words painted a vivid picture for the church in Galatia.

I travel the country coast-to-coast every year, speaking at conferences, teaching workshops, doing radio and television interviews, and more. Usually I fly, but sometimes I drive. My husband and I love to travel in our motorhome. It's far from new, but it's comfortable, and we love to take the whole family. I've driven through Nebraska perhaps a dozen times over the years, and it never looks the same way twice.

I've seen it freshly plowed, the rich, dark soil upturned under the spring sun. I've seen it with little corn plants only a few inches tall in early summer. I've seen corn that was knee-high by the fourth of July, and I've seen corn that was eight feet tall in the late summer. It's amazing to see the stalks and stubble after the enormous combines have harvested the crop in the fall. I've been privileged to catch a snapshot of each season of growth.

But for the farmer, the change is slow—almost imperceptible. From the exciting day of planting until the harvest is a long time. There are seasons of too much rain and times of drought. There are uncertainties about the harvest and a thousand variables that determine the outcome. But the farmer knows that in due season, if he doesn't give up, there *will* come a harvest.

I need to remember that. Perhaps you do too. All too often, the day-to-day routine of mothering wears on me, and I begin to doubt the harvest. Sometimes there's no visible progress, and giving up seems like the easiest route. As moms, our job is to sow. God's job is to produce a crop. What we sow in faith, we will reap. Patience is a fruit of the Spirit, and like a Nebraska farmer, we need to practice patience in faith. Our harvest will come.

In All Circumstances

Be thankful in all circumstances, for this is God's will for you who belong to Christ Jesus.

1 THESSALONIANS 5:18

WHO DOESN'T LOVE THE STORY OF David? Here's a young, obscure shepherd boy quietly minding his flock in anonymity. Then Samuel, the great and mighty man of God, begins to speak words of promise over this boy. Our hearts soar with the idea of being lifted out of obscurity, recognized by godly leaders around us, and promised a place of importance and visibility where our work will make a difference.

I love it when a story has a happy ending.

And sometimes that's exactly how it happens. When we're faithful in little, we may be given much. When we labor in obscurity, we may eventually be placed in the spotlight for all to see. But not always. Sometimes it's just the opposite. Perhaps no one knows this better than mothers. Most of what we do, day in and day out, goes unseen—even by the ones we are endeavoring to serve.

Maybe you have had the opportunity to serve in a place of visibility within the body of Christ, serving or leading in a ministry that is making a difference for all to see. And then, God asks you to step down to focus on your young children. Perhaps for a season. Or perhaps for an undefined period of time. Or perhaps . . . for good.

How should you respond? It's easy to love the "girl makes good" kind of story, but what about the other kind where you're moved to a season of hiddenness? Do you respond with the same enthusiasm and gratitude as when you were promoted? Or do you grumble and resist, feeling sorry for yourself or doubting what you've heard?

God's economy is different from our own. He moves people up, down, or laterally according to His plans. God's ways are not like our ways, precious mom— they're better.

No matter what circumstance you are facing, if you claim the name of Jesus, you are called to be thankful. Remember, mom—you can't pass on what you don't possess! Trust Him in every season and circumstance.

It's Okay to Take a Nap

Whether you eat or drink, or whatever you do, do it all for the glory of God.
1 CORINTHIANS 10:31

WHETHER I'M DECLUTTERING MY HOUSE (my stress reliever), writing a Bible study for MomStrong International, or homeschooling my children, I tend to throw myself into whatever is before me. I can't help it. My friends often poke fun at me for the pace I keep, saying they could never keep up with me. That's just the way I'm built. I'm wired to work, work, work. Even when I'm "on vacation," you will usually find me working on some sort of project. It's not necessarily a virtue, but it's the way God made me. Thank God He was kind enough to give me Jay—a husband who has a similar work ethic and who understands how I operate.

Given the choice to be a "Mary" or a "Martha," I'll usually pick Martha. Sometimes, though, my desire to "get something done" isn't what God wants me to do.

Many years ago, an elderly gentleman offered me some down-home wisdom that I've never forgotten. This old fellow was from the Deep South and had perhaps a third- or fourth-grade education, but he had walked with the Lord for many, many years. His words were always simple, but his thoughts were often profound.

He said, "Heidi, whether you raise the dead today or take a nap, the pay is the same as long as you're doing what the Lord asked you to do."

Why is this so hard for some of us to understand? If the Lord gave you the power and the faith to raise the dead and sent you to the grave of a Lazarus, that would seem like a pretty incredible experience. But it wouldn't be any more important or meaningful to the Lord than if He told you to put away the project you've been working on so intently and take a nap.

Obedience is what matters. The "what" isn't important. Some days He directs us to feed the poor, or sing songs of praise, or care for an elderly neighbor. Other days He may ask us to wait upon Him quietly or . . . yes . . . take a nap. I wonder if we could set our children free from the burden of "doing" all the time and instead practice simply *being*. God delights in us either way.

His pleasure with you isn't based on how public or how important your job was today. Even the smallest act done in complete hiddenness is just as pleasing to the Father, as long as we're doing what He asked of us.

Standing and Aware

Put on the full armor of God, so that you can take your stand against the devil's schemes.

EPHESIANS 6:11, NIV

MOST OF US ARE FAMILIAR WITH what it means to put on the full armor of God. We've heard the message preached from the pulpit, we've explored the armor of God in a church small group, and perhaps we've done a Bible study on God's armor.

But did you know there are two more parts to explore? First, we must take a stand. Putting on the full armor and then reclining on the couch will serve little purpose in the battle to advance the Kingdom of God. We are called to take a stand. Get up. Stand up. Stand firm.

Think of the guards standing resolutely at the gates of Buckingham Palace. Perhaps you've seen people try to get them to laugh or respond. It's pointless. These men are standing guard. They will not be moved while they are on duty. They have put on the uniform and the weapons assigned to them, and they are standing resolutely between you and the royal family. Are you taking a stand for God's Kingdom? Or are you easily distracted?

When I took my little children to the pool, I stood guard. As long as the kids were near the water, I kept my eyes on them. I wasn't reading a book or chatting with other mothers. I was ready and watching.

I was on guard to protect my children. Paul says it's not enough to put on the armor—we must also *stand guard*!

Of course, it's not enough to stand—we must also be aware, watching for any sign of the enemy. We're to be aware of the devil's schemes. Did you know he's scheming and planning ways to cause you to stumble or fail? Paul warns us that he is. Satan is watching you and your family, looking for weaknesses, probing and searching for areas that are unguarded.

Never doubt that your soul has an enemy—and never underestimate him.

But instead, put on the full armor, stand resolutely, watch for those schemes, and remember, we have the victory over the devil because of Jesus!

Sanctification

Sanctify them by the truth; your word is truth.

JOHN 17:17, NIV

HAVE YOU EVER STRUGGLED TO PASS on a spiritual truth to your kids because you were struggling to understand it yourself? I thank God for all the wonderful teachers who have helped me understand the deeper truths of the Bible.

Many years ago, I heard a great Bible teacher from England. He was in his late eighties, I would guess, and had walked with the Lord for more than fifty years. More than that, he had studied the Word of God diligently, teaching at a Bible college for many, many years and preaching regularly as well. I was in awe of his seemingly endless knowledge of Greek and Hebrew as he unpacked God's Word that day.

At one point, he came to the topic of sanctification. That word had always confused me, and although I had heard several preachers attempt to explain it, I was still struggling to grasp the concept. This wise, old man took off the thick, wire-rimmed glasses that he wore—his aged eyes rheumy and watery from years of reading God's Word. He placed the glasses on the top of the lectern where we all could see them, and he stood there quietly for several seconds.

I will never forget his words as he pointed at his glasses. He said, "These are unsanctified glasses sitting here. They're serving no purpose and are of no value."

He reached his wrinkled hand out, picked up the glasses, rested them gently on his nose, and stretched the wire frames behind his ears. "Now," he said, "these eyeglasses are sanctified. They are doing the thing for which they were created. Do you understand?"

Finally, I got it. The process of sanctification is the process of being conformed to the purpose for which we were created. Yes, that means sinning less, but more importantly, it means serving the One who made us. As you find your purpose and begin to walk in it, you are being sanctified day by day. As we walk in His truth, we find our way.

Understanding this has helped me teach my children the profound truth about the unique calling God has planned for their lives. I want them to know that as they grow, all the correction that they receive is part of the process of sanctification.

When we teach and correct our children, we are partnering with God for the beginning of our children's lives—but the process of sanctification goes on for a lifetime. God is always working to conform us into people who can be used for His glory.

No Fear in Love

There is no fear in love. But perfect love drives out fear, because fear has to do with punishment. The one who fears is not made perfect in love.

1 JOHN 4:18, NIV

MY FRIENDS STEVE AND JANE HAVE two little fluffy white dogs they are crazy about. I visit my friends often, and I love to watch my friends interact with those little dogs. They're both obedient little creatures and reasonably well trained to do as they're told. But one dog always cowers just a little bit, trembling on occasion and lowering its head as it scurries to obey a command. He's quick to obey, but there's something about that little dog's personality that causes it to respond out of fear more than love.

The other dog is much more upbeat—outgoing in every way, with its tail always wagging, ears always up, and almost smiling as it goes about its day. Like the other dog, this one also obeys promptly, but it obeys happily, eyes sparkling, and almost prancing to do the bidding of its owners. You can tell it wants to please my friends.

The dogs are both loved the same way by Steve and Jane. They receive equal amounts of love, affection, and training, but they respond very differently. One has a spirit that is free, while the other is dominated by false fear.

Maybe you have noticed this in your own children—or perhaps, in yourself. Sometimes when I obey the Lord, it's more out of fear than joy. I do what I know I'm supposed to do, but the joy of serving the Lord can be overshadowed by the fear of failing Him.

Other times, it truly delights me to do the will of the Father. I'm in a place of closeness, and there isn't anything I wouldn't do to please the Lord. Like those two little white dogs, obedience is always good, but obedience with a joyful heart and a desire to please the Master is always better than fearful or grudging obedience.

If you notice that your child is obeying you out of fear, you have an opportunity to teach them about the blessing of obedience—and also the opportunity to model the amazing love of Christ.

Remember that as you raise your children, you are also showing them who God is. He is love!

If you're the one who struggles to understand the heart of your heavenly Father, or if you tend to obey out of fear, look no further than the Cross. He loves you that much.

He Sees Every Tear

He will wipe away every tear from their eyes, and death shall be no more, neither shall there be mourning, nor crying, nor pain anymore, for the former things have passed away.

REVELATION 21:4, ESV

MY HUSBAND, JAY, AND I ATTENDED a funeral recently. It was hard. The woman who had passed away was too young. Her husband couldn't stop crying. I couldn't stop crying. I was glad we had left the girls at home with their grandma. We're never prepared for a loss like this.

As Jay and I sat quietly together at bedtime, I went over the funeral in my mind. The service had been beautiful. Each song was perfectly chosen. The eulogy was a wonderful tribute. The casket glistened, and the flowers were bountiful. But nothing could soften the reality of the permanence of death. There were tears—so many tears.

Like you, I long for the day we read about in Revelation. In that day, He will wipe our tears away and death will be no more. The Kingdom is not yet fully manifest. There is more to come—so much more. The Bible teaches us that this age of suffering will soon draw to a close. We live with one foot in the here and now and the other foot in eternity. Could there possibly be a greater promise than no more death, no more tears, no more mourning, and no more pain?

Because of sin, our world is a broken place, but the Lord assures us that not a single tear escapes His notice. In fact, Psalm 56:8 says, "You keep track of all my sorrows. You have collected all my tears in your bottle. You have recorded each one in your book."

Imagine that. Every. Single. Tear. I've cried a lot in my lifetime—including at that recent funeral. We all have. But God sees. He knows. One day soon, He will wipe away every tear. I said goodbye to my friend . . . for now. I cried until I couldn't cry anymore. But I know those tears counted for something. God saw them all. Because my faith and trust are in the Lord, I know I will see my friend again. I'm living for that day.

Rest in that truth, precious mom. Our tears matter—and Jesus understands. As you walk your children through times of grief, keep your eyes on Jesus. One day soon, He will return and make all things new. For now, we can be comforted to know that God sees our suffering, and He cares.

The Justice of God

God is just: He will pay back trouble to those who trouble you and give relief to you who are troubled, and to us as well.

2 THESSALONIANS 1:6-7, NIV

"GOD IS JUST." THOSE THREE WORDS nearly knocked me over as I was reading Scripture to my children this morning. I didn't even finish reading the verse. I turned to my youngest and repeated the words, "God is just." In my head, I've known that truth for years, but suddenly I knew it in my heart as well. God is the God of justice. He will set all things right in the end.

Oh, how we need to know this truth in the world right now.

When we say that God is just, we mean that He is perfectly righteous in His treatment of His creation. God shows no partiality. In Acts 10:34, we see this clearly: "Peter replied, 'I see very clearly that God shows no favoritism.'"

In Zechariah 7:10, He commands against the mistreatment of others: "Do not oppress widows, orphans, foreigners, and the poor. And do not scheme against each other." There are many more verses that reveal God's heart toward the oppressed and the oppressor. *True justice flows from God, not people.*

We have all heard the phrase *social justice* in recent years. Something in us cries out for justice. We want justice for the oppressed, justice for the innocent, justice for the weak among us. Many within the church and outside the family of Christ cry out relentlessly for social justice.

Even the most hardened sinners among us can't help but realize something isn't right. They intuitively sense that this world isn't just—it isn't fair. They long for what was meant to be in the Garden of Eden. They want justice, peace, joy, love. They want all the things that Jesus is. Jesus is peace. Jesus is love. Jesus is just. But instead of seeking Jesus for wisdom, many take it into their own hands to bring justice. There is no end to their schemes for a man-made utopia.

Of course, they will never create the justice they seek apart from Jesus. He is the only just One. When your heart aches and your soul hurts because of injustice, stand up and speak out. Fight injustice wherever you find it. But know this: a day is coming when all accounts will be settled in full. When Jesus returns, we shall *all* know justice at last. Nothing escapes Him. Nothing gets by Him. And justice will prevail, thank God.

Commanded to Forgive

Forgive others, and you will be forgiven.

LUKE 6:37

I THINK IF WE WERE HONEST WITH OURSELVES, we could all come up with a time when we were deeply hurt by someone. I know those are not fun times to remember, but as you do, take a moment to notice the emotions you feel. It's normal to feel angry, wanting revenge, hoping for calamity for your offender. Feelings of weariness, fear, and physical illness would also all be expected, judging by the world's standards.

Jesus, however, has different standards for when we think of those who have hurt us: "You must be compassionate, just as your Father is compassionate. Do not judge others, and you will not be judged. Do not condemn others, or it will all come back against you. Forgive others, and you will be forgiven" (Luke 6:36-37).

There's not much room for confusion there. We are to forgive others.

I believe one reason we are to forgive others is that it's best for *us*. God knows us so well. Harboring unforgiveness does not hurt the offender; it hurts the one holding the offense. The Lord is loving us in teaching us to forgive. He is saving us years of physical illness, emotional paralysis, stress, and anger—not to mention years void of joy.

Even in the context of Luke 6, the Lord is loving in the instruction He offers. He starts off by telling us to be compassionate. I have asked the Lord for years to help me see my offenders as He sees them. I am not particularly compassionate without the Lord's help, but with the Holy Spirit's work in me, I can see that my offender is hurting and truly want the best for him or her.

A compassionate person is much less likely to judge another, as we are more concerned with their well-being than their behavior, so it makes perfect sense that that is the next command.

First, we see someone with compassion. Then, we see without judgment. And finally, with a compassionate heart and without condemnation, we can forgive the person who has hurt us.

If this seems impossible, take it to the Lord in prayer. God will help you. You are not alone, and the Lord is a miracle worker.

Relationship > Ritual

The LORD will guide you always; he will satisfy your needs in a sun-scorched land and will strengthen your frame. You will be like a well-watered garden, like a spring whose waters never fail.

ISAIAH 58:11, NIV

HAVE YOU EVER ASKED FOR A promotion and watched it be given to a coworker? Or prayed for healing in a relationship that never came? Or watched your child face ridicule and rejection? Whatever it may be, we can all agree that suffering has affected each one of us.

Suffering isn't new. We see it in the Bible when Sarah goes years without a child, Esau is tricked out of his birthright by a conniving brother, Joseph's life is turned upside down by his jealous brothers, Tamar is rejected by her husband, the Jews are sent into exile, and the list could go on and on. History is full of people who have felt the sting of suffering.

In Isaiah, the people were upset when God didn't answer their fasting and prayers to their satisfaction: "'Why have we fasted,' they say, 'and you have not seen it? Why have we humbled ourselves, and you have not noticed?'" (Isaiah 58:3, NIV).

Just like the Israelites, when faced with suffering, I am prone to blame God and ask, *Why isn't He helping me?* But the first thing I should do is examine my heart. Not all suffering is caused by our own behavior, but it is always a good idea to ask God to show us any sin that may be hindering us.

I encourage you to read all of Isaiah 58. You'll see that the Lord tells His people their fasting is unfruitful because it is hypocritical. They were good at keeping the rituals and going through the motions. We can relate. We go through the motions when we head to church, sing worship songs, listen to the sermon, maybe even take some notes, then get the kids out of class and head back home, not opening the Word until the next Sunday. Yet, like the Israelites, we mistake rituals for a real and vibrant relationship with Christ.

When our rituals and habits are out of an overflow of our love for our Savior, we can truly know the Lord on an intimate level. We will find then that we ask fewer questions and we trust Him more. We learn to rest in the knowledge that God satisfies our needs and strengthens our hearts in troubling times.

Gray Is Good!

Gray hair is a crown of glory; it is gained in a righteous life.
PROVERBS 16:31, ESV

WHILE I WAS SHOPPING THE OTHER day with my oldest daughter, I saw an elderly woman. She appeared to be in her seventies, perhaps approaching eighty. She was dressed in the latest fashions, with frayed and ripped denim jeans, blonde hair extensions, gold high heels, and a designer purse. Signs of plastic surgery were evident, and yet—in spite of all her trying, she didn't look young. She looked like an old woman trying to look young.

We live in a world that is absolutely obsessed with staying young.

Now, to be fair, I can be as vain as the next woman. I try to keep up with fashion trends, and only my hairdresser knows for sure what color my hair actually is. But why are we so obsessed with youth? Why is it no longer acceptable to grow old gracefully? More importantly, what message are we sending to our children about aging?

Proverbs 16:31 reminds us that gray hair is something to be proud of. I've been a grandmother now for over ten years. As I get older, I appreciate this verse in Proverbs. God says growing old is glorious. Gray hair is like a crown on our heads. Those who live a righteous life earn that crown of glory. So why am I so vain at times? Why do I wrestle with aging?

Perhaps it's because I still have a young daughter at home, but I still think of myself as a young mother. Yet, at a recent meeting, someone said they wanted to hear from me because older women always have wisdom. I guess having a daughter in her thirties really does make me an "older" mom.

All of a sudden, I was feeling pretty good about being in my fifties! I mean, I learned a lot of things in fifty years! (Most of them the hard way!) You know what? That knowledge is worth something, mom!

I'm not saying we shouldn't update our wardrobes or use makeup. We shouldn't generally let ourselves go. But I admit that I'm challenged when the Lord says something I fight against is a good thing. As I grow older, I increasingly find myself making peace with the woman I'm becoming. Today, ask the Lord to help you see each wrinkle, each stretch mark, and each gray hair as the proof of a life well lived.

And smile! I'm aging too—right there with you.

Stay Out of the Mud!

Now you are free from the power of sin and have become slaves of God.

ROMANS 6:22

As a little girl, I used to love going to the zoo. A farm was almost as good. I just loved animals. Large or small, animals were my jam.

We can learn a lot from watching animals.

I remember being at a friend's farm one day. We had just had a heavy storm earlier in the day, and there was mud everywhere, but especially where her father had driven the tractor. The ruts were filled with mud the consistency of chocolate pudding. I watched, fascinated, as one of her brother's pigs settled down into the mud. The cool mud must have felt good. The pig wallowed as deep as he could get in that muddy rut, rolling from one side to the other. He was in no hurry to extricate himself. In fact, left to his own devices, he would have likely spent the rest of the day there, but my friend's brother came out of the barn and chased the filthy pig out of the rut and into a nearby pen.

Later, my friend's lamb was walking along that same area near the pasture gate and stepped into the mud. Immediately, that lamb leaped backward, shaking its foot furiously, trying to sling all the mud off its foot. It took the long way around to a high spot in the tractor ruts to avoid getting near the mud again as it made its way across the pasture. I remember thinking at the time how interesting it was that both the pig and the sheep wandered into that muddy rut, but the pig wallowed in it gleefully, while the sheep struggled to get free and clean as soon as possible and avoided the mud in the future.

People are like that. Those who have given themselves over to sin wallow in their brokenness with no desire to get out. But those of us who have found forgiveness in Christ have been freed "from the power of sin." We can find ourselves in the mud on occasion, but the difference is that, like that little lamb, our heart's desire is to get free and clean as quickly as possible because we are repulsed by the mud that so easily traps us.

Looking to the Strong One

The salvation of the righteous comes from the LORD;
he is their stronghold in time of trouble.

PSALM 37:39, ESV

I CAN'T COUNT THE TIMES AS a mom when I looked around and thought, *Oh, great—I'm the one in charge here.* The truth is, none of us feel as if we have our act together all the time as moms—not even close. Troubles seem too big, and the worries stack one on top of the other. The good news is that as big as our worries seem, they are flimsy in comparison to God's firm foundation.

Each of us can turn to God and stand strong when we understand two important truths: who God is and who God says we are. Who is God? The same God who strengthened the men and women of the Bible. He is just as strong today. Just as present. Who does God say we are? If we have submitted our lives to Him, He calls us righteous. He has brought us salvation by saving our souls, but He is also showing up day after day to save us in our times of trouble.

It's important to believe what God says about us as His righteous ones. We have to believe we're going to have weaknesses and failures, but God will be there to fill in with His strengths.

Today, consider yourself standing before God. Dare to see yourself as He sees you: righteous, loved, His. It's only when we see ourselves this way that we can approach God with boldness, seeking His help. As Hebrews 4:16 says, "Let us then approach God's throne of grace with confidence, so that we may receive mercy and find grace to help us in our time of need" (NIV).

So the truth is, even when you feel that you're alone, you're not. Yes, you do make decisions for yourself and your family, but God is always available to help you in every time of need.

The next time you start feeling overwhelmed, take time to pause. Prayer starts with pausing from feeling overwhelmed and actually looking to the One who can provide strength. God can be strong in your troubles, but you have to let Him. As a mom, if your troubles seem too big or your worries stacked too high, it's because you're not looking up to your God for help.

Come to think of it, let's ask Him for help right now:

Lord, forgive us for trying to tackle everything ourselves. Right now, we humble ourselves and ask You to be strong in our lives. We need You for all of our troubles, big or small.

Uniquely Created for His Glory

You made all the delicate, inner parts of my body
and knit me together in my mother's womb.

PSALM 139:13

HAVE YOU EVER HAD A SEASON of your adult life where you couldn't find your footing for who you really are? The battle of "too much" or "not enough" can render us impotent in our service to the Lord if we aren't careful. I firmly believe that every women's ministry event is a roomful of insecurity as if we were all back in the seventh-grade locker room!

The lesson we need to learn isn't that we need to find friends who like us, but that we are just fine the way the Lord made us. I'm not talking about behavior here, and certainly not about justifying sin. I'm talking about a deep knowing that the Lord created us with personality, gifts, and talents to use for His glory and that we need to be confident in who He made us to be. "We are God's masterpiece. He has created us anew in Christ Jesus, so we can do the good things he planned for us long ago" (Ephesians 2:10).

When we rest in who He created us to be, we can be free to serve as He leads us. Long ago, He planned good works for us to do. Surely He considered our personality when He did that!

As we learn who we really are and begin to walk confidently in who God created us to be, we can pass this on to our children. We can help them grow confidently into who God created them to be and help them bypass the insecurity and hesitation we went through.

God is a creative Creator, and He takes pleasure in watching His children serve Him in the ways He uniquely gifted them to do. Walk confidently in your unique giftedness!

Moms Need Help Too

Rulers lead with my help, and nobles make righteous judgments.
PROVERBS 8:16

MORNINGS ARE BUSY FOR MOTHERS WITH active households. Maybe your kids, like mine, seem to sense when you first open your eyes in the morning. You might be trying to read for a few minutes or get a moment to pray alone while your kids tiptoe into the kitchen to pour themselves a bowl of cereal or butter some toast. As a result, you might find crushed cereal on the kitchen floor, a broken dishwasher door, or milk spilled by a toddler chef in charge. And then you might wonder whether you should address the disobedience of climbing onto the dishwasher door to reach the bowl or applaud the independence and self-service of the four-year-old brother helping his younger sister! Mothers need new wisdom for each new day, don't we?

Even if it's the help of a toddler-turned-chef, sometimes we just need help.

It's okay to ask God for help. Even kings do. "Because of me, kings reign, and rulers make just decrees. Rulers lead with my help, and nobles make righteous judgments" (Proverbs 8:15-16).

This is the best part. The Creator of your children is waiting for you to ask Him for wisdom. He knows you need it, and it says in James 1:5 that He will give it in abundance.

Ask Him for help in all things: the sleep schedules for preschool twins, coupons for diapers, a babysitter for date nights, grace when you are weary, a chance to nap for twenty minutes, effective treatment for a chronic ear infection, a doctor who thinks outside the box, a husband to bring home pizza tonight, a best friend for your twelve-year-old, confidence for your five-year-old, a new home and a friend next door, grandparents full of vitality and a desire to be involved, godly spouses for your children, patience for your nineteen-year-old, and so much more. Yes, my list was all over the place. That's the point!

You need help with many things as a mom, and God is right there waiting to give it. Start your list today. Pray and watch to see where He will work!

Looking Forward to God's Glory

Since we have been made right in God's sight by faith, we have peace with God because of what Jesus Christ our Lord has done for us. Because of our faith, Christ has brought us into this place of undeserved privilege where we now stand, and we confidently and joyfully look forward to sharing God's glory.

We can rejoice, too, when we run into problems and trials, for we know that they help us develop endurance. And endurance develops strength of character, and character strengthens our confident hope of salvation. And this hope will not lead to disappointment. For we know how dearly God loves us, because he has given us the Holy Spirit to fill our hearts with his love.

ROMANS 5:1-5

ARE YOU NEEDING HOPE TODAY? This world is weighty when we consider all that we have in front of us. Focusing on our husbands, being an attentive mother, honoring our parents, being a diligent employee, and in the later years, parenting adult children and starting to worry about the grandchildren are enough to stress anyone out.

When we feel the threat of being swallowed up by the challenges of this temporary home, we need to get back to the basics.

What a story of hope Romans 5 gives us! We have been made righteous, and our days here on earth are only a short window of eternity. The troubles we encounter here develop endurance as we learn to rely on our Creator and trust in His plan for our lives. That endurance produces a strong character, less likely to waver when the raging storms come. This strong character fortifies our hope, and we settle on a firm foundation of salvation.

The journey from troubles to hope can seem like it will take us under, but we must remember that we are not alone. The Lord left us the Holy Spirit as a helper because He loves us so much. This world is not our home, and our hope and confidence are in what is to come: sharing God's glory for eternity!

When God Feels So Far Away

The LORD is righteous in everything he does; he is filled with kindness. The LORD is close to all who call on him, yes, to all who call on him in truth. He grants the desires of those who fear him; he hears their cries for help and rescues them.

PSALM 145:17-19

SOMETIMES IT CAN FEEL LIKE GOD is really far away. Our Bible sits on the nightstand, gathering dust. We pray but don't hear any answers. We go to church and sing the songs, but we don't connect to the words. We stop to pray before a meal, but it's just empty words said out of habit.

When we feel like God is distant, it's important to recognize that we are the ones who have wandered, not Him. Are you feeling far from God now? Take some time to think about when you began to wander.

Was there something God allowed that made you angry with or disappointed in Him? Take time to address that in prayer, recommitting your trust in His leadership in your life.

Did God ask you to do something, but you were disobedient and didn't follow His leading? Get to the bottom of that. Acknowledge your sinful disobedience, take courage, and obey, acting on God's direction to you.

Are you living in sin, ashamed to spend time with your Father? Confess your sin, turn from it, and accept God's loving forgiveness.

Is there a broken relationship you know you need to humbly repair? Set out to connect with that person, and do what you know you need to do to mend the relationship.

The Lord is always waiting on us to come to Him in prayer. When we set apart time to read His Word and pray, we are acknowledging His lordship in our lives, making ourselves vulnerable to His working in us and aligning our heart with His.

God is a forgiving Father waiting for you to call on Him. If He has been feeling distant, seek Him today. Like a good father, He is waiting. He loves you.

Be Strong and Courageous

> Be strong and courageous! Do not be afraid or discouraged. For the LORD your God is with you wherever you go.
>
> JOSHUA 1:9

LET'S TAKE A MOMENT TO READ Joshua 1:1-2, 5-7, 9: "After the death of Moses the LORD's servant, the LORD spoke to Joshua son of Nun, Moses' assistant. He said, 'Moses my servant is dead. Therefore, the time has come for you to lead these people, the Israelites, across the Jordan River into the land I am giving them. . . . No one will be able to stand against you as long as you live. For I will be with you as I was with Moses. I will not fail you or abandon you. Be strong and courageous, for you are the one who will lead these people to possess all the land I swore to their ancestors I would give them. Be strong and very courageous. Be careful to obey all the instructions Moses gave you. Do not deviate from them, turning either to the right or to the left. Then you will be successful in everything you do. . . . This is my command—be strong and courageous! Do not be afraid or discouraged. For the LORD your God is with you wherever you go.'"

God had given Joshua a tremendous command. As God was fulfilling His promise, He appointed Joshua to lead the Israelites to cross the Jordan and take the Promised Land, never mind fighting a few major battles in the process. It seems God knew that Joshua needed a pep talk, as He tells him in three different ways to "be strong and courageous."

Do you need a pep talk, precious mom?

God has given you your marching orders: "You must love the LORD your God with all your heart, all your soul, and all your strength. And you must commit yourselves wholeheartedly to these commands that I am giving you today. Repeat them again and again to your children. Talk about them when you are at home and when you are on the road, when you are going to bed and when you are getting up" (Deuteronomy 6:5-7).

Stand firm in Him. Do not turn to the right or to the left. Remember the instruction God has given you. There will be hard days and long nights.

You are not alone. Your precious children are God's treasure as well, and He will lead you as you raise them. Yes, you will have heartache, but you will have sweet victories as well.

Now march on, precious mama—with courage!

Let Them Fail

A prudent person foresees danger and takes precautions. The
simpleton goes blindly on and suffers the consequences.

PROVERBS 22:3

MY FRIEND'S THREE-YEAR-OLD SON HAD A favorite dump truck. He took it everywhere, including on a boat one Sunday afternoon. His parents warned him that it
was risky and that one bump over a wave would have that dump truck sinking to
the bottom of the lake. Unfortunately, he didn't heed their advice, and the truck
went swimming.

Children, like my friend's three-year-old, typically fit in the "simpleton" category. They're dependent on their parents and other trustworthy adults to guide
them and make sure they're safe. This simplemindedness is appropriate for some
years, but then they reach a point where it's time they move forward. How quickly
they move into the "prudent" category is largely dependent on what kind of parenting they have.

We've all heard of helicopter parents—the ones that run a forgotten lunchbox
or backpack over to school repeatedly. The ones who follow their six-year-old
around the playground like a shadow, making sure their child doesn't do anything
they've determined is dangerous. This form of parenting has proven to prevent
kids' development, as their lives are void of an excellent teaching tool: natural
consequences.

When children run too quickly down a driveway or climb a tree with weak
branches, they learn that it hurts if they misjudge the situation. When the eleven-
year-old forgets his lunch, going hungry for a few hours will help him learn the
importance of remembering it the next day. When our teenagers fail to commit
time to studying the booklet of driving laws, they learn they won't pass the test
and earn a permit. When a freshman in college doesn't turn their class registration
in on time, they learn that they have to sit out a semester.

It is failure that turns a simpleton into a prudent young person.

Don't buy a new dump truck. Be prepared to not bail them out. Let them
miss the deadline.

Without saying "I told you so," and with understanding, let them fail. You're
turning a simpleton into a prudent adult.

Make the Most of the Moments

Be careful how you live. Don't live like fools, but like those who are wise. Make the most of every opportunity in these evil days. Don't act thoughtlessly, but understand what the Lord wants you to do.

EPHESIANS 5:15-17

HAVE YOU EVER BEEN AT THE grocery store, putting your items on the conveyor belt while your toddler cries because you said no to the M&Ms, only to hear an older mom behind you say, "Enjoy every moment!" Or perhaps you've heard a couple in their golden years say, "The days are long, but the years are short." The sentiment is sweet, but there are times when we want the days to be short too—and that's okay.

In the early days with babies and toddlers, everything can seem overwhelming, and the last thing you feel like you can do is enjoy every moment! Yes, it's true that not every moment is enjoyable. But what those sweet older folks are really saying is that the time with their kids went too fast, and they wish they had slowed down to enjoy it more.

In today's Scripture passage, Paul is telling the Ephesian church something similar.

Don't be foolish with the time you have. It is limited, and there is much work to do.

Ask the Lord for strength to leave the dishes in the sink and read the next chapter of your current read-aloud or go run in circles with your children at the park. Prioritize church over sports and sleeping in. Choose wisely where they will spend their years in school. Be diligent about the time you spend in the Word with your children.

Ask God to give you wisdom in your child-rearing years. Spend time writing lists of and reviewing your priorities so you don't let the years go by without doing what is really important to you. Most importantly, let your children see you focus on the Bible and share your love of Christ with them and others.

Your time is short, precious mom, and it will go much more quickly than you think. Make the most of these years.

A Light in Your Eyes

With the Lord's authority I say this: Live no longer as the Gentiles do, for they are hopelessly confused. . . . Throw off your old sinful nature and your former way of life, which is corrupted by lust and deception. Instead, let the Spirit renew your thoughts and attitudes. Put on your new nature, created to be like God—truly righteous and holy.

EPHESIANS 4:17, 22-24

HAVE YOU EVER ENCOUNTERED SOMEONE WHO clearly had the light of Christ in them? You could tell even without interacting. Or maybe you've met someone who you were drawn to because they were warm and full of kindness?

The Internet has changed the way we interact as humans. We are disconnected, short-tempered, presumptuous, and ready to throw a one-line barb and walk away victoriously without looking over our shoulder for the damage. Add everyday stressors to this new culture of social media, and we are severely lacking in genuine communication and kindness.

We are told in today's passage from Ephesians to turn from the way we lived before we met Christ, as the Gentiles were living. Not only that, but to actively "throw off" the sinful ways and old nature and "put on" a righteous and holy nature.

This means there should be a difference, a *noticeable* difference, between the way we behave compared to our neighbor who doesn't know Christ. Are you willing to submit yourself for the Lord to renew your thoughts and attitudes?

When a bully is hurting our first-grader at school, the staff needs to see kindness in our defense. When our husband does something foolish at a barbecue, our friends need to see us treat him with honor and respect. When our three-year-old is pitching a fit in the grocery store, the mom walking by is desperate to see an example of a patient and gracious mom.

You will be the person with a bright light in your eyes that others will notice because you have the Holy Spirit in you!

Created for Good Works

God saved you by his grace when you believed. And you can't take credit for this; it is a gift from God. Salvation is not a reward for the good things we have done, so none of us can boast about it. For we are God's masterpiece. He has created us anew in Christ Jesus, so we can do the good things he planned for us long ago.

EPHESIANS 2:8-10

DO YOU EVER WONDER WHY YOU'RE HERE? Amid the dirty diapers, to-do lists, sports schedules, grocery runs, bedtime snuggles, and Band-Aids?

It's easy to feel undervalued and forgotten when you're in the throes of the busy mothering years, as the world spins around you, not stopping to notice all the heart and energy you pour into raising the next generation. It is easy to feel like your job is measured in the daily minutiae that often seem inconsequential.

But Paul reminds us in Ephesians that we are created for a very specific purpose. You, precious mama, were created by the God of the Universe! He knows every cell in your body and emotion in your heart. God stirred your heart to believe, and you were saved by His gift of grace. But that's not where He ended His story for your life.

God made you a new creation in Him, because He already had a plan for you. He knew you were coming, He knew what your life would require, He knew what talents and heart you would have to offer—and He took all that and put it together with the good works He had already laid out for you. So in your coming to Him, accepting His free gift of grace, and desiring to make Him the Lord of your life, you are walking in *His* purpose written for you long before you were even a thought!

Take heart if you are weary. Take courage if you are afraid. Stand strong if you are wavering. God created you for a specific time and for a specific role and for many good works. Walk in His purpose for you as you follow Him!

The Trap of Pride

Pride leads to conflict.

PROVERBS 13:10

JAY AND I GOT INTO A fight a few months ago. It was actually pretty silly. Our fight wasn't over anything important, really. And it never should have happened. But words were exchanged and feelings hurt. We each retreated to a different room in the house to lick our wounds.

As I sat there feeling sorry for myself, I felt the Lord nudge me. Have you ever felt that nudge? It's an uncomfortable "uh-oh" moment for me most of the time. The check in my spirit caused me to go back over the verbal exchange word for word. I wanted to defend myself but knew better.

As I went over the exchange, I came to one particular moment in the conversation. Jay had thrown out a point that contradicted what I had been saying. Instantly, I knew he was right. But I refused to admit it. I kept arguing my point, even though I knew I was wrong. Why? What had driven me? The point of the whole argument was insignificant. Why had I kept the fight going? The Lord nudged me again: pride.

Ugh! I knew instantly that was it. I had been too proud to admit I was wrong. I had argued too long and fought too hard for my point of view to suddenly acknowledge I had been wrong the entire time, so things spiraled downward for another ten minutes. I went to Jay and asked forgiveness and confessed my sin of pride. As always, Jay took me in his arms and forgave me. But we had wasted half an evening.

Pride is a trap. It snares marriage partners and parents alike. Pride can take a small disagreement and turn it into a major blowup.

Today's verse packs a punch. There's so much truth in so few words. As Proverbs 13:10 says, pride always leads to conflict. If you want to build a richer marriage or grow in your relationship with your children, flee from pride. Recognize it. Confess it. Run from it.

Jesus Is in the Resurrection Business

Jesus shouted, "Lazarus, come out!"

JOHN 11:43

WHEN JESUS FOUND OUT THAT HIS friend Lazarus was sick, He said, "This sickness will not end in death. No, it is for God's glory so that God's Son may be glorified through it" (John 11:4, NIV). Lazarus's friends and family must have been devastated when he died, but Martha still had faith that Jesus could do a miracle. When she saw Jesus, she said, "I know that even now God will give you whatever you ask" (John 11:22, NIV). Can you imagine what she thought when Jesus shouted, "Lazarus, come out!" from in front of the tomb? Has there ever been a more outrageous statement? If Lazarus hadn't come forth, Jesus would have looked pretty bad. But, of course, he did come out. Lazarus walked out of the grave alive, and when the cloth was removed from his face, he blinked his eyes, looking around at his family and making eye contact with Jesus. What an incredible answer to an incredible prayer. But that's who Jesus is. He's the One who calls forth life out of death. He brings that which is dead back to life.

What do you have in your life that is dead? What do you have that needs to be brought back to life? Perhaps it's your marriage or your relationship with one of your parents. Maybe it's your prayer life or your desire to serve in the body of Christ. Maybe your passion for homeschooling has faded away. Perhaps you've lost a relationship with your best friend.

Jesus is in the business of bringing dead things back to life. Set aside time each day to pray and ask the Lord to release His resurrection power on the dead areas of your life. Ask Him to bring life back into your marriage. Ask Him to build a bridge back to revive broken relationships with parents or friends or siblings. Pray for Him to bring freshness and breath back into your prayer and devotional life. Try God, precious mom, and see if He won't give you that "fresh wind" you need. After all, if Jesus can resurrect Lazarus, He can certainly resurrect these things too.

Are You Wearing the Right Equipment?

Since we are surrounded by such a huge crowd of witnesses to the life of faith, let us strip off every weight that slows us down, especially the sin that so easily trips us up. And let us run with endurance the race God has set before us.

HEBREWS 12:1

THERE ARE FEW THINGS MORE EXCITING to watch than a track event at the Olympics. World-class athletes, the best of the best in their sport, gather to compete against each other for the coveted gold medal. At least five to ten years of training comes down to one race that may be over in as little as ten seconds. The difference between first and last place may be measured in hundredths of a second. The runners settle into their starting blocks with every muscle tensed, waiting for the starter's gun.

Now, could you imagine seeing one of these runners competing while wearing a pair of heavy hiking boots and a full subzero parka? Of course not! Could you imagine a competitor's shoelaces tangled together or caught in the starting block? Definitely not! If they want to win, these runners wear shoes that weigh around three ounces each, with the tiniest sleeveless T-shirt and a pair of ultralight running shorts. They make sure they are prepared to win the race set before them.

Are you living the Christian life like an Olympic athlete? Are you carrying only the essentials in the race, or have you become encumbered by sins that entangle you and burdens you were never meant to carry? The author of Hebrews challenges each of us to look at our lives honestly. What are the things that are slowing you down today? What has been tripping you up and keeping you from running your race well? Take time each day for introspection, asking God to show you things that are getting in the way. As you purpose to "strip off every weight" that slows you down, the things of this world will begin to grow dim and fall away. Concentrate on the prize that awaits you, and begin to run the race you've been called to like an Olympic champion.

There Is One Thing That Never Changes

Jesus Christ is the same yesterday and today and forever.

HEBREWS 13:8, NIV

DID YOU CATCH THAT? I've known today's verse for more than forty years. I learned it as a child. Perhaps you did too. My grandmother often quoted Hebrews 13:8. It was one of her favorites. It's become one of my favorites too. But I never realized how precious God's unchanging nature would become to me until recently.

We live in a world of relentless change. And the rate of change is accelerating year by year. I've bought my favorite James Taylor album on vinyl, on 8-track, on cassette, on CD, and as an MP3 download. New formats are invented every year, it seems. Just as soon as I become comfortable with one social media platform, four new ones appear for me to figure out. The baby boy I used to hold in my arms is now a young married man with a home of his own. I am truly awash in a sea of change.

But there is one still point in a turning world. There is one thing that never, ever changes—Jesus Christ. He was the same in the beginning when it all began. He was the same when He walked the earth in human form. He was the same when He walked with the early church martyrs. And He is still the same with you and me today.

I love knowing there is one place I can always turn when the changes become too overwhelming. I can return to Him whom my soul loves. Don't you love that too?

Anytime the Lord seems to be retreating or perhaps feels far away, it's always me who has moved. It's never Him. He is the same, never wavering. And here's the really strange thing that defies all earthly laws of physics: no matter how far away I may have moved, it's never more than one step back to Him.

If you've moved away, or if you've been overwhelmed by today's chaotic world, take that step. Return to your first love, and rediscover the peace that comes when you're in His presence.

Stop and Notice the Extraordinary

Amazement seized them all, and they glorified God and were filled with awe, saying, "We have seen extraordinary things today."

LUKE 5:26, ESV

HAVE YOU SEEN EXTRAORDINARY THINGS TODAY? No, I'm not talking about your son putting his dirty clothes in the clothes hamper or your daughter loading her dirty bowl into the dishwasher, although those things are extraordinary when you're a mom. Instead, I'm talking about the extraordinary things that surround us in numbers so great we usually take them for granted.

I'm talking about things like Paul talks about in Romans 1:20: "The invisible things of him from the creation of the world are clearly seen, being understood by the things that are made, even his eternal power and Godhead; so that they are without excuse" (KJV). God's Word declares that the evidence of His mighty power is all around us. In our busy world, it's easy to fail to see it—but it's important that we do.

Last evening, Jay's mom called me from my desk to come and feast my eyes on a glorious sunset. And do you know what? It refreshed my soul. She was right to call me from my work of writing. It was a chance to hit the reset button—a chance to gain fresh perspective.

When you're overwhelmed, take a break. Go outside. Open your eyes. What do you see? Clouds? Evergreens? Fall leaves? Fresh fallen snow? A chipmunk gathering nuts for winter? A child skipping rope? An elderly neighbor walking their dog? They're all miracles. Every one of them is a miracle. Everywhere you look in God's creation you'll find a miracle. That should amaze you. It should leave you in awe.

Awe and wonder are natural by-products of the normal Christian life. To a small child, *everything* is amazing, from the sound of thunder to the dandelion seeds blowing in the breeze. As adults, we become bored and jaded. We get distracted by completing our to-do lists and fretting about the everyday challenges we all face. We lose the awe we were intended to have. Both Paul and Luke point us back toward a spirit of awe and wonder. If your relationship with the Lord is feeling a little stale, take time to "stop and smell the roses" today, worshiping their Creator for His extraordinary creativity and care. You may soon find yourself walking in a closer relationship with the Lord.

The Privilege of Laying Down Your Life

Greater love has no one than this, that a person will lay down his life for his friends.

JOHN 15:13, NASB

A YOUNG WOMAN I MET SEVERAL years ago shared her life's story with me. She had been raised in a home without television, but on a trip to her grandfather's house, she was able to watch a movie on television for the first time ever. The movie she watched was *The Miracle Worker,* starring Anne Bancroft and Patty Duke. The movie tells the story of Helen Keller, who was blind, deaf, and nonverbal, and Anne Sullivan, the woman who taught her to communicate and accompanied her for the rest of her life.

This new friend of mine relayed how she was impressed with all that Helen Keller was able to accomplish, but she was most impressed with Anne Sullivan. The thought that anyone would voluntarily choose to serve someone else for their entire lifetime seemed overwhelming to her young mind.

As the years progressed, she married and had two sons who were both severely autistic, unable to speak or express themselves. Remembering that movie from many years ago, this young woman cried out to the Lord to raise up an Anne Sullivan who would lay down her life to help her two sons. She sensed the Lord speaking to her, saying, "I have—and it's you." As the years went by, those boys learned to communicate as their mom laid down her life for them one day at a time.

Do you sometimes feel like Anne Sullivan? Who are you laying down your life to serve? We all serve someone. Sometimes we serve ourselves. Sometimes we serve sin. Sometimes we serve our spouse. Sometimes we serve our children. And sometimes we serve the Lord.

The story of Helen Keller is indeed amazing, but not nearly as amazing as the story of Anne Sullivan.

When we become Anne Sullivans, we are fulfilling the challenge to love one another in an extraordinary way. May the Lord help us to see where we're being called and to find the courage and faith to lay down our lives for those He has called us to serve.

Come to Me

Jesus said, "Come to me, all you who are weary and carry heavy burdens, and I will give you rest."

MATTHEW 11:28

I'VE SELDOM MET A MOTHER WHO WASN'T TIRED. Weariness goes hand in hand with motherhood. If you've been up twice in the middle of the night with a sick child, gotten up early to get your husband's lunch packed and send him off to work, run a dozen errands, and spent the day serving your children while trying to prepare breakfast, lunch, and dinner, you know what weariness is.

We long for rest. Our bodies crave a chance to relax, and our minds are sometimes desperate to find peace and quiet amid loud children and a noisy world. Our souls long to release the relentless burdens of motherhood. Precious mom, I have good news for you. Rest is available if you'll go to the One who created you.

While your responsibilities and duties may not disappear, God is there to give hope for every mother's weary soul. "But I don't have time to go to Him," you say. Friend, you don't have time to *not* go to Him. The busier your schedule is, the more important it is for you to carve out time to be alone with the Lord.

As with every season of life, some years and months it will be easier to set that time aside than other times. But lean in, precious mom—when it's hard to find the time, it's imperative that you do. Try getting up a little earlier or taking your Bible with you as you wait for a doctor's appointment or a music lesson. Maybe it's time to recalibrate your schedule so that you can find time to be with the lover of your soul. Time with Him really does change everything—from our perspectives to our ability to be patient with ourselves and with our children.

Perhaps you've seen the popular meme that asks if you need Jesus in order to go to heaven. The heartfelt response is "I need Jesus to go to Walmart!" Truer words have never been spoken.

Even if it's only five or ten minutes, a time of quietness, prayer, and worship will refresh you. The One who created you and cares for you is calling you. Can you hear Him? Run to Him now. Let Him refresh you. Lay your burdens down, and rest your weary head in His arms. Rest for your weary soul awaits.

Where Are You, God?

Every day I call to you, my God, but you do not answer.
Every night I lift my voice, but I find no relief.

PSALM 22:2

DURING MY QUIET TIME THIS MORNING, I was listening to some old gospel songs. The lyrics of one song caught my attention: "He may not come when you want Him, but He's right on time." Do you know the song? It's called "You Can't Hurry God." Find it and listen to it even if you know it.

Have you ever tried to hurry God? You can't do it. He's a God that can't be hurried. When a thousand years is as a day to Him, hurry isn't in God's vocabulary. But it's the second part of that lyric that holds the promise our souls long for: "He's right on time." Did you catch that? God always shows up right on time.

How I wish I'd known that deep in my soul years ago. I've spent too many years of my life being impatient with the Lord. Have you? We know something that needs to happen. We can see it clearly. It's so obvious. Why can't God see it? It's easy to get frustrated. WHERE IS GOD?

Perhaps no other question burns so deeply in our hearts: *Where is God when we need Him? Why isn't He responding?* Read again how David put it. In other words, he's asking, "Where are you, God?" David is almost accusatory in his plea.

But from before the dawn of Creation until today, God always shows up at the right time. You can bet your life on it. He is not bound by our sense of timing, nor is He obligated to appear upon our command. He is the great I Am. He comes when the time is perfect. Not a moment before. Never a moment after. He may not come when we want Him to, but He's right on time.

Rest in that knowledge as you lie down to sleep tonight. Like David, it's okay to cry out day and night, but rest in the knowledge that God has not forsaken you and He *will* show up right on time. Sleep well in that knowledge, friend.

He Will Equip You

May the God of peace, who through the blood of the eternal covenant brought back from the dead our Lord Jesus, that great Shepherd of the sheep, equip you with everything good for doing his will, and may he work in us what is pleasing to him.

HEBREWS 13:20-21, NIV

WHEN I WAS PREGNANT WITH OUR FIRST CHILD, I was terrified. I was worried I would not be a good mother. I was afraid I might be an awful parent. I didn't know if I could trust my parenting skills. My own childhood had been less than perfect in many ways, and I feared that I too might be ill equipped for parenthood.

But a dear friend pulled me aside one day and spoke life-giving words to me. She said, "Heidi, you're going to make a wonderful mother! Just because you weren't parented well doesn't mean you're going to be a bad parent too." And then she prayed for me. She prayed for exactly what I needed: wisdom and peace. You see, knowing that God will provide us with wisdom means He will equip us for the challenge of motherhood. And when we know we are equipped, we can be at peace. And while I may not have been the world's most perfect parent, I've never again doubted that I could do this special job that God had called me to do. He trains and equips those He calls.

What fears and doubts have shadowed you? What insecurities have lowered a veil of uncertainty over your life?

Read again how the author of Hebrews encourages us:

May the God of peace, who through the blood of the eternal covenant brought back from the dead our Lord Jesus, that great Shepherd of the sheep, equip you with everything good for doing his will, and may he work in us what is pleasing to him.

Did you catch that? God will equip you with *everything you need* to do His will. From the moment I began to carry life within my womb, the Lord was equipping me with everything I needed to be a good mother and to parent in a way that would be pleasing to Him. Whatever He calls you to do, He will equip you. You can rest on that promise, friend.

I Will Never Again Remember

I will forgive their wickedness, and I will never again remember their sins.

HEBREWS 8:12

THIS MORNING, WHILE I WAS WAITING for my youngest to brush her teeth and come downstairs, I read Hebrews 8:12 over and over. It struck me in a new way as I considered the depth of God's forgiveness.

Yes, God forgave my sins. I know that. It's a debt I can never repay, and I am constantly aware of this truth. But it's the next portion of the passage that left me stunned and speechless: "I will never again remember their sins."

God didn't say He would forget my sins. He said He would never again remember them. In our humanity, it's easy for us to forget things. In fact, that's a common saying, isn't it? We're often told to "forgive and forget." But anything you forget can be remembered again. Perhaps you've forgiven and even forgotten about a time of infidelity in a relationship or a betrayal by a friend. You purpose to leave it in the past. And yet, suddenly at the worst possible moment, it all comes rushing back again. You remember what the other person did. You remember how badly it hurt. And you have to begin dealing with it all over again. In fact, it may be far worse when you remember it than when you first dealt with it.

But God didn't merely say He would forget our sins and wickedness. He made a promise. He swore He would never again remember our failings. It will never come rushing back to His memory, and He will never again see us as sinners. Through the blood of Christ, we have been cleansed of all unrighteousness, and we have God's very word that we are forgiven and that we never have to worry about Him remembering our sin. Rest in that truth, friend. If you are in Christ, nothing can ever separate you from His love—including the sins in your past.

Consider Others More Significant

Do nothing from selfish ambition or conceit, but in humility count others more significant than yourselves. Let each of you look not only to his own interests, but also to the interests of others.

PHILIPPIANS 2:3-4, ESV

"MOM! SHE STOLE MY RED MARKER!"

"I needed it right now, and he wasn't using it."

"Yes, I was! I just set it down for a second. She's going to use it all up."

"No, I'm not!"

And on it goes. Sound familiar? How about this?

"I'm so exhausted. How come he gets to just go to bed whenever he wants to? Yet here I am, wrapping up the dishes, starting laundry, fighting with a cranky two-year-old who won't stay in bed. When do I get to just go to bed when I want to?"

In both cases, there are legitimate complaints, but the issue is how we handle our own response. We can choose to focus on ourselves and our desires: my son could choose to believe that his art project was more important than his sister's art project and that she was being selfish by taking the marker and using it when she knew full well he needed it. Or I could focus on how tired I was, how little help I was getting, and how many things I did that day for my husband.

The reality is that we can only control ourselves. We can't actually *make* someone else do what we want, so our control is limited to our own responses.

We are told the right choice is to focus on others: my children can choose to kindly consider their sibling having the desire for the same red marker at the same moment. I can choose to believe that my husband is exhausted after a long week at work and that God gifted us differently, so he doesn't notice all the things I see at ten o'clock every night.

This all rests on knowing that the Lord is responsible for meeting our own needs. When we are confident that the Lord will meet all of our needs, we can choose to focus on others instead of being hyperfocused on ourselves.

What do you choose today?

Look for the Lord

"I know the plans I have for you," says the LORD. "They are plans for good and not for disaster, to give you a future and a hope. In those days when you pray, I will listen. If you look for me wholeheartedly, you will find me."

JEREMIAH 29:11-13

WE LOVE TO TAKE HOLD OF Jeremiah 29:11 and quote it as an encouraging, feel-good verse, don't we? It *is* a comforting verse. But when we read the surrounding verses and put it into context, the message has so much more meaning.

In Jeremiah 29, the Lord is speaking to the Israelites who have been exiled to live in captivity under Babylonian rule—a culture that is not their own. God is pointing out that He does have good plans for the Israelites, for a future and a hope, but He is also making it clear that they will be staying put in Babylon for the next seventy years. This is no small thing He's doing! But He is there for them. He reminds them to pray and call out to Him, that He will be found by them.

We often find ourselves in the desert for what seems like a very long time. A husband has a decades-long pornography addiction, consequences of "sowing wild oats" are lifelong, we beg for children and the Lord says no, adult children squander their talents and walk away from the Lord, our parents suffer for years in the fallen state of dementia, we spend years desperately lonely surrounded by people because we are locked in depression.

When it seems like life's challenges are more than we can bear, we have to remember that God knows how hard this world is. He knows it's not our home, and He is saying to us, "I've got a plan." He encourages us, telling us, "I'm right here. Pray and I will hear you. Seek me and you will find me!"

You are the Lord's beloved, and He has good plans for you, even in the midst of troubling times. Look for Him.

Pray about the Small Stuff

Always be joyful. Never stop praying. Be thankful in all circumstances,
for this is God's will for you who belong to Christ Jesus.

1 THESSALONIANS 5:16-18

I LOVE THAT I CAN BE in constant communication with Jesus through prayer. No matter what I'm doing, I can thank and praise Him. Through prayer, I can ask God to help me align myself with His desires.

When I am getting ready for the day, I thank Him for rest, asking Him to encourage my hard-working husband who is buttoning his shirt next to me. When I hear the sliding door shut as my son leaves for work, I ask the Lord to give my teenager courage in his conversations with his friends today. Sometimes I can't find my keys when I'm running late, and one of my kids will remind me to ask the Lord to show me right where they are—He knows! I thank Him as He leads me right to them—and I often find them right by the glasses I forgot to grab in my rush. Thank you, Lord, for that!

I ask the Lord to make me more like Him. I ask Him to teach me parts of His character I've never known. I beg Him for wisdom and grace as I know I'm in short supply and He gives these in abundance. I ask Him to draw me nearer to Him.

On another day, I have a child with a confusing health need, and I ask for a specific answer that I know the doctors can't pinpoint, but I know the Lord knows, and I trust Him for an answer, because He created this child of mine! I thank the Lord the following day when He leads me right to the answer that makes sense, and again two days later when it proves to be true.

Precious mom, your Creator *knows* your need. He knows every detail of every day, every longing in your heart, and every answer to all the questions. But it's not about just asking for things. He does know those answers and He cares, but it's about asking for more of Him in your moments. He knows you and wants to walk with you in prayer—all day, every day.

Deeper Prayers

Teach me knowledge and good judgment, for I trust your commands.

PSALM 119:66, NIV

As MOMS, WE OFTEN HAVE A prayer list that we go through for our children: that they are healthy, safe, and (always!) that they are obedient. Yet often as we're praying for these ordinary, everyday things, we can miss out on more important prayers. We often find these types of prayers in Scripture. Here is one from Philippians 1:9-11: "This is my prayer: that your love may abound more and more in knowledge and depth of insight, so that you may be able to discern what is best and may be pure and blameless for the day of Christ, filled with the fruit of righteousness that comes through Jesus Christ—to the glory and praise of God" (NIV).

The older my kids have gotten, the more I've realized how vital abounding love, knowledge, and depth of insight are. When our children grow in these three areas, they *will* be able to discern what is best. Then, as the years pass, our children can grow into adults who will be pure and blameless for the day of Christ. This, of course, is what we want most for our kids.

Yes, it is important to pray about the daily things. I've prayed about potty training and driver's education, hormonal teen girls and thick-headed teen boys. Yet, all of us need to go deeper with our prayers. We can pray for our children to have high morals and righteous living even as we're watching them play on the playground or teaching them how to read.

Finally, we can pray these verses for ourselves too. Even today, we can pray that our own love will abound more and that we will grow in knowledge and depth of insight for all that we face. We can pray for discernment, which is something we all need. We can pray that our lives will be righteous, which is basically making good choices now so that we will be pure and blameless for the day of Christ when He comes.

Let's go deeper with our prayers today.

"Do Not Disturb" Prayers

Look to the LORD and his strength; seek his face always.

PSALM 105:4, NIV

As a kid, an adult in your life might have told you to kneel, fold your hands, and close your eyes when it was time to pray. Since you were also learning other things, you may have believed that's how prayer works. Yes, we can pray by kneeling, folding our hands, and closing our eyes at a scheduled time of day, but that's not the only way to pray. It can be a continual conversation with your Creator. It can even be the shortest cry, "Help!" when faced with a tantrumming toddler in the grocery store.

While we may want to set aside those longer times to pray, we can also blurt out short prayers whenever a worry fills our minds. Jesus' ear is always attuned to our smallest requests. There is no rule that says prayer must happen at a certain time of day. Jesus doesn't need an invitation, and we don't need to mark a time on our schedule. We can pray anytime, and He is there.

I love this prayer of David, shepherd and king, from Psalm 27: "My heart says of you, 'Seek his face!' Your face, LORD, I will seek" (verse 8, NIV). How would our prayer lives change if, as soon as our hearts felt troubled, we realized it was actually a signal to seek God right then? A sign to pray no matter where we were?

Susanna Wesley is a good example of someone who would pray at all times. She was a mom with a large family, and she sometimes had to run the household without her husband's help. It's noted that whenever she couldn't get away to pray alone, she would tell her children that if they saw her with her apron over her head, that meant she was praying. Basically, an apron over that mom's head was a "Do Not Disturb" sign. That's something that might be worth trying!

Whether you try the apron-over-your-head method or you get your own Do Not Disturb sign, work to make prayer your go-to habit to carry you through the day. Yes, do set aside times to spend with God, but also remember that He's always there. Prayer can happen when you're kneeling with your eyes closed, or it can happen during any other "eyes wide-open moment" of your day.

The Lord is always available to hear our cries for help. When our hearts feel troubled, it's a reminder to seek Him. Whether you have ten minutes or ten seconds, God will hear and care.

Prayer Changes Things

We also glory in our sufferings, because we know that suffering produces
perseverance; perseverance, character; and character, hope.

ROMANS 5:3-4, NIV

I HAVE A LARGE FAMILY THROUGH BIRTH, but many of my friends have grown their
families through adoption. I've cried and prayed with many friends who are adoptive parents, especially those who've adopted older kids. It's hard to raise kids as it
is, but there are added challenges to parenting kids whose childhoods have been
marked with pre-adoption trauma. While a child's actions and attitudes can be
painful to deal with, things get especially disheartening for adoptive parents when
it seems as if they've done everything right and their children's behavior does not
improve.

I have friends who have done all they could to bring their kids into a loving
and caring environment. They've put them in all the right therapies. Yet, even then,
there is no promise of miraculous transformation. As hard as it is to accept, no
number of "right" things adoptive parents do can completely erase all the "wrong"
that has been done to their kids in the past. Some things, like hearts and minds,
can't be mended quickly or completely.

Of course, this is true for every parent: we can do everything right for our
kids, but it still doesn't guarantee our children will make good choices as they
near or enter adulthood. Yet, all parents can find help and hope in the same place:
through prayer.

As James 5:16 says, "The prayer of a righteous person is powerful and effective"
(NIV). Sometimes our prayers will be powerful and effective for our kids, but they
will always be powerful and effective for us. When we pray, we build our faith.
Faith-filled people pray because they believe it makes a difference. Whether our
kids are adopted or biological, the sufferings can produce perseverance, character,
and hope in each mom. These things are wonderful answers to our prayers!

Sometimes you may not see good outcomes from your prayers in a week, in
a year, or even in your lifetime, but that doesn't mean they aren't effective. You'll
never know what difference your prayers will make in your children's lives. And
you can be sure that your prayers are making a difference for you.

Train Yourself for the Hills

Do you not know that in a race all the runners run, but only one gets the prize? Run in such a way as to get the prize.

1 CORINTHIANS 9:24, NIV

MY YOUNGEST SISTER HILARY LOVES TO climb mountains. Here in the Pacific Northwest, we have plenty. She's invited me, but mountain climbing is not my thing. I'd rather sit by the fire at the foot of the mountain with a steaming cup of coffee and a good book. I have several friends who are athletes like Hilary. I admire them, and I appreciate that their calling illustrates many things about motherhood. This life is a marathon, after all. It's one mountain after another.

If you're a long-distance runner or a climber, I'm guessing you've struggled with that last hill. As a mother, I'm always amazed by the number of challenging "hills" I've encountered along the path God has laid out for me. I don't ever ask for them, wish for them, or long for them. Yet, they always show up and leave me panting for air as I struggle to get over them.

You'd think I'd be an extraordinary "runner" for all the motherhood marathons I've run over the years, but the truth is there are times when I look at the mountain and want to give up. Hills in our parenting journey can catch even the most seasoned mom off guard and feeling untrained.

Yet, the Bible urges us to run the race that God has set before us. The race will often come with unseen obstacles. First Corinthians 9 tells us, "Everyone who competes in the games goes into strict training. They do it to get a crown that will not last, but we do it to get a crown that will last forever" (verse 25, NIV). Paul was so eager to serve God fully that his life was focused on eternity instead of things or circumstances of this world.

We are to be people who choose to train ourselves to be godly. How can we expect to be like Jesus and run the race if we aren't in His Word, the greatest training book of all time?

You and I can succeed, but we must choose to let God be in charge. A mother who surrenders to Him is drawn quite spontaneously into a great learning process that Christians call "sanctification." It's a process that's meant to make us more like Jesus. Once you have learned to conquer the hills with God's help, then you can help train the stragglers behind you.

Keep climbing, sweet mom! Keep running your race. The view from the top will be worth it.

I Will Not Be Shaken

LORD, you alone are my inheritance, my cup of blessing. You guard all that is mine. The land you have given me is a pleasant land. What a wonderful inheritance! I will bless the LORD who guides me; even at night my heart instructs me. I know the LORD is always with me. I will not be shaken, for he is right beside me.

PSALM 16:5-8

THIS WORLD IS FULL OF TROUBLE, and it seems to be growing. Does it feel that way to you? Sometimes it feels inescapable. Violence in the cities, corrupt politicians, natural disasters. On a personal level, we may be dealing with cancer, chronic illness, job loss, wayward adult children, constant family tension, marriages in crisis, broken friendships, emotional hurts, and more.

Most of us learn early in life that there is no guarantee that we will escape trouble because we are Christians. Jesus even warned us about this in John 16:33: "I have told you these things, so that in me you may have peace. In this world you will have trouble. But take heart! I have overcome the world" (NIV). Because He has overcome the world, we will too. Our calling is to learn to walk in the trouble with joy, hope, and a calm assurance that says, "All will be well." After all, God is doing something good in us through the hard times!

As we walk through trials and heal from wounds, they produce a deep, abiding faith in God that holds steady when the waves seem like they will overtake us.

As you shepherd your children through difficult times, it's important to keep your eyes on Jesus. He is the reason we have hope, and our children need to know this truth deep in their souls. The Lord says in His Word that He has an inheritance worth looking forward to! He is our inheritance, and everything else pales in comparison to what lies ahead for the Christian.

Even in the dark seasons, there is no need to be shaken, for we are not alone!

If you are weary and hurting, whether it's from a major crisis or a challenging day of parenting, His promise is for you. Maybe this is a good day to write today's verse on a card and put it on your bathroom mirror or by your kitchen sink. The Lord is your cup of blessing. He is always with you! Because of Him, we will not be shaken—no matter what comes.

Remember the Sacrifice

The LORD God has told us what is right and what he demands: "See that justice is done, let mercy be your first concern, and humbly obey your God."

MICAH 6:8, CEV

MY YOUNGEST SON TOTALED HIS CAR this week. All the airbags deployed, and the car was declared a complete loss. Miraculously, he walked away without a scratch. The car did what it was created to do, sacrificing itself to protect its occupants with precisely engineered "crumple zones" and safety equipment. As a mother, I am grateful for automotive engineers and their expertise. It could have ended very differently, and I don't want to think about what might have been.

As I was flipping through a Christian publication this week, I was mesmerized by a painting of Jesus on the cross. His body was wracked and folded awkwardly, His face bathed in sweat and tears, His wounds open and bleeding. And in truth, I'm sure it was a hundred times worse than the artist portrayed in this remarkable scene.

My mind flashed back to the photographs of my son's car from a few days ago, twisted and wrecked, fluids leaking out onto the pavement beneath it and the airbags deployed and shriveled, deflated on the seats. Like that car, Jesus had sacrificed His body to save my life. Of course, I've known that truth since I was a small child, but seeing the painting and remembering the photos of my son's car made me stop and catch my breath

I had been so grateful for the safety engineering and the incredible job the car had done in saving my boy's life. Am I that amazed at the incredible truth of what transpired on Calvary? That twisted body on the cross was sacrificed so that I might have life. I will never again take that truth for granted. We didn't deserve to walk away from the eternal consequences of sin without a mark on us. And He didn't deserve the Cross. Lord, help us to never forget what You've done for us.

Love and Respect

Again I say, each man must love his wife as he loves himself,
and the wife must respect her husband.

EPHESIANS 5:33

OUR CULTURE DOESN'T ENCOURAGE WOMEN TO respect men, and it shows. The feminist movement has done terrible damage to men. Fathers have been portrayed as idiots on TV since the beginning of sitcoms, and it has gone downhill from there. We are encouraged in our culture to mother our husbands, treat them as fools behind their backs, joke about their stupidity, and mock their weaknesses. We've attempted to tell men that they can have no say in what happens to their unborn children—never mind that it takes a man and a woman to create new life. Is it any wonder we have a generation of passive men?

When you read today's verse from Ephesians, you might have felt immediately excused because your husband may not be loving you as he is commanded. While you may *feel* justified, your husband's sin does not nullify Scripture. As his wife, you can respectfully disagree, get intervention for your marriage, and stand up for yourself when needed. But your responsibility is to respect your husband. It's clear and unequivocal.

Respect his needs, his desires, his hard work, his willingness to serve his family. Respect his choices, even if you think they are foolish. Respect his opinions, even if you disagree. Respect his efforts, even if they are unsuccessful. Do not discount the wounds of public humor at your husband's expense.

Respect him. Especially in front of others.

The Lord will meet your needs, so in this posture of respect, of course you can ask Him to grow your husband into a man who loves God and loves you as he should. Just respect your husband in the process.

I have spent plenty of time with women who do not act respectfully toward their husbands, and it is painful to witness. No man will continue standing tall for long when his wife mocks, nags, or mothers him. He will slink passively out of an emotional relationship with his wife and put distance between them. But a man who is respected will stand tall, serve graciously, and love his family. Do you long to be married to a diligent lover, a stronger leader, and a kind servant? It starts with respect.

Encourage One Another

Encourage each other and build each other up, just as you are already doing.

1 THESSALONIANS 5:11

I'VE READ 1 THESSALONIANS MANY TIMES OVER the course of my life. But this morning, during my quiet time, 1 Thessalonians 5:11 jumped off the page and caught my attention. Have you experienced that? Suddenly a familiar verse takes on a new urgency as the Lord highlights it in your personal devotion time.

I've always read that verse in the context of the body of believers at large. Paul is charging the believers in Thessalonica to await the Lord's return and to press on, remaining alert always and keeping their priorities straight. That's good advice.

But this morning, that verse suddenly spoke to me about my marriage. If there is one important "one another" in my life, it's my husband. How often do I intentionally encourage him? This verse isn't only about building up our brothers and sisters in Christ, as important as that is. It's a challenge to speak life to our partner on a daily basis.

All too often, it feels like we are pulling in opposite directions in this business of parenting. Every parent knows we often find ourselves in new and uncertain territory where we're not sure which way to turn. We need each other on this journey. It's so easy to find fault, to criticize, to become frustrated with our spouse. That's what the enemy of our souls wants. Nothing pleases him more than to sow division in marriage. Don't let him.

Encourage one another and build each other up. Each of us is all too familiar with the relentless inner monologue of the accuser. He never tires of reminding us of our failings and faults. We need someone in our corner who is just as relentless in building us up.

God is so good to show us where we need to improve, isn't He? The Holy Spirit used this passage to remind me that I need to be intentional about encouraging my husband. God's heart is that we would build our men up at every opportunity.

What are you waiting for? Today is a great day to encourage the precious people in your life. After all, a little encouragement can go a long way.

Growing in Parenting Wisdom

Teach us to realize the brevity of life, so that we may grow in wisdom.

PSALM 90:12

THERE'S NOTHING LIKE BECOMING A MOTHER to help us grasp the concept of the brevity of this life. One minute, we are holding a tiny infant, the next, a toddler. You blink, and that toddler is asking about driving your car—and shortly after that, they're picking out furniture for their own home. Life comes at you fast.

All of my grandparents are home with the Lord now—and I am a grandmother.

In today's verse, the psalmist exhorts us to grasp the brevity of life. In the New Testament, James reminds us, "Your life is like the morning fog—it's here a little while, then it's gone" (James 4:14).

Perhaps you've heard your parents or grandparents remark about how quickly life goes by. Seventy or eighty years isn't long in the scope of eternity. God's Word tells us to think about these things—things we prefer not to think about. Why? Because within that contemplation we will find wisdom.

Every parent knows that if there's one thing we need, it's wisdom. Which battles are worth fighting and which ones are meaningless? Parenting is a difficult job under the best of circumstances, but over the years and through many struggles and successes, I've found the Word of God to be true.

When I realize the brevity of life and think about how quickly the morning fog dissipates, I find my priorities beginning to fall into place. Have you noticed that too? Things that seemed so important before dim in the light of eternity. I encourage you to gain wisdom by prioritizing your parenting tasks in light of God's Word. In those words, you will find life and find it abundantly.

The Lord Directs Our Steps

We can make our plans, but the LORD determines our steps.
PROVERBS 16:9

ONE OF MY DEAREST FRIENDS AND his wife were gifted a trip to Cancún, Mexico, several years ago. They were to meet others there and spend a week at a high-end resort, eating amazing food and basking in the sun by the ocean. They had done extensive planning, booking a preliminary flight to San Diego, where they could spend the night at a beautiful resort before flying to Cancún the next morning.

After weeks of preparation, the big day arrived. They enjoyed a fabulous night in San Diego, packed the next morning, and headed to the airport. As they prepared to board the flight to their dream vacation, they discovered they had somehow lost one of their passports. After a frantic search and several phone calls, my friends were left in San Diego as their plane departed without them. All of their plans screeched to a halt.

As they prayerfully considered what to do, they realized their schedule was cleared and they were already on the west coast, so they booked a flight to come visit Jay and me in Washington. What looked like a disappointing disaster turned into one of the most fruitful weeks of their lives. Together, the four of us had a remarkable time of fellowship, ministry, and planning that would never have been possible if they had been in Mexico. They had planned their trip, but the Lord directed them in a new and unexpected direction.

Why am I telling you this story? Because knowing the Lord ultimately determines our steps gives us hope for the future. Too many believers live in a constant state of fear, perpetually anxious about tomorrow and what may happen. But in the Kingdom of God, we don't need to live under that crippling fear. Live in faith, knowing that even though you have carefully made plans, your life is in His hands.

If your plans are interrupted today, look to the Lord. You can trust that He will direct your steps. He has good plans for you.

Justice in Due Season

I also noticed that under the sun there is evil in the courtroom. Yes,
even the courts of law are corrupt! I said to myself, "In due season God
will judge everyone, both good and bad, for all their deeds."

ECCLESIASTES 3:16-17

I DON'T KNOW ABOUT YOU, but I have noticed a lot of injustice in the world lately. Watching the evening news can be incredibly frustrating when it seems there is no justice for those who have been hurt or harmed by another. Have you also noticed evil in the courtrooms these days? I am appalled at so many of the decisions coming out of today's justice system. Justice seems far from us all too often. I've wept over more than one verdict in recent years. Sometimes, it leaves me discouraged and wondering if there will ever be justice.

But the author of Ecclesiastes, who scholars believe was King Solomon, reminds us that nothing escapes God's justice forever. I've taught this truth to all of my children. I hope you have shared it with your children too. Children have a deep sense of justice. Especially young children. They are quick to say, "That's not fair!" or "That's not right!" I've felt that way too—more lately than in years past, it seems. I sometimes forget the truth that God's justice is coming when I'm in the middle of a frustrating moment.

Remind yourself and your children of Solomon's wisdom: nothing escapes the Lord's justice forever. And if you find yourself frustrated with the lack of justice reported on the nightly news, remind yourself as well. Whether it's the courtroom or the classroom—or the family room—justice is inescapable.

Whether it's the "trial of the century" on television, or a sibling taking advantage in an unjust way, the Lord sees all. Even in the workplace, when someone else gets credit for your work, or someone else gets the promotion although they didn't deserve it—the Lord sees. In due season, He will make everything right.

Ask Him

You parents—if your children ask for a loaf of bread, do you give them a stone instead? Or if they ask for a fish, do you give them a snake? Of course not! So if you sinful people know how to give good gifts to your children, how much more will your heavenly Father give good gifts to those who ask him.

MATTHEW 7:9-11

IF YOU WERE TEACHING A CHILD'S Sunday school lesson on Matthew 7:9-11, how do you think your class would respond to the message? My guess is that most kids would take what they heard, go home to their parents, and start explaining that they wanted a new bicycle for Christmas or a new iPhone for their birthday and that the Bible says their parents should buy it for them. When I was a child, that's how I saw it too.

Of course as we mature, we realize that we would be missing out on an important part of the passage if we focused only on verse 9. In verses 10 and 11, we see that the good gifts we "sinful people" give our children pale in comparison to the gifts our heavenly Father gives us. There's one "catch" to this encouraging verse, though. Check out the last two little words of verse 11: "ask him."

Yes, you can trust the Lord. Yes, He has wonderful plans for you. But the footnote is that He will give these things "to those who ask him." Just like gratitude and humility, *asking* is foundational to a healthy relationship with our heavenly Father. For some believers, their devotional life consists only of asking—constantly asking for everything under the sun and seldom expressing gratitude for the many blessings they have received. But others are hesitant to ask.

If you are hesitant to ask, I want to encourage you to ask the Lord for His blessing. As you thank Him for the things He has already done, humbly ask Him for His direction. Ask Him to be present with you during trials. Ask Him to bring you just the right used car. Ask Him to find just the right part-time job for your teenage son. Ask Him to find just the right husband for your daughter.

Like a wonderful Father, God delights in giving us good gifts, if only we ask Him.

Pressed but Not Crushed

We are pressed on every side by troubles, but we are not crushed. We are perplexed, but not driven to despair.

2 CORINTHIANS 4:8

IF YOU'VE WATCHED THE NEWS LATELY, this verse should catch your attention. Now more than in any season of my life, we seem to have troubles on every side: our economy, our border, our cities, our allies, our enemies, and so much more. Never mind the sad stories reported from my region of the country. I had to turn off the news this morning. It was too much to bear. I found myself overwhelmed and angry at the magnitude of troubles we all face.

But my daily reading brought me to 2 Corinthians, and this verse spoke to my heart. Let it speak to your heart too. I began to think about the troubles facing Paul and the apostles. Suddenly my troubles seemed less significant.

Three times I was beaten with rods. Once I was stoned. Three times I was shipwrecked. Once I spent a whole night and a day adrift at sea.
2 CORINTHIANS 11:25

And yet, Paul said he wasn't crushed. He admitted he was perplexed by all that had happened, but he wasn't despairing. Can you say that? I thought about those two verses often throughout the day. Yes, I am surrounded by troubles, but not the kind of troubles Paul was dealing with. Yes, I'm perplexed by what is happening in this world, but not as perplexed as Paul must have been. Yes, I worry about the world my children will be left with. But I will not despair. I choose not to be crushed. I will place my mind on the things above and move forward with the things God has called my attention to.

With God's help, I will love my husband. I will love and disciple my children in the ways of the Lord. I will love my neighbor. Let's commit again that we will worship our Savior—and as we do, we can purpose to give the troubles of this world to the One who knows and loves us best.

Honor the Young Ones

Don't let anyone think less of you because you are young. Be an example to all believers in what you say, in the way you live, in your love, your faith, and your purity.

1 TIMOTHY 4:12

MOTHERING IS A UNIQUE RESPONSIBILITY, and anyone who has mothered teenagers for five minutes will tell you it is an opportunity not to be taken lightly and often feels like wandering without a road map.

There aren't a lot of specifics in Scripture about how we are to carry out the daily responsibilities of keeping our children alive, so we ask for wisdom from God, ask for advice from women who have gone before us, and hang on for the ride!

What we do know is that Paul felt the need to encourage Timothy in today's verse, and if Paul is giving a young person this encouragement, mothers should listen and learn too.

There is tension as teens grow toward young adulthood. Parents still set the boundaries, responsibilities, consequences, and the like. And over a period of a few years, all of those loosen from the parents' grip, and the developing teen hopefully takes the reins and handles the new freedom well.

We can help this happen. We set them up for success and cheer for them loudly when they do well. We spend time training and guiding and then sit on the sidelines to let them move forward. What makes or breaks them is how we handle it when they mess up. We can laugh at them, shame them, or say the dreaded "I told you so." Or we can dust them off, lovingly walk through the failure with them and help them process it, and respectfully work through a better plan for next time.

This tension I mentioned is no small thing. Young women desire autonomy as they prepare to manage their own affairs. Young men especially need to be respected in order to grow into men who are worthy of respect.

We have the distinct honor of being the one who doesn't think less of them because they are young. What a privilege!

He Trains My Hands for Battle

He trains my hands for battle; my arms can bend a bow of bronze.

PSALM 18:34, NIV

I LOVE STATEMENT SHIRTS. If you have followed me for any length of time, you have probably seen me in a bunch of them. God put it on my heart to print today's verse on a shirt for my speaking season some years ago. My women's conference is called "Faith That Speaks," and each year, I ask God for a new theme. As I prayed, God impressed it on my heart to speak to mothers about walking onto the battlefield with confidence. We can have confidence because of who we are in Christ. It's not about us, after all. It's about Him.

It's easy to think that all the division in the world right now is simply because we are broken people. While that is certainly true, there is much more going on than meets the eye. We need to see the unseen. We need spiritual eyes. This is not an earthly war. It's a spiritual one. Consider the psalmist's insight as he considered the battles of his time: "He trains my hands for battle; my arms can bend a bow of bronze. You make your saving help my shield, and your right hand sustains me; your help has made me great. You provide a broad path for my feet, so that my ankles do not give way. I pursued my enemies and overtook them; I did not turn back till they were destroyed. I crushed them so that they could not rise; they fell beneath my feet. You armed me with strength for battle; you humbled my adversaries before me. You made my enemies turn their backs in flight, and I destroyed my foes" (Psalm 18:34-40, NIV).

When I read this, the word I see the most is the word *you*. *You* make your saving help my shield. *You* provide a broad path for my feet. *You* armed me with strength for battle. *You* humbled my adversaries.

We are no match for the war we are facing, that is true. But the war is no match for God. When we understand this, we give credit where it's due. It's with God's help that we win our battles. Today, make sure you ask God for His help as you take your place on the battlefield. And don't forget to give credit where it belongs: the battle belongs to the Lord.

When the Healing Doesn't Come

Peter asked them all to leave the room; then he knelt and prayed. Turning to the body he said, "Get up, Tabitha." And she opened her eyes! When she saw Peter, she sat up! He gave her his hand and helped her up. Then he called in the widows and all the believers, and he presented her to them alive. The news spread through the whole town, and many believed in the Lord.

ACTS 9:40-42

WE READ MANY STORIES IN THE gospels where Jesus heals people who believe in Him. In today's passage, we read about Peter using the power of God to bring Tabitha back to life. These miracles drew people to Jesus, and more people believed in Him after witnessing them. We learn that Jesus was filled with the power of His Father, which set Him apart from many other prophets of His day.

We have to realize, when we read the Word, that the lessons aren't always easy to scrape right off the surface. Sometimes we have to look a little deeper. The moral of these miracle stories cannot be "Ask God and He will heal you," because the fact of the matter is that many times He just doesn't. Many times, healing doesn't come until heaven.

Sometimes, people who haven't been healed are accused of not having enough faith. But it can't be about the people having enough faith to believe or about the healing. It has to be about God and His plans for us.

Jesus was truly a miracle worker who used His power to draw others to Himself and bolster the confidence of His disciples (who probably second-guessed their own faith a little each time they asked for healing!). Jesus as a healer was also all-knowing and sovereign, and that is where we have to settle with this.

The God of the Universe created each and every one of us for good works, which He prepared for us to do (see Ephesians 2:10). We have to believe with every ounce of our being that He knows what's best for us and remember that we are created for His glory. That is where our souls will find rest. He loves you more than you could ever imagine. He knows that His lack of healing hurts. But He also knows that you can walk with the Holy Spirit in you and glorify Him in the good works He set before you. Walk confidently in the knowledge that He chose you to glorify Him in this way. He is walking with you!

Leading by Example

Be strong in the Lord and in his mighty power. Put on the full armor of God, so that you can take your stand against the devil's schemes.

EPHESIANS 6:10-11, NIV

I HAVE FOUND, AS A MOTHER, that the spiritual warfare within parenting is very real, and in order to defeat it, we must use every piece of armor God provides. For starters, we must know and teach God's Word, the sword of the Spirit, to our children. I was teaching a group of women once and encouraging them to dive headfirst into the greatest book ever written.

That night as I drove home from teaching, the Spirit spoke to my heart so abruptly that I fought the urge to pull the car over. It was brought to my attention that I was teaching out of falsehood. I was encouraging others to dive into Scripture when I myself only pulled from the Word of God what I wanted to teach on. I, in fact, had never read the Bible front to back. Who was I to tell others to read the Word when I neglected it myself?

As a mother, I want my children to glean from my knowledge and love for Jesus. I long to have my kids pick up their faith with a fierce love and respect for Christ. I want them to arm themselves with the sword of the Spirit by reading God's Word, and I want them to learn from my example of regularly studying the Bible. I want them to want to obey God's laws for their lives, and I want them to have a fear of Him that fuels their walk to be leaders in a world full of darkness.

After I got home that night from my Bible study, I got on my knees and asked God to forgive my pride and to guide me as I opened His Word and started at the beginning, taking my time to study and come to know my Savior more intimately.

That year of growth was one of my favorite years. I gained a plethora of knowledge and grew to love the Old Testament.

Now when I teach my children and others, I teach from a passion, not an obligation. I walk fully clothed in the armor of God, relishing in the beauty that I am His and He is mine. When we have passion for the things of God, it encourages others to want what we have and encourages our kids to follow in our footsteps. If you aren't leading by example, then your children have no example. Teach them to live according to God's Word by doing it yourself.

Grace: The Gift That Keeps on Giving

By grace you have been saved through faith. And this is not your own doing;
it is the gift of God, not a result of works, so that no one may boast.

EPHESIANS 2:8-9, ESV

Born in Arkansas during the Great Depression, Bob had grown up dirt poor in what was then known as a "shotgun shack" among the rolling hills and piney woods of Arkansas. Bob only had a third-grade education, but he knew the Word of God, and he knew the principles of the Kingdom. Bob told me something I have never forgotten. Bob and I were talking about the words *mercy* and *grace*. I was rapidly reviewing all I had learned in Bible college about those two concepts, so I was caught completely off guard by Bob's simple country wisdom.

He looked me square in the eye as if he were talking to a child, and in his slow, rolling drawl he said, "Them there is easy to understand. When the Lord gives ya mercy, He don't give ya what ya had a-comin', an' when He gives ya grace, He gives ya what ya didn't have a-comin'."

In that one sentence, Bob summed up all that I had learned in Bible college in terms simple enough even a child (like me?) could understand. Besides a keen theological insight, I learned an important lesson that day. Never judge any of God's people by their background or appearance. God uses even those from the most unlikely background.

Have you experienced God's mercy in your life? I know I have, and I try to recognize it now and thank Him each time He extends new mercies to me. I deserve so many consequences that He has never demanded I pay. Instead, He freely gives me salvation from sin's eternal consequence.

How about His grace? I couldn't begin to name all the times the Lord has extended grace upon grace to me. How about you? Perhaps you can use those definitions Bob shared with me with your own children sometime. Give your children an example of ways you've experienced God's mercy and grace in your life, and help them be on the lookout for those gifts in their own lives. Their relationship with God will grow deeper as a result.

God Wants to Give Us Good Gifts

Which of you, if your son asks for bread, will give him a stone? Or if he asks for a fish, will give him a snake? If you, then, though you are evil, know how to give good gifts to your children, how much more will your Father in heaven give good gifts to those who ask him!

MATTHEW 7:9-11, NIV

WHEN OUR OLDEST DAUGHTER WAS AROUND TWELVE YEARS OLD, she developed a keen interest in African grey parrots. It was easy to see why—parrots are fascinating creatures. A few of the species (like the African grey) can speak almost as clearly as humans. Parrots make lifelong pets, sometimes outliving their owners. But as incredible as parrots are, they're not easy to care for. For example, if they don't have enough human interaction, they will become depressed and start plucking out their feathers. Large parrots need—you guessed it—large cages, not to mention specific food. It's a big responsibility to care for such an exotic animal, but our daughter was determined to save her money and buy one.

Eventually she saved almost enough to buy both the bird and the accessories. All that was needed was permission from her father and me—and a little more money. We told her repeatedly that we didn't think a parrot was a practical animal to have in our busy household. "Perhaps a gerbil or a hamster would be a better option," we said.

But as we watched her dedication to studying parrots, we saw how important this was to her. Like most parents, we love to give our children good gifts, especially when they have worked diligently toward a goal. We seldom indulge in extravagant purchases, but eventually we started to see how a parrot would be a good fit for our family. We wanted to reward Savannah's diligence, and we thought it would be a good way to teach her responsibility too. So on a warm autumn evening, after adding a little to Savannah's saved babysitting money, we adopted a young African grey parrot.

Rosie grew to become a beloved part of our family, and she gave me a thousand stories to tell out on the road too. Truly, Rosie was a good gift—not only for Savannah, but for our whole family.

The Bible teaches us that God loves to give His children good gifts. The next time you find yourself buying that pet you said you'd never purchase simply because it makes you smile to see your kids smile, remember that God loves you in the same way—in fact, He loves you even more! God delights in giving good gifts to His children.

Be Slow to Anger

Understand this, my dear brothers and sisters: You must all be quick to listen, slow to speak, and slow to get angry.

JAMES 1:19

TODAY'S VERSE IS CONVICTING FOR MOMS in every stage of parenting. The timeless biblical counsel to be "quick to listen" to our children, "slow to speak" when we want to spout off advice, and "slow to get angry" when we're feeling frustrated or impatient never seems to be out of season. We can all relate to the struggles of becoming easily irritated and angry, but God, in His mercy, offers help through the Bible.

James is offering us great advice for living the Christian life. More than that, he's offering us great advice for our relationship with our spouse. And perhaps most of all, he's offering us great advice for parenting our children.

I heard it put this way once. Suppose you come home, and your spouse says, "Jimmy totaled our brand-new car this afternoon. He's up in his room." What would be your first reaction? As the mother of several grown kids, let me just say that we've had a few fender benders in our family. Sometimes, it's the result of immaturity—other times, negligence. Sometimes, it's totally the fault of the other driver.

It's easy to react out of anger when we hear bad news, but the Bible warns us against being quick to become angry. Context in every situation is what wisdom requires. Slow down. Listen. Ask the Lord for wisdom.

Sometimes, the first words that come to our lips are the wrong words. Rather than live to regret the words you spoke in those first moments after hearing a disappointing outcome or hearsay from one of your other kids, be still. Stopping to listen often completely changes the way we see the story.

It's easy to become angry, but the Lord has challenged me again and again to follow the advice James is offering us. Over the years, I have asked the Lord many times to help me to listen more and talk less. We need His help to become slow to anger and quick to listen—especially when we're dealing with our husbands and children. Do I hear an amen?

Ask for Wisdom

If you need wisdom, ask our generous God, and he will give it to you. He will not rebuke you for asking.

JAMES 1:5

FOR PARENTS, I'M NOT SURE THERE is a more important verse anywhere in the Bible than today's verse. There isn't a single day in the life of a parent that we don't need godly wisdom.

When I had only one or two children, if I messed up, I used to explain to them, "Please give Mommy grace. This parenting thing is all new to me, and I'm learning as I go along." They would laugh—usually.

But when I got to children six and seven, I found that perhaps I hadn't learned as much along the way as I'd hoped. Oh, I knew a lot more about some of the parenting basics, but each child is unique, and every single one presents new, unexpected, and usually challenging opportunities for parents to deal with. Why did child number four suddenly decide everything in our house needed to be stuck in his ears? Why did child number five decide to bring every wild critter she found into my bedroom? I cried out to the Lord, asking Him for wisdom, plenty of times in those phases of parenting.

But thanks be to God that He is ready and waiting to offer His wisdom. In the world, there are a hundred new self-help books published each day. Many contain some of the worst advice ever given. And then there's your sister-in-law, your next-door neighbor, the self-proclaimed parenting expert you follow online, and even the family doctor. Sometimes you will get great wisdom from them. But all too often you don't. The only One who is 100 percent reliable for giving sound advice and wisdom is your heavenly Father.

The Lord is leaning forward on His throne, eager and waiting for you to ask Him for His wisdom. He is generous and wants to share, if only you'll ask. I'm reminding you (and I'm reminding myself) right now: ask for wisdom.

Draw Close

The LORD is close to all who call on him.

PSALM 145:18

PUMPKIN LATTE IN HAND, MY DAUGHTER sat looking at me from her seat in the car. It had been a rough week for my brown-eyed teen. She had made some poor choices in her friendships and found herself on the receiving end of gossip from a group of girls at church. My heart hurt to see how wounded she was.

After a few minutes, it became clear that for all my trying, nothing I said was making her feel any better. Her blank stare said it all; my advice felt worn-out and cliché to my fourteen-year-old.

Since my attempt at being "Dear Abby" wasn't well received, I decided to try another tactic: I asked her if she had talked to God about it. "After all," I said, "He is very aware of your circumstances. God can help you reconcile with your friends."

"But, Mom! He's so far away!" she said as the tears flowed freely. "He doesn't get it!"

Now *this* I understood.

"Oh, sweetheart! I understand how you feel," I said, leaning across the armrests. "And fortunately, God does too." For the next several minutes, I let my daughter see into my private struggle to set time aside for the Lord each day. I told her that when I neglect my time with the Lord, I also feel far away from His care and love. As we talked, her blank stare disappeared and her eyes brightened.

Over the years of parenting teens, I have learned that when I am transparent with them, it opens the door to being able to speak truth into their lives. This time, the truth I was able to share resonated with both of us: when we feel far away from God, it's because *we* have moved, not Him.

I reminded her that the Bible teaches us that God is near whenever we call—the key is to call. We talked about times we have moved from God. I related to her struggle, and she was glad to know that I struggle too.

The Bible teaches us that the Lord is near to us when we call on Him—and He is the best example of a parent we could ever want. If He draws close, we can too.

Around the Table

As they were eating, Jesus took some bread and blessed it. Then he broke it in pieces and gave it to the disciples, saying, "Take this and eat it, for this is my body."

MATTHEW 26:26

MY KIDS OFTEN MAKE FUN OF me when I talk about how awesome the hair and music was back in the eighties, but what they don't know is that many of those moments of my growing up shaped how we do life as a family today. For instance, I am just old enough to remember when most of my friends were home in time for dinner. The family dinner hour was important then, and it's been a precious time at our house too.

Jesus was often found breaking bread around a table with His earthly family, the motley crew of disciples and those who traveled with them. One of the most famous meals in the Bible included Jesus with His disciples around the dinner table in the upper room. It's known as the Last Supper.

Around the table you find conversation, connection, and love. I can imagine Jesus laughing with His dearest friends, talking about their travels, telling stories while they decompressed from a busy day of serving.

We've lost this connection over the years. Overloaded schedules and exhaustion have left us with so little time and energy to gather around anything, let alone a meal. I'm here to tell you that it's important, because it was important to Jesus.

It's also possible.

Put it on your calendar, and get the family to show up. It won't be precious every time—and I assure you someone will burp or fart or say something inappropriate, because it's real life. Bring some conversation starters or have everyone share a high from the day and a low from the day. Come prepared to look one another in the eyes as you share a simple meal. Put your phones away. (You can do it!) It just might change your family's life. I'm certain it changed the lives of the disciples.

Scripture tells us Jesus ate with His beloved disciples, and it even says we will feast together in heaven. Today, let's look at our ordinary, everyday mealtime as a chance to say, "I love you." I promise you, the investment you make in the family meal will pay dividends for generations to come.

A Fellowship of Believers

All the believers met together in one place and shared everything they had.
ACTS 2:44

LONELINESS HAS BECOME A PANDEMIC OF our time. For all our modern ways of connecting virtually through social media and Zoom, loneliness is a real issue for many mothers. There was a time when it was more common than not to see families and neighbors doing daily life together because survival required it. Ironically, what was viewed as necessary for survival ended up being the thing that built and sustained thriving communities. My grandparents loved to talk about life in their small Nebraska town of Fairbury. Neighbors would often be visiting on the sidewalk. It wasn't uncommon to get a knock at the door with a request for a cup of flour or some eggs. Communities grew and thrived because the people there valued relationship. They did life together.

Somehow, as we've grown more self-sufficient through technology, we've come to think that we don't need each other. That's a lie that we have believed for too long, and it is the work of the enemy of our souls. One of the greatest schemes of Satan is to get to us by first getting us alone. He loves isolation.

If we look at the early church, we see Christians doing life together. This was modeled best for them by the way Jesus spent His time on earth, with His disciples and the people He ministered to. In Acts, the early Christians are found going out into their villages and bringing people into their church communities. There, they cared for each other, ate together, worshiped together, and provided for each other's needs. If someone needed a goat, their neighbor gave them a goat. If they had an extra blanket, they gave it to the new baby up the road. It was the way they did life.

We were made for this kind of community—a fellowship of believers, to care and be cared for. All it takes is one brave person to make that first invitation. And yes, that brave soul is you. Moms get lonely and moms need community, even in a house full of humans. The best way to find a friend is to be a friend first. It's going to take us working together in order to fight off this loneliness pandemic. If you notice someone is struggling, consider inviting them to your home for dinner. If you're homeschooling, being involved in a homeschool community is an absolute must. Instead of living lives of isolation, the Creator would have us live as the early church did—in community. There really is a blessing in sharing our lives with others. Give it a try!

The Mom in the Mirror

Get rid of all evil behavior. Be done with all deceit, hypocrisy, jealousy, and all unkind speech.

1 PETER 2:1

ACCOMPLISHING THE ASSIGNMENT IN TODAY'S VERSE could keep me busy for the rest of my life. Wow! There are a dozen sermons just waiting to be preached on each of those subjects: evil behavior, deceit, hypocrisy, jealousy, and unkind speech!

More specifically, there could be a dozen sermons on how doing away with deceit will improve your marriage. Or how doing away with hypocrisy will improve your relationship with your children. I can picture a sermon titled "Seven Ways Jealousy Can Shipwreck Your Parenting." Or maybe one titled "Three Ways Unkind Speech Can Destroy Your Parenting Witness."

The list might feel overwhelming. Where do you even begin? As with everything, you begin wherever you find yourself. Take a look at the list once more. Which word leaps out at you? For me, it's the word *hypocrisy*. Occasionally, I have scolded one of my children about something they were doing wrong, knowing full well I'm guilty of that very thing myself. How much would my parenting score go up if I could be honest with my children in such a moment?

Rather than asking my child, "Why do you always procrastinate and wait till the last minute to do your chores?" I could instead say, "I know how easy it is to wait until the last minute to complete a task. It makes things so much harder. I can sympathize with your tendency to procrastinate. Maybe we can pray for each other, and both get better in the process. Will you pray for me?" Think of how different our conversation would go if I approached the topic with honesty about myself and my own failures rather than being a hypocrite while I lectured my child.

Look over Peter's list of relationship killers, and choose one to work on today.

Your husband may thank you. Or, he may not. Same with your children. But remember, at the end of the day, the blessing that's found in walking rightly before the Lord cannot be understated. God's ways build relationships. Try it and see for yourself!

Always Watching

Be careful to live properly among your unbelieving neighbors.

1 PETER 2:12

Do you remember the movie *Monsters, Inc.*? I loved it, with its quirky characters, funny turns and twists, and heartwarming moments. My kind of movie. But I gotta say, the thing I remember most was one line from the movie. "I'm watching you, Wazowski. Always watching. Always."

I can still hear the tone in Roz's voice. Do you remember it too? Roz was the grouchy, slug-like monster with the whiny, snarky voice and a perpetual frown. She worked at Monsters, Inc., and was the leader of the Child Detection Agency. They named her "Number One." It was her job to remind Mike Wazowski that he was always being watched.

Sometimes, I feel like people are watching me, and if I'm honest, I know they are.

In this age of social media, we all live in a fishbowl. Our thoughts and actions can instantly live forever on the Internet. We know our children are watching to see whether we walk the walk or just talk the talk. And our husbands watch—especially if they're unbelievers.

But the world is watching too. *Always watching.* Friends, neighbors, and relatives. Often the first step toward becoming a believer is observing someone who claims to be a Christ-follower. Do they live a disciplined, godly life or just attend church and spout Bible verses?

It would be easy to turn this truth into some sort of paranoid freak-out. That's not what Peter was suggesting in today's verse. As we begin to walk in a closer relationship with the Lord, walking the walk comes more naturally. This shouldn't be a matter of gritting our teeth and trying harder. The rhythms of grace come naturally as we spend time in His presence. Read the Word. Spend time in prayer. Worship Him. Ask Him to help you.

You're not accountable for the spiritual choices of your neighbors and relatives. But by living a more authentic Christian life, you may be instrumental in their salvation. And perhaps more importantly, you will experience a closer intimacy with Jesus. *He's watching too.* And He's rooting for you. The Bible even says He's praying for you.

I sometimes imagine that "great cloud of witnesses" from Hebrews watching. That seems a little more spiritual than imagining my next-door neighbor watching me. With them watching, do I really want to say what I was about to say? Do I really want to do what I was about to do? My walk is made straighter by knowing others are watching me. There are a lot of people watching. Live in a way that pleases God!

Heart Issues

Don't be concerned about the outward beauty of fancy
hairstyles, expensive jewelry, or beautiful clothes.

1 PETER 3:3

I HAVE FIVE DAUGHTERS. My daughters and I have talked about 1 Peter 3:3 dozens of times over the years. It's good for all of our kids to hear what my husband and I think about this important topic and to discuss it with us—because godly people can disagree as to how it should be applied.

A musician friend observed, "Anointed music is whatever kind of music you like." I'm not sure that's true, but this verse reminds me of that quip. Depending on where you live, go to church, work, and more, no two women can agree on exactly what this verse means.

Some would argue this verse means no makeup, no hair color, no necklaces, and only rugged, utilitarian clothes. Others might interpret it to mean no plastic surgery, no hair extensions, no diamonds over one carat, and no designer clothes that cost more than $1,000. The truth probably lies somewhere between those extremes. But like so many issues in the Kingdom of God, this is more of a heart issue than a legalism issue. What's in your heart when thinking about fashion?

Is your desire to draw attention to yourself, to make other women envious, or to cause men to give you admiring glances? Or are you dressing to please the Lord and your husband?

Mom—your daughters are watching you. As parents, we know our children often don't listen to much of what we tell them, but they're always watching what we do and how we live our lives. Your daughters are learning how to dress by watching you. Your sons are learning about what a lovely, godly woman wears by watching you as well.

Dress in a way that pleases you, pleases your husband, and pleases the Lord. My husband likes me to look nice. I love that about him. I want to dress to please him. I don't want him to ever stop looking at me with that little twinkle in his eye. He is always quick to compliment a dress he likes on me or the way I've done my hair—but he also wants me to dress modestly. I love that about him too.

At the end of the day, it's a heart issue, isn't it? It pleases the Lord when we seek His heart above all else.

Ready to Answer

If someone asks you about your hope as a believer, always be ready to explain it.

1 PETER 3:15

PERHAPS YOU'VE HEARD IT SAID, "We aren't called to go to church—we're called to be the church." In a world of increasing darkness, even the smallest bit of light is refreshing. We're called to be salt and light to those around us.

Our kids need to *see* this in action in our lives. In addition to being the church, we should be ready to explain our hope as believers. If you've never written out your testimony, you should.

I have always thought that my conversion story was sort of boring. I mean—it's not exciting. My grandmother led me to Christ when I was about four years old. I'll never forget that moment—my heart was broken for the love that Jesus showed me when He died for me. I still remember my grandmother's scent as she prayed with me. The moment of my salvation marked a change of direction in my young life. My hunch is that Grandma never thought I'd remember the details, but I do, more than fifty years later.

If you share your testimony with your kids, they will remember your story too. Write it down, mama! You don't have to include every detail. But as a believer, you should be able to quickly and clearly articulate your situation in life before salvation, what led you toward redemption, the choice you made, the prayer you prayed, and the changes you've experienced since rebirth.

Peter told us that we should always be ready to tell our salvation story to anyone who asks. It needn't take more than two minutes to tell your story in a way that's easily followed. Practice telling it. Perhaps tell it to a friend or fellow believer and ask them if the story is clear and understandable. Then tell your kids. See if you can share your story one night at dinner. While you needn't press them for a response, it never hurts to ask if they've ever had a similar experience of being born again.

It's important to be able to simply explain God's plan for salvation. We have all sinned. Sin separates us from a holy God. God sent His own son to take the punishment we deserved so that we might have our sins forgiven and might live with God forever. It's even more powerful if you can memorize four or five short verses to tell the salvation story.

At the end of the day, it's more than a suggestion. We are instructed to be ready to share our hope. Are you ready?

Whatever Is Good

Fix your thoughts on what is true, and honorable, and right, and pure, and lovely, and admirable. Think about things that are excellent and worthy of praise.

PHILIPPIANS 4:8

LIFE HAS BEEN CHALLENGING FOR ME LATELY. Usually I handle the ups and downs just fine, and I don't allow the hard times to sideline me. But in the past few weeks, I've struggled to come up for air from what feels like one hard thing after another: the loss of loved ones, illness, political upheaval, financial setbacks, and more.

Can you relate? Have you been through a difficult season in your life? In your marriage? Of course, you have. We all have.

As I was enjoying my first cup of coffee this morning before the sun had even come up, I read today's verse: "Fix your thoughts on what is true, and honorable, and right, and pure, and lovely, and admirable. Think about things that are excellent and worthy of praise" (Philippians 4:8).

I needed that reminder from Paul. It's so easy to let our minds drift to all that's wrong instead of all that's right, isn't it? It's all too easy to settle into a funk as we think about all the things that seem to be going so badly rather than fixing our eyes on what God is doing that is good. Precious mom, we can easily spiral out of control when we allow the devil to keep our eyes fixed on the hard things.

Remember, this is war! The enemy of our soul would like nothing more than to pull us down into an ever-tightening spiral of sadness, depression, and hopelessness.

If you're struggling with finances, think about all the good things that have happened in that area in the past or even in the present. Remind yourself that God is the provider. If you're in a season of marriage tension, focus your thoughts on all the good things about your spouse instead of things you might want to change.

Someone once said that life is ten percent about what happens to us and ninety percent about how we respond to what happens to us. There's a lot of wisdom in that. Join me today in focusing on the good instead of the bad.

The Secret

I have learned how to be content with whatever I have. I know how to live on almost nothing or with everything. I have learned the secret of living in every situation, whether it is with a full stomach or empty, with plenty or little. For I can do everything through Christ, who gives me strength.

PHILIPPIANS 4:11-13

As a pastor's wife for many years, I learned how to make every penny count. And I do mean *every* penny. As a young mother, I became an expert at navigating the thrift stores in my neighborhood—and you know what? I loved how God provided. It was like a treasure hunt. Funny thing—I still love thrift store shopping.

Thanks to some wonderful women in my life, I learned how to make lots of delicious, low-cost soups to feed our growing family. Did you know that taco soup can feed twenty-five college kids for about fifteen dollars? Funny thing—our family still loves soup!

Financial pressure is no fun, though. I remember times we wondered how we would pay our rent or where the grocery money would come from. Perhaps you've been in one of those seasons. Perhaps you're in one now. Hang in there, mama! Seasons are just that. They don't last forever.

It's been more than thirty years since Jay and I said "I do" and partnered together to face the ups and downs of life. While we've never been "rich," we've had times when money wasn't a constant worry. And do you know what I learned when we finally moved beyond the season of wondering where our provision was going to come from?

I learned that when we abide in Christ, there's not a great deal of difference between those seasons. My family was just as satisfied, and our dinner table conversation was just as rich over a pot of homemade soup as it was over steaks and baked potatoes. My front door looked just as nice with a used four-dollar Christmas wreath as it would have with a new twenty-four-dollar wreath. My children ran just as fast wearing a two-dollar pair of sneakers from the resale shop as they would have wearing a brand-new thirty-dollar pair of name-brand sneakers from the mall.

When we understand we can live a joyful, satisfying life through Christ, like Paul, we can live above our circumstances. If you're in a season of stretching, give thanks for the harvest to come. And if you're in a season of bounty, find your joy in Him rather than in those nice things.

Contentment in Christ is the same in every season.

In Pursuit of Humility

When pride comes, then comes disgrace, but with humility comes wisdom.

PROVERBS 11:2, NIV

FEW THINGS SHOULD DEFINE THE MATURE Christian life as much as humility. As a speaker and teacher, I've traveled the country doing workshops, radio interviews, and keynote addresses. I've been privileged to meet many leaders, both Christian and political, who are household names. I've spent time in the homes and offices of some who are rich beyond anything I can imagine.

And do you know what? When I think back over all those encounters, the people who stand out most in my mind are those who were humble servants of Christ. It's interesting to me that some of the richest, smartest, most famous people I've met were also the most unassuming, gentle, kind, humble people I've ever known.

God blesses humility. Our children are growing up in a very "me-centric" world. In an age of selfies and blatant love of self, we must teach our children that God honors humility. With it, the Bible says, comes wisdom.

So what does humility look like?

Paul puts it this way: "Don't be selfish; don't try to impress others. Be humble, thinking of others as better than yourself. Don't look out only for your own interests, but take an interest in others, too" (Philippians 2:3-4).

We know there's no future in living our lives trying to impress our neighbors and family. Even baby Christians learn that truth. But did you know that these principles apply to marriage and our parenting as well?

Nothing brings richness into a marriage relationship more than being humble, thinking of your spouse's needs more than your own, and taking an interest in the things that interest them. What does it look like to practice humility in parenting? Sometimes that seems difficult with a child who wants to be a know-it-all. But there is joy and redemption in preferring others in humility.

Ask the Lord to show you ways to put Paul's teaching into practice this week in your home. Write down how the Spirit prompts you to teach humility to your children, and then model it.

The results will speak for themselves.

Seek Wisdom

All Israel heard of the judgment which the king had rendered; and they feared the king, for they saw that the wisdom of God was in him to administer justice.

1 KINGS 3:28, NKJV

I ARRIVED HOME SOME DAYS AGO to a fairly loud, shall we say, "discussion" happening in my kitchen. Okay, let's be real: there was some yelling involved. And some hurt feelings. And maybe a broken mug. Clearly, these young people needed their mom to intervene.

I surveyed the emotional landscape, being careful not to step unintentionally onto a land mine and thereby ruin my chances at being an objective mediator. After several minutes of me asking all the standard questions (e.g., How did this start? Did anyone provoke you? Could you have reacted differently?), I realized that I was in over my head. Both kids were making credible cases for their point of view.

I needed wisdom. In fact, we all need the wisdom of Solomon. In 1 Kings 3:16-28, we read the story of two women who took a very challenging case before King Solomon. They each had newborn babies. One mom accidentally rolled over on her child and killed him. Both moms then laid claim to the living child.

What was Solomon to do? He wasn't there to witness the accident. He had no history with the women to recognize the child. The Bible records that Solomon asked God for wisdom—and God gave it to him. Read the passage with your kids today. It's a beautiful illustration of how God gives us wisdom when we ask Him.

As moms, we can't be everywhere at once and see everything. Sometimes we make wrong decisions. Sometimes, we misjudge the heart or intentions of our children. Like Solomon, we need counsel from God to administer judgment in our families.

That day, I sat with my kids and asked God to show me what had happened so that I could make a wise decision and shepherd my children with grace and understanding. You know what? God showed up. He gave me insight I would not have had apart from Him. He's good like that.

If This, Then That

"Honor your father and mother." This is the first commandment with a promise: If you honor your father and mother, "things will go well for you, and you will have a long life on the earth."

EPHESIANS 6:2-3

EPHESIANS 6:2-3 IS WHAT I CALL a boomerang verse. A boomerang verse is where we're eager to rightly apply it to someone else, and then suddenly the Lord sends it back and rightly applies it to us as well. Does that make sense?

As parents, we're quick to teach this verse to our children. "You need to be honoring your mother and father so that things will go well for you," we tell them. And of course, that's very true. When you have a child who consistently honors and respects you as a parent, you tend to bend over backward to be merciful toward that child and to help them in every way possible.

It's much more challenging to act that way with a disrespectful child, isn't it?

But that verse boomerangs back—and our kids notice. The Lord challenges us to honor *our* mother and father too. Sometimes that's hard. As our parents get older, they can become more difficult to deal with. As their health declines, they may not always be rational. As they become set in their ways, they may not be able to understand our choices sometimes. They may even vehemently disagree with how we're raising our children or how we're handling our finances.

There's a caveat to this biblical principle that I've been teaching moms for years. Honoring your parents does *not* mean that you become a doormat to an abusive parent. It doesn't mean that you must stay in relationship with a parent who has betrayed your trust. This verse isn't asking us to surrender our thoughts and blindly obey our parents. Not at all.

Paul is reminding us that honoring and respecting our parents is very important to God. We can watch what we say and be careful how we talk about our parents to our children and others. Guard against gossip and bitterness.

In truth, it wasn't so long ago when we were totally dependent on our parents for every little thing. It's a fine line. Even healthy parent/child relationships can be complicated! We need to learn to honor and respect our parents even when they challenge or disagree with us.

Phrases like "I appreciate why you would feel that way," or maybe "Thank you for sharing your thoughts on that," or perhaps "You know we always want to hear your input" will go a long way toward fulfilling Paul's admonition.

Becoming a Peace-Filled Parent

Fathers, do not provoke your children to anger by the way you treat them. Rather, bring them up with the discipline and instruction that comes from the Lord.

EPHESIANS 6:4

Oh boy! I don't know about you, but I need to print this verse out and stick it on my refrigerator door. I wish I didn't struggle with my sinful flesh. I've lived more than half a century, but when one of my children gets under my skin, I can act like a nine-year-old! It's embarrassing, really. Please tell me you understand.

I know this verse doesn't only apply to fathers. As a mother, I can be downright snarky with my kids. There are moments for all of us when we lose our temper or fall victim to our own need to be right. This is especially true after a long day or after what feels like the fiftieth time we have corrected a child.

And here's the crazy thing: when I've reached my breaking point, I know it. I can feel my snark-o-meter light up even before the words come out of my mouth. One moment I'm instructing my daughter with godly instruction and discipline, and when she doesn't respond in kind, I feel it in the back of my throat.

It's a little extra phrase, or tone of voice, or spiteful inflection on a certain word. I know before I say it that it's going to provoke my child to anger. And at that moment, I might even take some immature pleasure in the thought. I want them to feel the repercussions of their behavior and not simply be aware of what they've done wrong.

When I provoke my children to anger, the Bible says very plainly that I'm the one sinning in that moment.

Ouch.

In moments of frustration, we have a choice to make: either we can enrich our relationship with our children (or spouse!) or we can strain it. Yes—it's true. I've been known to provoke my husband to anger too. It's wrong with my children, and it's wrong with my husband.

Proverbs 15:1 tells us, "A gentle answer deflects anger, but harsh words make tempers flare."

God desires that we parent from a place of peace . . . His peace. May He imprint that truth on our hearts today.

Protect the Privilege

Understand this, my dear brothers and sisters: You must all be
quick to listen, slow to speak, and slow to get angry.

JAMES 1:19

MOTHERHOOD IS SANCTIFYING, ISN'T IT? I am known for telling women that the *best* way to see if they have any sin issues is simply to have children. Want to crank it up a notch? Homeschool said children. Being a mom has unearthed so many weaknesses and sins in my life—and homeschooling has upped the ante 100 percent!

Today's verse is a perfect example. According to James, I'm supposed to be "quick to listen [and] slow to speak."

Why do I get this backward so often? Why am I quick to get angry, shoot off my mouth, and not listen to others—especially my children—sometimes? It's because our relationships with our children are safe. I don't mean "safe" in the way you might expect either—I mean that they're safe places for us to be as ugly as our sin nature will allow. After all, what are they gonna do, go on strike and find a new mother? No—they're stuck with us.

It's the same reason our kids treat us badly sometimes—we're a safe place to vent their emotions, whether for good or bad. And, even when it's hard to be on the receiving end of the sanctification process, we need to remember what an incredible privilege it is to have such a profound influence in the lives of those closest to us. Being a safe place for our children is a privilege worth protecting.

We protect the privilege when we listen more than we talk. I can promise you—this is hard for me. I tend to be very quick with my words. It's easy for me to jump ahead of my kids and get to the "conclusion" that I assume they're heading toward. When I do this, I'm essentially saying, "You're taking too long; I'll finish for you."

When James says, "Be quick to listen," he is offering us great advice in living the Christian life. More than that, he's offering us great advice for marriage. And perhaps most of all, he's offering us great advice for parenting. The Lord has challenged me again and again to follow the advice James is offering us.

Lord, help me to listen more and talk less. Help me be slow to anger—especially when I'm dealing with my children. Do I hear an amen? Let's protect the privilege of motherhood by becoming better listeners.

Let Them Know

Beloved, let us love one another, for love is from God, and
whoever loves has been born of God and knows God.

1 JOHN 4:7, ESV

MY DAD AND I ALWAYS HAD a difficult relationship. Though we had moments of
calm, most of the time, our relationship was marked by stormy seas. Looking back,
I can see dysfunction has been a theme in my family for decades. Though I prayed
and worked to find some sort of common ground with my dad (and I think he
did too, in his own way), we never did have the kind of loving connection I so
desperately wanted. In 2021, Dad passed away after a long battle with his health.

The time for saying "I love you" is a short window, isn't it?

I know I'm not alone when it comes to the imperfect relationship that I
had with my dad. Truth is, many, many families experience the pain of broken
relationships—but the parental bond is possibly the most tender of all.

As my sisters and I reflected on our dad's passing, I could not help but think
about my precious relationships with my children and grandchildren. The reality
is that we have one opportunity to invest in our kids.

There is a common thread that I have observed in happy, successful families
over the years: they make sure to express the love they have for one another. They
take the time to invest in big and little ways. Truth is, someday, my kids will be
reflecting on my life. I want them to have good memories of me. I do not want a
hint of doubt in their minds as to how I felt about them. Something tells me you
feel the same way.

Do your kids know how much you love and enjoy them? What about the rest
of your family? Could your messaging be a little better or a little more consistent?
We have one chance to show love to our people, precious friends! Let's not miss
out on the opportunity.

Everything

Do everything without complaining and arguing.

PHILIPPIANS 2:14

I LIVE AT THE END OF A GRAVEL ROAD. Most of the time, I'm glad about that. My house is off the beaten path. I rarely hear traffic. But sometimes, that gravel road gets potholes that drive me crazy. Last summer, I was riding in the truck with Jay, and when we turned up our driveway, we hit a big ol' hole.

"*I hate this road!!* I hate it! Why can't we seem to keep it free from these gigantic holes?" I said in disgust as we tried in vain to avoid the bumps.

"I love it when you complain like that, Heidi," Jay said sarcastically. His sarcasm had a point. I was so frustrated by our road that every single time I was on it, I complained about it. It was wearing on my husband.

Few things cause more stress in a marriage or in a family than the tendency for one or more members to constantly complain about a situation they won't or can't change. Want to up the tension? Argue over every choice and every decision.

"Do *everything* without grumbling or complaining." *Everything? Are You sure, God?* I'm so very thankful for God's Word. It never ceases to amaze me how a single verse of Scripture can cut to the very core of an issue. Have you noticed that?

It doesn't say, "Try to complain a little less sometimes" or "Too much arguing can strain a relationship so just argue over the big things." No—it says, "DON'T DO IT! STOP IT! QUIT COMPLAINING AND ARGUING!"

When a Bible verse is that clear, with no hint of compromise or ambiguity, it behooves us to pay close attention. I have to admit I'm not always successful at obeying today's verse—but I'm much better than I was. And I can assure you, obedience reduces stress and strengthens relationships in both your marriage and your family.

Note that it does *not* say you should never discuss something. Nor does it say there isn't room for compromise to come to an agreement. It just says not to complain and argue in the process.

Perhaps you'd like to pray this prayer with me:

Lord, help me to be less argumentative. Help me to complain less and discuss more. Help me to watch my tongue so that my family and my marriage might be more pleasant for all of us. Amen.

The High Price of Sexual Sin

Let there be no sexual immorality, impurity, or greed among you.

EPHESIANS 5:3

LAST NIGHT, I RECEIVED A PHONE call from a friend in crisis. Her voice was shaking as she confessed that she had been unfaithful to her husband. As years of pent-up anger and emotional hurt tumbled out of her mouth, I began to pray for her family. I knew they would never be the same. In this case, the wife fell into sin, but sometimes it's a husband who is unfaithful. It could be a pastor or his wife, a homeschool mom, a community leader or a school bus driver or a physician or an auto mechanic.

The hurt is still the same. Sin hurts everyone.

My soul grows weary of the seemingly endless string of marriages shattered by sexual sin. The apostle Paul warns us over and over of the dangers of sexual temptation.

I wish none of us needed to be reminded of this verse. But statistics tell me we do. Without question, this verse speaks to men. Husbands and fathers have shipwrecked many a family because of sexual immorality. Sadly, it's become nearly as common for women to be at fault.

Women are viewing or reading sexually explicit materials too. This may not be the visual type we often think about. It may be written words of immorality. Erotica is an ever-growing form of literature, and most of it is aimed at women. How many Christians were among the millions of women who read *Fifty Shades of Grey*?

What begins as a passing thought or fantasy takes root and sooner or later leads to full-on infidelity. This breaks my heart for the many broken marriages. But even more heartbreaking are the millions of children whose lives have been damaged because of divorce. And it all began when someone entertained an impure thought.

Rarely do we consider what the cost might be if we continue to entertain such thoughts. Sadly, the cost is much more than we could ever imagine, until we're there.

Women, guard yourselves. Don't think this could never happen to you. Turn quickly from every impure thought, and resist the temptation to indulge in a fantasy life.

Your children need you to be strong and resist sexual sin, but just as important, they need you to teach this truth to them. We are always surrounded by sexual sin—but we have the Holy Spirit to help us say *no* to it.

Make the Most of Your Time

Make the most of every opportunity in these evil days.

EPHESIANS 5:16

I WAS IN A HURRY TO GET HOME from the grocery store and get dinner started last night. Somehow the day had gotten away from me, and I knew I had hungry children waiting at home. As I was getting ready to pay for my groceries, the cashier asked about the T-shirt I was wearing. It had an up arrow and said, "One Way." She looked confused. I knew by the way she was looking at my shirt that I might have an opportunity to share briefly about my faith in Jesus. But I was late. I was in a hurry.

Fortunately, she asked me where I got the shirt. I replied, "This shirt reminds me that Jesus is the one way to enter heaven. Do you know Jesus?" Her eyes misted up, and she said, "I used to." Fortunately, there was no one in line behind me, and I was able to spend two or three minutes reminding her that the Lord loves her very much. I don't know what happened with this young woman after that, but I was so glad the Lord gave me an opportunity to make the most of my quick grocery run.

In Ephesians 5:16, Paul exhorts us, "Make the most of every opportunity in these evil days." I knew there was an opportunity in that checkout line. It was inconvenient. But I'm thankful I didn't rush out and miss the chance the Lord gave me.

Making the most of opportunities isn't just about sharing our faith. As women of God, we have opportunities every day, but all too often we miss them. Whether it's an opportunity to show kindness to someone at the grocery store or to share God's wisdom with one of our children, God would have us be ready to seize those precious moments.

Opportunities present themselves every single day. Ask the Lord to help you see them. Learn to recognize them when they occur. Your actions can make all the difference in the world to the person on the receiving end.

Falsely Accused

The LORD will fight for you, and you have only to be silent.

EXODUS 14:14, ESV

HAVE YOU EVER HEARD THE PHRASE "Hurting people hurt people?" It's true.

Few things in this life are as painful as being falsely accused. Years ago, I was the victim of a horrific accusation. To make things worse, the two individuals at the root *knew* they were hurting me—and they didn't care, because what they really wanted was to hurt each other. They thought using my name would lend credibility to their family feud. In the end, selfishness prevented them from correcting the lie.

To make things worse, when I jumped into a Congressional race, the accusation resurfaced. The second time around, the damage was even greater because the stakes were higher. The anger I felt seemed to come in waves. First there was shock. I could not believe that a seven-year-old lie was being used against me in such a devastating way. Next came anger. Hot tears streamed down my face as I started to see the fallout online. Newspapers called. Reporters wanted interviews—all over a *lie*. I wanted to lash out. *Why would anyone do this to me?*

Finally, there was fear. I worried about what might happen to me as people read the false accusation. Would my family be affected? It was hard on my kids to read what people were writing about their mom. Would friends turn against me?

After several days of being constantly attacked, I was spiritually and emotionally exhausted. As I prayed, the Lord reminded me of a time when the Israelites were spiritually and emotionally tired too. With the Egyptian army bearing down, and the Red Sea in front of them, the Israelites needed God to act. There was no hope otherwise. Moses spoke the words of Exodus 14:14 *just before God parted the sea.*

That's our God, isn't it? In the end, He is the owner of the outcome, not me. For me, this meant I needed to stop worrying so much about a lie and, instead, focus on being an agent of hope and good leadership for the people of my state.

God really does have all things in His control. He can handle even the toughest situations. If we could grasp this amazing truth, we would experience much more peace and much less angst. If you're in a season of being falsely accused, rest in the Lord. He will fight for you. After all, you are His precious daughter.

Disloyalty

In fact, they did turn his heart away from the LORD.

1 KINGS 11:3

WANT TO KNOW WHAT CAN GO wrong when we stray from God's ways? Study the life of Solomon. Considering the great wisdom God granted him, it seems impossible that he could have been so foolish as to succumb to idolatry, and yet, that's exactly what he did.

Solomon's departure from God's law didn't happen overnight, of course—it rarely does. Instead, it happened slowly . . . one disobedience at a time. Let's look briefly at how his slow fade began: "King Solomon loved many foreign women. Besides Pharaoh's daughter, he married women from Moab, Ammon, Edom, Sidon, and from among the Hittites. The LORD had clearly instructed the people of Israel, 'You must not marry them, because they will turn your hearts to their gods.' Yet Solomon insisted on loving them anyway. He had 700 wives of royal birth and 300 concubines. And in fact, they did turn his heart away from the LORD" (1 Kings 11:1-3).

Solomon, who had been given so much from the Lord, was disloyal to God. He had been instructed *not* to marry foreign women, and yet, he did. First, it was tolerated in his household. Does this sound familiar? Moms, we must not tolerate *any* hint of sin. Not in our lives and not in the lives of our kids!

Once he and his family became accustomed to disobedience, they soon became comfortable with it. After that, he also began to participate in idolatry with his wives. This is exactly what the Lord had warned him about! The sad truth is that Solomon's fall from grace mirrors many Christians' experiences today.

Like many in the lukewarm church, Solomon never renounced the Lord, but his heart was not entirely devoted to Him either.

The attempt to mix godliness and worldliness plagues our churches today as it did in Solomon's time.

Solomon's life stands as a solemn warning against ungodly alliances and relationships that dishonor God. Solomon had sown disloyalty to God, and so he began to reap disloyalty.

God Delights in You!

Praise the LORD your God, who delights in you and has placed you on the throne of Israel.

1 KINGS 10:9

I LOVE THE WAY GOD'S NATURE is seen throughout Scripture! It should be a joy to read God's Word with our children. When our kids were little, we read about the queen of Sheba in 1 Kings 10. The girls loved to dig out their Aladdin and Jasmine costumes and pretend they were queen. And why not? The visit of the queen of Sheba is a graphic illustration of the fame of Solomon. The people were in awe at the reports of his wisdom and splendor.

Of course, there are many wonderful spiritual takeaways from this story, but the way I saw this when my kids were young might be different from what you'd expect.

After Solomon wows the queen of Sheba with his amazing intellect, she lavishes compliments on him: "She exclaimed to the king, 'Everything I heard in my country about your achievements and wisdom is true! I didn't believe what was said until I arrived here and saw it with my own eyes. In fact, I had not heard the half of it! Your wisdom and prosperity are far beyond what I was told. How happy your people must be! What a privilege for your officials to stand here day after day, listening to your wisdom! Praise the LORD your God, who delights in you and has placed you on the throne of Israel. Because of the LORD's eternal love for Israel, he has made you king so you can rule with justice and righteousness'" (1 Kings 10:6-9).

That's laying it on pretty thick, isn't it? After my kids were done imitating what that must have been like, verse 9 caught my eye: the queen of Sheba noted that God *delighted* in Solomon. Isn't that something? It's a little window into the heart of our heavenly Father. He loves us! The Lord delights in you!

We see this again in Zephaniah: "The LORD your God is living among you. He is a mighty savior. He will take delight in you with gladness" (Zephaniah 3:17).

The queen of Sheba had it right. Like every good father, God does delight in His children.

Mom, today, look your kids in the eyes and tell them that *God delights in them.* He does! And they need to know it.

Even When I'm Old and Gray

Now that I am old and gray, do not abandon me, O God. Let me proclaim your power to this new generation, your mighty miracles to all who come after me.

PSALM 71:18

WELL, IT HAPPENED. A LITTLE GRAY streak seemed to appear overnight just above my left eyebrow. I pulled out my magnifying mirror (which, by the way, has become a very good friend to my oldish eyes). It was gray, alright. I was about forty-six when the first gray hair appeared, so really, it was time.

The women in my family seem to take after my maternal grandmother. Don't be mad at me, but we really don't get gray hair at the usual age. My mom is in her seventies, but she looks younger. My grandma, who spent a few years at the end of her life looking very much like Mrs. Doubtfire, maintained her spunk and youthful appearance until she was well into her eighties.

At least that's how I remember her. It's funny that the things we worry so much about as adults really didn't factor into how we saw the adults in our lives when we were kids. Somewhere along the line, something changes. I have noticed something very precious that happens when godly women age: they become ambassadors to the generations behind them.

It's a sad fact of life that in this world, we value youth and strength. I thought it was something new to modern culture, but if you look at today's Scripture from David's psalm, he was worried that God might abandon him. I'm sure he could feel his strength failing.

Rather than turn inward, though, David turned his attention to the generations behind him. He wanted the Lord to give him strength for one primary purpose: so that he could proclaim the miracles of God to a new generation. As I think about it, that's what Jay's mom, Jerry, is doing for my children. It's what my mom is still doing and her mom before her did.

I can't help but think of all the wonderful grandparents that are spending their golden years teaching classes at our homeschool resource center in Vancouver. They have a wealth of knowledge and wisdom to pass on, and as they do, they are giving us a little bit of our history that we wouldn't have had otherwise. They are so precious to our kids!

Oh, that we could have that same heart as we get older. Rather than sink into a self-centered view of our life season, I pray we will see it as a time to pass on truth to the next generation.

Life has its challenges in every season, but God wants to be present in all of them.

A Theology for Suffering

Have mercy on me, O God, have mercy! I look to you for protection. I will hide beneath the shadow of your wings until the danger passes by.

PSALM 57:1

THE INTRODUCTION TO PSALM 51 OFFERS a bit of background, insight, and introduction about the life of David: "A psalm of David, regarding the time he fled from Saul and went into the cave."

In recent years, Christians have faced increasing persecution. The Bible offers us insight into how others handled suffering all throughout its pages. Try to picture a young David, on the run from King Saul because Saul wants to kill him. David is alone in a damp cave, and he has nowhere to run. He can't go home, because it will put his family in danger.

The city of Gath had become a refuge for David when he fled from King Saul, but now, King Achish of Gath was wary of him, having heard about his accomplishments in battle. Fearing for his life, David pretended to be insane so that the Philistine king would send him away.

And now, he is all alone. Can you see him now? A young man, alone in a cave, crying out to God: "Have mercy on me, O God, have mercy! I look to you for protection. I will hide beneath the shadow of your wings until the danger passes by" (Psalm 57:1).

Lately, I am hearing more and more Christians talking about being persecuted. Chinese Christians are in hiding or imprisoned. Christ-followers in Afghanistan are being hunted by the Taliban. Persecution, although not at the same level as other parts of the world, is even happening in the United States.

Yet God says, "I am here." David knew God's wings were big enough for him to hide under.

Mom, there may be tough times ahead for God's people. We are promised that there will be. Christians will be persecuted. Have you experienced persecution? Have your children? Do you have a theology for suffering? What I mean is, do your children know that they must look to God in every circumstance?

When life gets hard, remember David and look to your only true Refuge in times of trouble—God. We can hide under His wings until the danger passes by.

Who's Your Rescuer?

The LORD rescues the godly; he is their fortress in times of trouble. The LORD helps them, rescuing them from the wicked. He saves them, and they find shelter in him.

PSALM 37:39-40

THE WORLD CAN FEEL FRIGHTENING FOR MOTHERS. School shootings. Economic instability. Natural disasters. Government overreach. New illnesses come along, with conflicting opinions on how best to treat them.

There is no question that we are living in troubled times.

So, let me ask you, where do you turn in times of trouble? The answer to this reveals a lot. Throughout the Psalms, David often pointed out the differences between how the righteous handled trouble and how the wicked did.

According to David, the Lord rescues the godly. But what does that "rescue" look like? It's not always the ending that we want, is it? But one of the blessings of following God is the help that comes from the Lord. His help sometimes comes in the form of healing. Other times, it comes in the form of steadying our hearts as we endure hardship.

Isn't this exactly what we teach our children? We encourage them to follow God and trust Him to take care of them. But I wonder—are we living this out in our everyday lives? Do our kids see that we are giving praise to God for the daily rescue He provides?

Every day I need rescuing from so many things: my own sin, my immaturity, my lack of understanding, physical threats, emotional threats. I could go on and on, but you get the point. As moms, we are showing our children what it looks like to *find shelter* in the Lord, and we can't show them how to find that shelter unless we know how to nestle under His wings and rest too.

When you are in a fortress, you are secure. The same is true with our relationship with the Lord. Do we treat Him like He is our refuge and fortress? Our kids will see that we are safe when we behave like we believe it. If we're constantly worried, complaining, or afraid, the message they will get is that God can't really be trusted to protect them either. Our actions really do speak louder than our words. What are your actions saying about your trust in God?

Run to the Father

He returned home to his father. And while he was still a long way off, his father saw him coming. Filled with love and compassion, he ran to his son, embraced him, and kissed him.

LUKE 15:20

IT'S NOT A NEW CONCEPT, the prodigal son, the wayward child. It dates all the way back to the Garden of Eden with Adam and Eve. We, in fact, were wayward children ourselves, but God in His infinite love for us called us back to Himself and waited patiently for our return. Are you waiting on a wayward child? I get it, mom. It's hard when our children choose something different from what we'd hoped for them.

God understands how you feel as you wait for your child's return. He, too, identifies with His children being wayward, not choosing the best story He has for them. Consider this: you have a powerful love and concern for your child, but God loves them even more. Can you even imagine? The parable of the Prodigal Son best describes it!

After the Prodigal Son returns home, his father gives him the best robe, serves him the best food, and even throws him a party! This is how God feels when His children return. This is His desire for your child. He knows how you feel, because it's how He feels too. Let Him sit in your grief with you, let Him hear your prayers for your child, and let Him comfort you as their mom. His desire is to share in your grief and carry your burden. It is not yours to carry alone. He says in Matthew 11 that His yoke is easy and His burden is light. Give the burden of your wayward child back over to God, and wait expectantly for that child's return.

The Father knows your worry, your sadness, and your hopes for your child's eternity. It's hard for us to give our children back to God, but they were always His first. I anxiously await the day when we throw the biggest party at their return!

Mothering for Every Season

For everything there is a season, a time for every activity under heaven.

ECCLESIASTES 3:1

WITH CHILDREN OF ALL AGES AND STAGES, it's common for us as moms to fight against each season. There are a number of reasons why we push against a new season. Maybe it's because we don't like change, maybe we are afraid of what that new age or stage will hold, or maybe it's fear that our children will not need us as much or uncertainty of how they will handle that new season. With newness there is always a letting go, a shedding of the old.

Today's verse from the poetic book of Ecclesiastes tells us there is a new season for everything. In Ecclesiastes, we are reminded that even our lives themselves are seasons. So, we know it's inevitable and biblical and for our own good, yet we fight against it. Friend, what would it be like if you stopped fighting each new season of your child's life and instead embraced the beauty that it brings? Imagine the beauty that each day would bring if your prayer was "Show me what You have for me in this new season."

That doesn't mean that in beauty there is no difficulty. Ecclesiastes points out that with each new season there can be tears, scattering, grief, death, and fighting. (It's kind of like putting your toddler's pants on when they have learned to express their opinion on pant wearing!) The author is reminding us that, yes, there is bad with the good and good with the bad, but keep going, because it all gets us to the better story—eternity.

As you step into each season of your child's life, pray for your heart as you shed the old and embrace the beauty of the new. Believe that God has a purpose for your child as your child grows and you prepare them to take that new step forward toward the mission field God has planned for them, and for you.

Rest

Jesus said, "Come to me, all of you who are weary and carry heavy burdens, and I will give you rest.

MATTHEW 11:28

HAVE YOU EVER COME BACK FROM a vacation more tired than before you left? You start off thinking it's going to be this amazing, refreshing time—but it actually turns out to be the opposite. All the planning, packing, traveling to get to your destination, stopping for potty breaks, whining, arguing, and straining of your family budget can quickly take a vacation from restful to stressful.

Jesus doesn't promise us a vacation. But He does promise us rest.

Rest isn't found in an all-inclusive resort or an Airbnb on the top of a mountain. Rest isn't found in someone else folding the piles of laundry or having a date night out (although both of those are very nice things!). Rest is found in God Himself.

Notice how in today's verse, Matthew 11:28, Jesus says, "Come to *me*, all of you who are weary and carry heavy burdens, and *I* will give you rest" (emphasis added). Jesus is the source of our rest, and He is the fulfillment of our rest. Rest is inevitable when we come close to Him.

In Psalm 62:1 the psalmist says, "Truly my soul finds rest *in God*" (NIV, emphasis added). Rest isn't found in a place we go, but in a Person we meet.

A loving relationship with God is the most restful place to be. When life is overwhelming or exhausting, I find rest in knowing my eternity is secure with Jesus. The more I know Him—through reading my Bible, listening to worship music, filling my mind with Scripture, and praying as I go throughout my day— even the craziest days of my life can become restful.

May we find our rest not in our location or our circumstance but in knowing the Lord more. May we rest in Him and experience His peace in our everyday moments.

Your Mission

Go and make disciples of all the nations, baptizing them in the name of the Father and the Son and the Holy Spirit. Teach these new disciples to obey all the commands I have given you. And be sure of this: I am with you always, even to the end of the age.

MATTHEW 28:19-20

MISSIONARY STORIES ALWAYS MAKE ME A little starry eyed. I grew up reading about Elisabeth Elliot, Hudson Taylor, and Gladys Aylward, and their stories always hit me like a shot of adrenaline with a side of shame.

I can't believe how much Kingdom work they did in such a short amount of time! What should I be doing? Should I sell everything and go to China?

A few years ago, I stumbled across this quote by Jill Briscoe: "Your mission field is between your own two feet at any given time." In other words, your mission field is exactly where God has planted you, whether that's in your home, in the grocery store, or in another country. Hearing that was incredibly freeing.

When I read the great commission to "go and make disciples of all the nations" in today's Scripture, I immediately jump to grandiose Christian missions. But what if my mission is supposed to be simpler? What if it is a matter of making disciples and reflecting Jesus right where I am?

Can I let my kids see me reading my Bible today?

Can I send an encouraging text to a friend?

Can I pray for my brothers and sisters around the world who are experiencing persecution?

Can I turn on worship music when I'm stressed and change the mood of my home?

Can I promote kindness on social media?

Can I wash dishes with joy as I serve my family?

When I see the great commission not as a lofty charge but a simple daily commitment to sharing Jesus with those He has placed around me, it changes the storyline around the great commission from one of shame and overwhelm to one of joy and community.

The Lord will make you mindful today of the mission field He has for you. He will help you see each interaction as a holy moment of discipleship to bring His Kingdom here on earth.

God's Timing

The Lord isn't really being slow about his promise, as some people think. No, he is being patient for your sake. He does not want anyone to be destroyed, but wants everyone to repent.

2 PETER 3:9

Don't you love two-day shipping?

It always puts a big smile on my face when I can see my new hair straightener or favorite granola or new water bottle show up at my house just a couple days after I've ordered it. With some delivery options, you can order something late at night and have it sitting on your doorstep by the time you wake up the next morning. Talk about speedy delivery!

The problem with these conveniences, however, is that I can sometimes start expecting everything in my life to be that quick. I want my child to grow out of a challenging phase fast. I want healing to be fast. I want spiritual growth to be fast. I want the answers to the questions I have about my life, and I want them now!

But God doesn't operate on a two-day shipping guarantee. His way isn't always the easy way, and He operates on a timeline I can't even comprehend.

God's way is often the way that seems slow. Like the way you can look at a garden and it seems like each day nothing is happening—but growth is still coming. Or the way a child grows. Day by day, you don't even notice the changes until you look back and your baby is taking steps and going to kindergarten and then twirling in her prom dress.

God could totally grow us fast, but it wouldn't be best for us. God's patience, His ability to play the long game, is only for our good. When the world or our lives aren't going at the pace we prefer, we can remember that God's timeline is a kind gift worth waiting for.

When we long for fast and want to push our own timelines, let us trust in the Lord's patient heart, knowing He is working in our lives in His time.

Called to Courage

If you keep quiet at a time like this, deliverance and relief for the Jews will arise from some other place, but you and your relatives will die. Who knows if perhaps you were made queen for just such a time as this?

ESTHER 4:14

MY LIFE HAS BEEN FILLED WITH moments that have called me to courage. Moments where my body, mind, and heart were filled with fear. Fear of losing relationships, position, the love of parents. Standing up for what is right in situations where you have a lot to lose can be terrifying.

One of my friends had an found herself in a situation like this a couple years ago. She wrote:

My childhood was riddled with abuse. My father was abusive mentally, emotionally, physically, and sexually, and my mother did not keep us safe. At one point, my youngest sister ended up pregnant and was on her way to prison, and my parents decided that they would raise her baby. I knew I was called to stand up to my parents and tell them that they couldn't do this. I had to stand up for a baby that couldn't defend himself. But who was I to do this?

When they attempted to take the baby anyway, I knew I had to call Child Protective Services. TO CALL CPS. On my parents. Thirty-four years after my own abuse took place. Would they even believe me? Would I sound like a crazy person making up stories?

With a broken heart, I told my story to a woman in another state that I had never met. And she believed me. She walked away from our phone conversation and went to pick up my nephew. She took him to a place where he is safe.

What an honorable and humbling opportunity it is to be with God, in His will, even when standing up for what is right might cost us.

Esther had so much to lose. Addressing her husband, the king, came with the risk of death. But her people were at risk. She had a powerful opportunity to move past the fear and be the woman that God would use to save her people!

Like Esther, and like my friend, you have been placed here with a purpose. It will likely require courage for you too. What have you been placed on earth to do for such a time as this?

Speak the Truth in Love

Instead, we will speak the truth in love, growing in every way more and more like Christ, who is the head of his body, the church.

EPHESIANS 4:15

AS BELIEVERS, WE SOMETIMES STRUGGLE TO know how to speak like Jesus to a lost and dying world. As a spouse, as a parent, as a grandparent—how do we live? As an employee or employer, how do we interact with others in our workplaces? What about on social media? What are we sharing, and what is the tone of our posts on the various platforms?

Paul's words to the church in Ephesus can give us some help: *speaking the truth in love*. Those are five simple words, but they are so hard to live out in our own strength. As humans, we tend to do either one or the other.

First, some of us are very good at speaking the truth. Truth at any cost. Let the chips fall where they may. We are careless, brash, and maybe even rude or obnoxious. The person who prioritizes speaking the truth would probably say, "The truth is all that matters, right? If someone has an issue with how I say it, it's their problem."

Or, maybe we fall in the other camp, the one that prioritizes love over truth. We try so hard to love others that we overlook the truth. We skirt the issue, we ignore the truth, and we are unwilling to confront because we think love alone will carry the day. We see the current issues divide and polarize, but to avoid offending others, we hold our peace and love quietly. Sometimes we are so afraid to offend that we don't speak up and stand for biblical truth.

Both approaches are flawed. Truth without love hurts. Love without truth deceives. To grow more and more like Jesus, we have to speak the truth in love. Only then will truth be heard. Only then will love have a solid foundation.

Oh, how tempting it is to do only one of the two. But to grow more like Jesus, to speak as He would speak, we need to speak both truth and love!

When I Am a Fool

Control your temper, for anger labels you a fool.

ECCLESIASTES 7:9

HAVE YOU EVER COME TO THE end of your mental and emotional resources? Motherhood will do that to you! Sometimes, it's just too much, isn't it? Too many hard things, not enough rest. Too many kids needing wisely placed words to course-correct, to train, to encourage . . . and in a moment of frustration, my children see a version of me that I wish they hadn't.

If I'm honest, it's easy to just not care what comes out of my mouth when I'm angry. I mean, let's be real! Sometimes, it feels good to let those words rush out like a river—until the heat of the moment is gone, and I look like a fool, and I'm left wishing I had given myself a time-out before I opened my mouth. When I'm tempted to let out a string of angry words, the Holy Spirit reminds me that my children will very likely turn out to be just like me. And you know what? Sometimes it's not awesome.

Though we are often justified in our anger and frustration, it's important to remember that too many of these outbursts will damage our relationships. Releasing that pressure valve might feel good for a moment, but in the long run, it can injure the hearts of the ones we love most. Words spoken in truthful indignation literally apply unrest to the hearts of my children, when my goal upon waking was to apply peace!

Oh, how we need the Spirit of God to help us be wiser than our impulses! The next time events are out of your control and you're tempted to succumb to an impulse that will not yield "the peaceful fruit of righteousness" (Hebrews 12:11, ESV) that we're all after as moms, take a moment and ask for God's help. He is not out of control—and because of the Holy Spirit's help, we don't need to be either.

No Magic 8 Ball

I believe that I shall look upon the goodness of the LORD in the land of the living!
Wait for the LORD; be strong, and let your heart take courage; wait for the LORD!

PSALM 27:13-14, ESV

SOMETIMES I WISH THERE WAS A Magic 8 Ball for parenting: if I were facing a difficult decision or a parenting dilemma, I could ask the Magic 8 Ball a question, give it a good shake, and turn it upside down to find the answer. Wouldn't that be convenient? Life's decisions can be so tough or so cloudy sometimes. They can feel loaded and weighty, as if the whole of my child's future depends on this one decision I make about whether to do the dishes or take some time to play. *What if skipping one nap to visit friends results in my child never being a good sleeper? Will joining this church be the right decision for my child's spiritual walk?* We've all second-guessed our decision-making at some point in our motherhood journeys.

I'm a girl who likes to follow directions. In fact, sometimes I find myself wishing I could get simple, straightforward directions from God, as well. It would be great for God to just tell me what to do. I know that He does sometimes. The Bible falls open to just the right spot, or the pastor says exactly what I needed to hear. But more often than not, I'm waiting, watching, and walking.

I don't think it's a coincidence that in parenting and in our walk with God the answers aren't usually so readily available. What matters more is our unique relationship with God. We hear over and over that every kid is different, and the same can be said about each one of God's children and their relationship with Him. As we have to grow to learn who our children are, so we grow to learn what it means for us to walk with God, His spirit accompanying us through the days that He formed just for us.

When our hearts desire easy answers and quick fixes, may God remind us that He does have good things coming for us here on earth and in His Kingdom. He may not reveal the answers as quickly as we'd like, but we can trust Him and His unique plans for our lives as we walk with Him every step of the way.

Exactly As You Are

How foolish can you be? After starting your new lives in the Spirit, why
are you now trying to become perfect by your own human effort?

GALATIANS 3:3

To become perfect. That's quite a goal, isn't it? I think I could get there, with the
right balance of well rested, meditated, medicated, and caffeinated, with a slight tilt
in my messy mom bun to make it look like I'm not trying too hard.

The truth is that I couldn't get perfect *before* I had kids, much less after. In
today's verse, Paul is talking about being saved and born again in the Spirit, but
there's also a different kind of new life that comes when our kids arrive. We are
now Mom. You would think that experience would humble us: staring in the face
of a new human being, in awe of God and all of His miraculous power that is more
abundant than we could ask or imagine.

But too often, we act like God gave us this precious baby because we have a
handle on things. "Okay, God! Thanks for the gift! I'll take it from here!" We soon
realize, however, that we are not experts in parenting.

God did not give us our kids to leave us alone with our kids. (Thank heavens.)
The God that started this good work of our children will be faithful to complete
His good work in them *and* us (see Philippians 1:6).

He did not confuse us for someone else when He entrusted us with our children. In fact, He chose us to mother them, knowing that we were less than perfect.
He chose us exactly as we are, not to leave us but to use us as vessels for His love,
mercy, and grace.

God has chosen you to be your child's mother. Not the mom who seems to
have it all together—you. He does not expect you to be someone else, but He's
asking you to be a vessel of God's love. And, even when you feel overwhelmed and
less than perfect, know that He will never leave you alone.

Humiliation or Humility?

Humble yourselves under the mighty power of God, and at the right time he will lift you up in honor. Give all your worries and cares to God, for he cares about you.

1 PETER 5:6-7

HUMILITY SEEMS TO COME STANDARD WITH the Motherhood Membership. We lucky ones even get the Humiliation Bonus from time to time. Keeping the not-quite-big-kid locked with you in a bathroom stall from touching all the things, peeking under the dividing wall, or commenting on the odor associated with your current task definitely earns you the Humility Badge on your Mama Vest. Humbling ourselves under God's mighty power should be old hat for us then, right? Yes! And no.

Our sacred calling as mothers often leaves us feeling worn down and depleted. The daily grind, the repetitive chores, and the never-ending needs of our loved ones are more likely to make us feel humble, not prideful. But true humility isn't a matter of capacity or vigor, or even self-esteem. It isn't even a feeling. It is a reorienting of the mind; it is a decision to put God in His rightful place as King over our lives.

When we know God as the One in charge and ourselves as the ones in need, we can then submit to His sovereignty. Because our Heavenly Father really does care about us, know our worries, see the tears, and forgive the screams, we can come before Him in our weakness. In fact, He wants us to. Then we are already out of our own way, and He can show us His better way.

Sweet mom, there is peace in the act of humbling yourself before the Lord. And there is promise. At the right time—in God's perfect time—you will be lifted up in honor. It says so right there in His Word. That means we can trust it completely. It may not involve a couture gown or shiny award, but it will fill your heart with true joy and comfort. The dress would probably end up with ketchup on it anyway.

Stay Alert

Stay alert! Watch out for your great enemy, the devil. He prowls around like a roaring lion, looking for someone to devour. Stand firm against him, and be strong in your faith. Remember that your family of believers all over the world is going through the same kind of suffering you are.

1 PETER 5:8-9

MY FRIEND'S YOUNG SON LIKES TO SAY, "I hate Satan!" whenever he sees the results of sin in the world. I get it. Seeing and experiencing that evil often sends me looking for someone to blame too. Who better than the prince of darkness himself?

God did not give us a spirit of fear. He also doesn't want us sticking our heads in the sand or up in the clouds, behaving as though there is no battle surging for the right to our souls. So He gives us wisdom when we ask for it (see James 1:5). Wisdom unveils the real enemy. Wisdom shows us where to find the devil and how to arm ourselves against him. I love that God gives us the *how* as soon as He gives us the *what*.

Let's look more closely at the *how*:

Stay alert! Open your eyes! If we do not vet the information coming at our kids from all directions, they will be inundated with lies. Be the guardian at the gate, ready to catch and sift through the incoming messages and agendas.

Watch out. Don't be the ostrich! Be on the lookout! Just like we need to stay alert and not fall asleep at the wheel, we need to be aware of what threats look like. Pay attention to what is being taught to your children in school. Know what materials or programs are offered at your local library. Follow your lawmakers and the legislation they seek to pass.

Stand firm. Know the truth! Teach it to your kids! There is no way you will be able to tell truth from lies if you haven't learned it for yourself. You cannot pass on what you don't possess.

Remember. You are not alone! There really is strength in numbers. We can see the enemy fervently prowling and destroying in the Middle East, China, North Korea, and so many more countries. These are countries where believers have been specifically targeted and persecuted. Their experience can offer us strength, wisdom, and even comfort.

Recognize Satan when you see his destruction. Put on the full armor of God (see Ephesians 6:10-18) as you prepare to defend your people. Take comfort in knowing mamas all over the world, and all throughout time, have fought this very same enemy!

We Won't Suffer Forever

In his kindness God called you to share in his eternal glory by means of Christ Jesus. So after you have suffered a little while, he will restore, support, and strengthen you, and he will place you on a firm foundation. All power to him forever! Amen.

1 PETER 5:10-11

WE SOMETIMES TELL OUR KIDS (when they complain) that life isn't fair. (No? Just me?) Well, it isn't. God's Eden, His perfect world, never included suffering; yet we know it exists for each person on this side of the veil. If not from anecdotal evidence, we can see the truth of this in God's own Word.

While people easily believe the reality of the suffering spoken of in Scripture, they usually aren't as quick to believe the promises. What a good God we have who promises His glory, His *eternal* glory, at the end of our suffering! Yes, suffering is guaranteed. But so is restoration. So is support. So is strength.

All throughout Scripture, God pairs His promised redemption alongside the inevitable result of the Fall, of sin in the world. Because this kind King loves us so very much, He will not force us to believe in or choose Him. And so we suffer. And He hates it. Because He loves us so very much, He did not leave us to suffer alone or forever.

He sent His only Son, Christ Jesus, to bear the full burden of our sin. He suffered the consequences of all human sin to the extent of death so that we would have the choice to experience only the suffering of earth, followed by an eternity of His perfect plan (see John 3:16-17).

Not only are we given the choice to live with God forever, but we are allowed access to His power while on earth. He gave us His Advocate, the Holy Spirit, to abide with us while we wait for Jesus to return (see John 14:26; 15:26). And He gave us His inspired Word (see 2 Timothy 3:16-17). Together with Jesus, we can stand on the firm foundation of Truth, knowing that God already has victory in hand (see Revelation 20:10), and He has promised we will not have to suffer alone or forever. Amen and amen!

More Than Putting on Kindness

Since God chose you to be the holy people he loves, you must clothe yourselves with tenderhearted mercy, kindness, humility, gentleness, and patience. Make allowance for each other's faults, and forgive anyone who offends you. Remember, the Lord forgave you, so you must forgive others. Above all, clothe yourselves with love, which binds us all together in perfect harmony.

COLOSSIANS 3:12-14

TODAY'S SCRIPTURE TELLS US THAT BECAUSE God chose us to be the holy people He loves, we *must* clothe ourselves with the following attributes: mercy, kindness, humility, gentleness, patience, and forgiveness. Notice the verse says *must*, not *can*.

Even more important than the attributes I've listed, we must clothe ourselves in love. But have you ever stopped to consider that kindness and love are not the same thing?

For example, we can be kind to people, and they can be kind to us, but that doesn't mean we love each other. Not long ago, I kept seeing T-shirts, wall decor, notebooks, all sorts of things with "Be Kind" written on them. Something about it disturbed me, but I wasn't able to put my finger on it.

Upon reflection, I realized that the phrase "Be Kind," at least from a worldly perspective, isn't necessarily coming from a place of genuine love. God is love, and we must clothe ourselves in His love first. If we aren't living kindness from this place of love, then we run the risk of having selfishness be our motivation. When this happens, our kindnesses are often short lived. In some cases, we end up being nothing but a noisy gong (see 1 Corinthians 13:1). Anyone can be kind, whether they're a Christian or not. But what makes our kindness different from the world's is the place it comes from: God's love.

Jesus walked this earth in love. I want to be like that. I want love oozing out of me, so that people can see the goodness of God and be turned toward Him.

What is your motivation for the way you speak, act, and behave toward people? Oftentimes mine has been kindness. But stopping there and not pursuing love is simply not pursuing our highest calling. We're missing the best part.

Exercise Your Thinking Muscle

Now, dear brothers and sisters, one final thing. Fix your thoughts on what is true, and honorable, and right, and pure, and lovely, and admirable. Think about things that are excellent and worthy of praise.

PHILIPPIANS 4:8

WE HAVE SO MANY THOUGHTS THAT run through our minds every day, especially as moms. Our thoughts are powerful. They influence us to act or not act. They can encourage us or discourage us. How you think will affect how you feel. How you feel will affect what you do.

There is a reason for us to practice thinking on the things that are true and honorable, pure and lovely, excellent and worthy of praise. If we fix our thoughts on those things, we will strive for those things. We will believe those things. We will be those things. If we focus on things that aren't pure, that aren't honorable, then we will fall into those things. Where our thoughts go, our actions will follow. If we want to be like Christ, we need to think how He wants us to think.

If we are intentionally spending our time dwelling on things that are good, it leaves less room for the noise and negativity of the world. Spend time in Scripture, listen to praise and worship music, and spend time in prayer. Avoid gossip, mute your social media notifications, and turn off the news for a little while. Be intentional about counting your blessings instead of your trials.

That doesn't mean we won't get discouraged or have wrong thoughts. But we can choose to redirect those thoughts. We have the power to choose. We can choose to engage in gossip and negativity, or we can choose to build one another up, count our blessings, and give God the praise.

Changing our thoughts is like exercising a muscle. The more we practice thinking about good things, the easier it will get and the stronger our habit will be. The more we think like Christ, the more Christlike we will be.

Comfort in Times of Trouble

> He comforts us in all our troubles so that we can comfort others. When they are troubled, we will be able to give them the same comfort God has given us.
>
> **2 CORINTHIANS 1:4**

It's hard when we find ourselves in the midst of troubles and trials to think of anything other than the pain we are feeling. We sometimes even neglect the comfort that God Himself is trying to give us. Pain blinds us to truth and distorts the reality around us.

The old hymn "What a Friend We Have in Jesus" says it well:

O what peace we often forfeit
O what needless pain we bear
All because we do not carry
Everything to God in prayer

In those moments of raw pain, we can hide away. But the Holy Spirit is the Comforter, waiting for us to accept that peace that passes all understanding (see Philippians 4:7).

In His kindness, God offers another side to that comfort: the beauty that emerges from our trials. God is using this time of comfort to train us to be His hands of comfort to other people.

I know you have experienced the love of God through another person's actions too. That reassuring hand squeeze or hug that comes from someone who has already walked through the pain you are in. The testimony that stirs your heart to hope that you will see victory in your life. The Scripture someone sends you that is like a ray of light in the middle of a stormy day. All these moments remind us that behind the clouds and at the end of the trial there is joy, hope, a future, restoration, and Jesus!

Sometimes we don't have the strength to keep going in times of trouble. Perhaps these are the moments when we need to remember there is a purpose to the trouble. Something is being born in us. A hand squeeze, a testimony, a hug, or a song all say, "God knows! God sees! God wants to comfort you! I know because He did it for me!"

Learning to Walk in God's Will

Teach me to do your will, for you are my God. May your
gracious Spirit lead me forward on a firm footing.

PSALM 143:10

WE TALK ABOUT GOD'S WILL so much that sometimes we might forget what it actually means. It is so tempting in life to take *our* plans and just stamp the words "God's will" on them instead of following His lead. But learning to walk in God's will is not an easy task.

God's will often requires you to get off the bench in ways you may never have expected. His perfect will may involve asking you to do things that seem impossible or scary, and often it will push you out of your comfort zone.

Because of sin, we will always face a battle between our will and God's will. Just like a toddler, we need God to teach us obedience to His direction.

Today's verse from Psalm 143 recognizes God's graciousness toward us and His never-failing patience when we protest His plans. Our patient Father stands there waiting for us to stop our tantrum—all because He said no or He asked us to do something we didn't want to do.

It is scary to follow God's will, because we don't know the way ahead. We like to know what's going to happen ahead of time—the details, the schedule, all of it. But that isn't how God works. He asks us for faith even when nothing around us makes sense.

Sometimes we step out in His will, and rather than experience success, everything seems to go against us. *What is going on?* We know beyond a shadow of a doubt we heard God, and we did trust Him, and we did obey Him. Yes, Lord, send me! Then *bam!* Suddenly we get sideswiped, and now we don't know up from down.

But I love the plea in this verse—"lead me forward on a firm footing."

Lean in close, sweet mom, and remember that even when everything looks like it's not going according to plan, you can trust God. His gracious Spirit will teach you His will and give you a firm footing. Just keep putting one foot in front of the other, following His lead.

Inner Conflict

Now I appeal to Euodia and Syntyche. Please, because you belong to the Lord, settle your disagreement. And I ask you, my true partner, to help these two women, for they worked hard with me in telling others the Good News.

PHILIPPIANS 4:2-3

I THINK IT'S INTERESTING THAT PAUL called out Euodia and Syntyche by name in his letter to the Philippians. He didn't want them or anyone else to be confused about who he was talking to. We learn from Philippians 4:3 that these women meant a lot to Paul and had worked closely with him. It's safe to assume that he felt their quarrel was getting in the way of their work to expand God's Kingdom on the earth.

What happens when you get into conflict with someone? It can take over your brain, can't it? Whether it's a conversation that already happened or one that I'm anticipating, I can rehearse and rewrite the same script over and over again until it wears a path in my brain and it's about all I can think about.

And it is absolutely exhausting.

When we have these kinds of takeovers, it seriously limits our ability to minister. I can't minister to myself because my brain won't get quiet enough to hear from the Holy Spirit. I can't minister to other people because I'm not paying enough attention to get proper direction from the Holy Spirit. Heaven knows I'm not able to minister to these brothers or sisters in Christ because I'm too stinking mad.

Who is occupying your thoughts these days? Who besides the Holy Spirit have you let set up camp in your brain? Even if it's not someone in your immediate church family, is there a relationship in which you've let your differences and disagreements get in the way of the good work that needs to be done?

God knows your heart. Ask Him to show you if there are relationships getting in the way of sharing His love with the world. Ask Him to show you how to walk in that relationship in a way that brings Him glory.

Rooted

Let your roots grow down into him, and let your lives be built on him. Then your faith will grow strong in the truth you were taught, and you will overflow with thankfulness.

COLOSSIANS 2:7

As a mom, there have been times when I have set my own physical needs aside—even to the point that it compromises my health and well-being—for my kids to get what they need. When I read today's Scripture, it feels to me like I'm reading God's heart for me as I raise my kids. He wants me not to lack in my basic needs but rather to have everything I need in Him. It's His prescription for my spiritual nourishment.

There are two parts to today's verse. The first part—roots growing down and faith growing strong—is the rich inner work that people won't see. It's just between us and the Lord. The second part—overflowing with thankfulness—refers to the outer evidence of growth that we share with the world. The woman who shows up for her husband, family, church community, and neighbors with the fruit of the Spirit is someone who has first rooted herself in her heavenly Father.

It's like a duck paddling across the water. The duck looks like she's gliding effortlessly along. If you were to look underneath, she'd be furiously paddling, stirring up all kinds of water and silt.

There is lots of paddling, stirring, and hand-dirtying work for us to do if we want that life built on a solid foundation. God's burden is light, but we must do our part to stay yoked together with Him. There is peace in my paddling when I spend time with Him. But that peace can be quickly lost in the chaos of the day. I challenge you to take that peace with you today, with your life built on him and gratitude overflowing.

The Lord will gently guide you in this work of loving Him and the world He's built. He can show you how to grow your roots down so you can build your life on Him.

Refiner's Fire

Who will be able to endure it when he comes? Who will be able to stand
and face him when he appears? For he will be like a blazing fire that
refines metal, or like a strong soap that bleaches clothes.

MALACHI 3:2

THIS PASSAGE FROM THE OLD TESTAMENT describes Jesus in a way that is so different from our cultural depiction of Him that it borders on being comical. Jesus? Our homeless carpenter-King who hung around with fishermen and held children? He's like a blazing fire? Or bleach?

But it is His loving-kindness that blazes so brightly against the darkness of time, gently melting away our impurity, cleansing us from our sin, and refashioning us in His image.

Our children do this too, in their own way, don't they? The power they hold over us isn't one of strength and might. In fact, it's the opposite. It's their vulnerability and need that refine us. Our bodies are attuned to theirs as we care for them. We discover things about ourselves we didn't know were there, whether that's a lack of patience or a lack of humility. They help us become better versions of ourselves.

More than that, they are precious for the mere reason that they exist. No more, no less. And if they're precious because they exist, that must mean that we, too, are precious just for existing.

What does contemplating—and knowing—our own preciousness do to the power of shame that holds us in bondage? It breaks it. This is Jesus' love at work.

It's the Refiner's fire, making us more like Jesus.

Knowing this calls me to yield to the moments with my children, to let them be the refining fire when I'm irritated or impatient or insisting on my way, letting them soften my soul and turn my eye to the One who made them in His image.

Remember that, as God made our children in His image, He also made us. It's His fiery love that makes us in His image. May He remind us today as we go on our way that we are precious because we belong to Him.

A Repentant Parent

People who conceal their sins will not prosper, but if they confess and turn from them, they will receive mercy.

PROVERBS 28:13

In each age and stage, our children are going to mess up in different ways. Just like us, their sin takes different shapes and forms as they get older. In the younger years it's seemingly small things like sneaking an extra snack when they were told no or throwing a fit at bedtime. (I'll never understand why they despise bedtime; I love to go to bed!)

As our children get older, the dialogue changes to conversations around technology, relationships, things they're watching, words they are using, and life-altering decisions they are making. Things feel much heavier than in the younger years when it was more about how too much candy will hurt your tummy or obeying your mommy when she says it's time to pick up your toys. Either way, each stage of life will offer an opportunity to walk with our children through the process from disobedience to repentance and forgiveness. As their parent, we can be modeling this important process for them with our own shortcomings. Sounds like a lot of fun, right?

There have been many times as a parent, more times than I would care to admit, when I have had the opportunity to admit wrong and ask forgiveness from my children. When we never admit wrong to our kids, they never have the chance to see us modeling the process of repentance and forgiveness. When they experience us admitting imperfection, asking for forgiveness, and remedying the sin in our own life, it serves as an incredible example for them. The hard question is, are you acknowledging your own sin and receiving forgiveness and grace for the ways you fall short? This may take some work on your end as you prepare to lead your children through this process, but just imagine the freedom of not having to be the perfect parent.

Your prayer can simply be, *Lord help me model the process of forgiveness to my kids by walking it out with you authentically. Thank you, God, for forgiveness!*

Simply Stated, You Are Loved

God showed his great love for us by sending Christ to die for us while we were still sinners.

ROMANS 5:8

I REMEMBER WHEN MY FIRSTBORN CAME into the world. Seeing her for the first time took my breath away and filled me with a love I had never experienced before. It was overwhelming. I never thought I could love anything or anyone so much, but I loved that little girl more than I could have ever imagined. And with each new child that came into my life, my heart seemed to grow in its capacity to love. Even as my children get older, they still take my breath away. The love that we have for our children is simple, isn't it? No qualifiers, it just is.

It's hard to imagine, but God feels that way about us too. As moms, it's hard enough for us to wrap our minds around having that kind of love for our kids, but it's a lot more complicated when it comes to receiving that kind of love from God ourselves.

Read this sentence out loud: "I am loved." Say it again: "I am loved."

Somewhere along the line, we begin to deem ourselves unlovable, or we convince our souls that we don't really need that much love. Just like you never stop loving your child, God never runs out of love for you. His love is abundant and overflowing. On your worst day and your best day, His love is pouring over you and is there for the taking, but that's just it—you have to receive it.

You are part of the greatest love story ever told—the story that God sent His Son to die on a cross for you (even for you on your worst day) and He is still pursuing you in that love every day after that. Simply stated, you are audaciously loved every day. Every day, you take God's breath away. Start each day with this simple truth: "I am loved." Daily walking in that truth will change your life. You are loved.

Growing Trust

In panic I cried out, "I am cut off from the LORD!" But you heard my cry for mercy and answered my call for help.

PSALM 31:22

WHENEVER YOU ARE PHYSICALLY HURT—whether you've stubbed a toe or broken an arm—you have certain receptors in your brain that are triggered to let you know you are hurt and that something is wrong with your body.

Did you know that those same receptors fire when we feel rejected? Because community is essential to human survival, our brains perceive loss of community or relationship as being just as harmful to us as a physical injury.

In fact, studies have shown that you can take Tylenol to relieve the pain of rejection.

I think of a child experiencing separation anxiety. When her mom leaves the room, the child cries out in emotional pain. When the child cries out, unless otherwise unable to, her mom comes back to show her daughter that everything is okay. This back-and-forth throughout the child's early years develops a trusting relationship between her and her mom. She knows that no matter how many times Mom leaves the room, she always comes back.

I see this pattern in my relationship with God too. When I feel far from Him, I cry out, and I feel Him near again. It may not be right away, but soon enough, He makes Himself known. This back-and-forth develops a trusting relationship until I always know and trust that He's there. My brain will no longer perceive a loss of relationship with Him.

Take courage that when you feel far from God, it doesn't necessarily mean that something is wrong. It's a natural part of a relationship, and a time to build trust in the One who has already called you to Himself. He is never far from you.

When you feel like God is far away, pray this prayer: *God, I feel far from you, so I am crying out to You. Remind me that You are here, that You are good, and that You are trustworthy. I'm so thankful that You can be trusted in every situation I encounter. Thank You for being with me.*

Salty

Let your conversation be gracious and attractive so that
you will have the right response for everyone.

COLOSSIANS 4:6

ALTHOUGH THE NEW LIVING TRANSLATION USES the word "attractive" in today's verse, other translations use the phrase "seasoned with salt" to describe what our speech should be like. Isn't that such a great image? Sometimes salt is all that's needed to add some oomph to a bland dish. In the same way, conversations about God that are "seasoned with salt" are more attractive to their listeners. It's like our words are carefully prepared meals on their way to the table that the chef seasons at just the last second. We have in our mind what we want to say, we have our intentions, but when we cover our conversations in prayer, the Lord can see to it that our speech is what its listener needs.

And maybe if you're a really fast talker, He's there at the table with the salt shaker.

Isn't it amazing that it's possible for us to have the right response for everyone? Everyone includes in-laws, coworkers, kids, *in-laws*, spouse, neighbors, *in-laws*. (See what I did there?) When we submit our conversations to the Lord, the person we're talking to is not just hearing words from us to them but they're receiving a word from God to them.

I'm grateful I can rely on Him in that kind of way. It doesn't mean that I'll get everything perfect, but it does mean that I don't have to live in the anxiety and fear that comes with living on this earth and all its egos—mine included. When I do my part of abiding in Him, I can trust Him to guide me. I can rest in knowing that He covers things. When things are out of my control—like how those around me receive my words (especially my kids)—He can step in and use it for His purpose.

God goes before us always, even in our speech. Thank Him for speaking for you and through you, seasoning your words with salt. May He remind you of that truth today, so you can rest in Him.

My Unbelief

"What do you mean, 'If I can'?" Jesus asked. "Anything is possible if a person believes." The father instantly cried out, "I do believe, but help me overcome my unbelief!"

MARK 9:23-24

DID YOU KNOW THAT HOPE IS A SCIENCE? Researchers have studied hope and have found that someone can practice the art of hoping and grow in their ability to hope. I don't think anyone would be surprised to learn that hoping involves a goal, a will, and a way.

The father in Mark 9 was losing hope that his son would ever be well: "They brought the boy. But when the evil spirit saw Jesus, it threw the child into a violent convulsion, and he fell to the ground, writhing and foaming at the mouth. 'How long has this been happening?' Jesus asked the boy's father. He replied, 'Since he was a little boy. The spirit often throws him into the fire or into water, trying to kill him. Have mercy on us and help us, if you can'" (Mark 9:20-22).

The father had a goal, he had a will, but he had lost his way. He was like so many of us sloughing through the challenges of parenthood that have no easy solution or seemingly no end. Fortunately for this father, he was standing in front of the Way.

In Mark 9, we get a close look at an exhausted father. We can feel his torment and helplessness on the page as he's spent years trying to keep his son from harm. I think his sudden reaction to Jesus in verse 24 is what our souls do when we dialogue with our risen Savior. The tired man who is doubtful and done is suddenly awake.

This passage is the fight for my faith when the battle's raging in the lives of people I love, in the news headlines, when I'm praying for healing, when the world feels like it's on fire.

If you can. I do believe. Help me overcome my unbelief.

Help me overcome. Help me. Help.

I want God to wake us up to what He's capable of. There are things around us that shouldn't be, but we've grown so accustomed to them, we don't even notice them anymore.

May God wake us up to the things that are possible in Him. May He breathe His life and fire back into the places in our lives where we've grown accustomed to less than His desire for us.

When We're Misunderstood

After this, Jesus traveled around Galilee. He wanted to stay out of Judea, where the Jewish leaders were plotting his death. But soon it was time for the Jewish Festival of Shelters, and Jesus' brothers said to him, "Leave here and go to Judea, where your followers can see your miracles! You can't become famous if you hide like this! If you can do such wonderful things, show yourself to the world!" For even his brothers didn't believe in him.

JOHN 7:1-5

HAVE YOU EVER BEEN MISUNDERSTOOD BY someone you loved? I've been seriously misunderstood by people I love who I thought knew me well enough to understand me. There have been people I've tried hard to please, but in the end, it was like we were speaking a different language. Other times, I've had people angry at me because I took a path in obedience to the Lord that they did not agree with or understand. Have you been there too?

We need to have wisdom as we walk the Lord's path for us. We need to be in His Word, testing what we believe we're hearing from the Lord against Scripture, seeking wise counsel, and praying. But sometimes the Lord calls us on a different path than our brothers and sisters, familial and spiritual. It can be a very lonely journey when no one else understands our calling.

When I read today's Scripture, I can feel the sarcasm radiating from Jesus' brothers. Granted, Jesus's words and actions might not make sense to our human minds sometimes, but it's shocking to me that they grew up with the Son of Man—their big brother—and so misunderstood Him and His purpose.

I wonder if that made Jesus sad or if it hurt His feelings. Maybe He had such assurance that everything would come out right that it was okay, but I certainly feel sad as I read it.

If you are struggling with being misunderstood, here is my prayer for you:

Jesus, thank You that You see us, know us, and understand us. Forgive us when we mock our brothers and sisters who are following You the best they know how. Forgive us when we judge that path You've put someone else on. When we are the ones on a different path, help us to trust that You have good plans for us. Thank You that You lived on this earth and walked the ways that we walk and feel the things that we feel. Amen.

When Friendship Changes

Barnabas agreed and wanted to take along John Mark. But Paul disagreed strongly, since John Mark had deserted them in Pamphylia and had not continued with them in their work. Their disagreement was so sharp that they separated. Barnabas took John Mark with him and sailed for Cyprus. Paul chose Silas, and as he left, the believers entrusted him to the Lord's gracious care.

ACTS 15:37-40

OVER THE COURSE OF MY LIFE, I have been blessed with some truly wonderful friendships. A few have lasted decades and have witnessed (for better or worse!) the many phases of my life, from childhood adulthood. One group of friends comes to mind as I think about the situation between Paul and Barnabas in the book of Acts. For years, my husband and I did almost everything together with this couple—until at one point our friendship was challenged beyond what we could repair. Though we tried very hard to move beyond the situation, it eventually became clear that we would need to part ways. Similarly, I'm sure Paul and Barnabas never imagined not doing life alongside each other. It wasn't part of their plan, but there they were, going different ways.

Their paths eventually crossed again (see 1 Corinthians 9:5), but the Bible really doesn't tell us who was right and who was wrong. What we do know is that they did a lot of life together, there was a conflict, and then they split.

Friendships change because people change. As our lives ebb and flow through each new season, we will lose and gain friends. Losing important people in our lives, especially ones who we thought were in it for the long haul, is really hard. The encouragement I have for you is this: God brought new people into my life just a short season later. People who I would not have had the capacity to build a friendship with had I not lost a few friends along the way. God has a way of creating beauty out of hardship. Trust Him in that—He's been doing it since the beginning of time.

If you're struggling with the loss of a close friendship today, take it to the Lord in prayer. Pray for healing as you navigate the loss—and pray about the changes in life that made the friendship fall away. Pray and then trust God for a new beginning. When things change, it often means a new thing is coming. Trust God with your heart in this. His changes are always for our good.

Voices

My sheep listen to my voice; I know them, and they follow me. I give them eternal life, and they will never perish. No one can snatch them away from me, for my Father has given them to me, and he is more powerful than anyone else. No one can snatch them from the Father's hand.

JOHN 10:27-29

GOD CREATED US WITH THE ABILITY to listen to and know voices.

Babies can begin learning voices when they're still in the womb. Before they know exactly who those voices belong to, they know the voices. Once a baby is born, they can recognize their mother or father's voice because they've been listening to it in the womb. Once a baby is born, they can even recognize a song that they heard in the womb if they heard it often enough. Hearing the song can even calm a baby when they're upset. Amazing!

Babies aren't the only ones who need to hear reassuring voices. We moms need them too. One of my favorite things about being a part of a mom community is the encouragement it extends to new moms when they enter our fold. Hearing "You're doing a good job" from other moms becomes something of an encouraging refrain as they face the various challenges of motherhood for the first time. The assurance we help weave into the wee morning hours for new moms is the same assurance we can give when a mom of older children is up in the middle of the night worrying about them and wondering if she's doing enough. This is why it's important to invite moms into community and into the fold of Christian fellowship.

I want you to think, too, about what voices you're listening to in your life.

You can think first about where the voices are coming from. Are they coming from social media? A streaming service? Your faith community? God's Word?

How do you feel when you spend time in those places? How do you feel afterward? Do you feel refreshed? Encouraged? Challenged? Loved? Or sad? Discouraged? Drained?

What are some ways that you can gather godly voices around you? One way is through memorizing Scripture. I think today's Scripture is a good place to start, because it's a great reminder of who we are. It's the reassurance that not only can we hear God, but we can listen to Him and we can follow Him. No one can snatch us from our heavenly Father. Keep that refrain playing in your mind today.

Seeing Discipline as Love

Those who spare the rod of discipline hate their children. Those who love their children care enough to discipline them.

PROVERBS 13:24

WE USED TO BE IN A small Bible study with several other couples. We were all about the same age, and our children were all similar in age. It was a harmonious group, and we grew to love one another deeply.

But . . . there was one small fly in the ointment. One couple didn't believe in discipline. They would never dream of spanking a child and even hesitated to speak firmly to them. I would describe their approach to discipline as pleading for obedience with a touch of begging thrown in for good measure.

I remember one particular time when their two-year-old son deliberately poured a bowl of sugary cereal and milk from atop his high chair onto the shag carpet below. To my surprise, his mother simply said, "Please don't do that, Timothy. It makes a mess." She cleaned it up and made a second bowl of sugary cereal and milk for him, and before she could turn around, Timothy poured that bowl out slowly, watching it splatter onto the carpet below. Her response was baffling to me: "Please, Tim. Why do you do these things? You're making things so hard for Mommy." Wow! Do you think that changed her two-year-old's behavior?

Today's verse doesn't say failing to discipline isn't showing love. It says you *hate* your children if you don't discipline them. There's one thing I know for sure: if you don't discipline your children, lots of other folks are going to grow to hate them!

Talk with your husband about your approach to child discipline. Get on the same page. Settle on an approach that you both feel good about, and then practice consistency. Don't allow children to go from one parent to the other in order to get a different outcome. If you apply consistent discipline, you will be sowing the seeds that can bring a harvest of delight when your children grow up to be a joy to you and to others.

What Is Feeding Your Soul?

A wise person is hungry for knowledge, while the fool feeds on trash.

PROVERBS 15:14

HAVE YOU TURNED ON THE TELEVISION LATELY? Wow! Or have you looked through your social media feeds? Or listened to contemporary pop music? Or been to the theater to see the latest blockbuster movie? What in the world? I am constantly amazed at the amount of trash brought to us through secular media. Most of what passes for primetime entertainment today would have been banned and the creators prosecuted for obscenity just fifty years ago.

Do you think the writer of today's verse in Proverbs 15 was peeking into the future when he wrote this? While there are fools who rely on dumpster diving today, the masses feed on the trash of mainstream media, Hollywood, and social media.

If you want to improve the quality of family life, consider throwing out your television. Know which movies your children are watching. Limit their access to online content and social media. If they feed on enough of that trash, it will pollute their young minds. Replace the trash with the opportunity to learn and acquire knowledge. In our home, books abound. I have been collecting them for years from garage sales and secondhand stores. If we want our children to have less screen time, we need to give them alternatives.

The Lord created children with an enormous sense of curiosity. The average preschooler might ask nearly four hundred questions each day. Feed that curiosity. Introduce your children to resources rich in truth and information.

If you allow them to graze on the garbage of contemporary culture every day, that God-given curiosity will shrink and disappear entirely and be replaced by perversion and ignorance. It's not lost on me that many of the creators of electronic devices and media don't allow their own children to use the very platforms they created.

Remember, too, that as with everything else in parenting, we set the example. Banning them from media garbage when you yourself are feeding your own addiction won't go without notice by your children. As I've said so often, children seldom listen to their parents, but they watch them constantly. Set a good example!

Resigning to the Lord's Plans

We can make our plans, but the LORD determines our steps.

PROVERBS 16:9

Ever notice how the best planning can go awry in the twinkling of an eye?

You can't buy all the ingredients because your youngest child's temper tantrum is cutting your trip to the grocery store short, the funds for your vacation are depleted when you have to pay for unexpected car repairs, your teenager's date is the opposite of what you pictured, and it turns out retirement may never happen due to economic challenges. What happened to our plans?

God has a way of getting our attention in the area of planning. We can be as prepared as possible and the control freak of the year, but we still lack the power to make it all happen. We can yell at our kids, nag our husband, and even try to manipulate a situation to get a desired result, but we still can't control their decisions and actions. Come to think of it, the older I get, the more I realize how little control I had in the first place. At some point we learn that believing the lie that we are in control isn't helpful, and we learn to surrender our plans and submit to the authority of the Lord.

Isaiah 40:12 reminds us of our place in this world: "Who else has held the oceans in his hand? Who has measured off the heavens with his fingers? Who else knows the weight of the earth or has weighed the mountains and hills on a scale?"

The answer is the Lord God, the One who loves us and knows our heart's needs before we do. He will guide us and help us hold our plans loosely while we learn how to commit our many plans to Him. He knows what is best for us! "Commit everything you do to the LORD. Trust him, and he will help you" (Psalm 37:5).

Hold tight to Him, mom! Though our plans may fail, He never fails. He is always faithful. He is the Great Comforter, and he loves us. We can trust Him to help us.

Choose Who Walks with You

Walk with the wise and become wise; associate with fools and get in trouble.

PROVERBS 13:20

IF I COULD GIVE YOU ONE piece of advice to share with your children today, it might be this: think carefully about who you hang out with!

Years ago, a friend shared an analogy with me. He said, "Suppose I'm wanting to guide you to a better life, to be salt and light to you and to lift you up onto the higher ground I've found in Christ. Visualize me standing atop a high table, bending over and taking you by the hand. Now imagine that you want to pull me down to your level. You want to get your old friend back so we can party and live the crazy life we used to enjoy. Who do you think will be successful? The one pulling up, or the one pulling down?"

The people we choose to associate with will in large part determine the path we will walk. I love the wisdom that today's verse gives us.

Our children need to know that if they walk with the wise, they will become wise, and if they hang out with fools, they'll get in trouble. They need to have it indelibly written on their heart. And they need to see their parents modeling it. This is another one of those situations where wisdom is caught more than taught. Our children are watching us closely, and if we tell them one thing while doing another, they will see right through our charade.

Fortunately, the positive promise of this principle is just as true for us as it is for our children. Always try to associate with other couples who are ahead of you on the gospel road. Let them mentor you and guide your footsteps toward wisdom. The friends we choose can make all the difference.

It doesn't take a high level of discernment to tell which road friends are traveling on. You may find yourself needing to taper off old relationships and nurture new ones. Find friends who share your values and your goals if you want to arrive at your destination. Don't get sidetracked with fools who don't share your vision. Choose wisely!

An Attitude of Gratitude

I will give thanks to you, LORD, with all my heart.

PSALM 9:1, NIV

How often have you heard about having an "attitude of gratitude"? It's a cute saying that rolls off the tongue easily. It makes a great T-shirt slogan or a catchy sermon title. But have you ever really considered what having an attitude of gratitude would be like in your life? What might it look like to give thanks to the Lord with all your heart?

Perhaps you've heard it said that gratitude is less about having everything you want and more about being thankful for all that you have. It's about being content with the things God has given you. Perhaps you don't have the four-bedroom house you want, but you have a roof over your head and a warm place to sleep each night. Maybe you would love to have a nine-passenger van for your family, but you can be grateful for the reliable minivan that gets you and the kids around town. Perhaps you continue to struggle with the same recurring health concerns or a child who is difficult to parent even during the best of times. Instead of being discontent with your circumstances, what can you be grateful for?

Try making a list. Here are some ideas: Your salvation. The promise of eternity. The presence of the Holy Spirit. Your family. Your very life itself. The miracle of children. You have food on your table and fresh water to drink each day—things much of the world can't count on. Add to your list each day. The more you meditate on gratitude, the more things you'll find to be thankful for.

Thank God we've been given so much by His grace—and not been given what we deserve. We deserve condemnation and death. But by His mercy we've been given forgiveness and life. While you're keeping a gratitude journal, try writing out the desires of your heart. Rewrite them over time, and see which desires remain the same and which ones begin to change. You'll be surprised. Having an attitude of gratitude is more than just a T-shirt slogan. It's one of the most essential foundations for those who would live the Christian life.

Be a Generous Giver

The generous will prosper; those who refresh others will themselves be refreshed.

PROVERBS 11:25

ONE OF OUR DEAR FRIENDS USED to jokingly say, "I have the spiritual gift of receiving." We would all laugh. We were all poor as church mice at the time, and we understood what he meant. When someone would give us a used recliner or a smoked ham, we were always grateful to receive it.

The Lord has helped us find financial stability over the years, and along the way He has brought several wonderful friends into our lives who had the spiritual gift of giving. While it's wonderful to have the gift of receiving, it's even more wonderful to have the gift of giving.

As we watched the spirit of generosity at work in the lives of our friends, Jay and I purposed in our hearts that as the Lord prospered us, we would become generous givers too. By His grace, we've been able to do that. I can't tell you what joy it brings to be able to give to others in need.

Some seek to twist this principle into some sort of formula: if you give a certain amount, the Lord always gives you a certain amount back. But God doesn't work like that. This isn't some sort of divine ATM machine that spits out cash in exchange for deposits.

Yet the principle is truer than you might imagine. Jay and I have found that as we walk with the Holy Spirit and respond generously to His promptings to give, we ourselves suffer no financial lack. By helping to refresh those in need, we ourselves experience refreshment. It's uncanny how it works, but it has been a constant source of joy and delight in our marriage to see the Lord's hand in this way.

If this is a new concept to you, I challenge you. Don't give, expecting a certain return, but give out of generosity, expecting nothing in return. The response isn't instant, nor can it be calculated, but I promise you'll see the Lord's hand at work in unexpected ways. Be generous!

A Gold Ring in a Pig's Snout

A beautiful woman who lacks discretion is like a gold ring in a pig's snout.
PROVERBS 11:22

DOES SCRIPTURE MAKE YOU LAUGH OUT loud sometimes? I can't help but see the humor in the words from time to time. This morning in my devotion time, I was reading Proverbs 11. Verse 22 made me laugh out loud because it painted such an outrageous picture!

Think about it for a minute. Can you see a big fat pig, covered in dried mud, ears flopping, with its corkscrew tail? Perhaps it has some rotten cabbage leaves stuck on its forehead from foraging in the garbage. And there in the drooling, glistening snout is a beautiful gold ring. Ha!

I instantly went back twenty-five years to when my husband was new to full-time ministry. One of the most beautiful women in the church sang in the choir. She had perfect teeth, a flawless complexion, gorgeous hair, and a movie-star figure. She dressed to the nines and was always wearing the latest fashions. She was the kind of woman who could make anyone jealous. Except for one thing. She had absolutely no discretion and even less discernment.

She was always the first to share the latest gossip—the juicier, the better. She would pull you aside and say, "I certainly hope it's not true, but I heard that Jessica is blah, blah, blah." Her lack of discretion was so flagrant that it rendered her ugly despite her outward appearance. Every woman in the church knew her reputation and tried to steer clear of her. It was hard to reconcile how someone so beautiful on the outside could be ugly on the inside. It really was like putting a beautiful gold ring in a pig's snout.

If you want to be considered beautiful, practice discretion. Embrace discernment. Learn what is inappropriate to say, and avoid it. Your husband will love you for it, and your friends will know they can trust you with their heart of hearts. And the next time you are tempted to speak in an undiscerning way, just picture a filthy pig with a gold ring in its snout!

Listen Closely

My child, pay attention to what I say. Listen carefully to my words.

PROVERBS 4:20

SOME TIME AGO I WAS CHANNEL-SURFING and stumbled upon *Patch Adams*. It was that scene where he is in a therapy session, but he's being ignored. When he realizes it, he proceeds to say some pretty absurd and inappropriate things, just to see what the therapist's response will be. The therapist isn't even fazed.

Why? Because the therapist hasn't been listening to him. He's been hearing him, but not listening to him. There is a difference. Hearing is the awareness of sound. The ability to perceive sound with your ears. Listening is a conscious choice to make sense out of those sounds. You need to concentrate, focus, and process the words.

When it comes to parenting, we need to learn to listen to our children. Their words matter. They mean something. More than you can measure right now. As parents, we become comfortable with the idea that we know our children better than anyone, even than themselves. We assume that there is nothing new under the sun, so we shift ourselves out of listening mode and into hearing mode.

I remember a time when one of my daughters was telling me a story. She was so excited about it, but I was busy so I tuned her out. I felt guilty asking her if we could talk later, so I pretended to listen. When she was finished telling me her story, her face was lit up with excitement!

My heart sank. I knew I had just missed something important. I felt horrible. I had to admit that I hadn't paid attention to a single word she said. For a split second, she looked at me wondering if I was joking . . . but quickly realized I wasn't.

She was gracious enough to repeat what she had said with the same enthusiasm as the first time. We need to lean in and listen to our children. We must intentionally and purposefully listen to their words—each and every one. It's how we'll see deeper into their hearts—and how they'll know how special they are.

Influence

Don't just listen to God's word. You must do what it says.
Otherwise, you are only fooling yourselves.

JAMES 1:22

I LOVE JESUS. I WANT MY children to see that daily.

Not because I want them to say, "My mom loved Jesus." But because I want to show them Jesus. Children form their opinions on almost everything by watching their parents. They are imitators.

Are you scared of water? I bet your kid will be too, if they see you respond to water with fear. Do crowds make you panic? I bet they'll make your kids uneasy too, if they see you freak out every time you are in a crowded area.

When someone does something you don't like, how do you respond? How you respond will be your kids' instinctual response too. If you respond in love and patience, you've set the bar that high for them. But if you respond in anger and ill temper, you've set the bar too low for them.

We had a fly in our house for a few days once. I just couldn't manage to get it out. And my four-year-old was in a panic. She would run out of every room it was in, frightened and screaming! Finally one day I asked, "Why are you so scared of the fly?" To which she responded, "Because you don't like bugs, Mommy." Ouch.

So I said to her, "You know what? I bet he is more scared of you than you are of him." And with a deeply concerned look in her eyes and a soft voice, she said, "But WHY, Mommy? I'm not going to hurt him."

Her whole perspective changed because of what I told her.

Our children *listen t*o what we have to say.

Our children *watch* what we do.

Our words and actions are their biggest influence. Motherhood is humbling.

"All that I am, or hope to be, I owe to my angel mother," said Abraham Lincoln.

A mother's influence has a powerful impact on her children's hearts and lives. Use your influence wisely.

Seeing a New Side of God

I had only heard about you before, but now I have seen you with my own eyes.

JOB 42:5

THE STORY OF JOB'S TRIAL IS well known, but what is perhaps less familiar is that he submitted to God prior to the promised blessing. He did not know that restoration was on the horizon, but he recognized in the midst of his agony that he was seeing the righteousness of God in a new way. He ultimately describes being moved from an understanding of God into fully experiencing God's character.

Job had been a man of faith for a long time (see Job 1:1) before his testing. Job had heard about God and believed in Him. He was very well acquainted with God—so much so, in fact, that Satan sought to test Job's loyalty. However, it wasn't until the testing of his faith brought him into utter dependence on God that he was moved to seeing the reality of God's faithfulness in his life. He realized he was in the presence of a just, holy, and merciful Lord. His eyes were opened because he received the words God had spoken.

Maybe you, like Job, have been a person of faith for a long time. Perhaps today you are walking through the fire of life, or maybe you have in the past or will one day soon. Remember, it wasn't the healing that caused Job to see more of God; it was the trial and receiving of God's words. Allow yourself to be moved from just hearing and having a basic understanding of God into really seeing and experiencing His faithfulness, regardless of what you are going through in life. This undeniable understanding of God is unique to our perseverance through trials.

Job clearly says that his understanding of God at the very height of his agony was much deeper than it was prior to the trial. It was deeper because he was able to see the God of glory that he had heard about all those years.

Lean into and search the Scripture. Consider the preceding chapters in Job. Look for the Lord's character and holiness. He is waiting to reveal Himself to you.

Learning to Appreciate the Sharpening

As iron sharpens iron, so a friend sharpens a friend.

PROVERBS 27:17

SCRIPTURE HAS A LOT TO SAY about how we, as the body of believers, are to interact with one another. We're told to meet together often, to pray for one another, to bear one another's burdens, and to look to the needs of those outside of our household. While some of these can be challenging at times, we often feel good about fellowshipping with and serving our brothers and sisters.

We are blessed to be a blessing. But the Bible also tells us that we are to hold each other accountable and to sharpen one another as iron sharpens iron. I know, I know—we've been told judge not lest we be judged (see Matthew 7:1), right? What Jesus is actually pointing out in Matthew 7 is a self-righteous and hypocritical judgment that the Pharisees were known for. Their goal was not to help or sharpen those they rebuked; it was purely to make themselves look better and more holy.

What we are called to do is gently correct one another out of sincere love on things that Scripture makes clear are sinful, not on personal convictions or matters of Christian liberty.

Maybe even more uncomfortable than confronting a friend is accepting correction when a brother or sister comes to us in this way. The thing is, other believers are more likely to recognize our own ignorance or forgetfulness of Scripture than we are. Likewise, we will probably be able to see a fellow believer's blind spots much more easily than our own. This isn't a punishment; this is a gift! One of the reasons the Lord gives us the body of Christ is for our protection. We should not get bitter or angry at one another; we should appreciate and even desire loving correction.

Imagine you're in a rowboat, surrounded by friends, each in their own rowboats. You're just kicking back, reading a book, enjoying the sunshine with a glass of iced tea. After a little while, you look up to realize the current has pushed you a mile away from your group of friends, down the beach and farther out to sea. You hadn't felt a thing and had no idea how far you'd drifted because it was such a little bit at a time. Sound familiar? This is how sin works. Give it an inch, and it's taking a mile. Thankfully, the Lord has instructed believers to be the friends that call out to one another, "Hey, you're drifting away! Let me help you get back!"

Surround yourself with sharpening friends.

Letting Go of Perfection

"My grace is all you need. My power works best in weakness." So now I am glad to boast about my weaknesses, so that the power of Christ can work through me.

2 CORINTHIANS 12:9

MOTHERING IS HARD. IT IS ONE of the hardest things you will ever do—if it's not *the* hardest thing. It is also one of the best things you can invest yourself in. You have been entrusted with those little lives by the Creator.

There is an overwhelming amount of resources, from books to podcasts to social media influencers, available to help us do this mom thing well. But we often fall prey to the belief that by following these resources and becoming obsessed with the methods shared, we can achieve perfection. Striving for perfection—and subsequently failing—is what makes it the most overwhelming, isn't it?

We try to change ourselves, our home, and our surroundings to attain this idea of perfection we have mentally created because we allow ourselves to be influenced by others. The truth is that the Creator chose you, with your unique gifts, short-comings, and quirks, to be the mother of the children He gave you. And everything you need, you can find in Him.

Just lean in. Trust that before your first child was even a thought for you, before you were even a thought to your parents—He knew you would be your children's mother. He will equip you for this hard work and use you in spite of your weaknesses.

Give yourself grace, mom. Raising kids today is hard. With everything going on in the world, it makes the usual difficulties of parenting even heavier.

Don't give up. Keep going. If you fall, get back up. Put one foot in front of the other.

And you know what? It's okay if your kids see that you are weak, because they'll see His strength shine through you when He brings you forward. What matters is what you do from here on out.

Don't dwell on your weaknesses and seek to make yourself perfect. If you live there too long, you'll miss out on the present and the good gifts He's given you.

Cling to Christ

I cling to you; your strong right hand holds me securely.

PSALM 63:8

As a mom, what do you think of when you hear the word *cling*? You can probably think of the million times your kids have clung to you for something. Each time it boiled down to a basic need, right? It was either that your child needed you and only you for comfort, wanted something that they thought you could give them, or needed to feel safe in their mom's arms.

Remember the emotions you felt? Most of those times you probably swooned over your tiny treasure with your heart bursting at the seams with an insane amount of love for them as you provided just what they needed to be satisfied or comforted. Other times . . . well, you probably felt like ugly-crying at the amount of overwhelming fatigue you felt or the desire to have some personal space for just a minute. The struggle's real!

Motherhood is challenging, but God offers help. We desperately need to cling to someone to make it through this life. We need to cling to Christ to be healthy and whole. Just as our children cling to us because they trust us, let us run to our Father for our every need. *Cling* in today's verse means to adhere, to pursue closely, to cleave, to be glued, to follow closely. Today, let's adhere ourselves to Christ. Let's pursue Him closely.

Are you fighting paralyzing fear? Cling to Christ as you learn to let Him heal the wounded parts of you. Are you feeling irritated every second of the day? Cling to Christ as He restores your joy.

Are you worried about your kids? Cling to Christ as He shows you He can be trusted with them. Are you struggling with loneliness? Cling to Christ as you learn to be satisfied with Him and Him alone. Are you having a hard time trusting God? Cling to Him while He guides you through Truth.

There is nothing Jesus Christ cannot heal, mend, bind, or restore. Cling to Him as He tends to whatever has hurt you, held you back, or hindered you. He loves you ever so dearly!

The Habit of Anger

Don't sin by letting anger control you.

EPHESIANS 4:26

DID YOU KNOW THAT ANGER CAN control you? When we make a habit of indulging our anger, it becomes a habit, and that habit is inhabited by an enemy who seeks to destroy us and those around us.

My dad was raised by an unpredictable, angry father. As a result, I, too, grew up in a home marred by anger and unpredictability. Perhaps you have been witness to terrible anger in your own life. All of us have known someone who lived with a spirit of anger, allowing it to control them.

As a child, I couldn't understand why my father would have so many angry outbursts. There were times when I felt it must have been my fault. I would think that if I had been better or done something differently, he wouldn't have gotten angry. But as I grew older, I understood that his anger was not about, nor justified by, my behavior. It was something within him. It had nothing to do with me. It had nothing to do with the situation. This anger was simply there, under the surface and ready to strike out at anyone nearby.

Sometimes we can find ourselves succumbing to a habit of anger, am I right? It's like a cauldron of emotions under the surface, and if one of my kids strikes me wrong, they get the full (verbal) force of my lack of self-control. Our relationship is damaged as a result.

Anger is seldom a righteous act. Yes, there are situations that make us angry. But there is an enormous difference between being angry and allowing anger to control us. Watch your anger. Keep it in check. Resist the temptation to give it room to grow. When anger becomes our frequent attitude, we are far from the Spirit of God. Ask the Lord to help you resist the temptation to indulge your anger—even when it's justified. Your marriage, your family, and your friendships will all be better because of it.

You Are God's Masterpiece

We are God's masterpiece. He has created us anew in Christ Jesus,
so we can do the good things he planned for us long ago.
EPHESIANS 2:10

I WAS WALKING THROUGH THE National Gallery of Art in Washington, DC, last summer. There's never enough time when you're in an art gallery—especially the National Gallery. So little time. So much to see. As I wandered from room to room, I must have sounded like I suffered from asthma. I gasped again and again and again. Some of the most famous paintings in the world hung on every wall. It was impossible to take them all in—each one a masterpiece. The brilliance and creativity and passion of every artist were on display for all to see. I will never forget that afternoon, and someday perhaps I'll have a chance to revisit that magnificent gallery.

This morning in my devotion time I came across Ephesians 2:10. The words "God's masterpiece" touched my heart in a new way. My mind instantly raced back to last summer and the stunning beauty I saw that day. But God said *I* was His masterpiece! Me? I'm a mess sometimes. I'm broken in so many ways. I'm no masterpiece. Or at least that's how I see myself sometimes. Can you identify, friend? Do you see yourself as a masterpiece? Do you realize the Lord created you? You *are* a work of art. God loves His creation. As Max Lucado wrote, "If [God] had a refrigerator, your picture would be on it." Let that sink in.

Sometime today, underline Ephesians 2:10 in your Bible. Write it in your prayer journal. Meditate on it. If you need an extra reminder, write it on a Post-it and stick it on your bathroom mirror or steering wheel. The next time the enemy whispers in your ear, "You're a mess," remember this verse. You're God's masterpiece. Share this truth with your family. They are God's masterpieces too. Remember that the next time one of your family members does something without thinking. When they make a mistake, remind yourself: "They're God's masterpiece. And so am I!"

What Are You Sowing?

You will always harvest what you plant. Those who live only to satisfy their own sinful nature will harvest decay and death from that sinful nature. But those who live to please the Spirit will harvest everlasting life from the Spirit. So let's not get tired of doing what is good. At just the right time we will reap a harvest of blessing if we don't give up. Therefore, whenever we have the opportunity, we should do good to everyone—especially to those in the family of faith.

GALATIANS 6:7-10

LAST NIGHT MY FAMILY WAS WATCHING the movie *Secondhand Lions*. In one of the most memorable scenes, Robert Duvall and Michael Caine have planted a dozen different types of seeds they bought from a seed salesman. Now those seeds have all sprouted and begun to grow. Robert Duvall suddenly realizes they have been duped. Every row they planted is the same. The "beans" are corn. The "beets" are corn. The "tomatoes" are corn. The "carrots" are corn. "Corn! Corn! Corn!" he mutters in disgust before throwing down his hoe and walking toward the house.

This morning I came across Galatians 6 in my quiet time.

Of course, I thought back to last night's movie. Robert Duvall was sure he had planted many different crops, but God's immutable law of nature proved itself to be true. He harvested what he had planted. In his naivete, he had planted nothing but corn. And in due season he reaped what he had sown.

We will always reap what we have sown.

If we sow division, we will reap division. If we sow kindness, we will reap kindness. If we sow judgment, we will reap judgment. If we sow forgiveness, we will reap forgiveness.

As you contemplate the type of harvest you'd like to have in your marriage or from your children, think about what you need to be sowing. Don't be deceived. You cannot sow harshness and expect to reap a soft response. You cannot sow anger and reap peace. If you sow corn, corn, corn, you'll reap corn, corn, corn.

Let the Holy Spirit Guide You

L et the Holy Spirit guide your lives. Then you won't be doing what your sinful nature craves. The sinful nature wants to do evil, which is just the opposite of what the Spirit wants. And the Spirit gives us desires that are the opposite of what the sinful nature desires.

GALATIANS 5:16-17

JAY AND I HAD ONLY BEEN dating for a few weeks when I knew he was "the one." He knew it too. He gave me a ride to my parents' house one Sunday after church and stood awkwardly on the front steps. He knew it was time to meet my family, but Jay is a gentleman. He wasn't going to presume an invitation. I invited him in, and that, as they say, was how it all began.

The Holy Spirit is like that too. He is a gentleman. He seldom pushes his way into a situation without being invited.

How do you encourage the Holy Spirit to guide your life? You invite Him to come into situations just the way I invited Jay inside my parents' house that day so long ago. When you're in a difficult season of marriage, invite the Holy Spirit to guide you. In a tough season of parenting, invite the Holy Spirit to take control. When you've made some poor financial decisions, invite the Holy Spirit to help you sort out the mess you've made.

This request doesn't need to be a long, pious prayer. Your prayer can simply be, "Please come into this situation, Holy Spirit. I need your guidance. I want your help."

If you and your husband are in the habit of praying together, there is an even greater opportunity. Pray together, asking the Holy Spirit to step in. He will never take sides. Instead, He will take over. That's what our heart desires—to have the Holy Spirit take over and straighten out our sometimes chaotic lives.

Grace and Peace to You

May God our Father and the Lord Jesus Christ give you grace and peace.

ROMANS 1:7

During my teen years, whenever I'd leave the house, my mother would often say, "Have fun—and make good choices!" There's a lot of wisdom in that benediction, especially for a teen who's experiencing more independence. I can't tell you how many times my mom's voice echoed in my head as I was about to make a not-so-good choice. It's funny how we continue to hear our mom's voice as we grow older, isn't it? In fact, I've found myself saying the same thing to my kids as they've grown up.

But there are better ways to send out those you love. The apostle Paul was gifted with words, including the words in today's verse. I like his words above.

"May God . . . give you grace and peace." That pretty well covers all the bases, doesn't it? Grace is when we receive all the things that we don't deserve. And peace is the antidote to the chaos of this present world. To speak those words over someone we love bathes them in everything they need. If they have the grace and peace of Jesus, there's not much else they need.

When your husband leaves for work, speak the grace and peace of the Lord Jesus over his day. Give him a hug and speak the words aloud if you want. Or simply whisper them quietly to your heavenly Father above. Send your husband on his way with undeserved favor in every situation and peace to protect his day.

And your children? Bless them too. It's fine to tell them to have fun and make good choices. But it's better to speak grace and peace over their comings and goings, over their relationships and their encounters throughout the day. Whether they're leaving for school or their extracurricular activities, let them know what you're praying over them. We need to get into the habit of speaking the way Paul spoke. Paul earnestly believed in speaking a blessing and benediction over those he loved. He set an example worthy of following in our families. Speak life, precious mom! Little ears are listening!

You Have the Good News!

I am not ashamed of this Good News about Christ. It is the power of God at work, saving everyone who believes—the Jew first and also the Gentile. This Good News tells us how God makes us right in his sight. This is accomplished from start to finish by faith.

ROMANS 1:16-17

I BECAME BORN AGAIN AT THE AGE OF FOUR. It wasn't exactly life changing for me at that tender age, but it was definitely heart changing. I remember very clearly being broken over the sin in my life and wanting to serve Jesus with all my heart. As a young girl, I shared the gospel freely with others, even leading some of the neighborhood kids to Christ. But as I grew into my teen years, sharing my faith seemed intimidating and scary.

Like most teens, I struggled to find the courage to share my faith. Peer pressure often got the best of me, and I kept silent when I wanted to speak. But as I grew closer to the Lord, I was convicted that my real issue wasn't fear; it was embarrassment. I was worried about what others would think of me and my faith in Jesus. Can you relate?

Once I realized that this was my struggle, I confessed it to the Lord and asked for His help. I began to ask God for opportunities to share my faith. Over the years, He has been faithful to present me with unique chances to share the gospel—from airplanes to grocery stores. I am no longer ashamed of the gospel, and I don't wany my children to be ashamed either. I was reading Romans with my daughter this morning, and we came across the familiar passage above.

Beloved, are you ashamed of the Good News? Are you afraid to tell others what God has done in your life? I want to encourage you to become bold in your faith. The days are dark, and they're getting darker by the day. The Bible declares it, and we feel it: the world is dying. All of creation is groaning. The world is desperate for good news. And you have it!

This is not the time to be ashamed or awkward in your faith. Today, ask the Lord for opportunities to speak life to those who are dying. Ask Him to help you share the Good News with someone who needs to hear it. Remember, if you have Jesus, you have what the whole world needs.

The Goodness of Asking for Prayer

Finally, dear brothers and sisters, we ask you to pray for us.

2 THESSALONIANS 3:1

ARE YOU IN THE HABIT OF asking for prayer? There was a season in my life when I was grateful if someone asked to pray for me, but somehow it seemed wrong for me to ask others for prayer. I'm not sure whether I thought I didn't *need* prayer, or perhaps I was simply too afraid to admit my weakness.

But needing prayer isn't weakness. Neither is asking for prayer. In fact, asking for prayer comes from a place of strength. It comes from knowing who we are in Christ and from having respect for who others are in Christ.

Paul wrote approximately half of the New Testament. If anybody had his act together, it was Paul. But read again what he said above.

Why do you suppose Paul asked for prayer? I would submit that first, it was because he knew he needed it. He needed the Lord's strengthening to do the job set before him. Second, he knew prayer made a difference. Prayers are something far more than words mumbled into space. They affect much. And finally, Paul understood that when you pray for someone, you become invested in their life.

Have you thought about that? When you humble yourself and ask your husband or your children to pray for you about a situation, they become invested in your project. Whether it's a writing project you're involved in, an upcoming party that you're responsible for, or a class you're going to be teaching at church, having others pray for you makes a difference. It changes the outcome. It's a verbal acknowledgment that you need the Lord's help. And last of all, it invites others to share ownership with you in the task.

When days become stressful or your patience wears thin, if your husband and children have been praying for you regularly, they are also carrying the burden ahead of you. And they will be far more patient with you.

Asking for prayer is good, and it's good for your family to see you do it.

What Do You Want?

Jesus looked around and saw them following. "What do you want?" he asked them.

JOHN 1:38

EARLIER THIS WEEK THE DOORBELL RANG. That's unusual at my house. With seven children (three of whom are now married), four grandchildren, and lots of friends in our lives, we're used to people just walking through the front door unannounced.

As you might expect, I was a little surprised when the doorbell rang—and then I remembered my husband was expecting an insurance adjuster to come and look at the car my son wrecked. I was busy writing, but nobody else seemed to be home, so I got up and answered the door. I saw a gentleman standing there. Because I was anxious to keep writing, I said, "Just a moment. My husband will be right out." I closed the door and began to look for Jay. He was nowhere to be found. Now a little irritated, I returned to the front door and said, "I'm sorry. My husband doesn't seem to be here right now, but it's the white Volvo over there." He stared at me, obviously puzzled.

"You are the insurance adjuster here to see Jay and look at the car, right?"

He shook his head slowly. "No, ma'am. I'm a scheduler for Clean Windows, and I wondered if you'd be interested in having us wash your windows."

Well, that was embarrassing. I quickly apologized and assured the gentleman I have children to wash our windows. Returning to my writing desk, I put my hands over my face. I wish I would have listened before assuming I knew what the man wanted. I closed my computer and opened my Bible. I had been reading in the book of John.

Jesus knew everything. If ever there was someone who didn't need to ask questions, it was Jesus. And yet . . . He asked His disciples what they wanted. How much embarrassment would that simple question have saved me? By assuming I knew, I had embarrassed us both.

How much confusion could we prevent by asking the question "What do you want?" So many arguments and misunderstandings between husbands and wives or between parents and children occur because we anticipate what the other person wants. We make assumptions. We think we already know. And maybe we do. But so often we're wrong. Purpose in your heart to ask questions.

"How can I help you?"

"What can I do for you?"

"What do you need?"

What's in a Name?

Jesus said, "Your name is Simon, son of John—but you will
be called Cephas" (which means "Peter").

JOHN 1:42

Do you have a nickname? Do you know someone who has legally changed their name? Names are deeply personal. There was a time when I didn't like or appreciate that my parents named me Heidi. I don't know why. I guess it didn't help that the dog at Timberline Lodge, a giant Saint Bernard, was also named Heidi. If I had a nickel for every person who asked me if I knew the dog at Timberline who shared my name . . . well, I bet I would have been able to buy a car in high school.

My sister Hope purchased a plaque for me one Christmas that had the meaning of my name on it. To my surprise, I learned that Heidi means "noble one" or "honorable one." Learning the meaning of my name changed the way I saw myself. Names matter.

When He lived on the earth, Jesus was in the habit of changing names and nicknaming people. James and John became "the sons of thunder" (Mark 3:17). John 1:42 tells us that when Jesus first met Simon, he looked at him and said, "Your name is Simon, son of John—but you will be called Cephas (which means 'Peter')."

When Jesus looks closely at us, He sees beyond both the past and the present. He sees the future. He sees not only what has been, but what will be. And He calls forth what is to come from within us. He saw in John's son Simon a solid rock (*Petros* in Greek) who would be foundational in establishing Jesus' church among the Gentiles. Simon was more than he had been. He was more than he understood.

What's your name? What does it mean? Who is Jesus calling you to be? He probably won't rename you like Simon. But He can call forth a future you never dreamed imaginable. He can see not just who you've been or who you are but who you were meant to be.

Today, take a moment and ask Jesus who you are in Him. Ask Him who He has created you to be. God's heart for you is so big, precious mom! You were created to be far more than you ever imagined. Lean in and listen for His still, small voice today. Let the One who knew you before you were formed in your mother's womb speak to your heart. He knows your name.

Come and See

"Rabbi" (which means "Teacher"), "where are you staying?"

"Come and see," he said. It was about four o'clock in the afternoon when they went with him to the place where he was staying, and they remained with him the rest of the day.

JOHN 1:38-39

WHEN JESUS' DISCIPLES ASKED HIM WHERE He was staying, He replied, "Come and see." What an incredible invitation! There are no apparent limits to such an open invitation. Come and see. Look for yourself. Follow Me. Watch closely. See what you make of it all.

My grandpa studied the Word of God faithfully. He kept volumes of detailed journals of his devotions, sermons, and writings, and now they belong to me. Very few things are as precious to me as my grandpa's writings. And because he wrote down his thoughts and sermons, I have an open invitation to "come and see" his insights years after his passing. When I wonder what grandpa would say about the Twenty-third Psalm, his journals bid me to "come and see"!

As a little girl, I remember asking my grandpa, "Whatchadoin'?" One word that really meant, "Please invite me into what you're doing." Inevitably, he would say, "Come and see." My grandpa's open invitation to enter into his study and sit on his lap was an opportunity that I did not want to miss. He would show me what he was working on and teach me what God was teaching him. I will always treasure those moments with my grandpa, just as I treasure his journals. In those conversations and within those pages are answers that connect me to the man himself. Through them, my grandfather is still here beside me.

Jesus offers that same invitation. Just like He invited the disciples to "come and see" where He was staying in today's Scripture, He invites us to "come and see" what He's doing in our lives or what He has said about a topic in the Bible.

When you're facing a life challenge that doesn't seem to make much sense, you can always ask, "Jesus, whatchadoin'?" Then follow Him and wait on Him to help you understand. Or, like my grandpa's precious journals, open the Word of God and ask that same question: "God, whatchadoin'?" It's all in the book. Come and see.

No Need for Shame

Jesus said, . . . "You don't have a husband—for you have had five husbands, and you aren't even married to the man you're living with now."

JOHN 4:17-18

ONE OF MY FAVORITE VASES ALWAYS sat on the china cabinet where I could grab it quickly when I picked flowers from the garden or when my sweet husband brought me flowers.

One day when my son was seven or eight, he asked me where he could find a candlestick holder for a science experiment. He loved to create his own experiments. "It's on the china cabinet, next to the blue vase," I replied. The phone rang, and I went into the other room to take the call. I didn't think any more about it.

Jay came home that afternoon with a lovely bouquet of daisies. I went to the china cabinet to get my favorite vase. It was gone. Almost instantly, I connected the dots. I went out to the garage trash can and opened the lid. Sure enough, there was my vase—in pieces.

I went up to my son's room and asked, "Anything you want to tell me?" He looked nervous. I said, "When you borrowed the candlestick, you broke the blue vase while you were getting it down, and then you threw it in the trash can in the garage." He was astounded. How could I have known that?

Jesus had an encounter with a Samaritan woman at the well. As they dialogued, He told her the story of her life, saying, "You don't have a husband—for you have had five husbands, and you aren't even married to the man you're living with now" (John 4:17-18). The woman was astounded. How could Jesus have known this?

Here's the thing about knowing what seems to be unknowable. My son learned that day how important it is to be honest. I am keenly interested in what my children are doing. And Jesus is the same way. How often do we try to "hide" what we've been doing or how we've been feeling in hopes that He won't know? It never works. He always knows.

I've come to love that about Him. Don't you? We can always come clean. We never have to pretend. He already knows. There's nothing hidden between Him and me. Nothing I have ever done or thought or feared has escaped Him, and I never have to worry about Him being shocked at my failures. I can come to Him and be honest. You can too.

Jesus Is the Healer

Jesus told him, "Stand up, pick up your mat, and walk!" Instantly, the man was healed! He rolled up his sleeping mat and began walking!

JOHN 5:8-9

HAVE YOU EVER STRUGGLED TO FIND healing from a past hurt? Over the years, I have met many mothers who have noticed that past abuses, or even poor choices, can affect their everyday lives, even years later. Sometimes, we are victims of other people's choices—and sometimes, we suffer from our own sin and bad decisions. Over time, if we don't seek help, we can develop an emotional or spiritual limp of sorts.

Of course, it doesn't take years of abuse to develop a limp. Sometimes, just one encounter can result in a life-altering limp. For years, I've been on a healing journey with the Lord. Little by little, Jesus has been restoring my heart and my mind, because that's what He does. And while I still struggle with hurts from my past, the Lord uses every situation I encounter to mature and heal my mind and my heart.

Hurts are not always emotional or spiritual, though, are they? In John 5, at the pool of Bethesda, Jesus encounters a man who has been ill for thirty-eight years. When Jesus asks the man if he wants to be healed, the man explains his situation and why it would be too difficult to get him into the healing waters of the pool. Notice that Jesus cuts straight to the chase, saying, "Stand up, pick up your mat, and walk!"

You see, Jesus is in the business of healing the unwell—body, mind, and spirit. He delights in correcting a limp. No matter how long you may have suffered, Jesus can heal you, because He is the Healer. It's who He is. He delights in being merciful. If you have some emotional limps from past trauma, Jesus wants to heal you—and when He does, that healing has the blessing of extending to your children. When God heals a mother, her children are the first to benefit.

If you're hurting today, I encourage you to be honest with the Lord. Even situations that have been a hindrance for thirty-eight years, like the sick man's, aren't impossible for Him. You don't have to be debilitated by your situation forever. I know.

Pursue the Lamb

[Jesus said,] "You search the Scriptures because you think they give you eternal life. But the Scriptures point to me! Yet you refuse to come to me to receive this life."

JOHN 5:39-40

I WENT TO BIBLE COLLEGE IN the late eighties. To be honest, it wasn't my first choice for a college. I had applied to Oregon State University, but my application was denied based on my high school's accreditation status at the time. OSU said I needed one year at another college before I could apply there. We make our plans . . . but God directs our steps (see Proverbs 16:9).

As a Bible college student, I studied the Scriptures day and night. My classmates and I dug into the Hebrew of the Old Testament and the Greek of the New Testament. We listened to daily lectures from learned Bible scholars who unpacked the Word of God and made its meaning clear to rooms full of eager young adults. We thought we would find life in the Scriptures. And we did—sort of. The truth is, those Scriptures weren't the full picture of knowing Jesus. Instead, they pointed us to Life. They pointed us to Jesus, and *in Him* we found life.

Don't misunderstand. I loved studying God's Word. I still love it. I try to study it daily. I teach it regularly. I write about it extensively. But I never confuse the Word of God with the Living Word. They are one and the same—and yet they are different.

I've known people who were Bible scholars. They knew far more about the Scriptures than I will ever know. And yet they didn't know Jesus. They studied about Him for decades, but they had never met Him personally. Do you know someone like that?

Read again how Jesus put it in the Scripture above.

I encourage you to study God's Word at every opportunity. Read it. Meditate on it. Memorize it. Sing it. Write it down. But never let it keep you from a personal walk with the person of Jesus. Yes—He is the Word—the Living Word. The Scriptures point to Him from Genesis to Revelation. But there is more than simply becoming "knowledgeable" about Him. Knowing Jesus is more about a personal relationship than a degree in Bible scholarship. Pursue the Word of God. And pursue the Living Word too.

The Bread of Life

[Jesus said,] "I am the bread of life. Whoever comes to me will never be hungry again. Whoever believes in me will never be thirsty."

JOHN 6:35

PERHAPS YOU'VE SEEN THE FACEBOOK MEME that describes a mother's job as having to figure out what's for dinner every. single. night. for the rest of her life. Can you relate? I can. How many times can you order pizza or make mac and cheese? How do you accommodate the gluten allergy and the suddenly-vegetarian teenage daughter and the high-protein diet your son needs for football? And then there are the picky eaters . . . and the budget to balance . . . and a husband to please.

In the 1983 film *A Christmas Story*, the husband and two sons keep asking the mother for second helpings before she can take a bite of her dinner. The narrator observes, "My mother had not had a hot meal for herself in fifteen years." I can relate to that too.

I love the imagery of Jesus' encounter with the crowd at Capernaum. They had enjoyed the meal of fish and loaves the previous day, and they were hungry again. Sound familiar? "What's for dinner today, Jesus?"

Jesus looks at them and says, "I am the bread of life. Whoever comes to me will never be hungry again. Whoever believes in me will never be thirsty" (John 6:35).

As a mother of seven, that sounds like a dream come true to me. While that promise may not extend to my nightly dinner table, it's an invitation that stands open to my soul. Yours too. Each of us has a hunger deep inside us—a thirst for something clean and pure and right in a world polluted by sin. Jesus offers that to us.

Every time you feel that thirst returning or feel a hunger pang, turn toward Jesus. He is the eternal source. When you're hungry for a bigger house—turn to Him instead. When you're thirsty for a newer car—turn to the One who has satisfied that thirst. When you are desperate for a little recognition and a display of gratitude—let Him feed your soul.

There's nothing wrong with a bigger house or a newer car or a little appreciation once in a while. But those things will just leave you hungry again tomorrow for something else. Satisfy that hunger once and for all. Imagine never having to hear "What's for dinner, Mom?" again. It's an offer too good to turn down. Eat and drink at the Lord's table today.

From Nazareth

Philip went to look for Nathanael and told him, "We have found the very person Moses and the prophets wrote about! His name is Jesus, the son of Joseph from Nazareth."

"Nazareth!" exclaimed Nathanael. "Can anything good come from Nazareth?"

JOHN 1:45-46

I GREW UP IN BORING, OREGON. You read that right: Boring, Oregon. I took no small amount of teasing about that when I told people, as you can imagine. Of course, now I live in Battle Ground, Washington. It's not lost on me that God has taken me from Boring to Battle Ground!

Jesus grew up in Nazareth, a rural community of 400 to 500 people. It was like Mayberry, where Andy Taylor was sheriff. Or it was kind of like Boring, Oregon. People in Nazareth had an accent. It was easy enough to recognize anyone from there. They sounded different.

When Jesus began teaching in synagogues and declaring Himself to be the Messiah, people were dumbfounded. Some were quick to say, "How can the Messiah come out of a hick town like Nazareth? Surely God would bring Him forth from Jerusalem." But God's ways are not our ways. In the economy of God's Kingdom, the first shall be last and the least shall be greatest.

Where are you from? What was your family like? Were your parents college professors, or high school dropouts? Were you the wealthiest kid in school, or the poorest? Were you the debutante at the city ball, or were you the girl nobody asked on a date because your mother made you wear hand-me-downs? It doesn't matter whether you were the smartest kid in class or were held back a year. You are invaluable to God—because God has a plan and purpose for your life.

Jesus is in the business of breaking molds. He shattered everyone's expectations of what a Messiah should look and sound like and where He should come from. He's still doing that today. This is a wonderful truth to make sure you pass on to your children, also. When we see ourselves through the eyes of Jesus, our perspective is changed forever.

Whether you were raised in Nazareth or Jerusalem, God is at work. His plans are bigger than you can imagine and more loving than you will ever know this side of eternity. Today, remember that the world does not determine your worth or your path. God does. Ask Him to lead you and your children in His ways. Whether it's Boring or Battle Ground, God wants to use you right where you are for a purpose beyond what you can imagine or think.

He Is Still Speaking

The heavens proclaim the glory of God. The skies display his craftsmanship.
Day after day they continue to speak; night after night they make him known.
They speak without a sound or word; their voice is never heard. Yet their
message has gone throughout the earth, and their words to all the world.

PSALM 19:1-4

GOD IS SO MUCH BIGGER THAN we can wrap our finite minds around, isn't He? Some days God feels distant, like He is light-years away. We know He is supposed to be there, but like city light disguises the stars in the night sky, we can't see Him because the busyness and circumstances of life cloud our vision. We may feel alone and maybe even at our wit's end. Life might be beating us hard and we may feel lost, like we are living without direction.

The truth, however, is that just because we don't feel Him or see Him doesn't mean He is not there. It's actually the opposite. He is where He has always been.

Have you ever been in a place where there are no man-made lights? Maybe deep in the forest, on an ocean beach, or high up on a mountain after sundown? As darkness sets in, the brilliant night-sky canvas begins to take shape. A whole different world opens as we see the myriad of stars that were birthed by the words God spoke at Creation. God's majestic craftmanship silently shouts His glory across the universe.

As we tune out our circumstances, as we peer beyond our day-to-day haze, in the darkness, the creator of the universe can be found. Just like the North Star guiding sailors for centuries, He is there, constant, steadfast, shining His glorious light, just waiting to show us the "true" North in life. As mothers, we need His constant guidance, don't we? The never-ending changes in the culture provide new challenges that require fresh wisdom and insight . . . sometimes hourly!

While He might seem far, God stands ready to provide the insight we so desperately need. He is closer than a friend, never leaving us or forsaking us. If you can, try to get alone today, away from the noise and distraction. Push away all your pressing needs, and allow God to speak to you as you look up so that you can lock eyes with Him afresh. He's still speaking—and He wants to speak to you.

And Sin No More

"Where are your accusers? Didn't even one of them condemn you?" "No, Lord," she said. And Jesus said, "Neither do I. Go and sin no more."

JOHN 8:10-11

WE'RE ALL FAMILIAR WITH THE STORY of the woman caught in adultery. Caught in the act itself, she is dragged before Jesus, and the crowd challenges the Messiah that this woman deserves to be stoned. There is so much wrong with this whole picture that books have been written about it, but I want to focus on one thought today.

As her accusers disappear one by one, the woman eventually stands alone with Jesus. She's humiliated. Embarrassed. Tearful. Jesus asks her, "Where are your accusers? Didn't even one of them condemn you?" "No, Lord," she says. And Jesus tells her, "Neither do I. Go and sin no more" (see John 8:10-11).

Progressive churches are big on a loving God who doesn't condemn us for our sin. This emphasis has done a great deal of damage to the message of the gospel, because many progressive churches are failing to recognize sin as sin in the first place. They are all about the grace-bestowing Jesus. Of course, that's not completely wrong. Grace is real and available to anyone. But they're missing a key part: repentance. God's grace is sufficient for whatever you've done in the past—but that grace is connected to confessing your sin, asking for forgiveness, turning away from your sin, and moving forward.

A woman caught in adultery who was forgiven and immediately returned to her adulterous relationship would not fare so well the second time. We should call on God's mercy and His forgiveness quickly whenever we sin. But we mustn't skip over that last phrase: "and sin no more." To ignore that is to presume on cheap grace, and it cheapens the blood of Christ at Calvary.

There is nothing in your past, no sin you've ever committed, nothing you've ever done that isn't covered by the blood of Jesus—but we must turn from our sin. Own this imperative deep in your soul. And teach it to your children. Teach them God's principles. There is forgiveness when you confess and repent—but you need to purpose to sin no more. In teaching this truth, you are pointing your children toward eternity, precious mom.

Keep It Simple

[The man said,] "I was blind, and now I can see!"

JOHN 9:25

HAVE YOU EVER NOTICED THAT HUMAN beings have a tendency to overcomplicate things? When we're asked about our faith, it's tempting to use big words and grand theological truths and dogma when giving our answer. But most of the time, the simplest answer is the best answer.

Asked about his encounter with Jesus, the blind man in John 9 made no attempt to explain what had happened or to define whether Jesus was the Messiah or a false prophet. He cut to the chase: "All I know is I couldn't see before, and now I can!" So simple, even a child can understand it.

Sometimes that's all our children need from us. Actually, most of the time, a simple answer will do. When a child asks a question, it's easy to see it through adult eyes and want to give an adult response. When a friend or relative asks you about the change in your life since you "became religious," you don't have to unfold the full theology of sin and redemption right there on the spot. Sometimes a simple, "All I know is I was lost in my sin before, and now I am free."

As we grow in our walk with the Lord, we should become attuned to hearing His voice while we listen to the voices of those around us. When your child, or a friend, or your husband asks a question, listen with your ears and at the same time listen to the Holy Spirit. Ask the Lord to show you what the real question is about so that you can know what your answer should be.

When a child asks, "Why were you late picking me up from my tennis lesson?" maybe they want to know about traffic—or maybe they just want to know if they can count on you when they're a little uncertain.

Learn to give short answers when it's appropriate, and don't apologize for not being able to explain the second law of thermodynamics. If it was good enough for the blind man, it's probably good enough for you.

Seasons Change, Thankfully

The LORD corrects those he loves, just as a father corrects a child in whom he delights.

PROVERBS 3:12

HAVE YOU EVER BEEN THROUGH ONE of *those* seasons? You know, where that one particular child gets on your very last nerve—every single day. Where it just seems easier to let him go his own way and grow up to be a savage and live in the jungle. I have. Correction and discipline can be as wearying to the parent as they are to the child. Sometimes, I can wonder if all the work I'm putting into correcting a character flaw or pursuing academics is really worth it. Especially when I can't see the result I am hoping to see.

Several years ago, I was in one of those parenting seasons. I was bone weary of the endless cycle of correcting and disciplining my son and ending up right back where we started. Maybe you've been there too.

In my quiet time one morning during that difficult season, I stumbled upon our verse for today, perhaps *really* reading it for the first time in my life.

I sat up straight in my chair. Did I love my child? Of course, I did. Did I delight in my child? Well . . . some days I did. The implications were clear. For me to give up on disciplining my child would imply I no longer cared about him. Nothing could be further from the truth.

I recommitted to not growing weary in the process of correcting and disciplining. I would resist the urge to throw in the towel—even for a season. I would do what a parent does who loves her child—I would hang in there with him.

I'm happy to say that season passed—as all seasons do eventually. That son who drove me to hopelessness then is a wonderful, mature young man today. He truly is a friend, and I love spending time with him whenever time allows. Getting through the hard seasons reminds me of a truth that you may need to hear today, sweet mom: consistent discipline is an act of love. To fail to discipline is an act of indifference.

Mother, if you're weary, don't quit. If you're tired, don't despair. If you're discouraged, press on. This season will pass, and you will most likely reap the reward of a child who becomes both a blessing in your life and a friend too.

While We Wait

IT'S DECEMBER. MY FAMILY AND I are on a short holiday in Eastern Washington as I write this. We spent the day walking the streets of beautiful Leavenworth, taking in majestic views of this "Christmas town" and drinking artisan coffee. (It's a Pacific Northwest thing.) Now, the kids are playing games, and I'm snuggled into my place on the couch, reflecting on the day's events. Our goal was simple: to get away from "it all."

Christmas music is playing softly in the background, and it would be absolutely perfect—except for the fact that the headlines on the newspapers at the coffee shop reminded us that "peace on earth" is a rather elusive thing. We wanted to forget about all that . . . even if just for a moment.

Trouble is, we can't get away, can we?

Even though we try, the day's news reminds us that we simply cannot escape the evil around us. The headlines remind us that there is suffering in the world. I have met mothers who tell me that they are "done" having babies because they're fearful about the future—and I understand. It's tempting to become cynical and fearful. Our flesh groans under the weight of it all. I sometimes wonder why Jesus doesn't come back and sort it all out.

Lord! When will You return? Why do You delay?

If you're struggling with the timing of God, lean in, precious mom. God is not in a hurry. His timetable has been determined so that His faithfulness can be proclaimed to all generations. The Bible teaches us that He wants to be known by the generations.

And so while we wait, God says, "Trust Me." While we wait, we have an opportunity to be a light to the world around us. To offer hope, and to point people to the Healer.

Peter warned us that we would be mocked about the coming of our Lord Jesus: "So what's happened to the promise of his Coming?" (2 Peter 3:4, MSG). Trust God, beloved. There is a very good reason for the delay. The reason that the Lord has not come already is simple: He is giving people more time to repent.

While we wait for His return, let's make Him known. First to our children, and then to a weary world. Jesus is our hope. He is worth waiting for.

Pondering the Works of God

After seeing him, the shepherds told everyone what had happened and what the angel had said to them about this child. All who heard the shepherds' story were astonished, but Mary kept all these things in her heart and thought about them often.

LUKE 2:17-19

ONE YEAR AT CHRISTMAS, my family and I focused our daily devotions on the Advent season, and, of course, we read Luke 2. In verse 19, after the shepherds have run off to share the good news of Jesus' birth, we read, "Mary kept all these things in her heart and thought about them often."

Over the course of my lifetime, I've encountered the Lord in some of the most unlikely places and at the most unexpected times. Perhaps you have too. My tendency is to want to grasp eagerly onto these encounters and make major life changes instantly. If I read the great commission in Matthew 28, I may suddenly imagine selling our house and moving to some far-off land to share the gospel. Or after reading the biography of a great intercessor, I may be tempted to abdicate my parental responsibilities and spend every day in the forest behind our house lost in prayer.

In Luke 2:19, Mary had just seen and experienced God in a completely unprecedented way. How would she respond? What was she to do in light of all that had just happened?

I love the Word of God. The Bible tells us that Mary kept all that she had seen and experienced in her heart—and that she thought of it often, pondering what it all meant. I love Mary's response.

In a world where "ready, fire, aim" (yes, you read that correctly) is the norm for so many, we are called to something different. I have so many things that I'm still pondering and treasuring in my heart—waiting on the Lord for His perfect timing. Many of those things have unfolded and passed. Many still lie in the future. I love turning over those mysteries of God in my mind as I go about the mundane routine of daily life. Each of those thoughts links me to the mystery that is God and the promise of His return. The next time you encounter God, try doing what Mary did. Take time to ponder the blessings God has given you, and ask Him to help you with the challenges.

He is listening!

Seeking God

His purpose was for the nations to seek after God and perhaps feel their way toward him and find him—though he is not far from any one of us.

ACTS 17:27

Did you come to trust the Lord as a child or later in life? A dear friend of mine (I'll call her Lisa) recently shared her story with me of seeking after the Lord. It's a beautiful reminder of how He works in our lives to draw us nearer to Him.

Lisa's mom was saved when Lisa was just five years old. Until Lisa moved out of her mother's house, she attended church regularly on Sundays—regardless of her Saturday night escapades. She always felt the Lord's presence and saw Him working in those around her.

Though she never questioned whether God was real, as often happens, she didn't stop to *pursue* Him either. The result was that she set her relationship with the Lord aside as she ventured into adulthood. As the years went on and her twenties turned into her thirties, she began to attend church again. Like many, she attended group Bible studies and women's conferences to dig deeper into His Word. Women of the church invested in her, but she continued to struggle to seek Him and see Him in her daily life.

Like many of us, Lisa continued to pursue the world during these years, and it left her feeling empty and lost. Finally, Lisa yielded to the Lord's stirring in her heart, and she began to truly seek after Him. Funny how that works, isn't it? God is such a loving Father! Like a parent gently steering their child back onto the path, the Lord uses situations in our lives to draw us nearer to Him and make His presence known.

Eventually, Lisa realized that the Lord was pressing upon her heart the need to make some changes in her business venture—which required fully placing her trust in Him. She was uncertain how this would affect her future, but for the first time, she realized God was leading her. Why? Because she was seeking Him and learning to recognize His voice. She was ready to trust Him.

Knowing God is a journey, and it looks different for each of us, but there is a point at which we must decide we are fully ready to trust Him. That decision brings peace and rest. Take the time to listen for the Lord's voice today, precious mom. He wants to guide and direct you too.

Send In the Worshippers

The battle is not yours, but God's.

2 CHRONICLES 20:15

How are you doing today, sweet mama? Are you on top of the world, or are you ready to throw in the towel? While I do have many sweet days that make me so thankful for God's many blessings, some days, the world and its troubles feel like unbeatable odds. Those days I want to fight back like Joan of Arc. I may even have occasionally run through scenarios in my mind in case the need ever arises. I have, after all, watched a few fighting movies.

It's interesting that throughout the Bible, God's answer to difficult and even impossible situations is not for us to physically fight but to direct our focus upward. He asks us to turn our worry into worship. Our pain into praise.

When the enemies of God's people surrounded them and everyone knew doom was inevitable, God's people chose to sing praises to Him. What counterintuitive warfare! Surely the enemies of God's people looked on, bewildered. "What fools! What deserters of common sense! They are surely doomed!" But while God's people were praising, He caused their enemies to fight against each other (see 2 Chronicles 20:22).

God always responded with unnatural and unexpected action. Sometimes He would ask His people to fight, but often He would say, "The battle is not yours, but God's." He delights in seeing His children surrendered and trusting in Him! What better way to accomplish this than by lifting holy hands and raising songs of worship to our Deliverer? After all, we all have the same vulnerability and frailty.

We often feel our adversaries have an unfair advantage over us. But we all breathe the same air. We are all held together by the same Creator. A different perspective can assuage our fear. Remember, God is anxious to draw near to those who draw near to Him (see James 4:8). Now that's an unfair advantage!

Be encouraged, mom. The next time you're facing a struggle, instead of panicking, send in the worshippers! Lead a procession of praise around your kitchen and out into the front yard. Watch what God does next!

Contentment: True Wealth

True godliness with contentment is itself great wealth. After all, we brought nothing with us when we came into the world, and we can't take anything with us when we leave it. So if we have enough food and clothing, let us be content.

1 TIMOTHY 6:6-8

MAYBE PEOPLE ARE GROWING WEARY of the fast pace of modern living and the media saturation we are surrounded by these days, but I've noticed something beautiful happening everywhere I go: many moms are returning to a simpler way of living. From creating minimalist households to baking bread and tending gardens, there's something beautiful and peaceful about being content with simple things.

My friend Lylah has been showing women how to live simply ever since I met her nearly thirty years ago. On our last visit with Lylah and her husband, Michael, she sensed that my heart was weary. "When was the last time you loved being home? What new homemaking skills are you learning?" she asked me. Of course, I really do love being a homemaker. I also love being home. But I had become so busy that I lost sight of being content there.

In the months that followed, I asked the Lord to help me simplify my life, starting with my house. The kids and I spent a few weeks decluttering and paring down what we had so there was less to keep clean and tidy. I put what felt like a thousand pictures into albums and set them out for the kids to enjoy. After that, I started reading books and making sourdough bread at night instead of surfing the Internet. Sourdough takes time, and learning the art forced me to slow down.

Paul was right: godliness (the pursuit of God's ways) with contentment (being happy with what you have) really is great wealth. In a world that is constantly vying for your time and attention, ask the Lord where you should focus your heart and mind.

Something amazing happens when we focus on being content at home. For one thing, peace is a wonderful by-product of contentment. A mom at peace is more likely to have children at peace. A mom who is content is showing her children the blessing of being content.

Maybe it's time for you, like me, to slow down and turn your heart toward home again. If you're struggling with the hectic pace of your life, and if you long for peace, ask the Lord. God's desire is for you to pursue Him with your whole heart. And maybe, just maybe, you might consider learning to bake sourdough bread.

A Want or a Need?

Why do you have so little faith? So don't worry about these things, saying, "What will we eat? What will we drink? What will we wear?" These things dominate the thoughts of unbelievers, but your heavenly Father already knows all your needs. Seek the Kingdom of God above all else, and live righteously, and he will give you everything you need.

MATTHEW 6:30-33

WORRY MUCH? I GET IT. It's easy to worry and fret about having all you need for tomorrow and the days ahead. Unexpected expenses can really cause stress when we struggle to make a car payment or buy groceries for the week. As we get older, worries about retirement and our children's college tuition can make us feel insecure and tense.

In today's passage, we are reminded that God will provide for the righteous who are seeking Him. So what's a mom to do? Where is the disconnect?

I believe there are a couple, and I've fallen into the traps more than once myself.

If you're struggling with finances, start by asking yourself whether you're spending your money wisely. God may be giving you enough to meet your needs, but you may not be using His provision wisely.

In our culture of instant gratification, it's easy to lose sight of the very important distinction between a "need" and a "want." Mom, it's crucial that our children understand the difference. For decades, we Americans have set quite high expectations for our standard of living, and let's be honest: the game of "keeping up with the Joneses" is a real thing. As tempting as playing the game may be, it's important to notice that God doesn't tell us He will provide for us to keep up with the Joneses. He says He will provide all we *need.*

Today, spend some time asking the Lord to guide you in the area of your finances. Depending on Him as you discipline yourself is an exciting way to live. In fact, some of the stories our kids love to tell are about how God provided for us in times of need! Today, ask the Lord to help you learn the difference between wants and needs—and teach your children as you learn. God truly does provide for our needs!

A Desire for Holiness

Put on your new nature, created to be like God—truly righteous and holy.

EPHESIANS 4:24

WHAT'S MORE IMPORTANT: HAPPINESS OR HOLINESS? I've been pondering this quite a bit lately as my fifth child embarked on her first year of Bible college. *Oh, how I want her to be happy there—to make good friends and form lifelong ministry connections,* I thought. *But even more than that, I want her to run hard after God. I want her to pursue a life of holiness.*

In our culture of instant gratification, the pursuit of happiness has taken priority over the pursuit of holiness. Happiness is important—don't get me wrong! A study of God's Word will reveal that He cares deeply about happiness. But in God's economy, it's not the number one thing He wants us to desire. But in God's economy, it's not the number one thing He wants us to desire. God is resolutely committed to His own glory. He wants our lives to bring glory and honor to Him, no matter what circumstances we find ourselves in.

This takes time and intention. It also takes something called *sanctification,* which refers to the process of becoming more like Jesus. In other words, we are sanctified when we pursue a life of holiness.

As a mother, I want my children to be happy, but I also want them to desire holiness. Holiness is not only making the conscious choice to separate ourselves from sinful thoughts and actions; it's the pursuit of what God has set us apart to do. God wants to use the circumstances of our lives—including motherhood—to make us more like Jesus.

You see, God sees the big picture in our lives, and He can use anything to make us more like Him: failure, hunger, depression, heartache, wayward children, an abortion, divorce, abuse, abandonment, unfaithfulness, betrayal, or simply a terrible day of homeschooling.

All of these struggles that come as a result of this fallen world can cause us to run to Him, desperately cling to Him, and sometimes even need Him for our very next breath. As we pursue Him, we learn more about who He is. The pursuit of God's will for our lives and the desire to be more like Christ give birth to a life of holiness.

As you enter a new year, ask God to help you make a life of holiness a priority. If you're struggling with this, perhaps a place to start is to simply ask God to give you the genuine desire to pursue holiness. As you do, listen for the Holy Spirit's gentle prodding, always keeping in mind that your children are watching your walk. May our prayer for a new year include the desire to pursue holiness and a deeper walk with Jesus.

The God of New Beginnings

I will accomplish all my purpose.

ISAIAH 46:10, ESV

THE END OF THE YEAR SIGNIFIES that a change is coming. As one year quietly passes into the history books and a new year begins, I often find myself reflecting on the ever-changing seasons of motherhood.

Being a mom is an amazing journey, isn't it? It changes us. Motherhood brings us to our knees and reminds us that nothing stays the same. As things change, we learn to depend more on the Lord for each passing season of motherhood. Children grow quickly. Newborns are really only "newborns" for a few short weeks. Soon, they are babies who quickly become toddlers. Toddlers are only toddlers for a year or two, and shortly after that, wiggly teeth signify that yet another change is coming.

Elementary school, junior high, high school—gone before you know it. It can feel like a terrible loss when our kids leave home, but that loss is really the gateway to a beautiful new season of watching our children take flight and follow God on their own journeys.

Beautifully broken, our hearts learn to expand again. Mother's hearts are always expanding, after all. Soon our beautiful babies are having babies of their own—and it all starts over again.

As I have gotten older, I have come to appreciate the delicate nature of the transitory seasons of motherhood. As the year comes to a close, I hope you'll take just a few quiet moments to get alone with the Lord and let Him remind you of exactly how much He loves you.

A new beginning is here. God tells us in His Word that He is the God of new beginnings and that He will accomplish His purposes as we follow Him. The question is, will we lean into each new season and walk closer with God—or will we go our own way? Will we allow the Lord to teach us new things, take us new directions, and open new doors? By the grace of God, we will.

The new year will hold new challenges, but it will also hold new blessings. Hang on tight to the Lord, precious mom. The God of new beginnings will accomplish His purposes in you and in your family as you walk with Him every day. Good things are coming—you can count on it.

About the Author

BESTSELLING AUTHOR AND SPEAKER HEIDI ST. JOHN has been teaching on marriage, family, and cultural issues for more than twenty years. Through sound biblical insight and practical application, Heidi inspires audiences to pursue God's call on their lives wholeheartedly—starting at home.

Heidi has been married to Jay, her college sweetheart, since 1989. The St. Johns reside just outside beautiful Vancouver, Washington, where their nonprofit organization, Firmly Planted Family, and their homeschool resource center are based. The St. Johns have seven children, all of whom have been homeschooled, and several grandchildren.

Heidi is the author of several books, including *Becoming MomStrong: How to Fight with All That's in You for Your Family and Your Faith* and the corresponding *Becoming MomStrong Bible Study*, as well as *Prayers for the Battlefield* and *Bible Promises for Moms*.

Heidi's podcast, *Off the Bench with Heidi St. John*, has passed 16 million downloads and is available wherever podcasts can be found.

You can join Heidi online at momstronginternational.com, a Bible study ministry where thousands of women come together weekly to learn how the Bible can be applied to their everyday lives.